TYPE AND TYPOGRAPHY

TYPE AND TYPOGRAPHY

THE DESIGNER'S TYPE BOOK / BY BEN ROSEN   REVISED EDITION

Van Nostrand Reinhold Company

New York   Cincinnati   Toronto   London   Melbourne

Published in 1976 by Van Nostrand Reinhold Company
A division of Litton Educational Publishing, Inc.
450 West 33rd Street, New York, NY 10001

Van Nostrand Reinhold Limited
1410 Birchmount Road, Scarborough,
Ontario M1P 2E7, Canada

Van Nostrand Reinhold Australia Pty. Limited
17 Queen Street, Mitcham, Victoria 3132, Australia

Van Nostrand Reinhold Company Limited
Molly Millars Lane, Wokingham, Berkshire, England

16 15 14 13 12 11 10 9 8 7

This volume is concerned with type and typography. It is intended to serve as a practical workbook for the graphic designer.

It shows carefully selected, complete alphabets of the best type faces commonly available, or becoming available, in the United States.

These type faces, together with other relevant material, including information on sizes, comparisons of cuts, recognition traits, and some romantic and exotic faces are coordinated in a single volume.

The types represented here constitute the designer's basic arsenal of faces. A finely conceived, drawn and cut group, each face is shown in full alphabet, including numbers and punctuation.

The basic family groups are shown in sizes which range from 72 point down to 18 or 16 point in foundry or hand-set type. Within each font of foundry type, lines are separated by two points of lead or a hairline mounted on the up side of a 2 point body.

Where practical considerations allow, the showings include comparative cuts by different foundries.

From 14 point down to 8 or 6 point, each family face is set by machine in text form. To illustrate various text settings, the type is shown solid and both two and four points leaded.

A relatively full showing of individual types, plus the author's freedom to choose from many sources is a suitable framework in which to assemble a useful collection, selectively chosen for excellence. The type thus chosen has been set in a manner believed to be the most useful for readers.

A measure of perspective is provided by a brief look at the history of type, the origins of type, and its richly complex traditions. Technical data considered of use to the designer has also been included.

This volume attempts to focus on the day-to-day needs of graphic designers, art directors, industrial and architectural designers, advertising and promotion personnel, graphics students and many others concerned with type. It is directed to all those who, while daily serving in the market place, also do battle against banality and tastelessness.

A complete type library would include distinguished books encyclopedic in scale and specifically literary, historical, or esthetic in their frame of reference.

To round out a broad knowledge of the subject, typography students will find it to their advantage to consult the specialized periodicals and publications which show type in use.

Scholars, typophiles and others who may wish to pursue this subject further should consult the many fine works which bear the specialist's stamp.

It is hoped, however, that the type included here has been selected and presented in such a way that this volume will become an invaluable workbook in the designer's library.

Limitations of time, money, distance from sources — to name but a few — add to the complexity of producing such a work. The dependence of the author on the good will, cooperation and assistance of so many interested persons can hardly be overstated.

In preparing a work of this nature, the setting and proving of type is a highly critical function.

I therefore, with deep appreciation, thank the directors of The Composing Room for the interest, excellent craftsmanship and spirit of involvement with which the major portion of this volume was undertaken and executed.

To York Typesetting Co. for exercising the same virtues during the closing weeks of preparation, my gratitude.

I also take this opportunity to express appreciation to Richard K. Ansell, Vice President, Type Department, Amsterdam Continental; Sidney Minson, Executive Vice President, The Composing Room, Inc.; Sy Lemler, General Manager and Type Director, York Typesetting Company; and Milton Mandel, President, Ken-ro Typographic Service, Inc. for heartening support and practical assistance.

Richard K. Ansell, Vice President, Type Department, Amsterdam Continental; Jackson Burke, Director of Typographic Development, Mergenthaler Linotype Company; Marvin Corwin, Sales Manager, American Wood Type Manufacturing Company; Vincent Giannone, Sales Promotion Manager, Bauer Alphabets Inc.; Emil Klumpp, Sales Manager of the Type Division, American Type Founders Co., Inc.; R. Hunter Middleton, Director, Department of Typeface Design, Ludlow Typograph Company; and Sir Francis Stephenson, Stephenson Blake and Company, Ltd. have all contributed in one way or another, both encouragement and practical assistance, for which I acknowledge my gratitude.

In the important matter of general assistance in preparation and mechanical assembly, I am grateful to Claire Selley for the diligent effort she has applied to this book.

My thanks to Zenith Gross and Dorothy Willis for aid in editing and clarifying many of the ideas set forth here, and to Paula Kursh for help in many proving and secretarial chores.

It is my ardent desire that the reader will find many uses for this volume — thereby profiting from what is essentially a labor of love.

Ben Rosen

June 15, 1963

To the casual eye the imposing array of type faces in this volume is visual proof of the wealth which the interplay between creative urges and technological advances has produced over the last 150 years.

Each type face is a piece of history, like a colored stone chip in a mosaic that depicts the development of human communication. Each type face is also a visual record of the person who created it — his skill as a designer, his philosophy as an artist, his feeling for the relationship between the details of each letter and the resulting impressions of an alphabet or a text line.

It would, of course, be impossible to give in one book a **complete** record of what has happened to type since Didot's or Bodoni's time. The brush-stroke extravaganzas of an Eckman, or a Gaudi, the creations of Ehmcke, the polished brilliance of pen types by Schneidler, the early Bernhard type faces, along with many others, still await to be assembled in a form that is different from that of a book. And they must be logically linked with the currents of the time in which they were developed.

This book, "Type and Typography," has an important practical function in supplying the designer with visual information, so that he can assemble words and lines, chosing from a variety of faces and sizes. It is more complete than most books of this kind that I have seen. Its usefulness should be extensive, and lasting — the highest compliment which its author can receive for his diligent effort.

It appears appropriate to consider briefly the relationship between type and design in an attempt to evaluate where we stand now and in what direction we may be heading.

The enthusiastic clean-up of the twenties, associated with the De Stijl and Bauhaus period, brought forth a cultivation of sans-serif types which had a lasting impact on design. Traditionalist movements of the thirties and fifties had little effect on the use of the sans serifs in all the specialized segments of graphic design on a world-wide basis. Significant factors in this success undoubtedly were the enormous strides and the leveling influence of transportation and television.

This revolution was led originally by painters, architects and professional typographers. The increasing separation of the visual appearance of type (as the designer sees it) and type as a structural material (as the typesetter sees it) was facilitated by reproductive processes which no longer printed from type but from photographic compositions. Today's typographic design is, technically speaking, based on photocomposition, scissors, photostats and paste-ups, while previously the stern limits of type and spacing material controlled form.

In the twenties, the function of typography was outlined as the solving of reading and visual problems on the logical (werkgerecht) level of type **material.** Today, typographic design influenced by constructivism, surrealism and dadaism, has gained a freedom in terms of composition, size, color, weight and spacing of type that was hardly conceivable before. Whether this absence of limitation is a blessing or not is a question of more than academic importance, especially to education.

It is characteristic of the present state of transition, that this new freedom has not yet brought liberation from obsolescent reading organization. Contempt for reading functions is, however, much in evidence. Design seems to aim more often than not at developing visual riddles. In its eagerness to appear original, much recent magazine and advertising typography succeeds too often in being ugly, amateurish and unrelated to what is to be conveyed. The understanding of type and the ability to analyze a message coherently and in an original way is hard work. There is also no substitute for creative effort. When the only sense of order in recent American typographical exhibitions is that many entries appear to be more or less faithful copies of the same 1923 original, one realizes with a shock that the creative effort is absent. When the vaguely impressionistic type collage takes the place of type that is composed for reading, and the ripped-off fragment of a letter teases the eye rather than gives pleasure or a sense of ordered thought, we should question whether this is progress.

Preoccupation with the commercial aspects of design has led to preoccupation with the more formal aspects of a message as well as to shallow, muddled thinking. A commercial design can be a strong cultural force **and** — at the same time — sell well, if the designer understands the needs for both and is in command of his craft.

The very purpose of our alphabet is to give a visual structure to experiences, memory and abstract thought. A message which we hear is soon forgotten, but the one which we see and read is more permanent because it penetrates memory on more than one level and can be referred to over and over again. This explains the still growing significance of typography as a tool of world-wide communication — a tool which we must improve steadily by studying it as we use it.

The history of civilization and of life itself is one of continuous evolution. When this process is hindered, revolution occurs. Science helps us to evaluate and systematize, to plan and predict evolution. In addition to daily and more mundane tasks, art and typographic design have regained a **basic** importance as they can provide short-cuts to an easier understanding of this ever changing reality.

CONTENTS

In revising this edition for paperback production, a decision was made to respond to popular usage and include both text and display showings of the popular and beautiful Helvetica Series, and to set them in film type. These settings appear as a 16 pp. section beginning on p. 390.

*Text showing only.

Above: Sumerian hymn inscribed in clay.

Left: Impression from
Babylonian cylinder seal.

Below: Petroglyph found in Wyoming.

To inform, to explain, to exhort, to persuade, to sell —
all have become driving needs for most contemporary
societies.

If, as one modern writer suggested, human history
is a race between education and catastrophe, the
problem of communication may well be decisive in the
outcome of that race.

We see about us profound new developments, not
only in the physical sciences, but also in the areas of
religion, art, psychology, sociology and commerce.

Modern man focuses intently on how to understand
and to learn, and how to exchange with his fellows the
fruits of this understanding. He does this not only that
he may survive, but that his survival may have meaning and value.

With each significant advance in literacy and cul-
ture by the newly emerging nations and each leap for-
ward in science and invention by the industrialized
countries, there appear simultaneous needs to pro-
claim, instruct or convince.

A large share of this communication within and between the nations of the world is carried by graphic
designers of every level of skill and inventiveness, and
occasionally results in work of surpassing beauty and
refinement. This visually-oriented output attains a
staggering scale as it expands in response to the un-
precedented surge of the American economy, and
more recently, the European markets. The designer's
stature can be measured by his response to the present requirements of effective space advertising, con-
sumer publication needs, expanding communications
systems, package designing, promotion, direct mail
publications, architectural type forms, instruction
manuals of great complexity and fund raising and
opinion shaping programs of international scope.

In the United States, the economic structure is so
varied and its potential so dynamic that the creative
craftsman in every graphic field faces a kaleidoscope

of design problems. Many hazards also present themselves. Techniques of graphic selling can sometimes elevate ugliness and meaninglessness into dull national symbols.

The Designer Today

In terms of typography the designer should be familiar with the history of moveable type, which had its roots in antiquity and its first growth on the wave of Humanism which swept Europe in the fifteenth century.

The designer who understands and assimilates the experience of the past can best integrate that knowledge with current methods.

Originally intended as a means of speeding book production, type now pervades newspapers, magazines, television, packages, industrial design, many architectural forms, plus other aspects of our daily life.

Despite arguments that ugliness and poor design abound in every aspect of our daily lives here and abroad, I believe contemporary graphic methods which are evocative, visually intriguing, and functional without being banal, are exerting influence on more and more people. This hopeful turn of events is caused by many factors, including a lively public response to well designed products, improved advertising, better sales promotion and graphics in general. In my view, a slow but perceptible upgrading of mass taste is evident.

Many fine designers continue in the tradition of needing to do things well for the sake of the doing. Designers with skill, perseverance and dedication, are breaking through previously accepted academic boundaries. New applications of type and graphic methods in the past few decades have established a broader framework of design activities.

Thus designers are contributing much to the maturing of American taste. Their understanding and knowledgeable use of type is a vital part of that contribution.

The Designer Tomorrow

The designer must embrace the onrushing situations he will soon confront; new economic problems, new political and social ideas, new revolutions in education and science.

It is sobering to consider, for example, how a designer of the past might have reacted when confronted with the scientific and commercial reality of such concepts as atomic energy, satellite communications, jet rocketry and space ships to distant planets.

How could any designer of even the historically recent Victorian era imagine a national sub-culture such as our own 'teen-age group which would call for a whole economic, social and cultural climate of its own?

Indeed, how can a designer of today best prepare for what his work might be on behalf of major American philanthropic foundations a decade hence?

All we can be sure of is that much will be different, and a great deal of what is now accepted will change.

Yet the past offers illumination; we cannot summarily jettison it. Even viewed against the promise of the future, the past can be studied with profit by the contemporary designer.

As an example of such insights from the past let us recall the feat accomplished by Alcuin of York, abbot of St. Martin's monastery, who, at the command of Charlemagne, supervised the copying of all available manuscripts into a more uniform and legible style.

But perhaps the contemporary designer's interest in the type faces presented here will be heightened by a brief review of how the centuries of human progress produced first a variety of written communications and then, from them, the origins of type and typography. It becomes clear, as we survey studies of the origins of writing, that our present system of rigid alphabet structure, words, sentences, paragraphs, lines of words moving from left to right is only one possible arrangement.

Many other imaginative methods of arranging letters, lines, and symbols have been developed, such as Chinese ideograms, primitive picture writing, Egyptian hieroglyphics, cuneiform systems, the early Greek boustrophedon "plow" system in which the writing moves from left to right on one line and then alternates right to left on the next, and the Hebraic and Arabic (of Aramaic origin) which flows right to left.

All these varieties of writing emphasize for the designer that there are unlimited ways to express meaning graphically. A look at the most dynamic use of modern typography will show that this variety and spirit of abundant innovation is still being sought, found and successfully applied today.

Writing of Early Civilizations

As our outlook reaches across time, we may note the contributions to the history of writing made by the very earliest civilizations, such as the Mesopotamian cuneiform writing system of angular, debossed pictorial signs pressed into clay or carved in stone.

The ideograms of the ancient Egyptians cut into wood or stone were three dimensional and delightfully decorative. When drawn with a reed pen on papyrus, Egyptian writing was far more fluid and painting-like in quality. Here we see clearly how the tools of the craft have a most significant effect on form.

Very early, writing began to develop in the direction of the acrophonic principle, the system of using a pictorial symbol for the name of an object to represent the beginning sound of the name such as the use of a pen to represent the phonic value of P.

The Phoenicians, pressing further ahead on the path cleared by hieroglyphic and cuneiform writing, began the development of a phonetic system based to some extent on simplifications of earlier pictorial symbols. These are the roots of later Greek writing from which most Western written languages derive.

Any consideration of origins of writing, however restricted in scope, should not ignore the great contribution made by China. Nowhere else in the world has the art of writing enjoyed greater importance. Chinese writing is not alphabetic and uses thousands of symbols. The caligrapher enjoys a subtle rapport with meanings based on the way in which he draws each character and all the characters as a whole. As tone frequently gives various meanings to the spoken word, so character, weight, and style of drawing — in a few well controlled strokes — imply nuances of meaning

to the written word. Calligraphy, a form of art in China, is as highly esteemed as pictorial representation.

Japan and the Far Eastern countries offer much opportunity for rewarding investigation, but their influence on Western type and typography is comparatively limited and will not be explored here.

The life situation of early man made both writing and reading intensely significant rituals.

In primitive times, only a few persons were moved to record events. This record is best known as pictures of the hunt, the rain, the abundance or scarcity of food. We can guess how the drawings must have evoked passionate recognition, and re-created in the onlooker strong sensations of joy, fear or anger.

Written communication in prehistoric times was certainly not the daily casual attempt between and among all conditions of folk as it is in the twentieth century, but a recording of events and objects which profoundly involved the scribe and his audience.

Later, as early writing began to develop from varieties of symbols into more regularized, alphabetically constructed words, the acts of writing, reading aloud and listening remained essentially rare and precious activities. They gained additional force because it was usually only God's word, or the King's.

Since religion was the center of life in many early cultures, the sacred words held listeners in a dramatic, almost hypnotic, state of attention. Few could read except some members of the nobility and those of certain religious orders.

Hieratic inscription on papyrus. Egyptian, twentieth dynasty.

It is difficult to imagine today how ardent, how whole-souled the approach of earlier times was to the sacred acts of writing and then reading aloud the simplest pronouncements.

When we consider the outlook of the Medieval and early Renaissance periods, we can understand the seething excitement and suspense with which the first experimenters with moveable type must have approached their new power.

Since many of the innovators of printing were scholars in their own right, possessing most of what they held to be the world's store of knowledge, we can assume that they knew themselves to be benefactors of humanity, with a means at last for shedding light across the Western world. The potential of their new invention could have called forth only their best efforts, and these early efforts still shine with beauty and integrity across five hundred years.

Derivation of Form

The basic forms around which our types are constructed began to take shape in a clearly recognizable way with the advent of the developed Greek characters which, like our own, run from left to right. The Greek system of straight lines, curves and angles, organized into harmonious lines anticipated contemporary type forms and techniques by many centuries. To this day they wield a significant influence.

By 114 A.D. in Rome, out of the same classical tradition, Trajan's column was inscribed with perhaps the best known, and certainly among the most beautifully developed letters ever conceived. A classical propensity for form, proportion and beauty expressed in an orderly way, produced this inspiring model of Western letter forms. This was but one of many fine inscriptions, carved by skilled practitioners of the stone cutters' craft. These noble capital or majuscule letters were particularly well suited to represent the strength and order of Rome.

At about this time, writing began to branch out into many different paths. The course was one of testing, rejecting and revising a wealth of variations on basic techniques. Before the end of the second century the pen drawn imitations of stone inscribed letters made their appearance in at least five different forms: (1) Quadrata, or square letters; (2) Rustics, a condensed less stiff version of the Quadrata; (3) Uncials, which were rounder and more closely reflected a pen stroke with suggestions of ascenders and descenders; (4)

Half Uncials, a more exaggerated, looser style out of which our concept of lower case letters seems to have grown; and finally (5) Earlier and Later Roman Cursives, a form of writing comparatively fast and flowing, more closely related in character to our own writing although remote in letter form. The latter style also has contributed greatly to the creation of the over-all fabric of writing and consequently to type style.

Between the fifth and the ninth centuries, two other styles of writing emerged that were significant. First was the Irish and Anglo-Saxon Half Uncials which appeared in secular writings early in the eighth century and are known as the Irish-Anglo-Saxon Round Hand. In this style, as in the Book of Kells and the Lindisfarne Gospels, two well-known Celtic illuminated manuscripts of the Latin gospels, integration of ornamented letter form and illustration was carried to unsurpassed heights in the entire repertory of Western graphic art. In our time, graphic designers may still find sources of inspiration among these works.

The second style was the Carolingian Minuscule, a form of writing containing both capital and small letters which developed at the instigation of Charlemagne at the end of the eighth century. To overcome the confusion caused by the great diversity of writing styles then employed, and to achieve a measure of conformity in certain holy texts, he invited the Anglo-Saxon scholar and churchman Alcuin of York to take charge of the Abbey of St. Martin at Tours, and there to supervise the copying of all available texts into a unified style. The beautiful flowing and efficient letter forms that evolved became known as the Caroline Minuscule (named for Charlemagne). This significant style led directly through to the basic type styles of our day. Certainly no other style had greater influence on all the European calligraphic substyles that developed from the time of its birth into the early years of the Renaissance.

By the time printing was invented, a neo-Caroline style was employed in copying out rediscovered classical scripts since many of these earlier scripts were written in the Caroline Minuscule developed by Alcuin. Type styles of today are thus direct descendants of the Caroline Minuscule of the Middle-Ages.

The Renaissance fed on classical manifestations of many kinds. Men of that period had a taste for antiquity which led them to regard as good that which had been regarded as good in earlier periods — and this applied to the written scripts in the Carolingian style. These antique letters were believed to be the product of classical Rome and were identified as Littera Antiqua or white-letter in writing studies. They became the most admired style for secular transcriptions shortly after printing was invented.

The twelfth and thirteenth centuries produced a style of condensed letters with a heavier vertical stroke which, carried to excess, became the modified condensed form known as barbarous or Gothic black-letter script. Later, by the fifteenth century, most curves had disappeared and the letters became highly condensed, angular, black and somewhat hard to read. The latter style, called Textura, was widely employed and became identified with religious writings.

Thus at a time when printing from movable types was rapidly becoming a reality, the threads of many calligraphic styles were reconverging into two single strands, both serving as models for the form of printing types—the Gothic black letters and the Littera Antiqua white letters.

Late ninth century manuscript. St. Gall, Switzerland.

Invention of Printing

During the middle of the fifteenth century in Europe there was again demonstrated the truism that there is no greater power on earth than "an idea whose time has come."

The idea of printing the Word, heretofore so precious, and inaccessible, had now arrived and found its time in history; it now also found the men who were needed to bring it to fruition.

Two men are most often mentioned as the inventors of movable type and its corollary — printing.

Johann Gensfleish zum Gutenberg of Mainz is generally credited with the invention in 1440. But even a brief search into the many scholarly works on this subject turns up other claims. The invention has also been attributed to Laurens Janszoon Coster of Haarlem at about the same time.

Books printed with movable types between 1440 and 1500 became known as incunabula — a term meaning "swaddling clothes." These early products of printing are well represented in many collections throughout the world and are a constant source of delight to the serious student of graphics. As John R. Biggs points out in his excellent "Introduction to Typography," the first printers were largely scholars, excited by this new means for disseminating, in a comparatively rapid way, the new ideas of the Renaissance. Five hundred years later, their work still proclaims their skill and devotion to this matchless vehicle of mass learning.

The earliest printers tried to make their books look like manuscripts, using Gothic styles of type for sacred works, and the Littera Antiqua as the model for secular. At first, the text only was printed and space was left for large decorated initials to be drawn by hand. As printing began to develop, punch cutters departed more and more from the manuscripts of their time. Fewer ligatures were employed; more characters reflecting the special way in which types were formed crept into their product. By 1500, books were being produced in some of the most beautiful and legible types ever to be conceived and cut.

Gutenburg, Coster, Fust, and Schoeffer, Rusch, Nicolas Jenson, Aldus Manutius, Arrighi, Ratdolt, Garamond, Due Pre, Caxton, Pynson — the list of those whose inspired hands guided the development of type multiplies rapidly by the beginning of the sixteenth century.

As the pace of history quickened, in part due to the printing process itself, we find many great artists contributing to the progress of this invaluable tool of learning: Tory, Estienne, Didot, Fournier, Chochin, Plantin, Elzevir, Caslon, Baskerville; in many cases their names have come down to us associated with the beautiful types they created.

The craft flourished, but the art began to falter, as speed, experimentation and self-conscious implementation of detail and ornament increased, not always with the happiest results. Many works of the period from 1500 to 1750 are in a state of good repair and may be seen in fine libraries and collections in major cities of the U.S. and abroad.

A detailed discussion of this period, so rich in exploration of techniques and in the elaboration of the printer's art, is outside the province of this volume. However, in the light of the shift in typographic values and practices of the last three or four decades, I believe a complete and more favorable re-evaluation of the sixteenth and seventeenth century works will some day be a major contribution to type history.

By 1720 Caslon had arrived at his cut known as Old Face, a cut which Biggs credits largely to close observance of Dutch types preceding that time. Within fifty years, John Baskerville of Birmingham, England, had made his contribution in the form of a letter which started the transition from old style toward the form known as modern. This relatively heavy face with extreme thins, straight serifs and color based on a vertical stroke became basic in its use and had a wide influence on many derivative forms of letters in both text and display, down to our present era.

Revival

A revival in typography occurred late in the nineteenth century. The Industrial Revolution had crept into almost every aspect of life, corroding much that was craftsman-like, sensitively created and beautiful in the European and American scene. Typography suffered along with other art forms of the time.

One voice raised in England in the latter part of the nineteenth century to try to stem the creeping blight of industrial ugliness was that of William Morris, founder of the Kelmscott Press. For inspiration he looked, as had many before him, to the stately books produced in the fifteenth century in Italy. His efforts, no matter how some of today's design judgments may regard them, were based on a sincere desire to raise standards in this area.

Secuitur misse speciales ⁊ Et pmo
In dñica die de sca knitate Introit⁹

Enedicta sit sancta trinitas
atqȝ idiuisa vnitas rõfite-
bimᵘ ei quia fecit nobiscum
misericordiã suã ⁊ Bñdicam⁹ patrē
et filium cum sancto spiritu ⁊ Õro
õmipotēs sēpitne de⁹ qui dedisti
famuľ tuis in rõfessiõe vere fidei eterne knitatis gľiam agnoscere-
et in ptētia maiestatis adorare vni-
tatē qͣͫs ut eiusdē fidei firmitate ab
oñibȝ sēper muniam aduersis ⁊ Per
                                                dei
Kñs ⁊ O altitudo diui- Ad co-
tiaȝ sapiētie ⁊ sciētie· tȝ māos
icõphensibilia sũt iuditia ei⁹· ⁊ inues-
tigabiles vie ei⁹ ⁊ Quis eñ rognouit
seusũ dñi· aut quis õsiliari⁹ ei⁹ kuit·

EL PRINCI
PIO DIO creo
Il Cielo et La terra.
Et la terra era infru
ctuofa et uacua: et le
tenebre erano fopra
la faccia del abiffo.Et
il fpirito del Signo
re era menato fopra
le acque. Diffe dio. Sia facta la Luce. Et
facta e la Luce. Et uide dio la luce effer bu
ona: et diuife la Luce dalle tenebre:et ap
pello la Luce di: et le tenebre nocte. Et fa
cto e la Sera et Matina uno di.Etiam dif
fe dio. Sia facto il firmamento in mezo
dele acque:il quale diuida le acque dale ac
que. Et fece dio il firmamento. Et diuife
le acque che erano fopto il firmaméto da
quelle che erano fopra il firmamento. Et
facto e cofi:et chiamo dio il firmamento
cielo.Et facto e Sera et Matina il fecondo
di. Etiam diffe dio. Le acque che fo
no fopto il cielo fiano cógregate i uno lu
oco:et apparga la arida terra: et facto e co
fi:et chiamo dio la arida terra:et le cógre
gationi dele acque appello mare. Et uide

dio effer buono:Et diffe germine la terra
la herba uirête et facia il Seme:et il legno
pomifero che faci il fructo fecondo la fua
generatione: La femenza delquale fia in
fi medefimo fopra la terra:et cofi facto e.
Et la terra produffe la herba uirente et fa
ciente il feme fecondo la fua generatione
Et il legno faciente il fructo et hauendo
ciafcheduu il femente fecondo la fua fpe
tie. Et uide dio effer buono:et facto e Se
ra et Matina il terzo di. Etiam diffe dio.
Siano facte eluminarie nel firmamento
del cielo:Et feperino il di et la nocte.E fia
no infigni et tempi: et di et anni. Perche
refplendino nel firmamento del cielo: et
illumineno la terra.Et cofi facto e. Et fece
dio duo grädi Luminarii.Il luminare ma
iore che foprafteffi al di:et il luminare mi
nore che foprafteffi ala nocte. Et etiam fe
ce dio le Stelle. Et puofe quelle nel firma
mento del cielo:perche luceffono fopra la
terra:et fignorizaffeno al di et ala nocte:
et diuideffeno la Luce et le tenebre. Et ui
de dio effer buono:et facto e fera et mati
na il quarto di.Etiä diffe dio producano
le acque. il reptile del anima uiuente et

First printed Italian bible. Venice, 1471.

Goudy, Rogers, and many others followed but, by our contemporary measure of graphic design, their influence today is limited. Revivals which do not catch the essence of the time in which they arise appear transparent and even insignificant in later periods. It should be emphasized that these men of the nineteenth century classical revival brought the force of personal character to their demands for integrity to a field where this quality was not clearly in evidence.

Most accepted works on typography today take the view that there is little merit in nineteenth century romantic faces; I have heard authorities in the field malign this era in typography, particularly charging i with desecration of form and ruination of orderly, dignified traditional beauty.

So we find that bitter criticism and questioning c nineteenth century type standards have become, a so often happens with heresy, part of the academi dogma of our own time.

I believe that there is much to be found of inspiration and value in nineteenth century type styles. Robert N. Jones has well expressed this point of view in an article in "Print Magazine" for May, 1960, in which he stated: "It is my belief that there has never been a typeface cast that is so badly designed that it could not be handsomely and effectively used in the hands of the right printer or designer. Further, it is my belief that type was meant to serve more than one master. The original concept of type was most certainly for bookwork. However, as times changed so did the role of type. No one, least of all Mr. H. Ihlenburg, probably the most prolific of American type designers, or his contemporaries, would ever have suggested his "Bijou" or "Minster" for a setting of Chaucer. Ihlenburg, Herriet, Heyer, Ruthven, Smith, Rogers and others were designing type faces for printers who were producing printed persuasions for a vigorous and vital country that was expanding industrially and economically at a rate never before known in history. Ihlenburg and his contemporaries were engaged in trying to help satisfy the demands of what we have come to know as advertising typography.

"It is my conviction that advertising in all its many facets is as responsible for the literacy, the wealth and the strength of our country as any other factor save our natural resources.

"For whatever part these type designers played in developing our graphic arts, abuse should not be their reward."

Manuscript page from "The Four Gospels" in Latin. England, about 990-1000 A.D.

Today's alert designer, recognizing qualities in many type faces previously considered "out," can and does apply these types not only to advertising typography but across the spectrum of graphics.

Contemporary Typography

The Bauhaus of Weimar in the post-war Germany of the twenties was one of the first cohesive efforts to develop a quality of craftsmanship which uniquely related to the technological advances that were sweeping Europe and America. During the preceding revival men were repelled by visible changes they observed and sought to reinstate ancient concepts of truth and beauty. The Bauhaus, plus a handful of other individuals in Europe and America, sought new values in the time itself and in its technological manifestations — values that were a part of a new age.

Much has been published on the Bauhaus; its strengths and weaknesses have been well defined, but it continues to be important and influential in the graphic arts and in typography.

Certainly L. Moholy-Nagy's position is still helpful: "Typography must be clear communication in its most vivid form . . . for clarity is the essence of modern printing . . ."

The "new typography," pursued by the Bauhaus masters and students attempted to incorporate into printing all that was fresh and radical in our century's art, science, technology and psychology. It is interesting to note, for example, that Albert Einstein of Berlin was on the Board of Directors of a group called "Friends of the Bauhaus," which provided much financial and moral support for the institution.

New concepts in physics, mathematics and psychology were in the air. New visions of time, space, mass and energy formed the backdrop to experiments in scale and space relationships. These new currents also affected Bauhaus work in color, texture and other design facets. A new wave of materials and techniques flooded into modern consciousness through this exciting channel of creative activity.

Many of the leaders of the Bauhaus fled Hitler's Germany and came to America to teach, and to practice their crafts. Today they have become an integral part of our vigorous and productive graphic arts which they themselves so greatly influenced; their names will remain as worthy symbols of the bridges they tried to build between the artist and the industrial system, between the fine and applied arts, between modern man and his environment.

Some design schools in America and abroad have taken up the fight for vital and progressive concepts of graphic invention and are trying to couple their broad studies on this subject with highly disciplined skills. Their aim is to interweave a study of humanities with the craft of graphic design.

The work of designers trained in these schools bears witness to the strong effort being made to produce an American graphic design equal to our prime achievements in other fields.

The early manufacture of moveable type was carried out by hand. Molds were prepared, by means of which large quantities of types could be cast with a degree of precision that made printing possible. All the other prerequisites were on hand—paper, ink, the concept of the block print, and even printing presses of a primitive sort.

The first step in preparing types must have been the preparation of a drawn alphabet—a guide to the punch-cutter who was in some cases the designer, in other cases merely the one to execute a design. Following a prepared model, a counter punch was made and then driven into the end of an annealed steel tool. This counter punch forced the metal away from the inner and enclosed areas of such letters as a, e, and g. The finished punch was formed by cutting away the metal from the area outside each letter. By transferring an impression into soft material as the cutting progressed, a degree of control was exercised over the character of each letter while it was being refined. Tempering completed the punch. It was then ready to have its impression struck into a bar of softer metal. Once struck, the bar contained the matrix which, when properly fitted, caused the printing surface of the finished type to fall into proper alignment. When the matrix and mold were aligned properly the mold was ready to be poured.

In essence, this is the principle by which punch-cutters originally worked, though no doubt, each had his own ideas how to improve details of his task. Files, gravers, various methods of abrasion and large quantities of tender loving care went into varying this method as each separate challenge arose.

The type metal was poured, a process requiring skillful manipulation, then trimmed to a standard height. Although the tolerances were great by current industrial standards, the type was ready for use after various finishing procedures.

Current Processes

The principle of the pantograph in recent years has come to replace the punch-cutter's craft. The pantograph greatly speeds up the cutting practice and increases the precision with which a type may be cut. But it extracts its payment in terms of increased mechanization and a decrease in variation of letters to compensate for variation of letter size—a prin-

Punch of letter H.

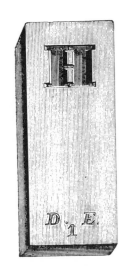

Matrix of letter H.

Type-mould without matrix, and with a type of the letter H in the mould.

ciple always considered by skilled punch-cutters.

A process employed by American Type Founders follows a somewhat different course designed to overcome some of these limitations. Greatly simplified, the process may be described as follows:

From a hand drawn master letter, a photographic image is transferred to a sensitized plate which is etched under carefully controlled conditions. The plate becomes a precise pattern for the Benton engraving machine, which is a routing device operating within an extremely fine tolerance, and working on the pantograph principle. The Benton can be adjusted to compensate for variables that occur when letter sizes change. The average size letter matrix from a typical alphabet will be precisely reproduced as originally drawn, while small sizes can become progressively more extended, and large sizes can be more condensed. Another advantage claimed for the Benton is that by routing the matrix, rather than striking a punch into it, there is less distortion.

After a painstaking fitting of matrix to mold the type is cast, finished and ready for distribution.

Most other foundries use a modified punch method to produce the matrix from which final types are cast, although comparison is unconclusive since the requirements of foundry and various machine types are different in so many ways.

As the name implies, linotype composition is set in single lines of type, each individual line being composed of one solid bar of type metal. Before casting, individual brass matrices are composed by the machine operator and then fed into the machine to be automatically justified, cast and trimmed. The individual matrices are then automatically redistributed to be used again. After printing, the type metal is melted down and reused.

The Ludlow Typograph machine is a device which makes large type available without the necessity of having to purchase multiple fonts of foundry type. It is a type-casting machine which produces individual lines of type as in linotype composition, but justification and distribution are performed manually, as in foundry composition.

The Lanston Monotype machine shares some of the automatic features of the linotype machine. By this process full lines of type are composed by the operator and fed into a casting device. The end product consists of individual letters, similar to foundry type, forming justified lines of type.

a.

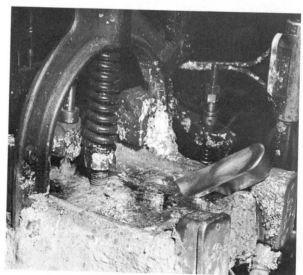

d.

a. The mechanical process of "cutting" the type face begins as each character is photographed, enlarged to about 3½ inches high and made into an etching which becomes a permanent pattern plate.

b. The zinc plate is used as a pattern in the ATF Benton engraving machine. Each slight move of the follower within the confines of the pattern plate is repeated in a reduced degree by a rapidly revolving cutting tool which engraves the matrix.

c. The engraved matrix.

d. Into the casting machines go pigs of metal.

e. The precision-cut matrix is inserted into the casting machine by experienced operators.

f. After casting, the type is moved past a series of trimming knives, the first of which removes the jet. Others groove the feet, trim the edges and kern the overhang. Photo shows the casting machine opened to expose knives.

b.

c.

e.

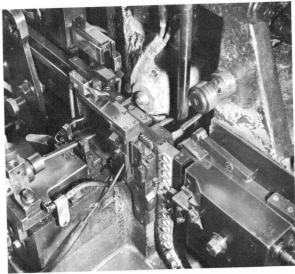

f.

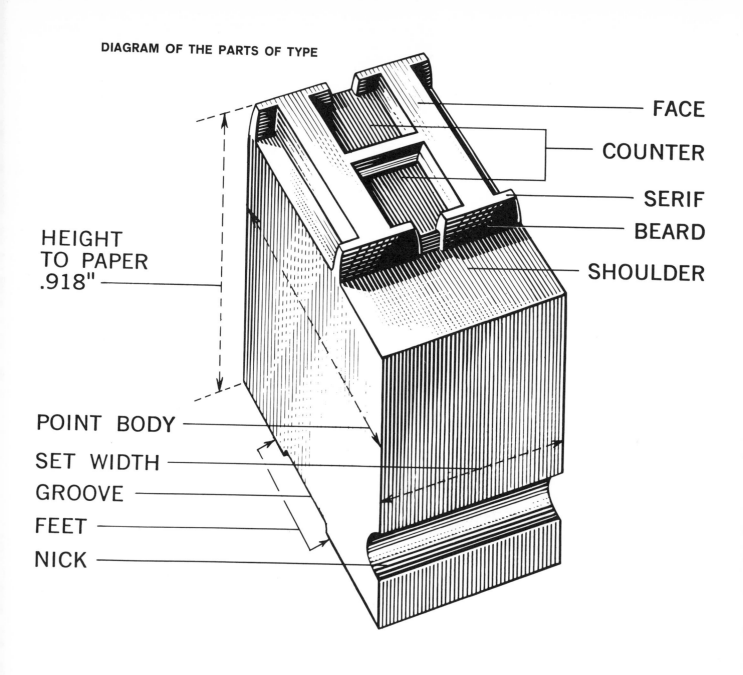

DIAGRAM OF THE PARTS OF TYPE

FACE

COUNTER

SERIF

BEARD

SHOULDER

HEIGHT
TO PAPER
.918"

POINT BODY

SET WIDTH

GROOVE

FEET

NICK

Measurement Data

English-American Point System

1 pt.	= 1/12 pica	**or**	1/72 inch	
6 pts.	= 1/2 pica	**or**	1/12 inch	
12 pts.	= 1 pica	**or**	1/6 inch	
72 pts.	= 6 picas	**or**	1 inch*	

Didot Point System

12 pts.	= 1 cicero or douze
1 pt.	= 0,3759 mm
8 pts.	= 3.007 mm
12 pts.	= 4.511 mm
1 mm	= 2.66 points
1 m	= 2660 points

Decimal Equivalents

1 inch	= 6 picas, 0 points
7/8 inch	= 5 picas, 3 points
3/4 inch	= 4 picas, 6 points
5/8 inch	= 3 picas, 9 points
1/2 inch	= 3 picas, 0 points
3/8 inch	= 2 picas, 3 points
1/4 inch	= 1 pica , 6 points
1/8 inch	= 0 picas, 9 points

*Seventy-two points measure .996 of an inch.

COPY CASTING

In order to convert original copy into type that will fit, look and function as desired, one should devise a system of efficient specification. Clear preparation of original copy that contains all the information a typographer needs to know is really all that is required. Here is one way to proceed.

Type up original copy. If possible, approximate the final form you want it to take. Common sense calls for preparation using flush or indented paragraphs, caps and lower case letters, correct details of spelling, punctuation, etc.–all typed as you wish the final job to be. Double space for clarity.

For a rough preliminary estimate you may assume that average typewritten copy will, when single spaced, be roughly equal to average 14 pt. type. If 12 pt. type is under consideration, assume about ¾ of the typed area and for 10 pt. type, ½ the area. This rule of thumb applies to single spaced typing and type set solid. Allowance must be made for variables. As useful as this may be for rough time-saving approximations, it is by no means accurate.

Original Copy

To cast with accuracy, consider that the most useful units of measurement are: (A) the individual line of type, and (B) the number of characters per line.

1. Start counting the original copy, taking two or three lines, and determine the average number of characters per line. Each letter, each punctuation mark, each space between words counts as one.

2. Multiply that number by the total number of lines per page on original copy. This will give you the number of characters per unit.

3. Multiply the number of characters per unit by the total number of units (pages) of the original copy and you have the total number of characters in your original copy.

Determine the Type

Now decide on the style of type to be used. Once again find (A) the measure (width) of line to be used, and (B) the number of characters per line. If text type, you will find a useful table listing the number of characters per line at the bottom of each page of text showing. Once you know the number of characters per line, divide this number into the total number of characters in the original copy and you have the number of lines of type your copy will set to.

All 12 point type is set on a 12 point body, 10 point type on a 10 point body, etc.* By allowing 12 points per line for 12 point type, you can readily determine the precise depth a given number of lines will occupy. This applies to all other sizes as well.

You will note that all text faces are shown 3 ways. 12 point type is designated 12/12, meaning no leading —a solid setting. Under this it is designated 12/14 and 12/16 indicating slugs that are 2 and 4 point leaded respectively.

For larger display faces, counting characters can be done with absolute accuracy by referring to the showings. Note that all display type is leaded 2 points. Where hairlines are used, they are always mounted on the up side of a 2 point body. This will be helpful in determining the position of the face on the body.

*Except where otherwise noted.

MARKING THE COPY

Each request for type may require the specifications listed below. Mark concisely, but fully, for best results.

1. **FACE** . . . Name the family or style: Garamond, Caslon, Latin Wide, etc.

2. **FOUNDRY** . . . For quality control, specify the foundry name which identifies each showing.

3. **SIZE** . . . Order exact sizes. Be specific—don't say "set larger."

4. **WEIGHT** . . . Faces come in Light, Book, Medium, Demibold, etc.

5. **STYLE** . . . Roman, Italic, Condensed, Extra Condensed, Wide, etc.

6. **LEADING** . . . State the amount you want in points or picas.

7. **LETTERSPACING** . . . Mark to set solid or letter spaced optically or to a certain measure.

8. **LAYOUT** . . . Make tissue showing positioning and alignments if required.

9. **WIDTH** . . . Mark the width of your lines on original copy and layout.

10. **CAPITALIZATION** . . . Mark for all caps, all lower case, caps and lower case, caps and small caps.

PROOFREADER'S MARKS

bf.	Reset in bold face	⌐	Move to right	⏀	Paragraph
X	Defective letter	///	Straighten lines	*no*⏀	No paragraph
⊥	Push down space	⊏	Move to left	*w.f.*	Wrong font
℔	Turn inverted letter	⯐	Indent 1 em	*tr.*	Transpose
ꝺ ℔	Delete	$\frac{1}{em}$	One-em dash	*caps*	Reset in capitals
⁂	Insert space	$\frac{2}{em}$	Two-em dash	*s.c.*	Reset in small capitals
⌣	Less space	⨀⁄	Insert semi-colon	*lc.*	Reset in lower case
⌒	Close up entirely	ⱽ	Insert apostrophe	*ital*	Reset in italic
⋀	Insert at this point	ⱽⱽ	Enclose in quotation marks	*Rom.*	Reset in Roman
⊙	Insert period	⩜	Insert hyphen	(?)	Verify
⋏	Insert comma	*stet*	Let it stand	*sp.*	Spell out
⊙	Insert colon	∽	Run in	*eq.*⁂	Equalize spacing

Suggested use:

⯐ ⌐In this introductory paragraph ⎯ and in the ad- $\frac{1}{em}$
vertisement reprinted below ⎯ we have purposely $\frac{1}{em}$
ital made typographic errors in order to show the most
ⱽ common proofreaders marks and how they are
used. These paragraphs are followed by the cor-
⊏rected copy, demonstrating precisely the meaning
of the marks and the changes they indicate. The ⏀ ⯐
advertisement is one that appeared as the frontis-
sp. piece of Volume ② of Typographia, by J. Johnson, ⱽⱽ⁄
⋏ a typographer, published in England in 1824. *bf*

s.c. J. Johnson embraces this opportunity of filling
up the present page, by announcing to the Ad-
Rom. mirers of the Typographic Art, and the Profession
in general, that he has now a subject in hand,
⊥ which ʰe flatters himself will not only eclipse all *stet*
his former productions, but like⌒wise any piece ⌒
that has ever yet appeared before the Public as a ℔
⨀⁄ Typographic Specimen. It will consist of an arch, *lc*
in perspective, supported by ten pillars, in centre *the*
will be a monument to the memory of William *eq#*
eq# Caxton, as the father of printing in this country,
together with the names of the principal early nurs ⩜
ers and improvers of our Art; the   whole will
be executed with brassrules and flowers; the size ⊙
will be eighteen and a quarter, by thirteen inches,
which will be printed on fine drawing paper. ∽ ⊙

no⏀ The above will appear in the course of the present
Cap summer.

In this introductory paragraph—and in the advertisement reprinted below—*we have purposely
made typographic errors* in order to show the most
common proofreader's marks and how they are
used. These paragraphs are followed by the cor-
rected copy, demonstrating precisely the meaning
of the marks and the changes they indicate.

The advertisement is one that appeared as the
frontispiece of Volume Two of **"Typographia"** by
J. Johnson, a typographer, published in England
in 1824.

J. Johnson embraces this opportunity of filling
up the present page, by announcing to the Admirers of the Typographic Art, and the Profession
in general, that he has now a subject in hand,
which he flatters himself will not only eclipse all
his former productions, but likewise any piece
that has ever yet appeared before the Public as a
Typographic Specimen; it will consist of an arch,
in perspective, supported by ten pillars, in the centre
will be a monument to the memory of William
Caxton, as the father of printing in this country,
together with the names of the principal early nurs-
ers and improvers of our Art; the whole will be
executed with brass rules and flowers: the size
will be eighteen and a quarter, by thirteen inches,
which will be printed on fine drawing paper. The
above will appear in the course of the present
Summer.

The following types, shown in a continuous
range of sizes in both Roman and Italic,
and in a variety of weights and size modifications
starting at 72 points for foundry showings
and progressing downward to 8 points or less
in machine sizes, are designated as families.

BASKERVILLE, ATF

EFGHIJKLMNO abcde

BASKERVILLE 353, MONOTYPE

EFGHIJKLMNO abcde

All comparisons are made on 24 point type.

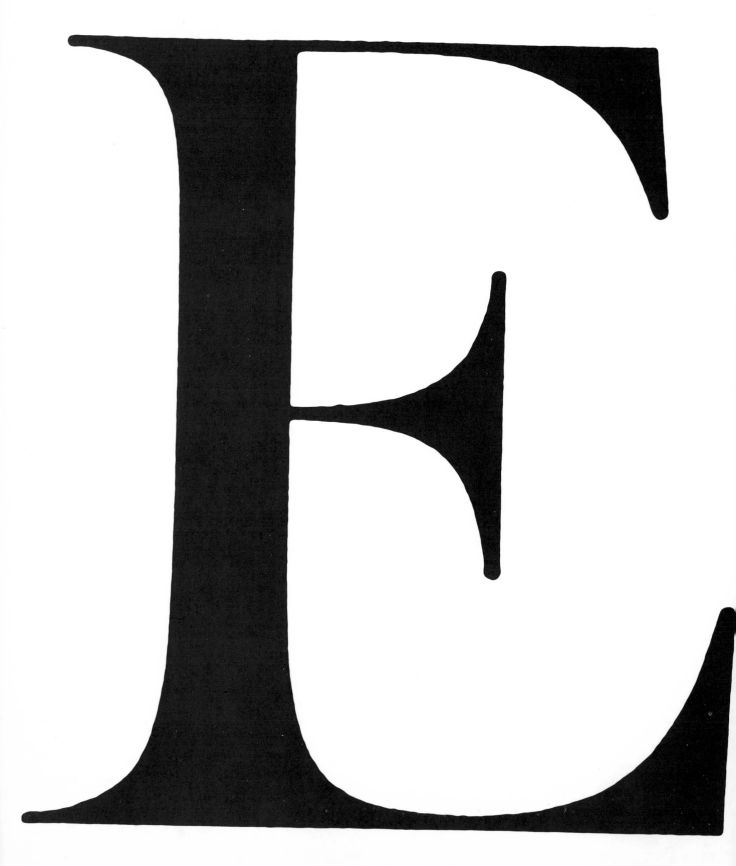

ABCDEFGH
IJKLMNOP
QRSTUVW
XYZ&abcdef
ghijklmnopqr
stuvwxyzfifffl
ffiffl123456789
0$., "-:;!¿?""''

72 POINT BASKERVILLE, ATF

ABCDEFGHIJK
LMNOPQRSTU
VWXYZ&abcde
fghijklmnopqrstu
vwxyzfifffflffffiffl123
4567890$.,"-:;!?""''

60 POINT BASKERVILLE, ATF

ABCDEFGHIJKLM
NOPQRSTUVWX
YZ&abcdefghijklmno
pqrstuvwxyzfifffflffffiffl1
234567890$.,"-:;!?""''

48 POINT BASKERVILLE, ATF

22

ABCDEFGHIJKLMNOPQ
RSTUVWXYZ&abcdefghij
klmnopqrstuvwxyzfifffflffffiffl12
34567890$.,"-:;!?"""

36 POINT BASKERVILLE, ATF

ABCDEFGHIJKLMNOPQRSTU
VWXYZ&abcdefghijklmnopqrstuvw
xyzfifffflffffiffl1234567890$.,"-:;!?""
1234567890

36 POINT BASKERVILLE ITALIC, MONOTYPE

ABCDEFGHIJKLMNOPQRSTU
VWXYZ&abcdefghijklmnopqrstuv
wxyzfifffflffffiffl1234567890$.,"-:;!?"""

30 POINT BASKERVILLE, ATF

ABCDEFGHIJKLMNOPQRSTUVWXY
Z&abcdefghijklmnopqrstuvwxyzfifffflffffiffl12345
67890$.,"-:;!?""1234567890

30 POINT BASKERVILLE ITALIC, MONOTYPE

ABCDEFGHIJKLMNOPQRSTUVWXYZ&
abcdefghijklmnopqrstuvwxyzfifffflffffiffl1234567890$
.,"-:;!?"""

24 POINT BASKERVILLE, ATF

ABCDEFGHIJKLMNOPQRSTUVWXYZ&abcdefghijklm
nopqrstuvwxyzfifffflffiffl1234567890$.,"-:;!?""``

18 POINT NO. 2 BASKERVILLE, ATF

ABCDEFGHIJKLMNOPQRSTUVWXYZ&abcdefghijklmno
pqrstuvwxyzfifffflffiffl1234567890$.,"-:;!?""``

18 POINT NO. 2 BASKERVILLE ITALIC, ATF

ABCDEFGHIJKLMNOPQRSTUVWXYZ&abcdefghijklmnopqrstuvwx
yzfifffflffiffl1234567890$.,'-:;!?""``

18 POINT NO. 1 BASKERVILLE, ATF

ABCDEFGHIJKLMNOPQRSTUVWXYZ&abcdefghijklmnopqrstuvwxy
zfifffflffiffl1234567890$.,"-:;!?""``

18 POINT NO. 1 BASKERVILLE ITALIC, ATF

14/14 Amongst the several mechanic Arts that have engaged my attention, there is no one which I have pursued with so much steadiness and pleasure, as that of Letter-Founding. Having been an early admirer of the beauty of Letters, I became insensibly desirous of contributing to the perfection of them. I formed to my self Ideas of greater accuracy than had yet appeared, and have endeavoured to produce a Sett *of Types according to what I conceived to be their true proportion.*

12/12 Amongst the several mechanic Arts that have engaged my attention, there is no one which I have pursued with so much steadiness and pleasure, as that of Letter-Founding. Having been an early admirer of the beauty of Letters, I became insensibly desirous of contributing to the perfection of them. I formed to my self Ideas of greater accuracy than had yet appeared, and have endeavoured to produce a Sett of Types according to what I conceived to be their true proportion.
Mr. Caslon is an Artist, to whom the Repub-*lic of Learning has great obligations; his ingenuity has left a fairer copy for my emulation,*

14/16 Amongst the several mechanic Arts that have engaged my attention, there is no one which I have pursued with so much steadiness and pleasure, as that of Letter-Founding. Having been an early admirer of the beauty of Letters, I became insensibly desirous of contributing to the perfection of them. I formed to my self Ideas *of Types according to what I conceived to be their true proportion.*

12/14 Amongst the several mechanic Arts that have engaged my attention, there is no one which I have pursued with so much steadiness and pleasure, as that of Letter-Founding. Having been an early admirer of the beauty of Letters, I became insensibly desirous of contributing to the perfection of them. I formed to my self Ideas of greater accuracy than had yet appeared, and have endeavoured to produce a *lic of Learning has great obligations; his ingenuity has left a fairer copy for my emulation,*

14/18 Amongst the several mechanic Arts that have engaged my attention, there is no one which I have pursued with so much steadiness and pleasure, as that of Letter-Founding. Having been an early admirer of the beauty of Letters, I became insensibly desirous of contributing to the per-*of Types according to what I conceived to be their true proportion.*

12/16 Amongst the several mechanic Arts that have engaged my attention, there is no one which I have pursued with so much steadiness and pleasure, as that of Letter-Founding. Having been an early admirer of the beauty of Letters, I became insensibly desirous of contributing to the perfection of them. I formed to my self Ideas of greater accuracy than had yet ap-*lic of Learning has great obligations; his ingenuity has left a fairer copy for my emulation,*

ABCDEFGHIJKLMNOPQRSTUV
ABCDEFGHIJKLMNOPQRSTUV
WXYZ&.,"-:;!?""''
WXYZ&.,"-:;!?""''
1234567890$1234567890$
1234567890$1234567890$
abcdefghijklmnopqrstuvwxyz
abcdefghijklmnopqrstuvwxyz

ABCDEFGHIJKLMNOPQRSTUVWXYZ
ABCDEFGHIJKLMNOPQRSTUVWXYZ
.,"-:;!?""''&1234567890$1234567890$
.,"-:;!?""''&1234567890$1234567890$
abcdefghijklmnopqrstuvwxyz
abcdefghijklmnopqrstuvwxyz

BASKERVILLE: LINOTYPE

PICAS	6	7	8	9	10	11	12	13	14	15	16	17	18	19	20	21	22	23	24	25	26	27	28	29	30
14 POINT	12	14	16	18	21	23	25	27	29	31	33	35	37	39	41	43	45	47	49	51	53	55	57	59	62
12 POINT	14	16	18	20	23	25	28	30	32	34	37	39	41	44	46	48	51	53	55	57	60	62	64	66	69

11/11
Amongst the several mechanic Arts that have engaged my attention, there is no one which I have pursued with so much steadiness and pleasure, as that of Letter-Founding. Having been an early admirer of the beauty of Letters, I became insensibly desirous of contributing to the perfection of them. I formed to my self Ideas of greater accuracy than had yet appeared, and have endeavoured to produce a Sett of Types according to what I conceived to be their true proportion.

Mr. Caslon is an Artist, to whom the Republic of Learning has great obligations; his ingenuity has left a fairer copy for my emulation, than any *other master. In his great variety of Characters I intend not to follow him; the Roman and Italic*

10/10
Amongst the several mechanic Arts that have engaged my attention, there is no one which I have pursued with so much steadiness and pleasure, as that of Letter-Founding. Having been an early admirer of the beauty of Letters, I became insensibly desirous of contributing to the perfection of them. I formed to my self Ideas of greater accuracy than had yet appeared, and have endeavoured to produce a Sett of Types according to what I conceived to be their true proportion.

Mr. Caslon is an Artist, to whom the Republic of Learning has great obligations; his ingenuity has left a fairer copy for my emulation, than any other master. In his great variety of Characters I intend not to follow him; the Roman and Italic are all I have hitherto *ment, it is probably more owing to that variety which divided his attention, than to any other cause. I honor*

11/13
Amongst the several mechanic Arts that have engaged my attention, there is no one which I have pursued with so much steadiness and pleasure, as that of Letter-Founding. Having been an early admirer of the beauty of Letters, I became insensibly desirous of contributing to the perfection of them. I formed to my self Ideas of greater accuracy than had yet appeared, and have endeavoured to produce a Sett of Types according to what I conceived to be their true proportion.

Mr. Caslon is an Artist, to whom the Republic *other master. In his great variety of Characters I intend not to follow him; the Roman and Italic*

10/12
Amongst the several mechanic Arts that have engaged my attention, there is no one which I have pursued with so much steadiness and pleasure, as that of Letter-Founding. Having been an early admirer of the beauty of Letters, I became insensibly desirous of contributing to the perfection of them. I formed to my self Ideas of greater accuracy than had yet appeared, and have endeavoured to produce a Sett of Types according to what I conceived to be their true proportion.

Mr. Caslon is an Artist, to whom the Republic of Learning has great obligations; his ingenuity has left a fairer copy for my emulation, than any other master. *ment, it is probably more owing to that variety which divided his attention, than to any other cause. I honor*

11/15
Amongst the several mechanic Arts that have engaged my attention, there is no one which I have pursued with so much steadiness and pleasure, as that of Letter-Founding. Having been an early admirer of the beauty of Letters, I became insensibly desirous of contributing to the perfection of them. I formed to my self Ideas of greater accuracy than had yet appeared, and have endeavoured to produce a Sett of Types according to what *other master. In his great variety of Characters I intend not to follow him; the Roman and Italic*

10/14
Amongst the several mechanic Arts that have engaged my attention, there is no one which I have pursued with so much steadiness and pleasure, as that of Letter-Founding. Having been an early admirer of the beauty of Letters, I became insensibly desirous of contributing to the perfection of them. I formed to my self Ideas of greater accuracy than had yet appeared, and have endeavoured to produce a Sett of Types according to what I conceived to be their true proportion.

Mr. Caslon is an Artist, to whom the Republic of *ment, it is probably more owing to that variety which divided his attention, than to any other cause. I honor*

ABCDEFGHIJKLMNOPQRSTUVWXYZ
ABCDEFGHIJKLMNOPQRSTUVWXYZ
&.,"-:;!?""1234567890$1234567890$
&.,"-:;!?""1234567890$1234567890$
abcdefghijklmnopqrstuvwxyz
abcdefghijklmnopqrstuvwxyz

ABCDEFGHIJKLMNOPQRSTUVWXYZ
ABCDEFGHIJKLMNOPQRSTUVWXYZ
.,"-:;!?""&1234567890$1234567890$
.,"-:;!?""&1234567890$1234567890$
abcdefghijklmnopqrstuvwxyz
abcdefghijklmnopqrstuvwxyz

BASKERVILLE : LINOTYPE

PICAS	6	7	8	9	10	11	12	13	14	15	16	17	18	19	20	21	22	23	24	25	26	27	28	29	30
11 POINT	15	17	20	22	25	27	29	31	34	36	39	41	44	46	49	51	54	56	59	61	64	66	69	71	74
10 POINT	16	18	21	23	26	28	31	33	36	39	42	44	47	49	52	54	57	59	62	65	68	70	73	75	78

9/9

Amongst the several mechanic Arts that have engaged my attention, there is no one which I have pursued with so much steadiness and pleasure, as that of Letter-Founding. Having been an early admirer of the beauty of Letters, I became insensibly desirous of contributing to the perfection of them. I formed to my self Ideas of greater accuracy than had yet appeared, and have endeavoured to produce a Sett of Types according to what I conceived to be their true proportion.

Mr. Caslon is an Artist, to whom the Republic of Learning has great obligations; his ingenuity has left a fairer copy for my emulation, than any other master. In his great variety of Characters I intend not to follow him; the Roman and Italic are all I have hitherto attempted; if in these he has left room for improvement, it is probably more owing to that variety which divided his attention, than to *any other cause. I honor his merit, and only wish to derive some small share of Reputation, from an Art which proves*

8/8

Amongst the several mechanic Arts that have engaged my attention, there is no one which I have pursued with so much steadiness and pleasure, as that of Letter-Founding. Having been an early admirer of the beauty of Letters, I became insensibly desirous of contributing to the perfection of them. I formed to my self Ideas of greater accuracy than had yet appeared, and have endeavoured to produce a Sett of Types according to what I conceived to be their true proportion.

Mr. Caslon is an Artist, to whom the Republic of Learning has great obligations; his ingenuity has left a fairer copy for my emulation, than any other master. In his great variety of Characters I intend not to follow him; the Roman and Italic are all I have hitherto attempted; if in these he has left room for improvement, it is probably more owing to that variety which divided his attention, than to any other cause. I honor his merit, and only wish to derive some small share of Reputation, from an Art which proves accidentally to have been the object of our mutual pursuit.

After having spent many years, and not a little of my fortune *in my endeavours to advance this art; I must own it gives me great Satisfaction, to find that my Edition of Virgil has been so*

9/11

Amongst the several mechanic Arts that have engaged my attention, there is no one which I have pursued with so much steadiness and pleasure, as that of Letter-Founding. Having been an early admirer of the beauty of Letters, I became insensibly desirous of contributing to the perfection of them. I formed to my self Ideas of greater accuracy than had yet appeared, and have endeavoured to produce a Sett of Types according to what I conceived to be their true proportion.

Mr. Caslon is an Artist, to whom the Republic of Learning has great obligations; his ingenuity has left a fairer copy for my emulation, than any other master. In his great variety of Characters I intend not to follow him; the Ro-*any other cause. I honor his merit, and only wish to derive some small share of Reputation, from an Art which proves*

8/10

Amongst the several mechanic Arts that have engaged my attention, there is no one which I have pursued with so much steadiness and pleasure, as that of Letter-Founding. Having been an early admirer of the beauty of Letters, I became insensibly desirous of contributing to the perfection of them. I formed to my self Ideas of greater accuracy than had yet appeared, and have endeavoured to produce a Sett of Types according to what I conceived to be their true proportion.

Mr. Caslon is an Artist, to whom the Republic of Learning has great obligations; his ingenuity has left a fairer copy for my emulation, than any other master. In his great variety of Characters I intend not to follow him; the Roman and Italic are all I have hitherto attempted; if in these he has left room for improvement, it is probably more owing to that variety which divided his attention, than to any other cause. I honor his merit, *in my endeavours to advance this art; I must own it gives me great Satisfaction, to find that my Edition of Virgil has been so*

9/13

Amongst the several mechanic Arts that have engaged my attention, there is no one which I have pursued with so much steadiness and pleasure, as that of Letter-Founding. Having been an early admirer of the beauty of Letters, I became insensibly desirous of contributing to the perfection of them. I formed to my self Ideas of greater accuracy than had yet appeared, and have endeavoured to produce a Sett of Types according to what I conceived to be their true proportion.

Mr. Caslon is an Artist, to whom the Republic of Learning has great obligations; his ingenuity has left a fairer *any other cause. I honor his merit, and only wish to derive some small share of Reputation, from an Art which proves*

8/12

Amongst the several mechanic Arts that have engaged my attention, there is no one which I have pursued with so much steadiness and pleasure, as that of Letter-Founding. Having been an early admirer of the beauty of Letters, I became insensibly desirous of contributing to the perfection of them. I formed to my self Ideas of greater accuracy than had yet appeared, and have endeavoured to produce a Sett of Types according to what I conceived to be their true proportion.

Mr. Caslon is an Artist, to whom the Republic of Learning has great obligations; his ingenuity has left a fairer copy for my emulation, than any other master. In his great variety of Characters I intend not to follow him; the Roman and Italic are all *in my endeavours to advance this art; I must own it gives me great Satisfaction, to find that my Edition of Virgil has been so*

ABCDEFGHIJKLMNOPQRSTUVWXYZ
ABCDEFGHIJKLMNOPQRSTUVWXYZ
.,"-:;!?""&1234567890$1234567890$
.,"-:;!?""&1234567890$1234567890$
abcdefghijklmnopqrstuvwxyz
abcdefghijklmnopqrstuvwxyz

ABCDEFGHIJKLMNOPQRSTUVWXYZ
ABCDEFGHIJKLMNOPQRSTUVWXYZ
.,"-:;!?""&1234567890$1234567890$
.,"-:;!?""&1234567890$1234567890$
abcdefghijklmnopqrstuvwxyz
abcdefghijklmnopqrstuvwxyz

BASKERVILLE: LINOTYPE

PICAS	6	7	8	9	10	11	12	13	14	15	16	17	18	19	20	21	22	23	24	25	26	27	28	29	30
9 POINT	17	20	23	26	29	32	35	38	41	43	46	49	52	55	58	61	64	67	70	72	75	78	81	84	87
8 POINT	19	22	25	28	32	35	38	41	44	47	50	54	58	61	64	66	69	72	76	79	82	85	88	91	95

14/14 Amongst the several mechanic Arts that have engaged my attention, there is no one which I have pursued with so much steadiness and pleasure, as that of Letter-Founding. Having been an early admirer of the beauty of Letters, I became insensibly desirous of contributing to the perfection of them. I formed to my self Ideas of greater accuracy than had yet appeared, and have endeavoured to *produce a Sett of Types according to what I conceived to be their true pro-*

14/16 Amongst the several mechanic Arts that have engaged my attention, there is no one which I have pursued with so much steadiness and pleasure, as that of Letter-Founding. Having been an early admirer of the beauty of Letters, I became insensibly desirous of contributing to the perfection of them. I formed to my *produce a Sett of Types according to what I conceived to be their true pro-*

14/18 Amongst the several mechanic Arts that have engaged my attention, there is no one which I have pursued with so much steadiness and pleasure, as that of Letter-Founding. Having been an early admirer of the beauty of Letters, I became insensibly desirous of contributing to *produce a Sett of Types according to what I conceived to be their true pro-*

12/12 Amongst the several mechanic Arts that have engaged my attention, there is no one which I have pursued with so much steadiness and pleasure, as that of Letter-Founding. Having been an early admirer of the beauty of Letters, I became insensibly desirous of contributing to the perfection of them. I formed to my self Ideas of greater accuracy than had yet appeared, and have endeavoured to produce a Set of Types according to what I conceived to be their true proportion.
    Mr. Caslon is an Artist, to whom the Re-*public of Learning has great obligations; his ingenuity has left a fairer copy for my emula-*

12/14 Amongst the several mechanic Arts that have engaged my attention, there is no one which I have pursued with so much steadiness and pleasure, as that of Letter-Founding. Having been an early admirer of the beauty of Letters, I became insensibly desirous of contributing to the perfection of them. I formed to my self Ideas of greater accuracy than had yet appeared, and have endeavoured to produce a *public of Learning has great obligations; his ingenuity has left a fairer copy for my emula-*

12/16 Amongst the several mechanic Arts that have engaged my attention, there is no one which I have pursued with so much steadiness and pleasure, as that of Letter-Founding. Having been an early admirer of the beauty of Letters, I became insensibly desirous of contributing to the perfection of them. I formed to my self Ideas of greater accuracy than had yet *public of Learning has great obligations; his ingenuity has left a fairer copy for my emula-*

ABCDEFGHIJKLMNOPQRSTUV
ABCDEFGHIJKLMNOPQRSTUV
&.,"-:;!?""1234567890$
&.,"-:;!?""1234567890$
abcdefghijklmnopqrstuvwxyz
abcdefghijklmnopqrstuvwxyz

ABCDEFGHIJKLMNOPQRSTUVWXYZ
ABCDEFGHIJKLMNOPQRSTUVWXYZ
&.,"-:;!?""1234567890$
&.,"-:;!?""1234567890$
abcdefghijklmnopqrstuvwxyz
abcdefghijklmnopqrstuvwxyz

BASKERVILLE BOLD: LINOTYPE

PICAS	6	7	8	9	10	11	12	13	14	15	16	17	18	19	20	21	22	23	24	25	26	27	28	29	30
14 POINT	12	14	16	18	20	22	24	26	28	30	32	34	36	38	40	42	44	46	48	50	52	54	56	58	60
12 POINT	14	16	19	21	23	25	28	30	32	35	37	39	41	44	46	48	51	53	55	58	60	62	65	67	69

10/10

Amongst the several mechanic Arts that have engaged my attention, there is no one which I have pursued with so much steadiness and pleasure, as that of Letter-Founding. Having been an early admirer of the beauty of Letters, I became insensibly desirous of contributing to the perfection of them. I formed to my self Ideas of greater accuracy than had yet appeared, and have endeavoured to produce a Sett of Types according to what I conceived to be their true proportion.

Mr. Caslon is an Artist, to whom the Republic of Learning has great obligations; his ingenuity has left a fairer copy for my emulation, than any other master. In his great variety of Characters I intend not to follow him; the Roman and Italic are all I *have hitherto attempted; if in these he has left room for improvement it is probably more owing to that*

8/8

Amongst the several mechanic Arts that have engaged my attention, there is no one which I have pursued with so much steadiness and pleasure, as that of Letter-Founding. Having been an early admirer of the beauty of Letters, I became insensibly desirous of contributing to the perfection of them. I formed to my self Ideas of greater accuracy than had yet appeared, and have endeavoured to produce a Sett of Types according to what I conceived to be their true proportion.

Mr. Caslon is an Artist, to whom the Republic of Learning has great obligations; his ingenuity has left a fairer copy for my emulation, than any other master. In his great variety of Characters I intend not to follow him; the Roman and Italic are all I have hitherto attempted; if in these he has left room for improvement, it is probably more owing to that variety which divided his attention, than to any other cause. I honor his merit, and only wish to derive some small share of Reputation, from an Art which proves accidentally to have been the object of our mutual pursuit.

After having spent many years, and not a little of my fortune *in my endeavours to advance this art; I must own it gives me great Satisfaction, to find that my Edition of Virgil has been so*

10/12

Amongst the several mechanic Arts that have engaged my attention, there is no one which I have pursued with so much steadiness and pleasure, as that of Letter-Founding. Having been an early admirer of the beauty of Letters, I became insensibly desirous of contributing to the perfection of them. I formed to my self Ideas of greater accuracy than had yet appeared, and have endeavoured to produce a Sett of Types according to what I conceived to be their true proportion.

Mr. Caslon is an Artist, to whom the Republic of Learning has great obligations; his ingenuity has *have hitherto attempted; if in these he has left room for improvement it is probably more owing to that*

8/10

Amongst the several mechanic Arts that have engaged my attention, there is no one which I have pursued with so much steadiness and pleasure, as that of Letter-Founding. Having been an early admirer of the beauty of Letters, I became insensibly desirous of contributing to the perfection of them. I formed to my self Ideas of greater accuracy than had yet appeared, and have endeavoured to produce a Sett of Types according to what I conceived to be their true proportion.

Mr. Caslon is an Artist, to whom the Republic of Learning has great obligations; his ingenuity has left a fairer copy for my emulation, than any other master. In his great variety of Characters I intend not to follow him; the Roman and Italic are all I have hitherto attempted; if in these he has left room for improvement, it is probably more owing to that variety which divided his attention, than to any other cause. I honor *in my endeavours to advance this art; I must own it gives me great Satisfaction, to find that my Edition of Virgil has been so*

10/14

Amongst the several mechanic Arts that have engaged my attention, there is no one which I have pursued with so much steadiness and pleasure, as that of Letter-Founding. Having been an early admirer of the beauty of Letters, I became insensibly desirous of contributing to the perfection of them. I formed to my self Ideas of greater accuracy than had yet appeared, and have endeavoured to produce a Sett of Types according to what I conceived to be their true proportion.

have hitherto attempted; if in these he has left room for improvement it is probably more owing to that

8/12

Amongst the several mechanic Arts that have engaged my attention, there is no one which I have pursued with so much steadiness and pleasure, as that of Letter-Founding. Having been an early admirer of the beauty of Letters, I became insensibly desirous of contributing to the perfection of them. I formed to my self Ideas of greater accuracy than had yet appeared, and have endeavoured to produce a Sett of Types according to what I conceived to be their true proportion.

Mr. Caslon is an Artist, to whom the Republic of Learning has great obligations; his ingenuity has left a fairer copy for my emulation, than any other master. In his great variety of Characters I intend not to follow him; the Roman and Italic *in my endeavours to advance this art; I must own it gives me great Satisfaction, to find that my Edition of Virgil has been so*

ABCDEFGHIJKLMNOPQRSTUVWXYZ
ABCDEFGHIJKLMNOPQRSTUVWXYZ
&.,"-:;!?""1234567890$
&.,"-:;!?""1234567890$
abcdefghijklmnopqrstuvwxyz
abcdefghijklmnopqrstuvwxyz

ABCDEFGHIJKLMNOPQRSTUVWXYZ
ABCDEFGHIJKLMNOPQRSTUVWXYZ
&.,"-:;!?""1234567890$
&.,"-:;!?""1234567890$
abcdefghijklmnopqrstuvwxyz
abcdefghijklmnopqrstuvwxyz

BASKERVILLE BOLD: LINOTYPE

PICAS	6	7	8	9	10	11	12	13	14	15	16	17	18	19	20	21	22	23	24	25	26	27	28	29	30
10 POINT	15	18	20	23	26	28	31	33	36	39	41	44	46	49	52	54	57	59	62	65	67	69	72	75	78
8 POINT	19	22	25	28	32	35	38	41	44	48	51	54	58	61	64	67	70	73	76	80	83	86	89	92	96

FIVE airplane wreck

QUICK SERVICE offices

BCDEF the established

BCDEF the established

MACHINE reference

BCDEF abcdefghrstuvw

All comparisons are made on 24 point type.

Bodoni is precise, somewhat aristocratic in character, imparting a quality of dignity.

ABCDEFGHIJK
LMNOPQRSTU
VWXYZ&abcdef
ghijklmnopqrstu
vwxyzfffiffiflffiffffffl12
34567890$.,""-.:;!?""

ABCDEFGHIJKLM
NOPQRSTUVWXY
Z&abcdefghijklmno
pqrstuvwxyzfffffiflffl
1234567890$.,"-:;!?""``

60 POINT BODONI, ATF

ABCDEFGHIJKLM
NOPQRSTUVWXY
Z&abcdefghijklmno
pqrstuvwxyzfifffflfffflffi
1234567890$.,"-:;!?""''

60 POINT BODONI ITALIC, ATF

Note the discrepancy in weights between Bauer Bodoni and ATF Bodoni.

ABCDEFGHIJKLMNOP QRSTUVWXYZ&abcdef ghijklmnopqrstuvwxyzfffi flffiffl1234567890$.,"-:;!?"""

48 POINT BODONI, ATF

ABCDEFGHIJKLMNOP QRSTUVWXYZ&abcdef ghijklmnopqrstuvwxyzfiff fflffifl1234567890$.,"-:;!?"""

48 POINT BODONI ITALIC, ATF

ABCDEFGHIJKLMNOPQRS TUVWXYZ&abcdefghijklm nopqrstuvwxyzfififfl1234567 890$.,"-:;!?""

42 POINT BODONI, BAUER

ABCDEFGHIJKLMNOPQ
RSTUVWXYZ&abcdefghijkl
mnopqrstuvwxyzfifffljft12345
67890$.,"-:,;!?""

42 POINT BODONI ITALIC, BAUER

ABCDEFGHIJKLMNOPQRSTUVWX
YZ&abcdefghijklmnopqrstuvwxyzfiffffl
1234567890$.,"-:,;!?""

30 POINT BODONI, BAUER

ABCDEFGHIJKLMNOPQRSTUV
WXYZ&abcdefghijklmnopqrstuvwxyz
fifffljft1234567890$.,"-:,;!?""

30 POINT BODONI ITALIC, BAUER

ABCDEFGHIJKLMNOPQRSTUVWXYZ&abcdefgh
ijklmnopqrstuvwxyzfifffl1234567890$.,"-:,;!?""

24 POINT BODONI, BAUER

ABCDEFGHIJKLMNOPQRSTUVWXYZ&abcdefgh
ijklmnopqrstuvwxyzfifffljft1234567890$,,"-:,;!?""

24 POINT BODONI ITALIC, BAUER

ABCDEFGHIJKLMNOPQRSTUVWXYZ&abcdefghijklmnopqrs
tuvwxyzfifffl1234567890$.,"-:,;!?""

18 POINT BODONI, BAUER

34

ABCDEFGHIJKLMNOPQRSTUVWXYZ&abcdefghijklmnop
qrstuvwxyzfifffflft1234567890$.,'‘-:.!?"“

18 POINT BODONI ITALIC, BAUER

ABCDEFGHIJKLMNOPQRSTUVWXYZ&abcdefghijklmnopqrstuvwxyz
fifffl1234567890$.,'‘-:;!?"“

16 POINT BODONI, BAUER

ABCDEFGHIJKLMNOPQRSTUVWXYZ&abcdefghijklmnopqrstuvwxyz
fifffflft1234567890$.,'‘-:;!?"“

16 POINT BODONI ITALIC, BAUER

14/14 From a translation of a letter to Mr. Francis Rosaspina by Bodoni dated Sept. 12, 1813:

You received with great courtesy the Rector of this our Imperial Lyceum in Parma; I am happy to think that you will extend the same courtesies to the Censor of said institute. Beside being my friend, and a very worthy ecclesiastic, he is the brother of a great friend of mine, who has a great name in the republic of letters, and *among the sacred orators living. Do please be liberal of your favors to him during the*

12/12 From a translation of a letter to Mr. Francis Rosaspina by Bodoni dated Sept. 12, 1813:

You received with great courtesy the Rector of this our Imperial Lyceum in Parma; I am happy to think that you will extend the same courtesies to the Censor of said institute. Beside being my friend, and a very worthy ecclesiastic, he is the brother of a great friend of mine, who has a great name in the republic of letters, and among the sacred orators living. Do please be liberal of your favors to him during the brief stay which he is planning to make in this your City, which is *counted among the most cultured in Europe. And now that I have sung the praises of my Rec-*

14/16 From a translation of a letter to Mr. Francis Rosaspina by Bodoni dated Sept. 12, 1813:

You received with great courtesy the Rector of this our Imperial Lyceum in Parma; I am happy to think that you will extend the same courtesies to the Censor of said institute. Beside being my friend, and a very worthy ecclesiastic, he is the *among the sacred orators living. Do please be liberal of your favors to him during the*

12/14 From a translation of a letter to Mr. Francis Rosaspina by Bodoni dated Sept. 12, 1813:

You received with great courtesy the Rector of this our Imperial Lyceum in Parma; I am happy to think that you will extend the same courtesies to the Censor of said institute. Beside being my friend, and a very worthy ecclesiastic, he is the brother of a great friend of mine, who has a great name in the republic of letters, and among the *counted among the most cultured in Europe. And now that I have sung the praises of my Rec-*

14/18 From a translation of a letter to Mr. Francis Rosaspina by Bodoni dated Sept. 12, 1813:

You received with great courtesy the Rector of this our Imperial Lyceum in Parma; I am happy to think that you will extend the same courtesies to the Censor of said institute. Beside being my friend, *among the sacred orators living. Do please be liberal of your favors to him during the*

12/16 From a translation of a letter to Mr. Francis Rosaspina by Bodoni dated Sept. 12, 1813:

You received with great courtesy the Rector of this our Imperial Lyceum in Parma; I am happy to think that you will extend the same courtesies to the Censor of said institute. Beside being my friend, and a very worthy ecclesiastic, he is the brother of a great friend of mine, who has a great *counted among the most cultured in Europe. And now that I have sung the praises of my Rec-*

ABCDEFGHIJKLMNOPQRSTUVWXY
ABCDEFGHIJKLMNOPQRSTUVWXY
&.,"-:;!?""'1234567890$
&.,"-:;!?""'1234567890$
abcdefghijklmnopqrstuvwxyz
abcdefghijklmnopqrstuvwxyz

ABCDEFGHIJKLMNOPQRSTUVWXYZ
ABCDEFGHIJKLMNOPQRSTUVWXYZ
&.,"-:;!?""'1234567890$
&.,"-:;!?""'1234567890$
abcdefghijklmnopqrstuvwxyz
abcdefghijklmnopqrstuvwxyz

BODONI: LINOTYPE

PICAS	6	7	8	9	10	11	12	13	14	15	16	17	18	19	20	21	22	23	24	25	26	27	28	29	30
14 POINT	12	14	16	18	20	22	24	26	28	30	32	34	36	38	40	42	44	46	48	50	52	54	56	58	60
12 POINT	16	18	20	23	25	27	29	32	34	36	39	41	43	46	48	50	53	55	57	59	62	64	66	69	74

10/10 From a translation of a letter to Mr. Francis Rosaspina, in Bologna, by Bodoni dated Sept. 12, 1813:

You received with great courtesy the Rector of this our Imperial Lyceum in Parma; I am happy to think that you will extend the same courtesies to the Censor of said institute. Beside being my friend, and a very worthy ecclesiastic, he is the brother of a great friend of mine, who has a great name in the republic of letters, and among the sacred orators living. Do please be liberal of your favors to him during the brief stay which he is planning to make in this your City, which is counted among the most cultured in Europe. And now that I have sung the praises of my Recommended, I will mention his name. He is Mr Abbé Guglielmo Leoni, very well known in Pied-*mont, and who holds a distinguished position among the literary men of Bormida and Tanaro. He will*

9/9 From a translation of a letter to Mr. Francis Rosaspina, in Bologna, by Bodoni dated Sept. 12, 1813:

You received with great courtesy the Rector of this our Imperial Lyceum in Parma; I am happy to think that you will extend the same courtesies to the Censor of said institute. Beside being my friend, and a very worthy ecclesiastic, he is the brother of a great friend of mine, who has a great name in the republic of letters, and among the sacred orators living. Do please be liberal of your favors to him during the brief stay which he is planning to make in this your City, which is counted among the most cultured in Europe. And now that I have sung the praises of my Recommended, I will mention his name. He is Mr Abbé Guglielmo Leoni, very well known in Piedmont, and who holds a distinguished position among the literary men of Bormida and Tanaro. He will give you detailed news of me, and of my joyful wife, and of our *friends; and will add that, as you have already received the most part of my Collection, so you will have the re-*

10/12 From a translation of a letter to Mr. Francis Rosaspina, in Bologna, by Bodoni dated Sept. 12, 1813:

You received with great courtesy the Rector of this our Imperial Lyceum in Parma; I am happy to think that you will extend the same courtesies to the Censor of said institute. Beside being my friend, and a very worthy ecclesiastic, he is the brother of a great friend of mine, who has a great name in the republic of letters, and among the sacred orators living. Do please be liberal of your favors to him during the brief stay which he is planning to make in this your City, which is counted among the most cultured in *mont, and who holds a distinguished position among the literary men of Bormida and Tanaro. He will*

9/11 From a translation of a letter to Mr. Francis Rosaspina, in Bologna, by Bodoni dated Sept. 12, 1813:

You received with great courtesy the Rector of this our Imperial Lyceum in Parma; I am happy to think that you will extend the same courtesies to the Censor of said institute. Beside being my friend, and a very worthy ecclesiastic, he is the brother of a great friend of mine, who has a great name in the republic of letters, and among the sacred orators living. Do please be liberal of your favors to him during the brief stay which he is planning to make in this your City, which is counted among the most cultured in Europe. And now that I have sung the praises of my Recommended, I will mention his name. He is Mr *friends; and will add that, as you have already received the most part of my Collection, so you will have the re-*

10/14 From a translation of a letter to Mr. Francis Rosaspina, in Bologna, by Bodoni dated Sept. 12, 1813:

You received with great courtesy the Rector of this our Imperial Lyceum in Parma; I am happy to think that you will extend the same courtesies to the Censor of said institute. Beside being my friend, and a very worthy ecclesiastic, he is the brother of a great friend of mine, who has a great name in the republic of letters, and among the sacred orators living. Do please be liberal of your favors to him during the *mont, and who holds a distinguished position among the literary men of Bormida and Tanaro. He will*

9/13 From a translation of a letter to Mr. Francis Rosaspina, in Bologna, by Bodoni dated Sept. 12, 1813:

You received with great courtesy the Rector of this our Imperial Lyceum in Parma; I am happy to think that you will extend the same courtesies to the Censor of said institute. Beside being my friend, and a very worthy ecclesiastic, he is the brother of a great friend of mine, who has a great name in the republic of letters, and among the sacred orators living. Do please be liberal of your favors to him during the brief stay which he is planning to make in this your City, which is counted among the most cul-*friends; and will add that, as you have already received the most part of my Collection, so you will have the re-*

ABCDEFGHIJKLMNOPQRSTUVWXYZ
ABCDEFGHIJKLMNOPQRSTUVWXYZ
&.,"-:;!?""''1234567890$
&.,"-:;!?""''1234567890$
abcdefghijklmnopqrstuvwxyz
abcdefghijklmnopqrstuvwxyz

ABCDEFGHIJKLMNOPQRSTUVWXYZ
ABCDEFGHIJKLMNOPQRSTUVWXYZ
&.,"-:;!?""''1234567890$
&.,"-:;!?""''1234567890$
abcdefghijklmnopqrstuvwxyz
abcdefghijklmnopqrstuvwxyz

BODONI: LINOTYPE

PICAS	6	7	8	9	10	11	12	13	14	15	16	17	18	19	20	21	22	23	24	25	26	27	28	29	30
10 POINT	17	20	22	25	27	30	32	35	37	40	42	45	47	50	52	55	57	60	62	65	67	70	72	75	77
9 POINT	17	20	22	25	28	31	34	36	39	42	45	48	50	53	56	59	62	64	67	70	73	76	78	81	84

8/8 From a translation of a letter to Mr. Francis Rosaspina, in Bologna, by Bodoni dated Sept. 12, 1813:

You received with great courtesy the Rector of this our Imperial Lyceum in Parma; I am happy to think that you will extend the same courtesies to the Censor of said institute. Beside being my friend, and a very worthy ecclesiastic, he is the brother of a great friend of mine, who has a great name in the republic of letters, and among the sacred orators living. Do please be liberal of your favors to him during the brief stay which he is planning to make in this your City, which is counted among the most cultured in Europe. And now that I have sung the praises of my Recommended, I will mention his name. He is Mr Abbé Guglielmo Leoni, very well known in Piedmont, and who holds a distinguished position among the literary men of Bormida and Tanaro. He will give you detailed news of me, and of my joyful wife, and of our friends; and will add that, as you have already received the most part of my Collection, so you will have the remainder. I shall be most happy to hear how you are getting on, and will rejoice to learn that you are enjoying, along *with florid health, a perfect contentment of the soul. Do not be surprised in finding that a friend's hand has written these lines*

6/6 From a translation of a letter to Mr. Francis Rosaspina, in Bologna, by Bodoni dated Sept. 12, 1813:

You received with great courtesy the Rector of this our Imperial Lyceum in Parma; I am happy to think that you will extend the same courtesies to the Censor of said institute. Beside being my friend, and a very worthy ecclesiastic, he is the brother of a great friend of mine, who has a great name in the republic of letters, and among the sacred orators living. Do please be liberal of your favors to him during the brief stay which he is planning to make in this your City, which is counted among the most cultured in Europe. And now that I have sung the praises of my Recommended, I will mention his name. He is Mr Abbé Guglielmo Leoni, very well known in Piedmont, and who holds a distinguished position among the literary men of Bormida and Tanaro. He will give you detailed news of me, and of my joyful wife, and of our friends; and will add that, as you have already received the most part of my Collection, so you will have the remainder. I shall be most happy to hear how you are getting on, and will rejoice to learn that you are enjoying, along with florid health, a perfect contentment of the soul. Do not be surprised in finding that a friend's hand has written these lines of recommendation, as for some time past I have had recourse to this help, for the reason that I am most busy; nor do I care to encroach upon the time which I need to bring to an end those typographical enterprises which I conceived, and indeed are now well on their way. Keep your friendship for me.

The bearer of this my letter will confirm that I, being very busy with my Typographical Manual, have absolutely no time to write at length, all the more so on account of my uncertain health, which prevents me to bend over my desk for any long time in writing; I only employ myself thus for the strictly indispensable.

You received with great courtesy the Rector of this our Imperial Lyceum in Parma: I am happy to think that you will extend the same courtesies to the

8/10 From a translation of a letter to Mr. Francis Rosaspina, in Bologna, by Bodoni dated Sept. 12, 1813:

You received with great courtesy the Rector of this our Imperial Lyceum in Parma; I am happy to think that you will extend the same courtesies to the Censor of said institute. Beside being my friend, and a very worthy ecclesiastic, he is the brother of a great friend of mine, who has a great name in the republic of letters, and among the sacred orators living. Do please be liberal of your favors to him during the brief stay which he is planning to make in this your City, which is counted among the most cultured in Europe. And now that I have sung the praises of my Recommended, I will mention his name. He is Mr Abbé Guglielmo Leoni, very well known in Piedmont, and who holds a distinguished position among the literary men of Bormida and Tanaro. He will give you detailed news of me, and of my *with florid health, a perfect contentment of the soul. Do not be surprised in finding that a friend's hand has written these lines*

6/8 From a translation of a letter to Mr. Francis Rosaspina, in Bologna, by Bodoni dated Sept. 12, 1813:

You received with great courtesy the Rector of this our Imperial Lyceum in Parma; I am happy to think that you will extend the same courtesies to the Censor of said institute. Beside being my friend, and a very worthy ecclesiastic, he is the brother of a great friend of mine, who has a great name in the republic of letters, and among the sacred orators living. Do please be liberal of your favors to him during the brief stay which he is planning to make in this your City, which is counted among the most cultured in Europe. And now that I have sung the praises of my Recommended, I will mention his name. He is Mr Abbé Guglielmo Leoni, very well known in Piedmont, and who holds a distinguished position among the literary men of Bormida and Tanaro. He will give you detailed news of me, and of my joyful wife, and of our friends; and will add that, as you have already received the most part of my Collection, so you will have the remainder. I shall be most happy to hear how you are getting on, and will rejoice to learn that you are enjoying, along with florid health, a perfect contentment of the soul. Do not be surprised in finding that a friend's hand has written these lines of recommendation, as for some time past I have had recourse to this help, for the reason that I am most busy; nor do I care to encroach upon

You received with great courtesy the Rector of this our Imperial Lyceum in Parma: I am happy to think that you will extend the same courtesies to the

8/12 From a translation of a letter to Mr. Francis Rosaspina, in Bologna, by Bodoni dated Sept. 12, 1813:

You received with great courtesy the Rector of this our Imperial Lyceum in Parma; I am happy to think that you will extend the same courtesies to the Censor of said institute. Beside being my friend, and a very worthy ecclesiastic, he is the brother of a great friend of mine, who has a great name in the republic of letters, and among the sacred orators living. Do please be liberal of your favors to him during the brief stay which he is planning to make in this your City, which is counted among the most cultured in Europe. And now that I have sung the praises of my Recommended, I will mention his name. He is Mr Abbé *with florid health, a perfect contentment of the soul. Do not be surprised in finding that a friend's hand has written these lines*

6/10 From a translation of a letter to Mr. Francis Rosaspina, in Bologna, by Bodoni dated Sept. 12, 1813:

You received with great courtesy the Rector of this our Imperial Lyceum in Parma; I am happy to think that you will extend the same courtesies to the Censor of said institute. Beside being my friend, and a very worthy ecclesiastic, he is the brother of a great friend of mine, who has a great name in the republic of letters, and among the sacred orators living. Do please be liberal of your favors to him during the brief stay which he is planning to make in this your City, which is counted among the most cultured in Europe. And now that I have sung the praises of my Recommended, I will mention his name. He is Mr Abbé Guglielmo Leoni, very well known in Piedmont, and who holds a distinguished position among the literary men of Bormida and Tanaro. He will give you detailed news of me, and of my joyful wife, and of our friends; and will add that, as you have already received the most part of my Collection, so you will have the remainder. I shall be most happy to hear how you are getting on, and will

You received with great courtesy the Rector of this our Imperial Lyceum in Parma: I am happy to think that you will extend the same courtesies to the

ABCDEFGHIJKLMNOPQRSTUVWXYZ
ABCDEFGHIJKLMNOPQRSTUVWXYZ
&.,"-:;!?""1234567890$
&.,"-:;!?""1234567890$
abcdefghijklmnopqrstuvwxyz
abcdefghijklmnopqrstuvwxyz

ABCDEFGHIJKLMNOPQRSTUVWXYZ
ABCDEFGHIJKLMNOPQRSTUVWXYZ
&.,"-:;!?""1234567890$
&.,"-:;!?""1234567890$
abcdefghijklmnopqrstuvwxyz
abcdefghijklmnopqrstuvwxyz

BODONI: LINOTYPE

PICAS	6	7	8	9	10	11	12	13	14	15	16	17	18	19	20	21	22	23	24	25	26	27	28	29	30
8 POINT	18	21	24	27	31	34	37	40	43	46	49	53	57	60	63	65	68	71	74	77	80	83	86	89	93
6 POINT	24	28	32	36	41	45	49	53	57	61	65	69	74	78	82	86	90	94	98	102	106	110	114	118	123

ABCDEFGHIJK
LMNOPQRSTU
VWXYZ&abcd
efghijklmnopqrs
tuvwxyzfiffffl123
4567890$.,"-:;!?""

60 POINT BODONI BOLD, BAUER

ABCDEFGHIJKLM
NOPQRSTUVWXY
Z&abcdefghijklmno
pqrstuvwxyzfifffl12
34567890$.,"-:;!?""

54 POINT BODONI BOLD, BAUER

ABCDEFGHIJKLMNOPQR
STUVWXYZ&abcdefghijkl
mnopqrstuvwxyzfifffl1234
567890$.,'-:;!?""

42 POINT BODONI BOLD, BAUER

ABCDEFGHIJKLMNOPQ
RSTUVWXYZ&abcdefghij
klmnopqrstuvwxyzfiffflft12
34567890$.,'-:;!?""

42 POINT BODONI BOLD ITALIC, BAUER

ABCDEFGHIJKLMNOPQRSTUV
WXYZ&abcdefghijklmnopqrstuvw
xyzfifffl1234567890$.,'‘-:;!?'""‘

30 POINT BODONI BOLD, BAUER

ABCDEFGHIJKLMNOPQRSTUV
WXYZ&abcdefghijklmnopqrstuvwx
yzfifffl1234567890$.,'‘-:;!?'""‘

30 POINT BODONI BOLD ITALIC, BAUER

ABCDEFGHIJKLMNOPQRSTUVWXYZ&abcdefg
hijklmnopqrstuvwxyzfifffl1234567890$-,'‘-:;!?'""‘

24 POINT BODONI BOLD, BAUER

ABCDEFGHIJKLMNOPQRSTUVWXYZ&abcdefg
hijklmnopqrstuvwxyzfiffflft1234567890$.,'‘-:;!?'""‘

24 POINT BODONI BOLD ITALIC, BAUER

41

14/14 From a translation of a letter to Mr. Francis Rosaspina, in Bologna, by Bodoni dated Sept. 12, 1813:

You received with great courtesy the Rector of this our Imperial Lyceum in Parma; I am happy to think that you will extend the same courtesies to the Censor of said institute. Beside being my friend, and a very worthy ecclesiastic, he is the brother of a great friend of mine, who *has a great name in the republic of letters, and among the sacred orators living.*

12/12 From a translation of a letter to Mr. Francis Rosaspina, in Bologna, by Bodoni dated Sept. 12, 1813:

You received with great courtesy the Rector of this our Imperial Lyceum in Parma; I am happy to think that you will extend the same courtesies to the Censor of said institute. Beside being my friend, and a very worthy ecclesiastic, he is the brother of a great friend of mine, who has a great name in the republic of letters, and among the sacred orators living. Do please be liberal of *your favors to him during the brief stay which he is planning to make in this your*

14/16 From a translation of a letter to Mr. Francis Rosaspina, in Bologna, by Bodoni dated Sept. 12, 1813:

You received with great courtesy the Rector of this our Imperial Lyceum in Parma; I am happy to think that you will extend the same courtesies to the Censor of said institute. Beside being my friend, *has a great name in the republic of letters, and among the sacred orators living.*

12/14 From a translation of a letter to Mr. Francis Rosaspina, in Bologna, by Bodoni dated Sept. 12, 1813:

You received with great courtesy the Rector of this our Imperial Lyceum in Parma; I am happy to think that you will extend the same courtesies to the Censor of said institute. Beside being my friend, and a very worthy ecclesiastic, he is the brother of a great friend of mine, who has a great name *your favors to him during the brief stay which he is planning to make in this your*

14/18 From a translation of a letter to Mr. Francis Rosaspina, in Bologna, by Bodoni dated Sept. 12, 1813:

You received with great courtesy the Rector of this our Imperial Lyceum in Parma; I am happy to think that you will extend the same courtesies to the Censor *has a great name in the republic of letters, and among the sacred orators living.*

12/16 From a translation of a letter to Mr. Francis Rosaspina, in Bologna, by Bodoni dated Sept. 12, 1813:

You received with great courtesy the Rector of this our Imperial Lyceum in Parma; I am happy to think that you will extend the same courtesies to the Censor of said institute. Beside being my friend, and a very *your favors to him during the brief stay which he is planning to make in this your*

ABCDEFGHIJKLMNOPQRSTUVW
ABCDEFGHIJKLMNOPQRSTUVW
&.,"-:;!?""1234567890$
&.,"-:;!?""1234567890$
abcdefghijklmnopqrstuvwxyz
abcdefghijklmnopqrstuvwxyz

ABCDEFGHIJKLMNOPQRSTUVWXYZ
ABCDEFGHIJKLMNOPQRSTUVWXYZ
&.,"-:;!?""1234567890$
&.,"-:;!?""1234567890$
abcdefghijklmnopqrstuvwxyz
abcdefghijklmnopqrstuvwxyz

BODONI BOLD: LINOTYPE

PICAS	6	7	8	9	10	11	12	13	14	15	16	17	18	19	20	21	22	23	24	25	26	27	28	29	30
14 POINT	11	13	15	17	20	22	24	26	28	30	32	34	36	38	39	41	43	45	47	49	51	53	55	57	59
12 POINT	12	14	16	18	21	23	25	28	31	33	35	37	39	42	44	46	48	50	52	54	56	58	60	63	65

10/10

From a translation of a letter to Mr. Francis Rosa-spina, in Bologna, by Bodoni dated Sept. 12, 1813:

You received with great courtesy the Rector of this our Imperial Lyceum in Parma; I am happy to think that you will extend the same courtesies to the Censor of said institute. Beside being my friend, and a very worthy ecclesiastic, he is the brother of a great friend of mine, who has a great name in the republic of letters, and among the sacred orators living. Do please be liberal of your favors to him during the brief stay which he is planning to make in this your City, which is counted among the most cultured in Europe. And now that I have sung the praises of my recom-*mended, will mention his name. He is Mr. Abbé Guglielmo Leoni, very well known in Piedmont,*

8/8

From a translation of a letter to Mr. Francis Rosaspina, in Bologna, by Bodoni dated Sept. 12, 1813:

You received with great courtesy the Rector of this our Imperial Lyceum in Parma; I am happy to think that you will extend the same courtesies to the Censor of said institute. Beside being my friend, and a very worthy ecclesiastic, he is the brother of a great friend of mine, who has a great name in the republic of letters, and among the sacred orators living. Do please be liberal of your favors to him during the brief stay which he is planning to make in this your City, which is counted among the most cultured in Europe. And now that I have sung the praises of my Recommended, I will mention his name. He is Mr. Abbé Guglielmo Leoni, very well known in Piedmont, and who holds a distinguished position among the literary men of Bormida and Tanaro. He will give you detailed news of me, and of my joyful wife, and of our friends; and will add that, as you have already received the most part of my Collection, so you will have the remainder. I shall be most *happy to hear how you are getting on, and will rejoice to learn that you are enjoying, along with florid health, a*

10/12

From a translation of a letter to Mr. Francis Rosa-spina, in Bologna, by Bodoni dated Sept. 12, 1813:

You received with great courtesy the Rector of this our Imperial Lyceum in Parma; I am happy to think that you will extend the same courtesies to the Censor of said institute. Beside being my friend, and a very worthy ecclesiastic, he is the brother of a great friend of mine, who has a great name in the republic of letters, and among the sacred orators living. Do please be liberal of your favors to him during the brief stay which he is *mended, will mention his name. He is Mr. Abbé Guglielmo Leoni, very well known in Piedmont,*

8/10

From a translation of a letter to Mr. Francis Rosaspina, in Bologna, by Bodoni dated Sept. 12, 1813:

You received with great courtesy the Rector of this our Imperial Lyceum in Parma; I am happy to think that you will extend the same courtesies to the Censor of said institute. Beside being my friend, and a very worthy ecclesiastic, he is the brother of a great friend of mine, who has a great name in the republic of letters, and among the sacred orators living. Do please be liberal of your favors to him during the brief stay which he is planning to make in this your City, which is counted among the most cultured in Europe. And now that I have sung the praises of my Recommended, I will mention his name. He is Mr. Abbé Guglielmo Leoni, very well known in Piedmont, and who holds a distinguished position among the literary men of Bor-*happy to hear how you are getting on, and will rejoice to learn that you are enjoying, along with florid health, a*

10/14

From a translation of a letter to Mr. Francis Rosa-spina, in Bologna, by Bodoni dated Sept. 12, 1813:

You received with great courtesy the Rector of this our Imperial Lyceum in Parma; I am happy to think that you will extend the same courtesies to the Censor of said institute. Beside being my friend, and a very worthy ecclesiastic, he is the brother of a great friend of mine, who has a great name in the republic of letters, and among the *mended, will mention his name. He is Mr. Abbé Guglielmo Leoni, very well known in Piedmont,*

8/12

From a translation of a letter to Mr. Francis Rosaspina, in Bologna, by Bodoni dated Sept. 12, 1813:

You received with great courtesy the Rector of this our Imperial Lyceum in Parma; I am happy to think that you will extend the same courtesies to the Censor of said institute. Beside being my friend, and a very worthy ecclesiastic, he is the brother of a great friend of mine, who has a great name in the republic of letters, and among the sacred orators living. Do please be liberal of your favors to him during the brief stay which he is planning to make in this your City, which is counted among the most cultured in Europe. And now that I have sung the praises of my Rec-*happy to hear how you are getting on, and will rejoice to learn that you are enjoying, along with florid health, a*

ABCDEFGHIJKLMNOPQRSTUVWXYZ
ABCDEFGHIJKLMNOPQRSTUVWXYZ
&.,"-:;!?""''1234567890$
&.,"-:;!?""''1234567890$
abcdefghijklmnopqrstuvwxyz
abcdefghijklmnopqrstuvwxyz

ABCDEFGHIJKLMNOPQRSTUVWXYZ
ABCDEFGHIJKLMNOPQRSTUVWXYZ
&.,"-:;!?""''1234567890$
&.,"-:;!?""''1234567890$
abcdefghijklmnopqrstuvwxyz
abcdefghijklmnopqrstuvwxyz

BODONI BOLD: LINOTYPE

PICAS	6	7	8	9	10	11	12	13	14	15	16	17	18	19	20	21	22	23	24	25	26	27	28	29	30
10 POINT	14	16	19	21	24	26	28	31	33	36	38	40	43	46	49	51	53	55	57	60	62	64	67	69	72
8 POINT	16	19	22	25	28	30	33	36	39	42	45	48	51	55	57	59	61	64	67	70	72	75	78	81	84

ABCDEFG
HIJKLMN
OPQRSTU
VWXYZ&
1234567890
$.,-:;!?'

72 POINT BODONI TITLE, BAUER

ABCDEFGHI
JKLMNOPQR
STUVWXYZ
&1234567890
$.,-:;!?'

60 POINT BODONI TITLE, BAUER

ABCDEFGHIJK
LMNOPQRSTU
VWXYZ&1234
567890$.,-:;!?'

54 POINT BODONI TITLE, BAUER

ABCDEFGHIJKLMNOPQ
RSTUVWXYZ&abcdefghij
klmnopqrstuvwxyzfffififlfffiffl
1234567890$.,"'-:;!?"""

48 POINT BODONI BOOK, ATF

ABCDEFGHIJKLMNOPQRSTUVW
XYZ&abcdefghijklmnopqrstuvwxyz
fffififlfffiffl1234567890$.,"'-:;!?"""

36 POINT BODONI BOOK, ATF

ABCDEFGHIJKLMNOPQRSTUVW
XYZ&abcdefghijklmnopqrstuvwxyz
fffififlfffiffl1234567890$.,"'-:;!?"""

36 POINT BODONI BOOK ITALIC, ATF

ABCDEFGHIJKLMNOPQRSTUVWXYZ&abcdefghi
jklmnopqrstuvwxyzfffififlfffiffl1234567890$.,"'-:;!?"""

24 POINT BODONI BOOK, ATF

ABCDEFGHIJKLMNOPQRSTUVWXYZ&abcdefghi
jklmnopqrstuvwxyzfffiflffiffl1234567890$.,"-:;!?""''

24 POINT BODONI BOOK ITALIC, ATF

ABCDEFGHIJKLMNOPQRSTUVWXYZ&abcdefghijklmnopqrstuv
wxyzfffiflffiffl1234567890$.,"-:;!?""''

18 POINT BODONI BOOK, ATF

ABCDEFGHIJKLMNOPQRSTUVWXYZ&abcdefghijklmnopqrstuv
wxyzfffiflffiffl1234567890$.,"-:;!?""''

18 POINT BODONI BOOK ITALIC, ATF

Quousque tandem abu-
têre, Catilina, patientiâ
nostrâ? quamdiu etiam
furor iste tuus nos elu-
det? quem ad finem sese
effrenata jactabit auda-
cia? nihilne te nocturnum
prœsidium Palatii, nihil

M. TULLIUS CICERO

ORATOR ATQUE PHILOS.

Page from the Bodoni Manuale Tipografico. Parma, 1818.

14/14 From a translation of a letter to Mr. Francis Rosaspina, in Bologna, by Bodoni dated Sept. 12, 1813:

You received with great courtesy the Rector of this our Imperial Lyceum in Parma; I am happy to think that you will extend the same courtesies to the Censor of said institute. Beside being my friend, and a very worthy ecclesiastic, he is the brother of a great friend of mine, who has a great name in the republic *of letters, and among the sacred orators living. Do please be liberal of your favors to him*

14/16 From a translation of a letter to Mr. Francis Rosaspina, in Bologna, by Bodoni dated Sept. 12, 1813:

You received with great courtesy the Rector of this our Imperial Lyceum in Parma; I am happy to think that you will extend the same courtesies to the Censor of said institute. Beside being my friend, and a very worthy *of letters, and among the sacred orators living. Do please be liberal of your favors to him*

14/18 From a translation of a letter to Mr. Francis Rosaspina, in Bologna, by Bodoni dated Sept. 12, 1813:

You received with great courtesy the Rector of this our Imperial Lyceum in Parma; I am happy to think that you will extend the same courtesies to the Censor of said institute. *of letters, and among the sacred orators living. Do please be liberal of your favors to him*

12/12 From a translation of a letter to Mr. Francis Rosaspina, in Bologna, by Bodoni dated Sept. 12, 1813:

You received with great courtesy the Rector of this our Imperial Lyceum in Parma; I am happy to think that you will extend the same courtesies to the Censor of said institute. Beside being my friend, and a very worthy ecclesiastic, he is the brother of a great friend of mine, who has a great name in the republic of letters, and among the sacred orators living. Do please be liberal of your favors to him during the brief stay which he is planning to make in this your City, which is *counted among the most cultured in Europe. And now that I have sung the praises of my Recom-*

12/14 From a translation of a letter to Mr. Francis Rosaspina, in Bologna, by Bodoni dated Sept. 12, 1813:

You received with great courtesy the Rector of this our Imperial Lyceum in Parma; I am happy to think that you will extend the same courtesies to the Censor of said institute. Beside being my friend, and a very worthy ecclesiastic, he is the brother of a great friend of mine, who has a great name in the republic of letters, and among the sa-*counted among the most cultured in Europe. And now that I have sung the praises of my Recom-*

12/16 From a translation of a letter to Mr. Francis Rosaspina, in Bologna, by Bodoni dated Sept. 12, 1813:

You received with great courtesy the Rector of this our Imperial Lyceum in Parma; I am happy to think that you will extend the same courtesies to the Censor of said institute. Beside being my friend, and a very worthy ecclesiastic, he is the brother of a great friend of mine, who has a great *counted among the most cultured in Europe. And now that I have sung the praises of my Recom-*

ABCDEFGHIJKLMNOPQRSTUVWXYZ
ABCDEFGHIJKLMNOPQRSTUVWXYZ
&.,"-:;!?""1234567890$
&.,"-:;!?""1234567890$
abcdefghijklmnopqrstuvwxyz
abcdefghijklmnopqrstuvwxyz

ABCDEFGHIJKLMNOPQRSTUVWXYZ
ABCDEFGHIJKLMNOPQRSTUVWXYZ
&.,"-:;!?""1234567890$
&.,"-:;!?""1234567890$
abcdefghijklmnopqrstuvwxyz
abcdefghijklmnopqrstuvwxyz

BODONI BOOK: LINOTYPE

PICAS	6	7	8	9	10	11	12	13	14	15	16	17	18	19	20	21	22	23	24	25	26	27	28	29	30
14 POINT	13	15	17	20	23	25	28	30	33	35	37	39	41	44	46	48	50	52	55	57	59	61	63	66	68
12 POINT	15	17	20	22	25	27	30	32	35	37	40	42	45	47	50	52	55	57	60	62	65	67	70	72	75

10/10

From a translation of a letter to Mr. Francis Rosaspina, in Bologna, by Bodoni dated Sept. 12, 1813:

You received with great courtesy the Rector of this our Imperial Lyceum in Parma; I am happy to think that you will extend the same courtesies to the Censor of said institute. Beside being my friend, and a very worthy ecclesiastic, he is the brother of a great friend of mine, who has a great name in the republic of letters, and among the sacred orators living. Do please be liberal of your favors to him during the brief stay which he is planning to make in this your City, which is counted among the most cultured in Europe. And now that I have sung the praises of my Recommended, I will mention his name. He is Mr. Abbé Guglielmo Leoni, very well known in Piedmont, and who holds a distinguished position *among the literary men of Bormida and Tanaro. He will give you detailed news of me, and of my joyful wife, and*

9/9

From a translation of a letter to Mr. Francis Rosaspina, in Bologna, by Bodoni dated Sept. 12, 1813:

You received with great courtesy the Rector of this our Imperial Lyceum in Parma; I am happy to think that you will extend the same courtesies to the Censor of said institute. Beside being my friend, and a very worthy ecclesiastic, he is the brother of a great friend of mine, who has a great name in the republic of letters, and among the sacred orators living. Do please be liberal of your favors to him during the brief stay which he is planning to make in this your City, which is counted among the most cultured in Europe. And now that I have sung the praises of my Recommended, I will mention his name. He is Mr. Abbé Guglielmo Leoni, very well known in Piedmont, and who holds a distinguished position among the literary men of Bormida and Tanaro. He will give you detailed news of me, and of my joyful wife, and of our friends; and will add that, as you have already *received the most part of my Collection, so you will have the remainder. I shall be most happy to hear how you are*

10/12

From a translation of a letter to Mr. Francis Rosaspina, in Bologna, by Bodoni dated Sept. 12, 1813:

You received with great courtesy the Rector of this our Imperial Lyceum in Parma; I am happy to think that you will extend the same courtesies to the Censor of said institute. Beside being my friend, and a very worthy ecclesiastic, he is the brother of a great friend of mine, who has a great name in the republic of letters, and among the sacred orators living. Do please be liberal of your favors to him during the brief stay which he is planning to make in this your City, which is counted among the most cultured in Europe. And now that I have *among the literary men of Bormida and Tanaro. He will give you detailed news of me, and of my joyful wife, and*

9/11

From a translation of a letter to Mr. Francis Rosaspina, in Bologna, by Bodoni dated Sept. 12, 1813:

You received with great courtesy the Rector of this our Imperial Lyceum in Parma; I am happy to think that you will extend the same courtesies to the Censor of said institute. Beside being my friend, and a very worthy ecclesiastic, he is the brother of a great friend of mine, who has a great name in the republic of letters, and among the sacred orators living. Do please be liberal of your favors to him during the brief stay which he is planning to make in this your City, which is counted among the most cultured in Europe. And now that I have sung the praises of my Recommended, I will mention his name. He is Mr. Abbé Guglielmo Leoni, *received the most part of my Collection, so you will have the remainder. I shall be most happy to hear how you are*

10/14

From a translation of a letter to Mr. Francis Rosaspina, in Bologna, by Bodoni dated Sept. 12, 1813:

You received with great courtesy the Rector of this our Imperial Lyceum in Parma; I am happy to think that you will extend the same courtesies to the Censor of said institute. Beside being my friend, and a very worthy ecclesiastic, he is the brother of a great friend of mine, who has a great name in the republic of letters, and among the sacred orators living. Do please be liberal of your favors to him during the brief stay which he is *among the literary men of Bormida and Tanaro. He will give you detailed news of me, and of my joyful wife, and*

9/13

From a translation of a letter to Mr. Francis Rosaspina, in Bologna, by Bodoni dated Sept. 12, 1813:

You received with great courtesy the Rector of this our Imperial Lyceum in Parma; I am happy to think that you will extend the same courtesies to the Censor of said institute. Beside being my friend, and a very worthy ecclesiastic, he is the brother of a great friend of mine, who has a great name in the republic of letters, and among the sacred orators living. Do please be liberal of your favors to him during the brief stay which he is planning to make in this your City, which is counted among the most cultured in Europe. And *received the most part of my Collection, so you will have the remainder. I shall be most happy to hear how you are*

ABCDEFGHIJKLMNOPQRSTUVWXYZ
ABCDEFGHIJKLMNOPQRSTUVWXYZ
&.,"-:;!?""1234567890$
&.,"-:;!?""1234567890$
abcdefghijklmnopqrstuvwxyz
abcdefghijklmnopqrstuvwxyz

ABCDEFGHIJKLMNOPQRSTUVWXYZ
ABCDEFGHIJKLMNOPQRSTUVWXYZ
&.,"-:;!?""1234567890$
&.,"-:;!?""1234567890$
abcdefghijklmnopqrstuvwxyz
abcdefghijklmnopqrstuvwxyz

BODONI BOOK: LINOTYPE

PICAS	6	7	8	9	10	11	12	13	14	15	16	17	18	19	20	21	22	23	24	25	26	27	28	29	30
10 POINT	20	22	25	27	30	32	35	37	40	42	45	47	50	52	55	57	60	62	65	67	70	72	75	77	83
9 POINT	18	21	25	28	31	34	36	39	42	45	48	50	53	56	59	62	64	67	70	73	76	78	83	86	89

8/8

From a translation of a letter to Mr. Francis Rosaspina, in Bologna, by Bodoni dated Sept. 12, 1813:

You received with great courtesy the Rector of this our Imperial Lyceum in Parma; I am happy to think that you will extend the same courtesies to the Censor of said institute. Beside being my friend, and a very worthy ecclesiastic, he is the brother of a great friend of mine, who has a great name in the republic of letters, and among the sacred orators living. Do please be liberal of your favors to him during the brief stay which he is planning to make in this your City, which is counted among the most cultured in Europe. And now that I have sung the praises of my Recommended, I will mention his name. He is Mr. Abbé Gugliel-mo Leoni, very well known in Piedmont, and who holds a dis-tinguished position among the literary men of Bormida and Tanaro. He will give you detailed news of me, and of my joyful wife, and of our friends; and will add that, as you have already received the most part of my Collection, so you will have the remainder. I shall be most happy to hear how you are getting on, and will rejoice to learn that you are enjoying, along with florid health, *a perfect contentment of the soul. Do not be surprised in finding that a friend's hand has written these lines of recommendation,*

6/6

From a translation of a letter to Mr. Francis Rosaspina, in Bologna, by Bodoni dated Sept. 12, 1813:

You received with great courtesy the Rector of this our Imperial Lyceum in Parma; I am happy to think that you will extend the same courtesies to the Censor of said institute. Beside being my friend, and a very worthy ecclesiastic, he is the brother of a great friend of mine, who has a great name in the republic of letters, and among the sacred orators living. Do please be liberal of your favors to him during the brief stay which he is planning to make in this your City, which is counted among the most cultured in, Europe. And now that I have sung the praises of my Recommended, I will mention his name. He is Mr. Abbé Guglielmo Leoni, very well known in Piedmont, and who holds a distinguished position among the literary men of Bormida and Tanaro. He will give you detailed news of me, and of my joyful wife, and of our friends; and will add that, as you have already received the most part of my Collection, so you will have the remainder. I shall be most happy to hear how you are getting on, and will rejoice to learn that you are enjoying, along with florid health, a perfect contentment of the soul. Do not be surprised in finding that a friend's hand has written these lines of recom-mendation, as for some time past I have had recourse to this help, for the reason that I am most busy; nor do I care to encroach upon the time which I need to bring to an end those typographical enterprises which I conceived, and indeed are now well on their way. Keep your friendship for me.

The bearer of this my letter will confirm that I, being very busy with my Typo-graphical Manual, have absolutely no time to write at length, all the more so on account of my uncertain health, which prevents me to bend over my desk for any long time in writing; I only employ myself thus for the strictly indispensable.

You received with great courtesy the Rector of this our Imperial Lyceum on Parma; I am happy to think that you will extend the same courtesies to the Censor of said institute. Beside being my friend, and a very worthy ecclesiastic,

8/10

From a translation of a letter to Mr. Francis Rosaspina, in Bologna, by Bodoni dated Sept. 12, 1813:

You received with great courtesy the Rector of this our Im-perial Lyceum in Parma; I am happy to think that you will extend the same courtesies to the Censor of said institute. Beside being my friend, and a very worthy ecclesiastic, he is the brother of a great friend of mine, who has a great name in the republic of letters, and among the sacred orators living. Do please be liberal of your favors to him during the brief stay which he is planning to make in this your City, which is counted among the most cul-tured in Europe. And now that I have sung the praises of my Recommended, I will mention his name. He is Mr. Abbé Gugliel-mo Leoni, very well known in Piedmont, and who holds a dis-tinguished position among the literary men of Bormida and Tanaro. He will give you detailed news of me, and of my joyful wife, and *a perfect contentment of the soul. Do not be surprised in finding that a friend's hand has written these lines of recommendation,*

6/8

From a translation of a letter to Mr. Francis Rosaspina, in Bologna, by Bodoni dated Sept. 12, 1813:

You received with great courtesy the Rector of this our Imperial Lyceum in Parma; I am happy to think that you will extend the same courtesies to the Censor of said institute. Beside being my friend, and a very worthy ecclesiastic, he is the brother of a great friend of mine, who has a great name in the republic of letters, and among the sacred orators living. Do please be liberal of your favors to him during the brief stay which he is planning to make in this your City, which is counted among the most cultured in Europe. And now that I have sung the praises of my Recommended, I will mention his name. He is Mr. Abbé Guglielmo Leoni, very well known in Piedmont, and who holds a distinguished position among the literary men of Bormida and Tanaro. He will give you detailed news of me, and of my joyful wife, and of our friends; and will add that, as you have already received the most part of my Collection, so you will have the remainder. I shall be most happy to hear how you are getting on, and will rejoice to learn that you are enjoying, along with florid health, a perfect contentment of the soul. Do not be surprised in finding that a friend's hand has written these lines of recom-mendation, as for some time past I have had recourse to this help, for the reason that I am most busy; nor do I care to encroach upon the time which I need to *Parma; I am happy to think that you will extend the same courtesies to the Censor of said institute. Beside being my friend, and a very worthy ecclesiastic,*

3/12

From a translation of a letter to Mr. Francis Rosaspina, in Bologna, by Bodoni dated Sept. 12, 1813:

You received with great courtesy the Rector of this our Im-perial Lyceum in Parma; I am happy to think that you will extend the same courtesies to the Censor of said institute. Beside being my friend, and a very worthy ecclesiastic, he is the brother of a great friend of mine, who has a great name in the republic of letters, and among the sacred orators living. Do please be liberal of your favors to him during the brief stay which he is planning to make in this your City, which is counted among the most cul-tured in Europe. And now that I have sung the praises of my Recommended, I will mention his name. He is Mr. Abbé Gugliel-*a perfect contentment of the soul. Do not be surprised in finding that a friend's hand has written these lines of recommendation,*

6/10

From a translation of a letter to Mr. Francis Rosaspina, in Bologna, by Bodoni dated Sept. 12, 1813:

You received with great courtesy the Rector of this our Imperial Lyceum in Parma; I am happy to think that you will extend the same courtesies to the Censor of said institute. Beside being my friend, and a very worthy ecclesiastic, he is the brother of a great friend of mine, who has a great name in the republic of letters, and among the sacred orators living. Do please be liberal of your favors to him during the brief stay which he is planning to make in this your City, which is counted among the most cultured in Europe. And now that I have sung the praises of my Recommended, I will mention his name. He is Mr. Abbé Guglielmo Leoni, very well known in Piedmont, and who holds a distinguished position among the literary men of Bormida and Tanaro. He will give you detailed news of me, and of my joyful wife, and of our friends; and will add that, as you have already received the most part of my Collection, so you will have the remainder. I shall be most happy to hear how you are getting on, and will rejoice to learn that *Parma; I am happy to think that you will extend the same courtesies to the Censor of said institute. Beside being my friend, and a very worthy ecclesiastic,*

ABCDEFGHIJKLMNOPQRSTUVWXYZ
ABCDEFGHIJKLMNOPQRSTUVWXYZ
&.,"-:;!–""1234567890$
&.,"-:;!–""1234567890$
abcdefghijklmnopqrstuvwxyz
abcdefghijklmnopqrstuvwxyz

ABCDEFGHIJKLMNOPQRSTUVWXYZ
ABCDEFGHIJKLMNOPQRSTUVWXYZ
&.,"-:;!?""1234567890$
&.,"-:;!?""1234567890$
abcdefghijklmnopqrstuvwxyz
abcdefghijklmnopqrstuvwxyz

BODONI BOOK: LINOTYPE

PICAS	6	7	8	9	10	11	12	13	14	15	16	17	18	19	20	21	22	23	24	25	26	27	28	29	30
8 POINT	19	23	26	29	33	36	39	42	46	49	52	56	60	63	66	69	72	76	79	82	85	89	92	95	99
6 POINT	25	29	33	37	42	46	50	54	58	63	67	71	76	80	84	88	92	96	100	105	109	113	117	121	126

ABCDEFGHIJK
LMNOPQRSTU
VWXYZ&abcd
efghijklmnopq
rstuvwxyzffffifl
1234567890
$.,'-:;!?

60 POINT BODONI EXTRA BOLD, BAUER

ABCDEFGHI
JKLMNOPQR
STUVWXYZ&
abcdefghijkl
mnopqrstuvv
wwxyzfffffffflfl
1234567890
$.,'-:;!?

60 POINT BODONI EXTRA BOLD ITALIC, BAUER

ABCDEFGHIJKLM
NOPQRSTUVWXY
Z&abcdefghijklmn
opqrstuvwxyzffffifl
1234567890
$.,'-:;!?

48 POINT BODONI EXTRA BOLD, BAUER

ABCDEFGHIJKL
MNOPQRSTUV
WXYZ&abcdefg
hijklmnopqrstuv
vwwxyzffffifflfft123
4567890$.,'-:;!?

48 POINT BODONI EXTRA BOLD ITALIC, BAUER

ABCDEFGHIJKLMNOPQRSTUVWXYZ&abcd
efghijklmnopqrstuvwxyzfffifl1234567890
$.,'-:;!?

24 POINT BODONI EXTRA BOLD, BAUER

ABCDEFGHIJKLMNOPQRSTUVWXYZ&abc
defghijklmnopqrstuvvwxyzfffifllft12345678
90$.,'-:;!?

24 POINT BODONI EXTRA BOLD ITALIC, BAUER

10/10

From a translation of a letter to Mr. Francis Rosaspina, in Bologna, by Bodoni dated Sept. 12, 1813:

You received with great courtesy the Rector of this our Imperial Lyceum in Parma; I am happy to think that you will extend the same courtesies to the Censor of said institute. Beside being my friend, and a very worthy ecclesiastic, he is the brother of a great friend of mine, who has a great name in the republic of letters, and among the sacred orators living. Do please be liberal of your favors to him during the brief stay which he is planning to make in this your City, *which is counted among the most cultured in Europe. And now that I have*

8/8

From a translation of a letter to Mr. Francis Rosaspina, in Bologna, by Bodoni dated Sept. 12, 1813:

You received with great courtesy the Rector of this our Imperial Lyceum in Parma; I am happy to think that you will extend the same courtesies to the Censor of said insitute. Beside being my friend, and a very worthy ecclesiastic, he is the brother of a great friend of mine, who has a great name in the republic of letters, and among the sacred orators living. Do please be liberal of your favors to him during the brief stay which he is planning to make in this your City, which is counted among the most cultured in Europe. And now that I have sung the praises of my Recommended, I will mention his name. He is Mr. Abbe Guglielmo Leoni, very well known in Piedmont, and who holds a distinguished position among the literary men of *Bormida and Tanaro. He will give you detailed news of me, and of my joyful wife, and of our*

10/12

From a translation of a letter to Mr. Francis Rosaspina, in Bologna, by Bodoni dated Sept. 12, 1813:

You received with great courtesy the Rector of this our Imperial Lyceum in Parma; I am happy to think that you will extend the same courtesies to the Censor of said institute. Beside being my friend, and a very worthy ecclesiastic, he is the brother of a great friend of mine, who has a great name in the republic of letters, and among the sacred orators liv-*which is counted among the most cultured in Europe. And now that I have*

8/10

From a translation of a letter to Mr. Francis Rosaspina, in Bologna, by Bodoni dated Sept. 12, 1813:

You received with great courtesy the Rector of this our Imperial Lyceum in Parma; I am happy to think that you will extend the same courtesies to the Censor of said insitute. Beside being my friend, and a very worthy ecclesiastic, he is the brother of a great friend of mine, who has a great name in the republic of letters, and among the sacred orators living. Do please be liberal of your favors to him during the brief stay which he is planning to make in this your City, which is counted among the most cultured in Europe. And now that I have sung the praises *Bormida and Tanaro. He will give you detailed news of me, and of my joyful wife, and of our*

10/14

From a translation of a letter to Mr. Francis Rosaspina, in Bologna, by Bodoni dated Sept. 12, 1813:

You received with great courtesy the Rector of this our Imperial Lyceum in Parma; I am happy to think that you will extend the same courtesies to the Censor of said institute. Beside being my friend, and a very worthy ecclesiastic, he is the brother of a great friend of mine, who *which is counted among the most cultured in Europe. And now that I have*

8/12

From a translation of a letter to Mr. Francis Rosaspina, in Bologna, by Bodoni dated Sept. 12, 1813:

You received with great courtesy the Rector of this our Imperial Lyceum in Parma; I am happy to think that you will extend the same courtesies to the Censor of said insitute. Beside being my friend, and a very worthy ecclesiastic, he is the brother of a great friend of mine, who has a great name in the republic of letters, and among the sacred orators living. Do please be liberal of your favors to him during the brief *Bormida and Tanaro. He will give you detailed news of me, and of my joyful wife, and of our*

ABCDEFGHIJKLMNOPQRSTUVWXYZ
ABCDEFGHIJKLMNOPQRSTUVWXYZ
&.,"'-:;!?""1234567890
&.,"'-:;!?""1234567890
abcdefghijklmnopqrstuvwxyz
abcdefghijklmnopqrstuvwxyz

ABCDEFGHIJKLMNOPQRSTUVWXYZ
ABCDEFGHIJKLMNOPQRSTUVWXYZ
&.,"'-:;!?""1234567890$
&.,"'-:;!?""1234567890$
abcdefghijklmnopqrstuvwxyz
abcdefghijklmnopqrstuvwxyz

ULTRA BODONI: LINOTYPE

PICAS	6	7	8	9	10	11	12	13	14	15	16	17	18	19	20	21	22	23	24	25	26	27	28	29	30
10 POINT	11	13	15	17	19	20	22	24	26	28	30	32	34	36	38	39	41	43	45	47	49	51	53	55	57
8 POINT	14	16	18	20	23	25	27	29	32	34	36	39	43	46	48	50	53	55	57	59	62	64	66	69	71

Hic ille est Magnus, typica quo nullus in arte
Plures depromsit divitias, veneres.

Engraved portrait of Bodoni from the Manuale Tipografico. Parma, 1818.

Superior In Quality

USEFUL fine

DURING earliest

All comparisons are made on 24 point type.

A useful face with an antique, oldstyle feel, Bookman is both charming and useful.

ABCDEFGHI
JKLMNOPQ
RSTUVWX
YZ&abcdefgh
ijklmnopqrstu
vwxyzfifffflffi
ffl1234567890
$.,'-:;!? A Mr
R y of & The

72 POINT BOOKMAN, ATF

ABCDEFG
HIJKLMNO
PQRSTUV
WXYZ&abc
defghijklmno
pqrstuvwxyz
fiffflffifflff1234
567890$.,'-:,:!?

72 POINT BOOKMAN ITALIC, ATF

ABCDEFGHIJK
LMNOPQRSTU
VWXYZ&abcde
fghijklmnopqrstu
vwxyzfifffflffifffl12
34567890$.,'-:;!?
A MR ry of
The &

60 POINT BOOKMAN, ATF

ABCDEFGHIJ
KLMNOPQRS
TUVWXYZ&
abcdefghijklmn
opqrstuvwxyzfi
ffflffiffl123456 7
890$.,'-;.:!?

60 POINT BOOKMAN ITALIC, ATF

ABCDEFGHIJKLM
NOPQRSTUVWX
YZ&abcdefghijklmno
pqrstuvwxyzfifffflffifffl
1234567890$.,'-:;!? A
MR ry of & The

48 POINT BOOKMAN, ATF

ABCDEFGHIJKL
MNOPQRSTUVW
XYZ&abcdefghijkl
mnopqrstuvwxyzfiff
flfffiffl1234567890$
.,-':;!?

48 POINT BOOKMAN ITALIC, ATF

ABCDEFGHIJKLMNOPQ
RSTUVWXYZ&abcdefgh
ijklmnopqrstuvwxyz123456
7890$.,-';:!?

36 POINT BOOKMAN, LUDLOW

ABCDEFGHIJKLMNOPQ
RSTUVWXYZ&abcdefgh
ijklmnopqrstuvwxyz12345
67890$.,-';:!?

36 POINT BOOKMAN ITALIC, LUDLOW

ABCDEFGHIJKLMNOPQRSTUV
WXYZ&abcdefghijklmnopqrstuvwxy
z1234567890$.,-';:!?

24 POINT BOOKMAN, LUDLOW

ABCDEFGHIJKLMNOPQRSTUVW
XYZ&abcdefghijklmnopqrstuvwxyz1
234567890$.,-';:!?

24 POINT BOOKMAN ITALIC, LUDLOW

ABCDEFGHIJKLMNOPQRSTUVWXYZ&abcdefghijklm
nopqrstuvwxyz1234567890$.,-';:!?

14 POINT BOOKMAN, LUDLOW

ABCDEFGHIJKLMNOPQRSTUVWXYZ&abcdefghijklm
nopqrstuvwxyz1234567890$.,-';:!?

14 POINT BOOKMAN ITALIC, LUDLOW

14/14 A Dissertation Upon English Typographical Founders and Founderies., by Edward Rowe Mores, 1778. The late MR CASLON, the *Coryphaeus* of Letterfounders, was not trained to this business. he was originally a *Gun-lock-graver,* and was taken from that instrument to an instrument of very different tendency, *the propagation of the Christian faith.*

In the y. 1720 the London Soc. for promoting Christian Knowledge in

12/12 A Dissertation Upon English Typographical Founders and Founderies., by Edward Rowe Mores, 1778. The late MR CASLON, the *Coryphæus* of Letterfounders, was not trained to this business. he was originally a *Gun-lock-graver,* and was taken from that instrument to an instrument of very different tendency, *the propagation of the Christian faith.*

In the y. 1720 the London Soc. for promoting Christian Knowledge in consequence of a representation made by Mr Salomon Negri a native of Damascus in Syria, well skilled in the oriental languages, who had

14/16 A Dissertation Upon English Typographical Founders and Founderies., by Edward Rowe Mores, 1778. The late MR CASLON, the *Coryphaeus* of Letterfounders, was not trained to this business. he was originally a *Gun-lock-graver,* and was taken from that instrument to an instrument of

In the y. 1720 the London Soc. for promoting Christian Knowledge in

12/14 A Dissertation Upon English Typographical Founders and Founderies., by Edward Rowe Mores, 1778. The late MR CASLON, the *Coryphæus* of Letterfounders, was not trained to this business. he was originally a *Gun-lock-graver,* and was taken from that instrument to an instrument of very different tendency, *the propagation of the Christian faith.*
Negri a native of Damascus in Syria, well skilled in the oriental languages, who had

14/18 A Dissertation Upon English Typographical Founders and Founderies., by Edward Rowe Mores, 1778. The late MR CASLON, the *Coryphaeus* of Letterfounders, was not trained to this business. he was originally a *Gun-lock-graver,* and was taken from

In the y. 1720 the London Soc. for promoting Christian Knowledge in

12/16 A Dissertation Upon English Typographical Founders and Founderies., by Edward Rowe Mores, 1778. The late MR CASLON, the *Coryphæus* of Letterfounders, was not trained to this business. he was originally a *Gun-lock-graver,* and was taken from that instrument to an instrument of very different tendency, *the propagation of the Chris-*
Negri a native of Damascus in Syria, well skilled in the oriental languages, who had

ABCDEFGHIJKLMNOPQRSTU
ABCDEFGHIJKLMNOPQRSTU
&.,"-:;!?""1234567890$
&.,"-:;!?""1234567890$
abcdefghijklmnopqrstuvwxyz
abcdefghijklmnopqrstuvwxyz

ABCDEFGHIJKLMNOPQRSTUVWXY
ABCDEFGHIJKLMNOPQRSTUVWXY
&.,"-:;!?""1234567890$
&.,"-:;!?""1234567890$
abcdefghijklmnopqrstuvwxyz
abcdefghijklmnopqrstuvwxyz

BOOKMAN: LINOTYPE

PICAS	6	7	8	9	10	11	12	13	14	15	16	17	18	19	20	21	22	23	24	25	26	27	28	29	30
14 POINT	10	12	14	16	18	19	21	23	25	27	28	30	32	34	36	37	39	41	43	45	46	48	50	52	54
12 POINT	13	15	17	19	22	24	26	28	30	33	35	37	39	41	44	46	48	50	52	55	57	59	61	63	66

11/11

A Dissertation Upon English Typographical Founders and Founderies., by Edward Rowe Mores, 1778. The late MR CASLON, the *Coryphæus* of Letterfounders, was not trained to this business. he was originally a *Gun-lock-graver*, and was taken from that instrument to an instrument of very different tendency, *the propagation of the Christian faith.*

In the y. 1720 the *London Soc. for promoting Christian Knowledge* in consequence of a representation made by *Mr Salomon Negri* a native of *Damascus* in *Syria,* well skilled in the oriental languages, who had been professor of *Arab.* in places of note for a great part of his life, deemed it expedient to print for the use of

10/10

A Dissertation Upon English Typographical Founders and Founderies., by Edward Rowe Mores, 1778. The late MR CASLON, the *Coryphæus* of Letterfounders, was not trained to this business. he was originally a *Gun-lock-graver*, and was taken from that instrument to an instrument of very different tendency, *the propagation of the Christian faith.*

In the y. 1720 the *London Soc. for promoting Christian Knowledge* in consequence of a representation made by *Mr Salomon Negri* a native of *Damascus* in *Syria,* well skilled in the oriental languages, who had been professor of *Arab.* in places of note for a great part of his life, deemed it expedient to print for the use of the *Eastern* churches *the N. Test. and Psalt. in the Arab. language for the benefit of the poor Christians in Palestine, Syria,*

11/13

A Dissertation Upon English Typographical Founders and Founderies., by Edward Rowe Mores, 1778. The late MR CASLON, the *Coryphæus* of Letterfounders, was not trained to this business. he was originally a *Gun-lock-graver,* and was taken from that instrument to an instrument of very different tendency, *the propagation of the Christian faith.*

In the y. 1720 the *London Soc. for promoting Christian Knowledge* in consequence of a representation made by *Mr Salomon Negri* a *Arab. in places of note for a great part of his life, deemed it expedient to print for the use of*

10/12

A Dissertation Upon English Typographical Founders and Founderies., by Edward Rowe Mores, 1778. The late MR CASLON, the *Coryphæus* of Letterfounders, was not trained to this business. he was originally a *Gun-lock-graver,* and was taken from that instrument to an instrument of very different tendency, *the propagation of the Christian faith.*

In the y. 1720 the *London Soc. for promoting Christian Knowledge* in consequence of a representation made by *Mr Salomon Negri* a native of *Damascus* in *Syria,* well skilled in the oriental lan- *the N. Test. and Psalt. in the Arab. language for the benefit of the poor Christians in Palestine, Syria,*

11/15

A Dissertation Upon English Typographical Founders and Founderies., by Edward Rowe Mores, 1778. The late MR CASLON, the *Coryphæus* of Letterfounders, was not trained to this business. he was originally a *Gun-lock-graver,* and was taken from that instrument to an instrument of very different tendency, *the propagation of the Christian faith.*

In the y. 1720 the *London Soc. for promot-* *Arab. in places of note for a great part of his life, deemed it expedient to print for the use of*

10/14

A Dissertation Upon English Typographical Founders and Founderies., by Edward Rowe Mores, 1778. The late MR CASLON, the *Coryphæus* of Letterfounders, was not trained to this business. he was originally a *Gun-lock-graver,* and was taken from that instrument to an instrument of very different tendency, *the propagation of the Christian faith.*

In the y. 1720 the *London Soc. for promoting Christian Knowledge* in consequence of a represen- *the N. Test. and Psalt. in the Arab. language for the benefit of the poor Christians in Palestine, Syria,*

ABCDEFGHIJKLMNOPQRSTUVWXYZ
ABCDEFGHIJKLMNOPQRSTUVWXYZ
&.,"-:;!?""1234567890$
&.,"-:;!?""1234567890$
abcdefghijklmnopqrstuvwxyz
abcdefghijklmnopqrstuvwxyz

ABCDEFGHIJKLMNOPQRSTUVWXYZ
ABCDEFGHIJKLMNOPQRSTUVWXYZ
&.,"-:;!?""1234567890$
&.,"-:;!?""1234567890$
abcdefghijklmnopqrstuvwxyz
abcdefghijklmnopqrstuvwxyz

BOOKMAN: LINOTYPE

PICAS	6	7	8	9	10	11	12	13	14	15	16	17	18	19	20	21	22	23	24	25	26	27	28	29	30
11 POINT	13	16	18	20	23	25	27	29	32	34	36	39	41	43	46	48	50	53	55	57	59	62	64	66	69
10 POINT	15	18	20	23	26	28	31	33	36	39	41	44	46	49	52	54	57	59	62	65	67	69	72	75	78

9/9

A Dissertation Upon English Typographical Founders and Founderies., by Edward Rowe Mores, 1778. The late MR CASLON, the *Coryphæus* of Letterfounders, was not trained to this business. he was originally a *Gun-lock-graver,* and was taken from that instrument to an instrument of very different tendency, *the propagation of the Christian faith.*

In the y. 1720 the *London Soc. for promoting Christian Knowledge* in consequence of a representation made by *Mr Salomon Negri* a native of *Damascus* in *Syria,* well skilled in the oriental languages, who had been professor of *Arab.* in places of note for a great part of his life, deemed it expedient to print for the use of the *Eastern* churches the *N. Test.* and *Psalt.* in the *Arab.* language for the benefit of the poor Christians in *Palestine, Syria, Mesopotamia, Arabia* and *Egypt;* the constitution of which countries allows of no printing: and Mr Caslon was pitched upon to cut a fount.

8/8

A Dissertation Upon English Typographical Founders and Founderies., by Edward Rowe Mores, 1778. The late MR CASLON, the *Coryphæus* of Letterfounders, was not trained to this business. he was originally a *Gun-lock-graver,* and was taken from that instrument to an instrument of very different tendency, *the propagation of the Christian faith.*

In the y. 1720 the *London Soc. for promoting Christian Knowledge* in consequence of a representation made by *Mr Salomon Negri* a native of *Damascus* in *Syria,* well skilled in the oriental languages, who had been professor of *Arab.* in places of note for a great part of his life, deemed it expedient to print for the use of the *Eastern* churches the *N. Test.* and *Psalt.* in the *Arab.* language for the benefit of the poor Christians in *Palestine, Syria, Mesopotamia, Arabia* and *Egypt;* the constitution of which countries allows of no printing: and *Mr Caslon* was pitched upon to cut a fount.

He cut the *Eng. Arabic* which we see in his specimens. this was after the y. 1721 and before the y. 1726. in which latter *y. the Soc. had procured "two new founts of Arab. types, viz. One from the Polyglott matrices; and Another of a lesser size*

9/11

A Dissertation Upon English Typographical Founders and Founderies., by Edward Rowe Mores, 1778. The late MR CASLON, the *Coryphæus* of Letterfounders, was not trained to this business. he was originally a *Gun-lock-graver,* and was taken from that instrument to an instrument of very different tendency, *the propagation of the Christian faith.*

In the y. 1720 the *London Soc. for promoting Christian Knowledge* in consequence of a representation made by *Mr Salomon Negri* a native of *Damascus* in *Syria,* well skilled in the oriental languages, who had been professor of *Arab.* in places of note for a great part of his life, deemed it expedient to print for the use of the *East-which countries allows of no printing: and Mr Caslon was pitched upon to cut a fount.*

8/10

A Dissertation Upon English Typographical Founders and Founderies., by Edward Rowe Mores, 1778. The late MR CASLON, the *Coryphæus* of Letterfounders, was not trained to this business. he was originally a *Gun-lock-graver,* and was taken from that instrument to an instrument of very different tendency, *the propagation of the Christian faith.*

In the y. 1720 the *London Soc. for promoting Christian Knowledge* in consequence of a representation made by *Mr Salomon Negri* a native of *Damascus* in *Syria,* well skilled in the oriental languages, who had been professor of *Arab.* in places of note for a great part of his life, deemed it expedient to print for the use of the *Eastern* churches the *N. Test.* and *Psalt.* in the *Arab.* language for the benefit of the poor Christians in *Palestine, Syria, Mesopotamia, Arabia* and *Egypt; y. the Soc. had procured "two new founts of Arab. types, viz. One from the Polyglott matrices; and Another of a lesser size*

9/13

A Dissertation Upon English Typographical Founders and Founderies., by Edward Rowe Mores, 1778. The late MR CASLON, the *Coryphæus* of Letterfounders, was not trained to this business. he was originally a *Gun-lock-graver,* and was taken from that instrument to an instrument of very different tendency, *the propagation of the Christian faith.*

In the y. 1720 the *London Soc. for promoting Christian Knowledge* in consequence of a representation made by *Mr Salomon Negri* a native of *Damascus* in *Syria,* well skilled in the oriental languages, who had been pro-*which countries allows of no printing: and Mr Caslon was pitched upon to cut a fount.*

8/12

A Dissertation Upon English Typographical Founders and Founderies., by Edward Rowe Mores, 1778. The late MR CASLON, the *Coryphæus* of Letterfounders, was not trained to this business. he was originally a *Gun-lock-graver,* and was taken from that instrument to an instrument of very different tendency, *the propagation of the Christian faith.*

In the y. 1720 the *London Soc. for promoting Christian Knowledge* in consequence of a representation made by *Mr Salomon Negri* a native of *Damascus* in *Syria,* well skilled in the oriental languages, who had been professor of *Arab.* in places of note for a great part of his life, deemed it expedient to print for the use of the *Eastern* churches the *N. Test.* and *y. the Soc. had procured "two new founts of Arab. types, viz. One from the Polyglott matrices; and Another of a lesser size*

ABCDEFGHIJKLMNOPQRSTUVWXYZ
ABCDEFGHIJKLMNOPQRSTUVWXYZ
&.,,"-:;!?""1234567890$
&.,,"-:;!?""1234567890$
abcdefghijklmnopqrstuvwxyz
abcdefghijklmnopqrstuvwxyz

ABCDEFGHIJKLMNOPQRSTUVWXYZ
ABCDEFGHIJKLMNOPQRSTUVWXYZ
&.,,"-:;!?""1234567890$
&.,,"-:;!?""1234567890$
abcdefghijklmnopqrstuvwxyz
abcdefghijklmnopqrstuvwxyz

BOOKMAN: LINOTYPE

PICAS	6	7	8	9	10	11	12	13	14	15	16	17	18	19	20	21	22	23	24	25	26	27	28	29	30
9 POINT	16	19	22	25	28	30	33	36	39	42	44	47	50	53	56	58	61	64	67	70	72	75	78	81	89
8 POINT	18	21	24	27	31	34	37	40	43	46	49	52	56	59	62	65	68	71	74	77	80	83	86	89	93

CASLON 540, ATF
ABCDE established

AMERICAN CASLON 637, MONOTYPE
TYPE USERS advantage

TRUE-CUT CASLON, LUDLOW
TYPE finer design

ENGLISH CASLON OLDSTYLE 37, MONOTYPE
RECEIVES ervonth

CASLON OLDSTYLE 337, MONOTYPE
YOUR NEXT urdes

All comparisons are made on 24 point type.

Highly individual 72 pt.
Caslon Q increased over 4 diameters.

ABCDEFGH
IJKLMNOP
QRSTUVW
XYZ&abcdef
ghijklmnopqrs
tuvwxyzfifffflffi
ffl1234567890
$.,"-..!?""''
.;..

72 POINT CASLON 540, ATF

ABCDEFGHI
JKLMNOPQ
RSTUVWX
YZ&abcdefghijk
lmnopqrstuvwxy
zfifffflffiflffl123456
7890$.,"-.;:!?"''

72 POINT CASLON 540 ITALIC, ATF

ABCDEFGHIJ
KLMNOPQRS
TUVWXYZ&a
bcdefghijklmnop
qrstuvwxyzfiffl
ffiffffl1234567890$
'' ' _.. !? " "
., .; ..

60 POINT CASLON 540, ATF

ABCDEFGHIJK
LMNOPQRSTU
VWXYZ&abcdefg
hijklmnopqrstuvwx
yzfifflfffiffl1234567
890$., "-.;:!?" "

60 POINT CASLON 540 ITALIC, ATF

ABCDEFGHIJKL
MNOPQRSTUV
WXYZ&abcdefghij
klmnopqrstuvwxyzfi
ffflffiffl1234567890$.,
"-.;:!?""

48 POINT CASLON 540, ATF

ABCDEFGHIJKL
MNOPQRSTUVWX
YZ&abcdefghijklmnopq
rstuvwxyzfiffflfffiffl12345
67890$.,"-.;.!?""''

48 POINT CASLON 540 ITALIC, ATF

ABCDEFGHIJKLMN
OPQRSTUVWXYZ&
abcdefghijklmnopqrstuv
wxyzfiffflfffiffl123456789
0$.,"-.;!?""''

42 POINT CASLON 540, ATF

ABCDEFGHIJKLMN
OPQRSTUVWXYZ&a
bcdefghijklmnopqrstuvwxyz
fifffifffiffl1234567890$.,'-:;!
?"''

42 POINT CASLON 540 ITALIC, ATF

ABCDEFGHIJKLMNOP
QRSTUVWXYZ&abcdefg
hijklmnopqrstuvwxyzfifffl
ffiffl1234567890$.,'-:;!?"''

36 POINT CASLON 540, ATF

ABCDEFGHIJKLMNOP
QRSTUVWXYZ&abcdefghi
jklmnopqrstuvwxyzfifffflffiffl12
34567890$.,'-:;!?"''

36 POINT CASLON 540 ITALIC, ATF

ABCDEFGHIJKLMNOPQRST
UVWXYZ&abcdefghijklmnopqr
stuvwxyzfifffflffifffl1234567890$
.,"‘-:;!?’"‘‘

30 POINT CASLON 540, ATF

ABCDEFGHIJKLMNOPQ
RSTUVWXYZ&abcdefghijklmn
opqrstuvwxyzfifffflffifffl1234567890$
.,"‘-:;!?’"‘‘

30 POINT CASLON 540 ITALIC, ATF

ABCDEFGHIJKLMNOPQRSTUVWXY
Z&abcdefghijklmnopqrstuvwxyzfifffflffifffl
1234567890$.,"‘-:;!?’"‘‘

24 POINT CASLON 540, ATF

ABCDEFGHIJKLMNOPQRSTUVW
XYZ&abcdefghijklmnopqrstuvwxyzfifffflffifffl
1234567890$.,"‘-:;!?’"‘‘

24 POINT CASLON 540 ITALIC, ATF

ABCDEFGHIJKLMNOPQRSTUVWXYZ&abcdefghi
jklmnopqrstuvwxyzfifffflffifffl1234567890$.,"‘-:;!?’"‘‘

18 POINT CASLON 540, ATF

ABCDEFGHIJKLMNOPQRSTUVWXYZ&abcdefg
hijklmnopqrstuvwxyzfifffflffifffl1234567890$.,"‘-:;!?’"‘‘

18 POINT CASLON 540 ITALIC, ATF

14/14 From a letter to John Baskerville by Benjamin Franklin dated 1760:

Let me give you a pleasant Instance of the Prejudice some have entertained against your Work. Soon after I returned, discoursing with a Gentleman concerning the Artists of Birmingham, he said you would [be] a Means of blinding all the Readers in the Nation; for the Strokes of your Letters, *being too thin and narrow, hurt the Eye, and he could never read a Line of*

14/16 From a letter to John Baskerville by Benjamin Franklin dated 1760:

Let me give you a pleasant Instance of the Prejudice some have entertained against your Work. Soon after I returned, discoursing with a Gentleman concerning the Artists of Birmingham, he said you would [be] a Means *being too thin and narrow, hurt the Eye, and he could never read a Line of*

14/18 From a letter to John Baskerville by Benjamin Franklin dated 1760:

Let me give you a pleasant Instance of the Prejudice some have entertained against your Work. Soon after I returned, discoursing with a Gentleman concerning the Artists of Birming- *being too thin and narrow, hurt the Eye, and he could never read a Line of*

12/12 From a letter to John Baskerville by Benjamin Franklin dated London, 1760:

Let me give you a pleasant Instance of the Prejudice some have entertained against your Work. Soon after I returned, discoursing with a Gentleman concerning the Artists of Birmingham, he said you would· [be] a Means of blinding all the Readers in the Nation; for the Strokes of your Letters, being too thin and narrow, hurt the Eye, and he could never read a Line of them without Pain. "I thought," said I, "you were going *to complain of the Gloss of the Paper, some object to." "No, no," says he, "I have heard*

12/14 From a letter to John Baskerville by Benjamin Franklin dated London, 1760:

Let me give you a pleasant Instance of the Prejudice some have entertained against your Work. Soon after I returned, discoursing with a Gentleman concerning the Artists of Birmingham, he said you would [be] a Means of blinding all the Readers in the Nation; for the Strokes of your Letters, be- *to complain of the Gloss of the Paper, some object to." "No, no," says he, "I have heard*

12/16 From a letter to John Baskerville by Benjamin Franklin dated London, 1760:

Let me give you a pleasant Instance of the Prejudice some have entertained against your Work. Soon after I returned, discoursing with a Gentleman concerning the Artists of Birmingham, he said you would [be] a Means of blinding all the Readers in the *to complain of the Gloss of the Paper, some object to." "No, no," says he, "I have heard*

ABCDEFGHIJKLMNOPQRSTU
ABCDEFGHIJKLMNOPQRSTU
&.,"-:;!?""1234567890$1234567890$
&.,"-:;!?""1234567890$1234567890$
abcdefghijklmnopqrstuvwxyz
abcdefghijklmnopqrstuvwxyz

ABCDEFGHIJKLMNOPQRSTUVW
ABCDEFGHIJKLMNOPQRSTUVW
&.,"-:;!?""1234567890$
&.,"-:;!?""1234567890$
abcdefghijklmnopqrstuvwxyz
abcdefghijklmnopqrstuvwxyz

CASLON: LINOTYPE

PICAS	6	7	8	9	10	11	12	13	14	15	16	17	18	19	20	21	22	23	24	25	26	27	28	29	30
14 POINT	10	12	14	16	18	19	21	23	25	27	28	30	32	34	36	37	39	41	43	45	46	48	50	52	54
12 POINT	13	15	18	20	22	24	26	28	31	33	35	37	40	42	44	46	48	50	53	55	57	59	62	64	66

From a letter to John Baskerville by Benjamin Franklin
10/10 dated London, 1760:

Let me give you a pleasant Instance of the Prejudice some have entertained against your Work. Soon after I returned, discoursing with a Gentleman concerning the Artists of Birmingham, he said you would [be] a Means of blinding all the Readers in the Nation; for the Strokes of your Letters, being too thin and narrow, hurt the Eye, and he could never read a Line of them without Pain. "I thought," said I, "you were going to complain of the Gloss of the Paper, some object to." "No, no," says he, "I have heard that mentioned, but it is not that; it Is in the Form and Cut of the Letters themselves; they have not that Height and Thickness of the Stroke, which make the common Printing so much the more comfortable to *the Eye." You see this Gentleman was a Connoisseur. In vain I endeavoured to support your character against the*

From a letter to John Baskerville by Benjamin Franklin
10/12 dated London, 1760:

Let me give you a pleasant Instance of the Prejudice some have entertained against your Work. Soon after I returned, discoursing with a Gentleman concerning the Artists of Birmingham, he said you would [be] a Means of blinding all the Readers in the Nation; for the Strokes of your Letters, being too thin and narrow, hurt the Eye, and he could never read a Line of them without Pain. "I thought," said I, "you were going to complain of the Gloss of the Paper, some object to." "No, no," says he, "I have heard that mentioned, but it is not that; it Is in *the Eye." You see this Gentleman was a Connoisseur. In vain I endeavoured to support your character against the*

From a letter to John Baskerville by Benjamin Franklin
10/14 dated London, 1760:

Let me give you a pleasant Instance of the Prejudice some have entertained against your Work. Soon after I returned, discoursing with a Gentleman concerning the Artists of Birmingham, he said you would [be] a Means of blinding all the Readers in the Nation; for the Strokes of your Letters, being too thin and narrow, hurt the Eye, and he could never read a Line of them without Pain. "I thought," said I, "you were going to complain of the *the Eye." You see this Gentleman was a Connoisseur. In vain I endeavoured to support your character against the*

ABCDEFGHIJKLMNOPQRSTUVWXYZ
ABCDEFGHIJKLMNOPQRSTUVWXYZ
&.,"-:;!?""1234567890$
&.,"-:;!?""1234567890$
abcdefghijklmnopqrstuvwxyz
abcdefghijklmnopqrstuvwxyz

From a letter to John Baskerville by Benjamin Franklin dated
8/8 London, 1760:

Let me give you a pleasant Instance of the Prejudice some have entertained against your Work. Soon after I returned, discoursing with a Gentleman concerning the Artists of Birmingham, he said you would [be] a Means of blinding all the Readers in the Nation; for the Strokes of your Letters, being too thin and narrow, hurt the Eye, and he could never read a Line of them without Pain. "I thought," said I, "you were going to complain of the Gloss of the Paper, some object to." "No, no," says he, "I have heard that mentioned, but it is not that; it Is in the Form and Cut of the Letters themselves; they have not that Height and Thickness of the Stroke, which make the common Printing so much the more comfortable to the Eye." You see this Gentleman was a *Connoisseur.* In vain I endeavoured to support your character against the Charge; he knew what he felt, and could see the Reason of it, and several other Gentlemen among his Friends had made the same Observation, &c.

Yesterday he called to visit me, when, mischievously bent to try his Judgment, I stept into my Closet, tore off the Top of

From a letter to John Baskerville by Benjamin Franklin dated
8/10 London, 1760:

Let me give you a pleasant Instance of the Prejudice some have entertained against your Work. Soon after I returned, discoursing with a Gentleman concerning the Artists of Birmingham, he said you would [be] a Means of blinding all the Readers in the Nation; for the Strokes of your Letters, being too thin and narrow, hurt the Eye, and he could never read a Line of them without Pain. "I thought," said I, "you were going to complain of the Gloss of the Paper, some object to." "No, no," says he, "I have heard that mentioned, but it is not that; it Is in the Form and Cut of the Letters themselves; they have not that Height and Thickness of the Stroke, which make the common Printing so much the more comfortable to the Eye." You see this Gentleman was a *Connoisseur.* In vain I endeav-

Yesterday he called to visit me, when, mischievously bent to try his Judgment, I stept into my Closet, tore off the Top of

From a letter to John Baskerville by Benjamin Franklin dated
8/12 London, 1760:

Let me give you a pleasant Instance of the Prejudice some have entertained against your Work. Soon after I returned, discoursing with a Gentleman concerning the Artists of Birmingham, he said you would [be] a Means of blinding all the Readers in the Nation; for the Strokes of your Letters, being too thin and narrow, hurt the Eye, and he could never read a Line of them without Pain. "I thought," said I, "you were going to complain of the Gloss of the Paper, some object to." "No, no," says he, "I have heard that mentioned, but it is not that; it Is in the Form and Cut of the Letters themselves; they have

Yesterday he called to visit me, when, mischievously bent to try his Judgment, I stept into my Closet, tore off the Top of

ABCDEFGHIJKLMNOPQRSTUVWXYZ
ABCDEFGHIJKLMNOPQRSTUVWXYZ
&.,"-:;!?""1234567890$
&.,"-:;!?""1234567890$
abcdefghijklmnopqrstuvwxyz
abcdefghijklmnopqrstuvwxyz

CASLON: LINOTYPE

PICAS	6	7	8	9	10	11	12	13	14	15	16	17	18	19	20	21	22	23	24	25	26	27	28	29	30
10 POINT	17	19	22	25	28	30	33	36	39	41	44	47	50	52	55	57	61	63	66	69	72	74	77	80	83
8 POINT	19	22	25	28	31	33	37	40	43	46	50	53	56	59	62	65	68	71	74	77	81	84	87	90	93

ABCDEFGHI
JKLMNOPQR
STUVWXYZ
&abcdefghijklm
nopqrstuvwxyz
1234567890$.,"-:;!
?""

60 POINT CASLON, NEW, ATF

ABCDEFGHIJKL
MNOPQRSTUVW
XYZ&abcdefghijkl
mnopqrstuvwxyz123
4567890$.,"-:;!?""

48 POINT CASLON, NEW, ATF

ABCDEFGHIJKL
MNOPQRSTUVW
XYZ&abcdefghijklmn
opqrstuvwxyzfifffflffifffl
1234567890$., "-:;!?""

48 POINT CASLON, NEW ITALIC, ATF

ABCDEFGHIJKLMNOPQRSTUVW
XYZ&abcdefghijklmnopqrstuvwxyz1234
567890$.,"-:;!?""

24 POINT CASLON, NEW, ATF

ABCDEFGHIJKLMNOPQRSTUVWXYZ
&abcdefghijklmnopqrstuvwxyzfifffflffifffl12345
67890$.,"-:;!?""

24 POINT CASLON, NEW ITALIC, ATF

14/14 From a letter to John Baskerville by Benjamin Franklin dated 1760:

Let me give you a pleasant Instance of the Prejudice some have entertained against your Work. Soon after I returned, discoursing with a Gentleman concerning the Artists of Birmingham, he said you would [be] a Means of blinding all the Readers *in the Nation; for the Strokes of your Letters, being too thin and nar-*

14/16 From a letter to John Baskerville by Benjamin Franklin dated 1760:

Let me give you a pleasant Instance of the Prejudice some have entertained against your Work. Soon after I returned, discoursing with a Gentleman concerning the Artists of Birmingham, he said you would [be] a Means of blinding all the Readers *in the Nation; for the Strokes of your Letters, being too thin and nar-*

14/18 From a letter to John Baskerville by Benjamin Franklin dated 1760:

Let me give you a pleasant Instance of the Prejudice some have entertained against your Work. Soon after I returned, discoursing with a Gentleman concerning the Artists of *in the Nation; for the Strokes of your Letters, being too thin and nar-*

12/12 From a letter to John Baskerville by Benjamin Franklin dated London, 1760:

Let me give you a pleasant Instance of the Prejudice some have entertained against your Work. Soon after I returned, discoursing with a Gentleman concerning the Artists of Birmingham, he said you would [be] a Means of blinding all the Readers in the Nation; for the Strokes of your Letters, being too thin and narrow, hurt the Eye, and he could never read a Line of them without Pain. "I thought," *said I, "you were going to complain of the Gloss of the Paper, some object to." "No,*

12/14 From a letter to John Baskerville by Benjamin Franklin dated London, 1760:

Let me give you a pleasant Instance of the Prejudice some have entertained against your Work. Soon after I returned, discoursing with a Gentleman concerning the Artists of Birmingham, he said you would [be] a Means of blinding all the Readers in the Nation; for the Strokes of your Letters, being too thin and narrow, *said I, "you were going to complain of the Gloss of the Paper, some object to." "No,*

12/16 From a letter to John Baskerville by Benjamin Franklin dated London, 1760:

Let me give you a pleasant Instance of the Prejudice some have entertained against your Work. Soon after I returned, discoursing with a Gentleman concerning the Artists of Birmingham, he said you would [be] a Means of blinding all the Readers in the Nation; for the Strokes of *said I, "you were going to complain of the Gloss of the Paper, some object to." "No,*

ABCDEFGHIJKLMNOPQRST
ABCDEFGHIJKLMNOPQRST
&.,"-:;!?""1234567890$
&.,"-:;!?""1234567890$
abcdefghijklmnopqrstuvwxyz
abcdefghijklmnopqrstuvwxyz

CASLON 3: LINOTYPE

ABCDEFGHIJKLMNOPQRSTUVW
ABCDEFGHIJKLMNOPQRSTUVW
&.,"-:;!?""1234567890$
&.,"-:;!?""1234567890$
abcdefghijklmnopqrstuvwxyz
abcdefghijklmnopqrstuvwxyz

PICAS	6	7	8	9	10	11	12	13	14	15	16	17	18	19	20	21	22	23	24	25	26	27	28	29	30
14 POINT	11	13	15	17	18	20	22	23	25	27	28	30	32	34	35	37	39	40	42	44	45	47	50	52	54
12 POINT	13	15	17	19	21	23	25	27	30	31	34	36	38	40	42	44	46	48	50	52	55	57	59	61	63

10/10

From a letter to John Baskerville by Benjamin Franklin dated London, 1760:

Let me give you a pleasant Instance of the Prejudice some have entertained against your Work. Soon after I returned, discoursing with a Gentleman concerning the Artists of Birmingham, he said you would [be] a Means of blinding all the Readers in the Nation; for the Strokes of your Letters, being too thin and narrow, hurt the Eye, and he could never read a Line of them without Pain. "I thought," said I, "you were going to complain of the Gloss of the Paper, some object to." "No, no," says he, "I have heard that mentioned, but it is not that; it Is in the Form and Cut of the Letters themselves; they have not that *Height and Thickness of the Stroke, which make the common Printing so much the more comfort-*

8/8

From a letter to John Baskerville by Benjamin Franklin dated London, 1760:

Let me give you a pleasant Instance of the Prejudice some have entertained against your Work. Soon after I returned, discoursing with a Gentleman concerning the Artists of Birmingham, he said you would [be] a Means of blinding all the Readers in the Nation; for the Strokes of your Letters, being too thin and narrow, hurt the Eye, and he could never read a Line of them without Pain. "I thought," said I, "you were going to complain of the Gloss of the Paper, some object to." "No, no," says he, "I have heard that mentioned, but it is not that; it Is in the Form and Cut of the Letters themselves; they have not that Height and Thickness of the Stroke, which make the common Printing so much the more comfortable to the Eye." You see this Gentleman was a *Connoisseur.* In vain I endeavoured to support your character against the Charge; he knew what he felt, and could see the Reason of it, and several other Gentlemen among his Friends had made the same Observation, &c.
Yesterday he called to visit me, when, mischievously bent to try his Judgment, I stept into my Closet, tore off the Top of

10/12

From a letter to John Baskerville by Benjamin Franklin dated London, 1760:

Let me give you a pleasant Instance of the Prejudice some have entertained against your Work. Soon after I returned, discoursing with a Gentleman concerning the Artists of Birmingham, he said you would [be] a Means of blinding all the Readers in the Nation; for the Strokes of your Letters, being too thin and narrow, hurt the Eye, and he could never read a Line of them without Pain. "I thought," said I, "you were going to complain of the Gloss of the Paper, some object *Height and Thickness of the Stroke, which make the common Printing so much the more comfort-*

8/10

From a letter to John Baskerville by Benjamin Franklin dated London, 1760:

Let me give you a pleasant Instance of the Prejudice some have entertained against your Work. Soon after I returned, discoursing with a Gentleman concerning the Artists of Birmingham, he said you would [be] a Means of blinding all the Readers in the Nation; for the Strokes of your Letters, being too thin and narrow, hurt the Eye, and he could never read a Line of them without Pain. "I thought," said I, "you were going to complain of the Gloss of the Paper, some object to." "No, no," says he, "I have heard that mentioned, but it is not that; it Is in the Form and Cut of the Letters themselves; they have not that Height and Thickness of the Stroke, which make the common Printing so much the more comfortable to the Eye." You see this Gentleman was a *Connoisseur.* In vain I endeav-
Yesterday he called to visit me, when, mischievously bent to try his Judgment, I stept into my Closet, tore off the Top of

10/14

From a letter to John Baskerville by Benjamin Franklin dated London, 1760:

Let me give you a pleasant Instance of the Prejudice some have entertained against your Work. Soon after I returned, discoursing with a Gentleman concerning the Artists of Birmingham, he said you would [be] a Means of blinding all the Readers in the Nation; for the Strokes of your Letters, being too thin and narrow, hurt the Eye, and he could never read a Line of them without-
Height and Thickness of the Stroke, which make the common Printing so much the more comfort-

8/12

From a letter to John Baskerville by Benjamin Franklin dated London, 1760:

Let me give you a pleasant Instance of the Prejudice some have entertained against your Work. Soon after I returned, discoursing with a Gentleman concerning the Artists of Birmingham, he said you would [be] a Means of blinding all the Readers in the Nation; for the Strokes of your Letters, being too thin and narrow, hurt the Eye, and he could never read a Line of them without Pain. "I thought," said I, "you were going to complain of the Gloss of the Paper, some object to." "No, no," says he, "I have heard that mentioned, but it is not that; it Is in the Form and Cut of the Letters themselves; they have
Yesterday he called to visit me, when, mischievously bent to try his Judgment, I stept into my Closet, tore off the Top of

ABCDEFGHIJKLMNOPQRSTUVWXYZ
ABCDEFGHIJKLMNOPQRSTUVWXYZ
&.,"-:;!?""1234567890$
&.,"-:;!?""1234567890$
abcdefghijklmnopqrstuvwxyz
abcdefghijklmnopqrstuvwxyz

ABCDEFGHIJKLMNOPQRSTUVWXYZ
ABCDEFGHIJKLMNOPQRSTUVWXYZ
&.,"-:;!?""1234567890$
&.,"-:;!?""1234567890$
abcdefghijklmnopqrstuvwxyz
abcdefghijklmnopqrstuvwxyz

CASLON 3: LINOTYPE

PICAS	6	7	8	9	10	11	12	13	14	15	16	17	18	19	20	21	22	23	24	25	26	27	28	29	30
10 POINT	14	17	19	22	24	26	29	31	34	36	38	40	43	45	48	50	53	55	58	60	62	64	67	69	72
8 POINT	19	22	25	28	31	34	37	40	43	46	50	53	56	59	62	65	68	71	74	77	81	84	87	90	93

ABCDEFGHIJ
KLMNOPQRS
TUVWXYZ&
abcdefghijklm
nopqrstuvwx
yz1234567890
$., "-.;!?""

60 POINT CASLON BOLD, ATF

Dear Sr   Birmingham 2 Oct. 1752

To remove in some Measure Yr Impatience, I have
sent You an Impression of 14 Punches of the two lines
Great Primer, which have been begun & finish'd in 9 Days
only, & contain all the Letters Roman necessary in the Titles & half
Titles. I can't forbear saying they please Me, as I can make
nothing more Correct, nor shall You see any thing of mine,
much less so. You'll observe they strike the Eye much more
sensibly than the smaller Characters tho Equally perfect, till
the press shews them to more Advantage; The Press is creeping slowly towards Perfection; I flatter my self with being
able to print nearly as good a Colour & smooth a stroke
as the inclos'd; I should esteem it a favour if You'd send
me the Initial Letters of all the Canto's, lest they should
not be included in the said 14, & three or four pages of
any part of the Poem, from whence to form a Bill for the
Casting a suitable Number of each Letter. The R. wants
a few slight Touches & the Y. half an hour's Correction.
This Day we have resolutely set about 15 of the same
Siz'd Italick Capitals, which will not be at all inferior to
the Roman, & I doubt not to compleat them in a fortnight.
You need therefore be in no pain about our being ready by
the time appointed. Our best Respects to Mrs Dodsley &
our friend Mr Beckett concludes me
                    Yr most obedt Servt John Baskerville
                                                              Verte

Postscript reads "Pray put it in no One's power to let Mr. Caslon see them"

Pray put it in no One's power to let Mr Caslon see them

ABCDEFGHIJKL MNOPQRSTUV WXYZ&abcdefghi jklmnopqrstuvwx yz1234567890$.,"-: .,!?""

48 POINT CASLON BOLD, ATF

ABCDEFGHIJK LMNOPQRSTU VWXYZ&abcdef ghijklmnopqrstuv wxyz123456789 0$., "-:,!?""

48 POINT CASLON BOLD ITALIC, ATF

ABCDEFGHIJKLMNOPQRSTUVW
XYZ&abcdefghijklmnopqrstuvwxyz12
34567890$.,"-:;!?""''

24 POINT CASLON BOLD, ATF

ABCDEFGHIJKLMNOPQRSTUV
WXYZ&abcdefghijklmnopqrstuvwxy
z1234567890$.,"-:;!?""''

24 POINT CASLON BOLD ITALIC, ATF

ABCDEFGHIJKLM
NOPQRSTUVWX
YZ&abcdefghijklm
nopqrstuvwxyz123
4567890$.,"-:;!?""

60 POINT CASLON BOLD CONDENSED, ATF

ABCDEFGHIJKLMNOP
QRSTUVWXYZ&abcdef
ghijklmnopqrstuvwxyz
1234567890$.,"-:;!?""

48 POINT CASLON BOLD CONDENSED, ATF

ABCDEFGHIJKLMNOPQRSTUVWXYZ&abcdefgh
ijklmnopqrstuvwxyz1234567890$.,"-:;!?""

24 POINT CASLON BOLD CONDENSED, ATF

ABCDEFGHIJKLMNOP QRSTUVWXYZ&abcdefg hijklmnopqrstuvwxyz123456 7890$.,'-:;!?""''

48 POINT CASLON ANTIQUE, ATF

ABCDEFGHIJKLMNOPQRSTUVWXYZ&abcdef ghijklmnopqrstuvwxyz1234567890$.,'-:;!?""''

24 POINT CASLON ANTIQUE, ATF

ABCDEFGHIJKLMNOPQRSTUVWXYZ&abcdefghijklmnopqrstuvwxyz1234567890$.,'-:;!?""''

12 POINT CASLON ANTIQUE, ATF

CENTURY EXPANDED, LUDLOW
COMPOSITOR mixed
CENTURY EXPANDED, ATF
BRAZIL civilization
CENTURY EXPANDED 20, MONOTYPE
SERIES Printing
All comparisons are made on 24 point type.

Highly versatile, legible and handsome, Century Expanded serves many design needs.

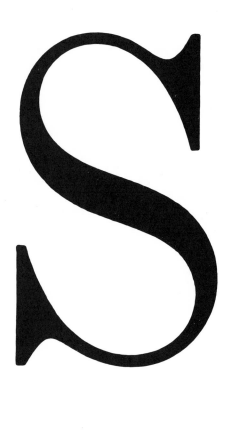
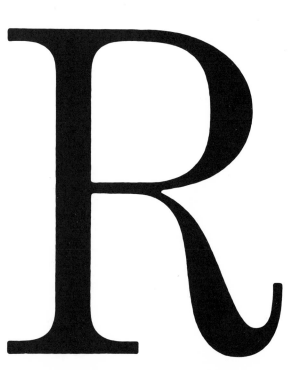

ABCDEFGHI
JKLMNOPQ
RSTUVWXY
Z&abcdefghij
klmnopqrstuv
wxyzfifffflflffifflffl1
234567890$.,"-:;
!?""''
..

72 POINT CENTURY EXPANDED, ATF

ABCDEFGH
IJKLMNOPQ
RSTUVWX
YZ&abcdefgh
ijklmnopqrst
uvwxyzfiffflflffi
ffl1234567890$
,"-..!?"""
., .,.

72 POINT CENTURY EXPANDED ITALIC, ATF

ABCDEFGHIJK
LMNOPQRSTU
VWXYZ&abcdef
ghijklmnopqrstu
vwxyzfifffflffifff12
34567890$.,"-:;!?""

60 POINT CENTURY EXPANDED, ATF

ABCDEFGHIJ
KLMNOPQRST
UVWXYZ&abc
defghijklmnopqr
stuvwxyzfiffflffiffl
1234567890$.,"-:;!
?"''
·

60 POINT CENTURY EXPANDED ITALIC, ATF

ABCDEFGHIJKLM
NOPQRSTUVWXYZ
&abcdefghijklmnopq
rstuvwxyzfiffflffiffl12
34567890$.,"-:;!?""

48 POINT CENTURY EXPANDED, ATF

ABCDEFGHIJKLM
NOPQRSTUVWXY
Z&abcdefghijklmnop
qrstuvwxyzfifffflffiffl12
34567890$.,'-.:,!?'''

48 POINT CENTURY EXPANDED ITALIC, ATF

ABCDEFGHIJKLMNOP
QRSTUVWXYZ&abcdef
ghijklmnopqrstuvwxyzfi
ffflffiffl1234567890$.,'-.:,!?'''

42 POINT CENTURY EXPANDED, ATF

ABCDEFGHIJKLMNO
PQRSTUVWXYZ&abcd
efghijklmnopqrstuvwxyz
fifffflffiffl1234567890$.,'-.:;
!?''''

42 POINT CENTURY EXPANDED ITALIC, ATF

ABCDEFGHIJKLMNOPQR
STUVWXYZ&abcdefghijkl
mnopqrstuvwxyzfifffflffifffl123
4567890$.,"-:;!?"''

36 POINT CENTURY EXPANDED, ATF

ABCDEFGHIJKLMNOPQ
RSTUVWXYZ&abcdefghijkl
mnopqrstuvwxyzfifffflffifffl1234
567890$.,"-:;!?"''

36 POINT CENTURY EXPANDED ITALIC, ATF

ABCDEFGHIJKLMNOPQRSTUV
WXYZ&abcdefghijklmnopqrstuvw
xyzfifffflffifffl1234567890$.,"-:;!?"''

30 POINT CENTURY EXPANDED, ATF

ABCDEFGHIJKLMNOPQRSTU
VWXYZ&abcdefghijklmnopqrstuv
wxyzfifffflffifffl1234567890$.,"-:;!?"''

30 POINT CENTURY EXPANDED ITALIC, ATF

ABCDEFGHIJKLMNOPQRSTUVWXYZ&
abcdefghijklmnopqrstuvwxyzfifffiflffiffl1234
567890$.,"-:;!?"""

24 POINT CENTURY EXPANDED, ATF

ABCDEFGHIJKLMNOPQRSTUVWXY
Z&abcdefghijklmnopqrstuvwxyzfifffiflffiffl12
34567890$.,"-:;!?"""

24 POINT CENTURY EXPANDED ITALIC, ATF

ABCDEFGHIJKLMNOPQRSTUVWXYZ&abcdefghijkl
mnopqrstuvwxyzfifffiflffiffl1234567890$.,"-:;!?"""

18 POINT CENTURY EXPANDED, ATF

ABCDEFGHIJKLMNOPQRSTUVWXYZ&abcdefghij
klmnopqrstuvwxyzfifffiflffiffl1234567890$.,"-:;!?"""

18 POINT CENTURY EXPANDED ITALIC, ATF

14/14 From a letter by Benjamin Franklin to B. Vaughan dated Apr. 21, 1785:

If the Irish can manufacture cottons, stuffs and silks, and linens, and cutlery, and toys, and books etc. etc. etc., so as to sell them cheaper in England than the *manufacturers* of England sell them, is not this good for the *people* of England who are not manufacturers? and will not *even the manufacturers themselves share the benefit? Since if cottons*

12/12 From a letter by Benjamin Franklin to B. Vaughan Esq. dated Apr. 21, 1785:

If the Irish can manufacture cottons, stuffs and silks, and linens, and cutlery, and toys, and books etc. etc. etc., so as to sell them cheaper in England than the *manufacturers* of England sell them, is not this good for the *people* of England who are not *manufacturers? and will not even the manufacturers themselves share the benefit? Since if cottons are cheaper, all the other manufacturers who wear cottons will save *in that article, and so of the rest. If books can be had much cheaper from Ireland,*

14/16 From a letter by Benjamin Franklin to B. Vaughan dated Apr. 21, 1785:

If the Irish can manufacture cottons, stuffs and silks, and linens, and cutlery, and toys, and books etc. etc. etc., so as to sell them cheaper in England than the *manufacturers* of England sell them, is not this good *even the manufacturers themselves share the benefit? Since if cottons*

12/14 From a letter by Benjamin Franklin to B. Vaughan Esq. dated Apr. 21, 1785:

If the Irish can manufacture cottons, stuffs and silks, and linens, and cutlery, and toys, and books etc. etc. etc., so as to sell them cheaper in England than the *manufacturers* of England sell them, is not this good for the *people* of England who are not *manufacturers? and will not even the manin that article, and so of the rest. If books can be had much cheaper from Ireland,*

14/18 From a letter by Benjamin Franklin to B. Vaughan dated Apr. 21, 1785:

If the Irish can manufacture cottons, stuffs and silks, and linens, and cutlery, and toys, and books etc. etc. etc., so as to sell them cheaper in England than the *manufacturers* of *even the manufacturers themselves share the benefit? Since if cottons*

12/16 From a letter by Benjamin Franklin to B. Vaughan Esq. dated Apr. 21, 1785:

If the Irish can manufacture cottons, stuffs and silks, and linens, and cutlery, and toys, and books etc. etc. etc., so as to sell them cheaper in England than the *manufacturers* of England sell them, is not this good for the *people* of England who are not *in that article, and so of the rest. If books can be had much cheaper from Ireland,*

ABCDEFGHIJKLMNOPQRSTUV
ABCDEFGHIJKLMNOPQRSTUV
&.,"-:;!?""1234567890$
&.,"-:;!?""1234567890$
abcdefghijklmnopqrstuvwxyz
abcdefghijklmnopqrstuvwxyz

ABCDEFGHIJKLMNOPQRSTUVWXY
ABCDEFGHIJKLMNOPQRSTUVWXY
&.,"-:;!?""1234567890$
&.,"-:;!?""1234567890$
abcdefghijklmnopqrstuvwxyz
abcdefghijklmnopqrstuvwxyz

CENTURY EXPANDED: INTERTYPE

PICAS	6	7	8	9	10	11	12	13	14	15	16	17	18	19	20	21	22	23	24	25	26	27	28	29	30
14 POINT	11	12	14	16	18	20	21	23	25	27	29	30	32	34	36	38	39	41	43	45	47	48	50	52	54
12 POINT	13	15	17	19	21	23	25	27	30	32	34	36	38	40	42	45	47	49	51	53	55	57	59	61	63

11/11
From a letter by Benjamin Franklin to B. Vaughan Esq. dated April 21, 1785:

If the Irish can manufacture cottons, stuffs and silks, and linens, and cutlery, and toys, and books etc. etc. etc., so as to sell them cheaper in England than the *manufacturers* of England sell them, is not this good for the *people* of England who are not *manufacturers?* and will not even the manufacturers themselves share the benefit? Since if cottons are cheaper, all the other manufacturers who wear cottons will save in that article, and so of the rest. If books can be had much cheaper from Ireland, *(which I believe for I bought Blackstone there for 24/- when it was sold in England at four*

10/10
From a letter by Benjamin Franklin to B. Vaughan Esq. dated April 21, 1785:

If the Irish can manufacture cottons, stuffs and silks, and linens, and cutlery, and toys, and books etc. etc. etc., so as to sell them cheaper in England than the *manufacturers* of England sell them, is not this good for the *people* of England who are not *manufacturers?* and will not even the manufacturers themselves share the benefit? Since if cottons are cheaper, all the other manufacturers who wear cottons will save in that article, and so of the rest. If books can be had much cheaper from Ireland, (which I believe for I bought Blackstone there for 24/- when it was sold in England at four guineas) is not this an advantage not to *English booksellers indeed, but to English readers and to learning. And of all the complainants*

11/13
From a letter by Benjamin Franklin to B. Vaughan Esq. dated April 21, 1785:

If the Irish can manufacture cottons, stuffs and silks, and linens, and cutlery, and toys, and books etc. etc. etc., so as to sell them cheaper in England than the *manufacturers* of England sell them, is not this good for the *people* of England who are not *manufacturers?* and will not even the manufacturers themselves share the benefit? Since if cottons are cheaper, all the other manufacturers who wear cottons *(which I believe for I bought Blackstone there for 24/- when it was sold in England at four*

10/12
From a letter by Benjamin Franklin to B. Vaughan Esq. dated April 21, 1785:

If the Irish can manufacture cottons, stuffs and silks, and linens, and cutlery, and toys, and books etc. etc. etc., so as to sell them cheaper in England than the *manufacturers* of England sell them, is not this good for the *people* of England who are not *manufacturers?* and will not even the manufacturers themselves share the benefit? Since if cottons are cheaper, all the other manufacturers who wear cottons will save in that article, and so of the rest. If books can be had much cheaper *English booksellers indeed, but to English readers and to learning. And of all the complainants*

11/15
From a letter by Benjamin Franklin to B. Vaughan Esq. dated April 21, 1785:

If the Irish can manufacture cottons, stuffs and silks, and linens, and cutlery, and toys, and books etc. etc. etc., so as to sell them cheaper in England than the *manufacturers* of England sell them, is not this good for the *people* of England who are not *manufacturers?* and will not even the manufacturers themselves *(which I believe for I bought Blackstone there for 24/- when it was sold in England at four*

10/14
From a letter by Benjamin Franklin to B. Vaughan Esq. dated April 21, 1785:

If the Irish can manufacture cottons, stuffs and silks, and linens, and cutlery, and toys, and books etc. etc. etc., so as to sell them cheaper in England than the *manufacturers* of England sell them, is not this good for the *people* of England who are not *manufacturers?* and will not even the manufacturers themselves share the benefit? Since if cottons are cheaper, all the other manufacturers *English booksellers indeed, but to English readers and to learning. And of all the complainants*

ABCDEFGHIJKLMNOPQRSTUVWXYZ
ABCDEFGHIJKLMNOPQRSTUVWXYZ
&.,"-:;!?""1234567890$
&.,"-:;!?""1234567890$
abcdefghijklmnopqrstuvwxyz
abcdefghijklmnopqrstuvwxyz

ABCDEFGHIJKLMNOPQRSTUVWXYZ
ABCDEFGHIJKLMNOPQRSTUVWXYZ
&.,"-:;!?""1234567890$
&.,"-:;!?""1234567890$
abcdefghijklmnopqrstuvwxyz
abcdefghijklmnopqrstuvwxyz

CENTURY EXPANDED: INTERTYPE

PICAS	6	7	8	9	10	11	12	13	14	15	16	17	18	19	20	21	22	23	24	25	26	27	28	29	30
11 POINT	14	16	18	21	23	25	28	30	32	35	37	39	41	44	46	48	51	53	55	57	60	62	64	67	69
10 POINT	14	17	19	22	24	27	29	31	34	36	39	41	43	46	48	51	53	55	58	60	63	65	67	70	73

9/9

From a letter by Benjamin Franklin to B. Vaughan Esq. dated April 21, 1785:

If the Irish can manufacture cottons, stuffs and silks, and linens, and cutlery, and toys, and books etc. etc. etc., so as to sell them cheaper in England than the *manufacturers* of England sell them, is not this good for the *people* of England who are not *manufac*turers? and will not even the manufacturers themselves share the benefit? Since if cottons are cheaper, all the other manufacturers who wear cottons will save in that article, and so of the rest. If books can be had much cheaper from Ireland, (which I believe for I bought Blackstone there for 24/- when it was sold in England at four guineas) is not this an advantage not to English booksellers indeed, but to English readers and to learning. And of all the complainants perhaps these booksellers are least worthy of consid*eration. The catalogue you last sent me amazes me by the high prices (said to be the lowest) affixed to each*

8/8

From a letter by Benjamin Franklin to B. Vaughan Esq. dated April 21, 1785:

If the Irish can manufacture cottons, stuffs and silks, and linens, and cutlery, and toys, and books etc. etc. etc., so as to sell them cheaper in England than the *manufacturers* of England sell them, is not this good for the *people* of England who are not *manufac*turers? and will not even the manufacturers themselves share the benefit? Since if cottons are cheaper, all the other manufacturers who wear cottons will save in that article, and so of the rest. If books can be had much cheaper from Ireland, (which I believe for I bought Blackstone there for 24/- when it was sold in England at four guineas) is not this an advantage not to English booksellers indeed, but to English readers and to learning. And of all the complainants perhaps these booksellers are least worthy of consideration. The catalogue you last sent me amazes me by the high prices (said to be the lowest) affixed to each article. And one can scarce see a new book, without observing the excessive *artifices may use use of to puff up a paper of verses into a pamphlet, a pamphlet into an octavo, and an octavo into*

9/11

From a letter by Benjamin Franklin to B. Vaughan Esq. dated April 21, 1785:

If the Irish can manufacture cottons, stuffs and silks, and linens, and cutlery, and toys, and books etc. etc. etc., so as to sell them cheaper in England than the *manufacturers* of England sell them, is not this good for the *people* of England who are not *manufac*turers? and will not even the manufacturers themselves share the benefit? Since if cottons are cheaper, all the other manufacturers who wear cottons will save in that article, and so of the rest. If books can be had much cheaper from Ireland, (which I believe for I bought Blackstone there for 24/- when it was *eration. The catalogue you last sent me amazes me by the high prices (said to be the lowest) affixed to each*

8/10

From a letter by Benjamin Franklin to B. Vaughan Esq. dated April 21, 1785:

If the Irish can manufacture cottons, stuffs and silks, and linens, and cutlery, and toys, and books etc. etc. etc., so as to sell them cheaper in England than the *manufacturers* of England sell them, is not this good for the *people* of England who are not *manufac*turers? and will not even the manufacturers themselves share the benefit? Since if cottons are cheaper, all the other manufacturers who wear cottons will save in that article, and so of the rest. If books can be had much cheaper from Ireland, (which I believe for I bought Blackstone there for 24/- when it was sold in England at four guineas) is not this an advantage not to English booksellers indeed, but to English readers and to learning. And of all the complainants perhaps *artifices may use use of to puff up a paper of verses into a pamphlet, a pamphlet into an octavo, and an octavo into*

9/13

From a letter by Benjamin Franklin to B. Vaughan Esq. dated April 21, 1785:

If the Irish can manufacture cottons, stuffs and silks, and linens, and cutlery, and toys, and books etc. etc. etc., so as to sell them cheaper in England than the *manufacturers* of England sell them, is not this good for the *people* of England who are not *manufac*turers? and will not even the manufacturers themselves share the benefit? Since if cottons are cheaper, all the other manufacturers who wear cottons will save in that article, and so of the rest. If books can *eration. The catalogue you last sent me amazes me by the high prices (said to be the lowest) affixed to each*

8/12

From a letter by Benjamin Franklin to B. Vaughan Esq. dated April 21, 1785:

If the Irish can manufacture cottons, stuffs and silks, and linens, and cutlery, and toys, and books etc. etc. etc., so as to sell them cheaper in England than the *manufacturers* of England sell them, is not this good for the *people* of England who are not *manufac*turers? and will not even the manufacturers themselves share the benefit? Since if cottons are cheaper, all the other manufacturers who wear cottons will save in that article, and so of the rest. If books can be had much cheaper from Ireland, (which I believe for I bought Blackstone there for 24/- when it was *artifices may use use of to puff up a paper of verses into a pamphlet, a pamphlet into an octavo, and an octavo into*

ABCDEFGHIJKLMNOPQRSTUVWXYZ
ABCDEFGHIJKLMNOPQRSTUVWXYZ
&.,"-:;!?""1234567890$
&.,"-:;!?""1234567890$
abcdefghijklmnopqrstuvwxyz
abcdefghijklmnopqrstuvwxyz

ABCDEFGHIJKLMNOPQRSTUVWXYZ
ABCDEFGHIJKLMNOPQRSTUVWXYZ
&.,"-:;!?""1234567890$
&.,"-:;!?""1234567890$
abcdefghijklmnopqrstuvwxyz
abcdefghijklmnopqrstuvwxyz

CENTURY EXPANDED: INTERTYPE

PICAS	6	7	8	9	10	11	12	13	14	15	16	17	18	19	20	21	22	23	24	25	26	27	28	29	30
9 POINT	16	19	21	24	27	29	32	35	37	40	43	46	48	51	54	56	59	61	64	67	70	72	75	78	81
8 POINT	17	20	23	26	29	32	35	37	40	43	46	49	52	55	57	60	63	66	69	72	75	78	81	83	87

From a letter by Benjamin Franklin to B. Vaughan Esq. dated April 21, 1785:

7/7

If the Irish can manufacture cottons, stuffs and silks, and linens, and cutlery, and toys, and books etc. etc. etc., so as to sell them cheaper in England than the *manufacturers* of England sell them, is not this good for the *people* of England who are not *manufacturers*? and will not even the manufacturers themselves share the benefit? Since if cottons are cheaper, all the other manufacturers who wear cottons will save in that article, and so of the rest. If books can be had much cheaper from Ireland, (which I believe for I bought Blackstone there for 24/- when it was sold in England at four guineas) is not this an advantage not to English booksellers indeed, but to English readers and to learning. And of all the complaints perhaps these booksellers are least worthy of consideration. The catalogue you last sent me amazes me by the high prices (said to be the lowest) affixed to each article. And one can scarce see a new book, without observing the excessive artifices may use of to puff up a paper of verses into a pamphlet, a pamphlet into an octavo, and an octavo into a quarto, with scab boardings, white lines, sparse titles of chapters, and exorbitant margins, to such a degree, that the selling of paper seems now the object and *printing on it only the pretence. I inclose the copy of a page in a late comedy. Between every two lines there is a white space*

From a letter by Benjamin Franklin to B. Vaughan Esq. dated April 21, 1785:

7/9

If the Irish can manufacture cottons, stuffs and silks, and linens, and cutlery, and toys, and books etc. etc. etc., so as to sell them cheaper in England than the *manufacturers* of England sell them, is not this good for the *people* of England who are not *manufacturers*? and will not even the manufacturers themselves share the benefit? Since if cottons are cheaper, all the other manufacturers who wear cottons will save in that article, and so of the rest. If books can be had much cheaper from Ireland, (which I believe for I bought Blackstone there for 24/- when it was sold in England at four guineas) is not this an advantage not to English booksellers indeed, but to English readers and to learning. And of all the complaints perhaps these booksellers are least worthy of consideration. The catalogue you last sent me amazes me by the high prices (said to be the lowest) affixed to each article. And one can scarce see a new *printing on it only the pretence. I inclose the copy of a page in a late comedy. Between every two lines there is a white space*

From a letter by Benjamin Franklin to B. Vaughan Esq. dated April 21, 1785:

7/11

If the Irish can manufacture cottons, stuffs and silks, and linens, and cutlery, and toys, and books etc. etc. etc., so as to sell them cheaper in England than the *manufacturers* of England sell them, is not this good for the *people* of England who are not *manufacturers*? and will not even the manufacturers themselves share the benefit? Since if cottons are cheaper, all the other manufacturers who wear cottons will save in that article, and so of the rest. If books can be had much cheaper from Ireland, (which I believe for I bought Blackstone there for 24/- when it was sold in England at four guineas) is not this an advantage not to English booksellers indeed, but to English *printing on it only the pretence. I inclose the copy of a page in a late comedy. Between every two lines there is a white space*

ABCDEFGHIJKLMNOPQRSTUVWXYZ
ABCDEFGHIJKLMNOPQRSTUVWXYZ
&.,."-:;!?"''1234567890$
&.,."-:;!?"''1234567890$
abcdefghijklmnopqrstuvwxyz
abcdefghijklmnopqrstuvwxyz

From a letter by Benjamin Franklin to B. Vaughan Esq. dated Apr. 21, 1785:

6/6

If the Irish can manufacture cottons, stuffs and silks, and linens, and cutlery, and toys, and books etc. etc. etc., so as to sell them cheaper in England than the *manufacturers* of England sell them, is not this good for the *people* of England who are not *manufacturers*? and will not even the manufacturers themselves share the benefit? Since if cottons are cheaper, all the other manufacturers who wear cottons will save in that article, and so of the rest. If books can be had much cheaper from Ireland, (which I believe for I bought Blackstone there for 24/- when it was sold in England at four guineas) is not this an advantage not to English booksellers indeed, but to English readers and to learning. And of all the complaints perhaps these booksellers are least worthy of consideration. The catalogue you last sent me amazes me by the high prices (said to be the lowest) affixed to each article. And one can scarce see a new book, without observing the excessive artifices may use of to puff up a paper of verses into a pamphlet, a pamphlet into an octavo, and an octavo into a quarto, with scab boardings, white lines, sparse titles of chapters, and exorbitant margins, to such a degree, that the selling of paper seems now the object and printing on it only the pretence. I inclose the copy of a page in a late comedy. Between every two lines there is a white space equal to another line. You have a law, I think, against butchers blowing of veal to make it look fatter; why not one against booksellers blowing of books to make them look bigger. All this to *yourself;* you can easily guess the reason.
My grandson is a little indisposed, but sends you two pamphlets, Fig- *aro and Le Roy Voyageux. The first is a play of Beaumarchais, which has had a great run here. The other a representation of all the supposed*

From a letter by Benjamin Franklin to B. Vaughan Esq. dated Apr. 21, 1785:

6/8

If the Irish can manufacture cottons, stuffs and silks, and linens, and cutlery, and toys, and books etc. etc. etc., so as to sell them cheaper in England than the *manufacturers* of England sell them, is not this good for the *people* of England who are not *manufacturers*? and will not even the manufacturers themselves share the benefit? Since if cottons are cheaper, all the other manufacturers who wear cottons will save in that article, and so of the rest. If books can be had much cheaper from Ireland, (which I believe for I bought Blackstone there for 24/- when it was sold in England at four guineas) is not this an advantage not to English booksellers indeed, but to English readers and to learning. And of all the complaints perhaps these booksellers are least worthy of consideration. The catalogue you last sent me amazes me by the high prices (said to be the lowest) affixed to each article. And one can scarce see a new book, without observing the excessive artifices may use of to puff up a paper of verses into a pamphlet, a pamphlet into an octavo, and an octavo into a quarto, with scab boardings, white lines, sparse titles of chapters, and exorbitant margins, to such a degree, that *aro and Le Roy Voyageux. The first is a play of Beaumarchais, which has had a great run here. The other a representation of all the supposed*

From a letter by Benjamin Franklin to B. Vaughan Esq. dated Apr. 21, 1785:

6/10

If the Irish can manufacture cottons, stuffs and silks, and linens, and cutlery, and toys, and books etc. etc. etc., so as to sell them cheaper in England than the *manufacturers* of England sell them, is not this good for the *people* of England who are not *manufacturers*? and will not even the manufacturers themselves share the benefit? Since if cottons are cheaper, all the other manufacturers who wear cottons will save in that article, and so of the rest. If books can be had much cheaper from Ireland, (which I believe for I bought Blackstone there for 24/- when it was sold in England at four guineas) is not this an advantage not to English booksellers indeed, but to English readers and to learning. And of all the complaints perhaps these booksellers are least worthy of consideration. The catalogue you last sent me amazes me by the high prices (said to be the lowest) affixed to each article. And one can scarce *aro and Le Roy Voyageux. The first is a play of Beaumarchais, which has had a great run here. The other a representation of all the supposed*

ABCDEFGHIJKLMNOPQRSTUVWXYZ
ABCDEFGHIJKLMNOPQRSTUVWXYZ
&.,."-:;!?"''1234567890$
&.,."-:;!?"''1234567890$
abcdefghijklmnopqrstuvwxyz
abcdefghijklmnopqrstuvwxyz

CENTURY EXPANDED: INTERTYPE

PICAS	6	7	8	9	10	11	12	13	14	15	16	17	18	19	20	21	22	23	24	25	26	27	28	29	30
7 POINT	19	22	26	29	32	35	38	42	45	48	51	54	58	61	64	67	70	73	77	80	83	86	90	93	96
6 POINT	22	25	29	32	36	40	43	47	51	54	58	61	65	68	72	76	79	83	87	90	94	97	101	105	108

ABCDEFGHIJKLM NOPQRSTUVWXYZ &abcdefghijklmnopq rstuvwxyzfifffflffiffl123 4567890$.,"-:;!?"""

48 POINT CENTURY SCHOOLBOOK, ATF

ABCDEFGHIJKLM NOPQRSTUVWXY Z&abcdefghijklmnopq rstuvwxyzfifffflffiffl123 4567890$.,"-:;!?"""

48 POINT CENTURY SCHOOLBOOK ITALIC, ATF

ABCDEFGHIJKLMNOPQR
STUVWXYZ&abcdefghijklm
nopqrstuvwxyzfifffflffifffl12345
67890$.,"-:;!?"""

36 POINT CENTURY SCHOOLBOOK, ATF

ABCDEFGHIJKLMNOPQR
STUVWXYZ&abcdefghijklm
nopqrstuvwxyzfiffflffiffl123456
7890$.,"-:;!?"""

36 POINT CENTURY SCHOOLBOOK ITALIC, ATF

ABCDEFGHIJKLMNOPQRSTUV
WXYZ&abcdefghijklmnopqrstuvw
xyzfiffflffiffl1234567890$.,"-:;!?"""

30 POINT CENTURY SCHOOLBOOK, ATF

ABCDEFGHIJKLMNOPQRSTUV
WXYZ&abcdefghijklmnopqrstuvwx
yzfiffflffiffl1234567890$.,"-:;!?"""

30 POINT CENTURY SCHOOLBOOK ITALIC, ATF

ABCDEFGHIJKLMNOPQRSTUVWXYZ&
abcdefghijklmnopqrstuvwxyzfifffflffiffl12345
67890$.,"-:;!?""''

24 POINT CENTURY SCHOOLBOOK, ATF

ABCDEFGHIJKLMNOPQRSTUVWXYZ
&abcdefghijklmnopqrstuvwxyzfifffflffiffl1234
567890$.,"-:;!?"''

24 POINT CENTURY SCHOOLBOOK ITALIC, ATF

ABCDEFGHIJKLMNOPQRSTUVWXYZ&abcdefghijk
lmnopqrstuvwxyzfifffflffiffl1234567890$.,"-:;!?""''

18 POINT CENTURY SCHOOLBOOK, ATF

ABCDEFGHIJKLMNOPQRSTUVWXYZ&abcdefghij
klmnopqrstuvwxyzfifffflffiffl1234567890$.,"-:;!?"''

18 POINT CENTURY SCHOOLBOOK ITALIC, ATF

14/14 FOURNIER ON TYPEFOUND-ING. Finding myself attached by profession and inclination to the art of founding letters, I have applied myself first of all to finding out their beauties and defects, and to observing the alterations which might be made in them. In the next place I have attempted to combine the art of cutting letters with that of found-*ing them, that I might be in a position to put my observations into*

12/12 FOURNIER ON TYPEFOUNDING. Finding myself attached by profession and inclination to the art of founding letters, I have applied myself first of all to finding out their beauties and defects, and to observing the alterations which might be made in them. In the next place I have attempted to combine the art of cutting letters with that of founding them, that I might be in a position to put my observations into practice without needing the intervention of an alien hand. With this in *view I gathered together specimens or examples of the most beautiful letters of va-*

14/16 FOURNIER ON TYPEFOUND-ING. Finding myself attached by profession and inclination to the art of founding letters, I have applied myself first of all to finding out their beauties and defects, and to observing the alterations which might be made in them. In the next place I *ing them, that I might be in a position to put my observations into*

12/14 FOURNIER ON TYPEFOUNDING. Finding myself attached by profession and inclination to the art of founding letters, I have applied myself first of all to finding out their beauties and defects, and to observing the alterations which might be made in them. In the next place I have attempted to combine the art of cutting letters with that of founding them, that I *view I gathered together specimens or examples of the most beautiful letters of va-*

14/18 FOURNIER ON TYPEFOUND-ING. Finding myself attached by profession and inclination to the art of founding letters, I have applied myself first of all to finding out their beauties and defects, and to observing the alterations which might be *ing them, that I might be in a position to put my observations into*

12/16 FOURNIER ON TYPEFOUNDING. Finding myself attached by profession and inclination to the art of founding letters, I have applied myself first of all to finding out their beauties and defects, and to observing the alterations which might be made in them. In the next place I have attempted to combine the art of cutting *view I gathered together specimens or examples of the most beautiful letters of va-*

ABCDEFGHIJKLMNOPQRSTU
ABCDEFGHIJKLMNOPQRSTU
&.,"-:;!?""1234567890$
&.,"-:;!?""1234567890$
abcdefghijklmnopqrstuvwxyz
abcdefghijklmnopqrstuvwxyz

ABCDEFGHIJKLMNOPQRSTUVWX
ABCDEFGHIJKLMNOPQRSTUVWX
&.,"-:;!?""1234567890$
&.,"-:;!?""1234567890$
abcdefghijklmnopqrstuvwxyz
abcdefghijklmnopqrstuvwxyz

CENTURY SCHOOLBOOK: INTERTYPE

PICAS	6	7	8	9	10	11	12	13	14	15	16	17	18	19	20	21	22	23	24	25	26	27	28	29	30
14 POINT	11	13	14	16	18	20	22	23	25	27	29	31	32	34	36	38	40	41	43	45	47	49	50	52	54
12 POINT	13	15	17	19	21	23	25	27	29	32	34	36	38	40	42	44	46	48	50	53	55	57	59	61	63

FOURNIER ON TYPEFOUNDING. Finding myself attached by profession and inclination to the art of founding letters, I have applied myself first of all to finding out their beauties and defects, and to observing the alterations which might be made in them. In the next place I have attempted to combine the art of cutting letters with that of founding them, that I might be in a position to put my observations into practice without needing the intervention of an alien hand. With this in view I gathered together specimens or examples of the most beautiful letters of various foundries *both in France and countries abroad, and I took from each what seemed to me to be good with-*

11/11

FOURNIER ON TYPEFOUNDING. Finding myself attached by profession and inclination to the art of founding letters, I have applied myself first of all to finding out their beauties and defects, and to observing the alterations which might be made in them. In the next place I have attempted to combine the art of cutting letters with that of founding them, that I might be in a position to put my observations into practice without needing the intervention of an alien hand. With this in view I gathered together specimens or examples of the most beautiful letters of various foundries *both in France and countries abroad, and I took from each what seemed to me to be good with-*

11/13

FOURNIER ON TYPEFOUNDING. Finding myself attached by profession and inclination to the art of founding letters, I have applied myself first of all to finding out their beauties and defects, and to observing the alterations which might be made in them. In the next place I have attempted to combine the art of cutting letters with that of founding them, that I might be in a position to put my *both in France and countries abroad, and I took from each what seemed to me to be good with-*

11/15

FOURNIER ON TYPEFOUNDING. Finding myself attached by profession and inclination to the art of founding letters, I have applied myself first of all to finding out their beauties and defects, and to observing the alterations which might be made in them. In the next place I have attempted to combine the art of cutting letters with that of founding them, that I might be in a position to put my observations into practice without needing the intervention of an alien hand. With this in view I gathered together specimens or examples of the most beautiful letters of vari- *came especially devoted to the roman letter of those letter-cutters of whom I have spoken, for-*

10/10

FOURNIER ON TYPEFOUNDING. Finding myself attached by profession and inclination to the art of founding letters, I have applied myself first of all to finding out their beauties and defects, and to observing the alterations which might be made in them. In the next place I have attempted to combine the art of cutting letters with that of founding them, that I might be in a position to put my observations into practice without needing the intervention of an alien hand. With this in view I gathered together specimens or examples of the most beautiful letters of vari- *came especially devoted to the roman letter of those letter-cutters of whom I have spoken, for-*

10/12

FOURNIER ON TYPEFOUNDING. Finding myself attached by profession and inclination to the art of founding letters, I have applied myself first of all to finding out their beauties and defects, and to observing the alterations which might be made in them. In the next place I have attempted to combine the art of cutting letters with that of founding them, that I might be in a position to put my observations into practice without needing the intervention of an alien hand. *came especially devoted to the roman letter of those letter-cutters of whom I have spoken, for-*

10/14

ABCDEFGHIJKLMNOPQRSTUVWXYZ
ABCDEFGHIJKLMNOPQRSTUVWXYZ
&.,"-:;!?""1234567890$
&.,"-:;!?""1234567890$
abcdefghijklmnopqrstuvwxyz
abcdefghijklmnopqrstuvwxyz

ABCDEFGHIJKLMNOPQRSTUVWXYZ
ABCDEFGHIJKLMNOPQRSTUVWXYZ
&.,"-:;!?""1234567890$
&.,"-:;!?""1234567890$
abcdefghijklmnopqrstuvwxyz
abcdefghijklmnopqrstuvwxyz

CENTURY SCHOOLBOOK: INTERTYPE

PICAS	6	7	8	9	10	11	12	13	14	15	16	17	18	19	20	21	22	23	24	25	26	27	28	29	30
11 POINT	14	16	19	21	24	26	28	31	33	35	38	40	42	45	47	49	52	54	56	59	61	63	66	68	71
10 POINT	15	17	20	22	25	27	29	31	34	36	39	41	44	46	49	51	54	56	59	61	64	66	69	71	74

9/9 FOURNIER ON TYPEFOUNDING. Finding myself attached by profession and inclination to the art of founding letters, I have applied myself first of all to finding out their beauties and defects, and to observing the alterations which might be made in them. In the next place I have attempted to combine the art of cutting letters with that of founding them, that I might be in a position to put my observations into practice without needing the intervention of an alien hand. With this in view I gathered together specimens or examples of the most beautiful letters of various foundries both in France and countries abroad, and I took from each what seemed to me to be good without becoming a slave to any. I became especially devoted to the roman letter of those letter-cutters of whom I have spoken, foreigners having never done *anything as good. Therefore, I have approximated to these as nearly as I could, taking care, at the same*

8/8 FOURNIER ON TYPEFOUNDING. Finding myself attached by profession and inclination to the art of founding letters, I have applied myself first of all to finding out their beauties and defects, and to observing the alterations which might be made in them. In the next place I have attempted to combine the art of cutting letters with that of founding them, that I might be in a position to put my observations into practice without needing the intervention of an alien hand. With this in view I gathered together specimens or examples of the most beautiful letters of various foundries both in France and countries abroad, and I took from each what seemed to me to be good without becoming a slave to any. I became especially devoted to the roman letter of those letter-cutters of whom I have spoken, foreigners having never done anything as good. Therefore I have approximated to these as nearly as I could, taking care, at the same time, to make certain changes in them which seemed *to me necessary, such as making the capitals range at the top with the lower-case ascenders. This change makes*

9/11 FOURNIER ON TYPEFOUNDING. Finding myself attached by profession and inclination to the art of founding letters, I have applied myself first of all to finding out their beauties and defects, and to observing the alterations which might be made in them. In the next place I have attempted to combine the art of cutting letters with that of founding them, that I might be in a position to put my observations into practice without needing the intervention of an alien hand. With this in view I gathered together specimens or examples of the most beautiful letters of various foundries both in France and countries abroad, and I took from each what seemed to me to be good *anything as good. Therefore, I have approximated to these as nearly as I could, taking care, at the same*

8/10 FOURNIER ON TYPEFOUNDING. Finding myself attached by profession and inclination to the art of founding letters, I have applied myself first of all to finding out their beauties and defects, and to observing the alterations which might be made in them. In the next place I have attempted to combine the art of cutting letters with that of founding them, that I might be in a position to put my observations into practice without needing the intervention of an alien hand. With this in view I gathered together specimens or examples of the most beautiful letters of various foundries both in France and countries abroad, and I took from each what seemed to me to be good without becoming a slave to any. I became especially devoted to the roman letter of those *to me necessary, such as making the capitals range at the top with the lower-case ascenders. This change makes*

9/13 FOURNIER ON TYPEFOUNDING. Finding myself attached by profession and inclination to the art of founding letters, I have applied myself first of all to finding out their beauties and defects, and to observing the alterations which might be made in them. In the next place I have attempted to combine the art of cutting letters with that of founding them, that I might be in a position to put my observations into practice without needing the intervention of an alien hand. With this in view I gathered together specimens or examples of the most beautiful letters of var- *anything as good. Therefore, I have approximated to these as nearly as I could, taking care, at the same*

8/12 FOURNIER ON TYPEFOUNDING. Finding myself attached by profession and inclination to the art of founding letters, I have applied myself first of all to finding out their beauties and defects, and to observing the alterations which might be made in them. In the next place I have attempted to combine the art of cutting letters with that of founding them, that I might be in a position to put my observations into practice without needing the intervention of an alien hand. With this in view I gathered together specimens or examples of the most beautiful letters of various foundries both in France and countries abroad, and I took from each what seemed *to me necessary, such as making the capitals range at the top with the lower-case ascenders. This change makes*

ABCDEFGHIJKLMNOPQRSTUVWXYZ
ABCDEFGHIJKLMNOPQRSTUVWXYZ
&.,"-:;!?""'"1234567890$
&.,"-:;!?""'"1234567890$
abcdefghijklmnopqrstuvwxyz
abcdefghijklmnopqrstuvwxyz

ABCDEFGHIJKLMNOPQRSTUVWXYZ
ABCDEFGHIJKLMNOPQRSTUVWXYZ
&.,"-:;!?""'"1234567890$
&.,"-:;!?""'"1234567890$
abcdefghijklmnopqrstuvwxyz
abcdefghijklmnopqrstuvwxyz

CENTURY SCHOOLBOOK: INTERTYPE

PICAS	6	7	8	9	10	11	12	13	14	15	16	17	18	19	20	21	22	23	24	25	26	27	28	29	30
9 POINT	16	19	21	24	27	29	32	34	37	40	42	45	48	50	53	56	58	61	64	66	69	72	74	77	80
8 POINT	17	20	23	26	29	31	34	37	40	43	46	49	51	54	57	60	63	65	68	71	74	77	80	83	86

ABCDEFGHIJKLMNOPQR
STUVWXYZ&abcdefghijklm
nopqrstuvwxyzfifffflffiffll23456
7890$.,"-:;!?""''

36 POINT CENTURY BOLD, ATF

ABCDEFGHIJKLMNOPQR
STUVWXYZ&abcdefghijkl
mnopqrstuvwxyzfifffflffiffll123
4567890$.,"-:;!?""''

36 POINT CENTURY BOLD ITALIC, ATF

ABCDEFGHIJKLMNOPQRSTUVWXYZ&
abcdefghijklmnopqrstuvwxyzfifffflffiffll12345
67890$.,"-:;!?""''

24 POINT CENTURY BOLD, ATF

ABCDEFGHIJKLMNOPQRSTUVWXYZ
&abcdefghijklmnopqrstuvwxyzfifffflffiffll12
34567890$.,"-:;!?""''

24 POINT CENTURY BOLD ITALIC, ATF

ABCDEFGHIJKLMNOPQRSTUVWXYZ&abcdefghijklmnopqrstuvw
xyzfifffflffiffll1234567890$.,"-:;!?""''

14 POINT CENTURY BOLD, ATF

ABCDEFGHIJKLMNOPQRSTUVWXYZ&abcdefghijklmnopqrst
uvwxyzfifffflffiffll1234567890$.,"-:;!?""''

14 POINT CENTURY BOLD ITALIC, ATF

ABCDEFGHIJKLMNOPQ
RSTUVWXYZ&abcdefgh
ijklmnopqrstuvwxyzfifffl
ffifffl1234567890$
"_•·!?""«
•9 •9··

60 POINT CENTURY BOLD CONDENSED, ATF

ABCDEFGHIJKLMNOPQRSTU
VWXYZ&abcdefghijklmnopqrs
tuvwxyzfifffflfffiffl1234567890$
"_••!?""«
•9 •9··

48 POINT CENTURY BOLD CONDENSED, ATF

ABCDEFGHIJKLMNOPQRSTUVWXYZ&
abcdefghijklmnopqrstuvwxyzfffififlffifffl123
4567890$.,-'!?

36 POINT CENTURY BOLD CONDENSED, ATF

A Yonge man that called was melibeus the whiche was myghty & ryche begat a doughter vpon his wyf that callyd was prudence whiche doughter callyd was Sophye/Vpon a day befyl that he for his disporte wente hym in to the feldys for to playe/his wyf & his doughter hath he lefte within his hous of whiche the dores were fast shytte/Thre of his olde foes hath hit aspyed & setten ladders vnto the walles of his hous & by the wyndowes ben entryd in/& bete his wyf/& wounded his doughter with fyue mortel woundes in v sondrye places/that is to say in her feet/in her hondes/in her eeres/in her nose/and in her mouthe/and leften her for dede and wenten her way/whan melibeus retorned was in to hys hous and sawe al thys myschyef/he like a mad man rentynge his clothes began to wepe and crye

P Rudence his wyf as ferforth as she durst besoughte hym of his wepynge to stynte/But not forthy he began to wepe and crye euer lenger the more/Thys noble wyf prudence remembryd her vpon the sentence of Ouyde in hys book that clepyd is the Remedye of loue/where

A j

ABCDEFGHIJKLMNOPQRSTUVWXYZ&abcdefghijklmnopqrst
uvwxyzfifffflffiffl1234567890$.,"-:;!?""
24 POINT CENTURY BOLD CONDENSED, ATF

ABCDEFGHIJKLMNOPQ
RSTUVWXYZ&abcdefghij
klmnopqrstuvwxyzfifffflffi
ffl1234567890$.,"-:;!?""
36 POINT CENTURY SCHOOLBOOK BOLD, ATF

ABCDEFGHIJKLMNOPQRSTUVWXY
Z&abcdefghijklmnopqrstuvwxyzfifffflffi
ffl1234567890$.,"-:;!?""
24 POINT CENTURY SCHOOLBOOK BOLD, ATF

ABCDEFGHIJKLMNOPQRSTUVWXYZ&abcdefghijklmnopqr
stuvwxyzfifffflffiffl1234567890$.,"-:;!?""
14 POINT CENTURY SCHOOLBOOK BOLD, ATF

FUTURA MEDIUM, BAUER
Books Reading

TEMPO MEDIUM, LUDLOW
LANDMARK tourist

SPARTAN MEDIUM, ATF
BRAZIL countries

AIRPORT GOTHIC, MONOTYPE
ABCDEFG abcdefgh

All comparisons are made on 24 point type.

Designed within the framework of "form follows function." Futura remains one of the most widely used faces.

tg

g

ABCDEFGHIJKL
MNOPQRSTU
VWXYZ&abcd

efghijklmnopqr

stuvwxyzﬀﬃﬁﬂﬅ

1234567890

$.,'-:;!?

72 POINT FUTURA MEDIUM, BAUER

ABCDEFGHIJKLM
NOPQRSTUVWX
YZ&abcdefghijklm
nopqrstuvwxyzfffi
ﬀﬁ1234567890
$.,'-:;!?

60 POINT FUTURA MEDIUM, BAUER

ABCDEFGHIJKLMNOP
QRSTUVWXYZ&abcde
fghijklmnopqrstuvwxyz
ﬀﬁﬂﬁ1234567890
$.,'-:;!?

48 POINT FUTURA MEDIUM, BAUER

ABCDEFGHIJKLMNOP QRSTUVWXYZ&abcde fghijklmnopqrstuvwxyz

 fffifl ﬀ 1234567890

$.,'-:;!?

48 POINT FUTURA MEDIUM ITALIC, BAUER

ABCDEFGHIJKLMNOPQRSTU VWXYZ&abcdefghijklmnopqr stuvwxyzfffiflﬀ1234567890

$.,'-:;!?

36 POINT FUTURA MEDIUM, BAUER

ABCDEFGHIJKLMNOPQRSTU VWXYZ&abcdefghijklmnopqrs tuvwxyzfffiflﬀ1234567890

$.,'-:;!?

36 POINT FUTURA MEDIUM ITALIC, BAUER

113

ABCDEFGHIJKLMNOPQRSTUVWXYZ
&abcdefghijklmnopqrstuvwxyzfffififlfl
1234567890$.,'-:;!?

30 POINT FUTURA MEDIUM, BAUER

ABCDEFGHIJKLMNOPQRSTUVWXYZ
&abcdefghijklmnopqrstuvwxyzfffififl
1234567890$.,'-:;!?

30 POINT FUTURA MEDIUM ITALIC, BAUER

ABCDEFGHIJKLMNOPQRSTUVWXYZ&abcdefghijk
lmnopqrstuvwxyzfffififlfl1234567890$.,'-:;!?

24 POINT FUTURA MEDIUM, BAUER

ABCDEFGHIJKLMNOPQRSTUVWXYZ&abcdefghijk
lmnopqrstuvwxyzfffififl1234567890$.,'-:;!?

24 POINT FUTURA MEDIUM ITALIC, BAUER

ABCDEFGHIJKLMNOPQRSTUVWXYZ&abcdefghijklmnopqrstu
vwxyzfffififlfl1234567890$.,'-:;!?

18 POINT FUTURA MEDIUM, BAUER

ABCDEFGHIJKLMNOPQRSTUVWXYZ&abcdefghijklmnopqrstuvw
xyzfffififlfl1234567890$.,'-:;!?

18 POINT FUTURA MEDIUM ITALIC, BAUER

114

12/12 The present popularity of the old style has encouraged French type-founders to revive other early printed forms, but they seem to regard the imitation of early manuscript forms as a reversion to barbarism and ugliness. But this imitation has been cleverly done by artists who have undertaken to make designs for book titles and book covers. Some have gone far beyond early typographic models, selecting the early Roman letter—the plain capital without serif or hair line, with an almost absolute uniformity of thick line. Others have copied and exaggerated *the mannerisms of mediaeval copyists and engravers, with all their faults, bundling words*

10/10 The present popularity of the old style has encouraged French type-founders to revive other early printed forms, but they seem to regard the imitation of early manuscript forms as a reversion to barbarism and ugliness. But this imitation has been cleverly done by artists who have undertaken to make designs for book titles and book covers. Some have gone far beyond early typographic models, selecting the early Roman letter—the plain capital without serif or hair line, with an almost absolute uniformity of thick line. Others have copied and exaggerated the mannerisms of mediaeval copyists and engravers, with all their faults, bundling words together without proper relief between lines, dividing them by periods and not by spaces, until they are almost *unreadable. The closely huddled and carelessly formed letters of Botticelli and other early Italian engravers are*

12/14 The present popularity of the old style has encouraged French type-founders to revive other early printed forms, but they seem to regard the imitation of early manuscript forms as a reversion to barbarism and ugliness. But this imitation has been cleverly done by artists ·who have undertaken to make designs for book titles and book covers. Some have gone far beyond early typographic models, selecting the early Roman letter—the plain capital without serif or hair *line, with an almost absolute uniformity of thick line. Others have copied and exaggerated*

10/12 The present popularity of the old style has encouraged French type-founders to revive other early printed forms, but they seem to regard the imitation of early manuscript forms as a reversion to barbarism and ugliness. But this imitation has been cleverly done by artists who have undertaken to make designs for book titles and book covers. Some have gone far beyond early typographic models, selecting the early Roman letter—the plain capital without serif or hair line, with an almost absolute uniformity of thick line. Others have copied and exaggerated the mannerisms of mediaeval copyists and engravers, with all their faults, bundling words *together without proper relief between lines, dividing them by periods and not by spaces, until they are almost*

12/16 The present popularity of the old style has encouraged French type-founders to revive other early printed forms, but they seem to regard the imitation of early manuscript forms as a reversion to barbarism and ugliness. But this imitation has been cleverly done by artists who have undertaken to make designs for book titles and book covers. Some have gone far beyond early typographic models, selecting the early Roman *letter—the plain capital without serif or hair line, with an almost absolute uniformity of thick*

10/14 The present popularity of the old style has encouraged French type-founders to revive other early printed forms, but they seem to regard the imitation of early manuscript forms as a reversion to barbarism and ugliness. But this imitation has been cleverly done by artists who have undertaken to make designs for book titles and book covers. Some have gone far beyond early typographic models, selecting the early Roman letter—the plain capital without serif or hair line, with an almost absolute uniformity of thick line. Others have copied *and exaggerated the mannerisms of mediaeval copyists and engravers, with all their faults, bundling words*

ABCDEFGHIJKLMNOPQRSTUVWXYZ
ABCDEFGHIJKLMNOPQRSTUVWXYZ
&.,''-:;!?'''''1234567890$
&.,''-:;!?'''''1234567890$
abcdefghijklmnopqrstuvwxyz
abcdefghijklmnopqrstuvwxyz

ABCDEFGHIJKLMNOPQRSTUVWXYZ
ABCDEFGHIJKLMNOPQRSTUVWXYZ
&.,''-:;!?'''''1234567890$
&.,''-:;!?'''''1234567890$
abcdefghijklmnopqrstuvwxyz
abcdefghijklmnopqrstuvwxyz

FUTURA MEDIUM: INTERTYPE

PiCAS	6	7	8	9	10	11	12	13	14	15	16	17	18	19	20	21	22	23	24	25	26	27	28	29	30
12 POINT	15	17	19	22	24	27	29	31	34	36	39	41	44	46	48	51	53	56	58	61	63	65	68	70	73
10 POINT	17	20	23	26	29	32	34	37	40	43	46	49	52	55	57	60	63	66	69	72	75	77	80	83	86

ABCDEFGHIJKLMN
OPQRSTUVWXYZ
&abcdefghijklmnop
qrstuvwxyzfffifl Aﬃﬂ12
34567890$.,'-:;!?

60 POINT FUTURA LIGHT, BAUER

ABCDEFGHIJKLMNOPQRSTU
VWXYZ&abcdefghijklmnopqrs
tuvwxyzfffiflA1234567890
$.,'-:;!?

36 POINT FUTURA LIGHT, BAUER

ABCDEFGHIJKLMNOPQRSTUV
WXYZ&abcdefghijklmnopqrstuv
wxyzfffiflA1234567890$.,'-:;!?

36 POINT FUTURA LIGHT ITALIC, BAUER

116

ABCDEFGHIJKLMNOPQRSTUVWXYZ & abcdefghijkl
mnopqrstuvwxyz ffffiflft1234567890$.,'-:;!?

24 POINT FUTURA LIGHT, BAUER

*ABCDEFGHIJKLMNOPQRSTUVWXYZ&abcdefghijklm
nopqrstuvwxyz ffffiflft1234567890$.,'-:;!?*

24 POINT FUTURA LIGHT ITALIC, BAUER

ABCDEFGHIJKL
MNOPQRSTUV
WXYZ&abcdefg
hijklmnopqrstuv
wxyzffffiflft12345
67890$.,'-:;!?

60 POINT FUTURA DEMIBOLD, BAUER

ABCDEFGHIJKL
MNOPQRSTUV
WXYZ&abcdefg
hijklmnopqrstuv
wxyzfffififlfl12345
67890$.,'-:;!?""

60 POINT FUTURA DEMIBOLD ITALIC, BAUER

ABCDEFGHIJKLMNOPQRST
UVWXYZ&abcdefghijklmn
opqrstuvwxyzfffififlfl123456
7890$.,'-:;!?

36 POINT FUTURA DEMIBOLD, BAUER

ABCDEFGHIJKLMNOPQRS TUVWXYZ&abcdefghijklmn opqrstuvwxyzfffifIfI123456 7890$.,'-:;!?""

36 POINT FUTURA DEMIBOLD ITALIC, BAUER

ABCDEFGHIJKLMNOPQRSTUVWXYZ&abcdefgh
ijklmnopqrstuvwxyzfffifIfI1234567890$.,'-:;!?

24 POINT FUTURA DEMIBOLD, BAUER

ABCDEFGHIJKLMNOPQRSTUVWXYZ&abcdef
ghijklmnopqrstuvwxyzfffifIfI1234567890
$.,'-:;!?""

24 POINT FUTURA DEMIBOLD ITALIC, BAUER

12/12
The present popularity of the old style has encouraged French type-founders to revive other early printed forms, but they seem to regard the imitation of early manuscript forms as a reversion to barbarism and ugliness. But this imitation has been cleverly done by artists who have undertaken to make designs for book titles and book covers. Some have gone far beyond early typographic models, selecting the early Roman letter—the plain capital without serif or hair line, with an almost absolute uniformity of thick line. Others have copied

10/10
The present popularity of the old style has encouraged French type-founders to revive other early printed forms, but they seem to regard the imitation of early manuscript forms as a reversion to barbarism and ugliness. But this imitation has been cleverly done by artists who have undertaken to make designs for book titles and book covers. Some have gone far beyond early typographic models, selecting the early Roman letter—the plain capital without serif or hair line, with an almost absolute uniformity of thick line. Others have copied and exaggerated the mannerisms of mediaeval copyists and engravers, with all their faults, bundling words together without proper relief between lines, dividing them by periods and not

12/14
The present popularity of the old style has encouraged French type-founders to revive other early printed forms, but they seem to regard the imitation of early manuscript forms as a reversion to barbarism and ugliness. But this imitation has been cleverly done by artists who have undertaken to make designs for book titles and book covers. Some have gone far beyond early typographic models, selecting the early Roman letter—the plain capital without serif or

10/12
The present popularity of the old style has encouraged French type-founders to revive other early printed forms, but they seem to regard the imitation of early manuscript forms as a reversion to barbarism and ugliness. But this imitation has been cleverly done by artists who have undertaken to make designs for book titles and book covers. Some have gone far beyond early typographic models, selecting the early Roman letter—the plain capital without serif or hair line, with an almost absolute uniformity of thick line. Others have copied and exaggerated the mannerisms of mediaeval copyists and engravers, with all their faults,

12/16
The present popularity of the old style has encouraged French type-founders to revive other early printed forms, but they seem to regard the imitation of early manuscript forms as a reversion to barbarism and ugliness. But this imitation has been cleverly done by artists who have undertaken to make designs for book titles and book covers. Some have gone far beyond early typographic models, selecting the early Roman let-

10/14
The present popularity of the old style has encouraged French type-founders to revive other early printed forms, but they seem to regard the imitation of early manuscript forms as a reversion to barbarism and ugliness. But this imitation has been cleverly done by artists who have undertaken to make designs for book titles and book covers. Some have gone far beyond early typographic models, selecting the early Roman letter—the plain capital without serif or hair line, with an almost absolute uniformity of thick line. Others have copied and

ABCDEFGHIJKLMNOPQRSTUVWXYZ
ABCDEFGHIJKLMNOPQRSTUVWXYZ
&.,'`-:;!?''""1234567890$
&.,'`-:;!?''""1234567890$
abcdefghijklmnopqrstuvwxyz
abcdefghijklmnopqrstuvwxyz

ABCDEFGHIJKLMNOPQRSTUVWXYZ
ABCDEFGHIJKLMNOPQRSTUVWXYZ
&.,'`-:;!?''""1234567890$
&.,'`-:;!?''""1234567890$
abcdefghijklmnopqrstuvwxyz
abcdefghijklmnopqrstuvwxyz

FUTURA BOLD: INTERTYPE

PICAS	6	7	8	9	10	11	12	13	14	15	16	17	18	19	20	21	22	23	24	25	26	27	28	29	30
12 POINT	14	16	18	21	23	25	28	30	32	35	37	39	41	44	46	48	51	53	55	58	60	62	64	67	69
10 POINT	16	18	21	23	26	28	31	34	36	39	41	44	47	49	52	54	57	59	62	65	67	70	73	75	78

ABCDEFGHIJKL
MNOPQRSTUV
WXYZ&abcdef
ghijklmnopqrs
tuvwxyzfffifltt
1234567890
$.,'-:;!?

60 POINT FUTURA BOLD, BAUER

ABCDEFGHIJKL MNOPQRSTUV WXYZ&abcde fghijklmnopqrs tuvwxyzfffifl 1234567890 $.,'-:;!?

60 POINT FUTURA BOLD ITALIC, BAUER

ABCDEFGHIJKLMNOPQR STUVWXYZ&abcdefghij klmnopqrstuvwxyzfffifl fl1234567890$.,'-:;!?

36 POINT FUTURA BOLD, BAUER

ABCDEFGHIJKLMNOPQR STUVWXYZ&abcdefghij klmnopqrstuvwxyzfffi flft1234567890$.,'-:;!?

36 POINT FUTURA BOLD ITALIC, BAUER

ABCDEFGHIJKLMNOPQRSTUVWXYZ&abc defghijklmnopqrstuvwxyzfffififlft1234567 890$.,'-:;!?

24 POINT FUTURA BOLD, BAUER

ABCDEFGHIJKLMNOPQRSTUVWXYZ&abc defghijklmnopqrstuvwxyzfffififlft 1234567890$.,'-:;!?

24 POINT FUTURA BOLD ITALIC, BAUER

12/12

The present popularity of the old style has encouraged French type-founders to revive other early printed forms, but they seem to regard the imitation of early manuscript forms as a reversion to barbarism and ugliness. But this imitation has been cleverly done by artists who have undertaken to make designs for book titles and book covers. Some have gone far beyond early typographic models, selecting the early Roman letter—the plain capital without serif or hair line, with an almost absolute uniformity of thick line. Others *have copied and exaggerated the mannerisms of mediaeval copyists and engravers, with all*

10/10

The present popularity of the old style has encouraged French type-founders to revive other early printed forms, but they seem to regard the imitation of early manuscript forms as a reversion to barbarism and ugliness. But this imitation has been cleverly done by artists who have undertaken to make designs for book titles and book covers. Some have gone far beyond early typographic models, selecting the early Roman letter—the plain capital without serif or hair line, with an almost absolute uniformity of thick line. Others have copied and exaggerated the mannerisms of mediaeval copyists and engravers, with all their faults, bundling words together without proper relief between lines, dividing them by periods and not by spaces, until they are almost *unreadable. The closely huddled and carelessly formed letters of Botticelli and other early Italian*

12/14

The present popularity of the old style has encouraged French type-founders to revive other early printed forms, but they seem to regard the imitation of early manuscript forms as a reversion to barbarism and ugliness. But this imitation has been cleverly done by artists who have undertaken to make designs for book titles and book covers. Some have gone far beyond early typographic models, selecting the early Roman letter—the plain *capital without serif or hair line, with an almost absolute uniformity of thick line. Others*

10/12

The present popularity of the old style has encouraged French type-founders to revive other early printed forms, but they seem to regard the imitation of early manuscript forms as a reversion to barbarism and ugliness. But this imitation has been cleverly done by artists who have undertaken to make designs for book titles and book covers. Some have gone far beyond early typographic models, selecting the early Roman letter—the plain capital without serif or hair line, with an almost absolute uniformity of thick line. Others have copied and exaggerated the mannerisms of mediaeval copyists and engravers, *with all their faults, bundling words together without proper relief between lines, dividing them*

12/16

The present popularity of the old style has encouraged French type-founders to revive other early printed forms, but they seem to regard the imitation of early manuscript forms as a reversion to barbarism and ugliness. But this imitation has been cleverly done by artists who have undertaken to make designs for book titles and book covers. Some have gone far beyond early typographic models, *selecting the early Roman letter—the plain capital without serif or hair line, with an*

10/14

The present popularity of the old style has encouraged French type-founders to revive other early printed forms, but they seem to regard the imitation of early manuscript forms as a reversion to barbarism and ugliness. But this imitation has been cleverly done by artists who have undertaken to make designs for book titles and book covers. Some have gone far beyond early typographic models, selecting the early Roman letter—the plain capital without serif or hair line, with an almost absolute uniformity *of thick line. Others have copied and exaggerated the mannerisms of mediaeval copyists and engrav-*

ABCDEFGHIJKLMNOPQRSTUVWXYZ
ABCDEFGHIJKLMNOPQRSTUVWXYZ
&.:'`-:;!?''''''1234567890$
&.:'`-:;!?''''''1234567890$
abcdefghijklmnopqrstuvwxyz
abcdefghijklmnopqrstuvwxyz

ABCDEFGHIJKLMNOPQRSTUVWXYZ
ABCDEFGHIJKLMNOPQRSTUVWXYZ
&.,'`-:;!?''''''1234567890$
&.,'`-:;!?''''''1234567890$
abcdefghijklmnopqrstuvwxyz
abcdefghijklmnopqrstuvwxyz

FUTURA DEMIBOLD: INTERTYPE

PICAS	6	7	8	9	10	11	12	13	14	15	16	17	18	19	20	21	22	23	24	25	26	27	28	29	30
12 POINT	12	14	16	18	20	22	24	26	28	30	32	34	36	38	40	42	44	46	48	50	51	53	55	57	59
10 POINT	14	17	19	22	24	26	29	31	34	36	38	41	43	46	48	50	53	55	58	60	62	65	67	70	72

ABCDEFGHIJKLMNOPQRSTUV
WXYZ&abcdefghijklmnopqrstuv
wxyzfffiflfft1234567890$.,'-:;!?

36 POINT FUTURA BOOK, BAUER

ABCDEFGHIJKLMNOPQRSTU
VWXYZ&abcdefghijklmnopqrst
uvwxyzfffiflfft1234567890
$.,'-:;!?

36 POINT FUTURA BOOK ITALIC, BAUER

ABCDEFGHIJKLMNOPQRSTUVWXYZ&abcdefghijklmn
opqrstuvwxyzfffiflfft1234567890$.,'-:;!?

24 POINT FUTURA BOOK, BAUER

ABCDEFGHIJKLMNOPQRSTUVWXYZ&abcdefghijklm
nopqrstuvwxyzfffiflfft1234567890$.,'-:;!?

24 POINT FUTURA BOOK ITALIC, BAUER

12/12

The present popularity of the old style has encouraged French type-founders to revive other early printed forms, but they seem to regard the imitation of early manuscript forms as a reversion to barbarism and ugliness. But this imitation has been cleverly done by artists who have undertaken to make designs for book titles and book covers. Some have gone far beyond early typographic models, selecting the early Roman letter—the plain capital without serif or hair line, with an almost absolute uniformity of thick line. Others have copied and exaggerated the mannerisms of mediaeval copyists and engravers, with all their faults, bundling words together without proper relief between lines, dividing them by periods and not by spaces, until they are almost unreadable. The closely huddled and carelessly formed letters of Botticelli and

10/10

The present popularity of the old style has encouraged French type-founders to revive other early printed forms, but they seem to regard the imitation of early manuscript forms as a reversion to barbarism and ugliness. But this imitation has been cleverly done by artists who have undertaken to make designs for book titles and book covers. Some have gone far beyond early typographic models, selecting the early Roman letter—the plain capital without serif or hair line, with an almost absolute uniformity of thick line. Others have copied and exaggerated the mannerisms of mediaeval copyists and engravers, with all their faults, bundling words together without proper relief between lines, dividing them by periods and not by spaces, until they are almost unreadable. The closely huddled and carelessly formed letters of Botticelli and other early Italian engravers are even preferred by many artists to the simple, severe, and easily read letters of chiseled inscriptions on the stones of ancient Rome. There has been an eccentric departure in another direction. Some designer has asked these questions: Why copy letter forms of any origin? Why should letters always

12/14

The present popularity of the old style has encouraged French type-founders to revive other early printed forms, but they seem to regard the imitation of early manuscript forms as a reversion to barbarism and ugliness. But this imitation has been cleverly done by artists who have undertaken to make designs for book titles and book covers. Some have gone far beyond early typographic models, selecting the early Roman letter—the plain capital without serif or hair line, with an almost absolute uniformity of thick line. Others have copied and exaggerated the mannerisms of mediaeval copyists and engravers, with all their faults, bundling words together without proper relief between lines, dividing them by periods

10/12

The present popularity of the old style has encouraged French type-founders to revive other early printed forms, but they seem to regard the imitation of early manuscript forms as a reversion to barbarism and ugliness. But this imitation has been cleverly done by artists who have undertaken to make designs for book titles and book covers. Some have gone far beyond early typographic models, selecting the early Roman letter—the plain capital without serif or hair line, with an almost absolute uniformity of thick line. Others have copied and exaggerated the mannerisms of mediaeval copyists and engravers, with all their faults, bundling words together without proper relief between lines, dividing them by periods and not by spaces, until they are almost unreadable. The closely huddled and carelessly formed letters of Botticelli and other early Italian engravers are even preferred by many artists to the simple, severe, and easily read letters of chiseled inscrip-

12/16

The present popularity of the old style has encouraged French type-founders to revive other early printed forms, but they seem to regard the imitation of early manuscript forms as a reversion to barbarism and ugliness. But this imitation has been cleverly done by artists who have undertaken to make designs for book titles and book covers. Some have gone far beyond early typographic models, selecting the early Roman letter—the plain capital without serif or hair line, with an almost absolute uniformity of thick line. Others have copied and exaggerated the mannerisms of mediaeval copyists and engravers, with all their faults, bundling words together

10/14

The present popularity of the old style has encouraged French type-founders to revive other early printed forms, but they seem to regard the imitation of early manuscript forms as a reversion to barbarism and ugliness. But this imitation has been cleverly done by artists who have undertaken to make designs for book titles and book covers. Some have gone far beyond early typographic models, selecting the early Roman letter—the plain capital without serif or hair line, with an almost absolute uniformity of thick line. Others have copied and exaggerated the mannerisms of mediaeval copyists and engravers, with all their faults, bundling words together without proper relief between lines, dividing them by periods and not by spaces, until they are almost unreadable. The closely huddled and carelessly formed letters of Botti-

ABCDEFGHIJKLMNOPQRSTUVWXYZ
&.,^-:;!?'"'`1234567890$
abcdefghijklmnopqrstuvwxyz

ABCDEFGHIJKLMNOPQRSTUVWXYZ
&.,^-:;!?'"'`1234567890$
abcdefghijklmnopqrstuvwxyz

FUTURA MEDIUM CONDENSED: INTERTYPE

PICAS	6	7	8	9	10	11	12	13	14	15	16	17	18	19	20	21	22	23	24	25	26	27	28	29	30
12 POINT	19	22	25	28	31	34	37	40	44	47	50	53	56	59	62	65	68	72	75	78	81	84	87	90	93
10 POINT	22	26	30	33	37	41	44	48	52	56	59	63	67	70	74	78	81	85	89	93	96	100	104	107	111

ABCDEFGHIJKLMNOPQRSTUVWXYZ&abcde
fghijklmnopqrstuvwxyzfffifl ft1234567890
$.,'-:;!?

36 POINT FUTURA MEDIUM CONDENSED, BAUER

ABCDEFGHIJKLMNOPQRSTUVWXYZ
&abcdefghijklmnopqrstuvwxyzfffifl ft
1234567890$.,'-:;!?

36 POINT FUTURA BOLD CONDENSED, BAUER

ABCDEFGHIJKLMNOPQRSTUVW
XYZ&abcdefghijklmnopqrstu
vwxyzfffiflflft1234567890
$.,´-:;!?

36 POINT FUTURA DISPLAY, BAUER

ABCDEFGHIJKLMNOPQR
STUVWXYZ&abcdefghijkl
mnopqrstuvwxyzfffifl fl
1234567890$.,'-:;!?

36 POINT FUTURA BLACK, BAUER

127

12/12

The present popularity of the old style has encouraged French type-founders to revive other early printed forms, but they seem to regard the imitation of early manuscript forms as a reversion to barbarism and ugliness. But this imitation has been cleverly done by artists who have undertaken to make designs for book titles and book covers. Some have gone far beyond early typographic models, selecting the early Roman letter—the plain capital without serif or hair line, with an almost absolute uniformity of thick line. Others have copied and exaggerated the mannerisms of mediaeval copyists and engravers, with all their faults, bundling words together without proper relief between lines, dividing them by periods and not by spaces, until they

10/10

The present popularity of the old style has encouraged French type-founders to revive other early printed forms, but they seem to regard the imitation of early manscript forms as a reversion to barbarism and ugliness. But this imitation has been cleverly done by artists who have undertaken to make designs for book titles and book covers. Some have gone far beyond early typographic models, selecting the early Roman letter—the plain capital without serif or hair line, with an almost absolute uniformity of thick line. Others have copied and exaggerated the mannerisms of mediaeval copyists and engravers, with all their faults, bundling words together without proper relief between lines, dividing them by periods and not by spaces, until they are almost unreadable. The closely huddled and carelessly formed letters of Botticelli and other early Italian engravers are even preferred by many artists to the simple, severe, and easily read letters of chis-

12/14

The present popularity of the old style has encouraged French type-founders to revive other early printed forms, but they seem to regard the imitation of early manuscript forms as a reversion to barbarism and ugliness. But this imitation has been cleverly done by artists who have undertaken to make designs for book titles and book covers. Some have gone far beyond early typographic models, selecting the early Roman letter—the plain capital without serif or hair line, with an almost absolute uniformity of thick line. Others have copied and exaggerated the mannerisms of mediaeval copyists and engravers, with all their faults, bundling

10/12

The present popularity of the old style has encouraged French type-founders to revive other early printed forms, but they seem to regard the imitation of early manscript forms as a reversion to barbarism and ugliness. But this imitation has been cleverly done by artists who have undertaken to make designs for book titles and book covers. Some have gone far beyond early typographic models, selecting the early Roman letter—the plain capital without serif or hair line, with an almost absolute uniformity of thick line. Others have copied and exaggerated the mannerisms of mediaeval copyists and engravers, with all their faults, bundling words together without proper relief between lines, dividing them by periods closely huddled and carelessly formed letters of Botticelli and other early Italian engravers are even preferred by many

12/16

The present popularity of the old style has encouraged French type-founders to revive other early printed forms, but they seem to regard the imitation of early manuscript forms as a reversion to barbarism and ugliness. But this imitation has been cleverly done by artists who have undertaken to make designs for book titles and book covers. Some have gone far beyond early typographic models, selecting the early Roman letter—the plain capital without serif or hair line, with an almost absolute uniformity of thick line. Others have copied and exaggerated the mannerisms of mediaeval

10/14

The present popularity of the old style has encouraged French type-founders to revive other early printed forms, but they seem to regard the imitation of early manuscript forms as a reversion to barbarism and ugliness. But this imitation has been cleverly done by artists who have undertaken to make designs for book titles and book covers. Some have gone far beyond early typographic models, selecting the early Roman letter—the plain capital without serif or hair line, with an almost absolute uniformity of thick line. Others have copied and exaggerated the mannerisms of mediaeval copyists and engravers, with all their faults, bundling words together without proper relief between lines, dividing them by periods

ABCDEFGHIJKLMNOPQRSTUVWXYZ
&.:'`-:;!?'"\1234567890$
abcdefghijklmnopqrstuvwxyz

ABCDEFGHIJKLMNOPQRSTUVWXYZ
&.,'`-:;!?'"\1234567890$
abcdefghijklmnopqrstuvwxyz

FUTURA BOLD CONDENSED: INTERTYPE

PICAS	6	7	8	9	10	11	12	13	14	15	16	17	18	19	20	21	22	23	24	25	26	27	28	29	30
12 POINT	17	19	22	25	28	31	33	36	39	42	44	47	50	53	56	58	61	64	67	70	72	75	79	81	83
10 POINT	19	22	25	28	31	34	37	40	44	47	50	53	56	59	62	65	68	72	75	78	81	84	87	90	93

ABCDEFGHIJKLMNOP QRSTUVWXYZ&12345 67890$.,'-:;!?

36 POINT FUTURA INLINE, BAUER

GARAMOND; LUDLOW

ABCDEF the established

GARAMOND, MONOTYPE

ABCDEF abcdefghijk

GARAMOND, ATF

ABCDEF abcdefghijk

All comparisons are made on 24 point type.

ABCDEFGHIJ

KLMNOPQRS

TUVWXYZ&a

bcdefghijklmno

pqrstuvwyz1234

567890$.,'‘–·.!?"''

72 POINT GARAMOND, MONOTYPE

ABCDEFGHIJ
KLMNOPQRS
TUVWXYZ&
abcdefghijklmnopq
rstuvwxyz1234567
890$.,"-.:,!?""''

72 POINT GARAMOND ITALIC, MONOTYPE

ABCDEFGHIJKL
MNOPQRSTUV
WXYZ&abcdefghi
jklmnopqrstuvwxy
z1234567890$.,'-:;!?

60 POINT GARAMOND, MONOTYPE

ABCDEFGHIJKL
MNOPQRSTUV
WXYZ&abcdefghij
klmnopqrstuvwxyz123
4567890$.,"-:;!?""

60 POINT GARAMOND ITALIC, MONOTYPE

ABCDEFGHIJKLMNOP
QRSTUVWXYZ&abcdefg
hijklmnopqrstuvwxyzfifl123
4567890$.,"-:;!?""''

48 POINT GARAMOND, ATF

ABCDEFGHIJKLMNOPQ
RSTUVWXYZ&abcdefghijkl
mnopqrstuvwxyzfifl1234567890
$., "-:;!?""''

48 POINT GARAMOND ITALIC, ATF

ABCDEFGHIJKLMNOPQRSTUV
WXYZ&abcdefghijklmnopqrstuvw
xyzfifl1234567890$.,"-:;!?""''

36 POINT GARAMOND, ATF

ABCDEFGHIJKLMNOPQRSTUVW
XYZ&abcdefghijklmnopqrstuvwxyzfifl12
34567890$.,"-:;!?"""

36 POINT GARAMOND ITALIC, ATF

ABCDEFGHIJKLMNOPQRSTUVWXY
Z&abcdefghijklmnopqrstuvwxyzfifl1234567
890$.,"-:;!?""

30 POINT GARAMOND, ATF

ABCDEFGHIJKLMNOPQRSTUVWXYZ
&abcdefghijklmnopqrstuvwxyzfifl1234567890$.,'
-:;!?"""

30 POINT GARAMOND ITALIC, ATF

ABCDEFGHIJKLMNOPQRSTUVWXYZ&abcdef
ghijklmnopqrstuvwxyzfifl1234567890$.,"-:;!?""

24 POINT GARAMOND, ATF

ABCDEFGHIJKLMNOPQRSTUVWXYZ&abcdefghij
klmnopqrstuvwxyzfifl1234567890$.,"-:;!?"""

24 POINT GARAMOND ITALIC, ATF

ABCDEFGHIJKLMNOPQRSTUVWXYZ&abcdefghijklmnopqrstu
vwxyzfifl1234567890$.,"-:;!?""

18 POINT GARAMOND, ATF

ABCDEFGHIJKLMNOPQRSTUVWXYZ&abcdefghijklmnopqrstuvwxy
zfifl1234567890$.,"-:;!?"""

18 POINT GARAMOND ITALIC, ATF

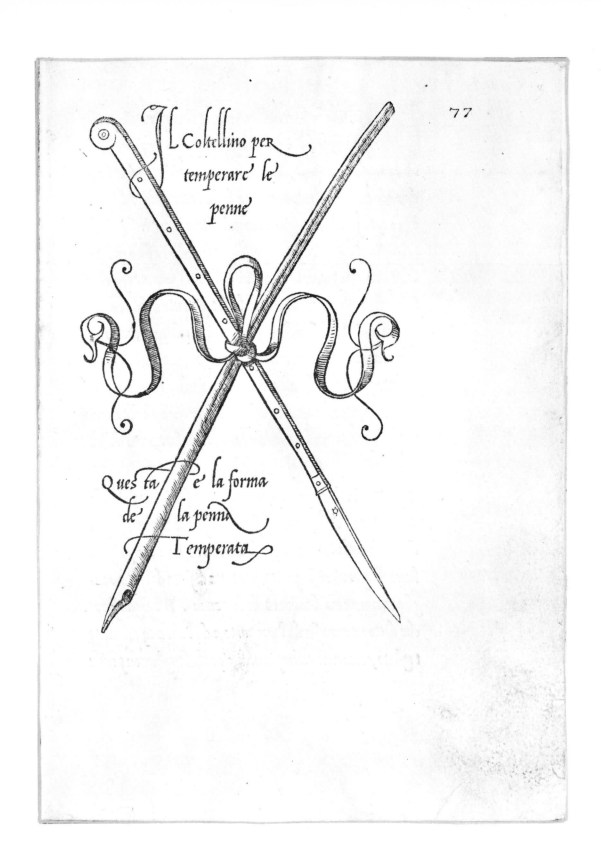

Il Coltellino per temperare le penne

Questa è la forma de la penna Temperata

77

Arrighi, page from ''Il Modo de Temperare le Penne,'' 1523.

14/15 From a letter by Benjamin Franklin to Noah Webster dated Dec. 26, 1789:

In examining the English Books, that were printed between the Restoration and the Accession of George the 2d, we may observe, that all *Substantives* were begun with a capital, in which we imitated our Mother Tongue, the German. This was more particularly useful to those, who were not well acquainted with the Eng-*lish; there being such a prodigious Number of our Words, that are both Verbs and*

12/13 From a letter by Benjamin Franklin to Noah Webster dated Dec. 26, 1789:

In examining the English Books, that were printed between the Restoration and the Accession of George the 2d, we may observe, that all *Substantives* were begun with a capital, in which we imitated our Mother Tongue, the German. This was more particularly useful to those, who were not well acquainted with the English; there being such a prodigious Number of our Words, that are both *Verbs* and *Substan-tives, and spelt in the same manner, tho' often accented differently in Pronunciation.*

14/16 From a letter by Benjamin Franklin to Noah Webster dated Dec. 26, 1789:

In examining the English Books, that were printed between the Restoration and the Accession of George the 2d, we may observe, that all *Substantives* were begun with a capital, in which we imitated our Mother Tongue, the German. This was *lish; there being such a prodigious Number of our Words, that are both Verbs and*

12/14 From a letter by Benjamin Franklin to Noah Webster dated Dec. 26, 1789:

In examining the English Books, that were printed between the Restoration and the Accession of George the 2d, we may observe, that all *Substantives* were begun with a capital, in which we imitated our Mother Tongue, the German. This was more particularly useful to those, who were not well acquainted with the English; there being such a prodigious Number *tives, and spelt in the same manner, tho' often accented differently in Pronunciation.*

14/18 From a letter by Benjamin Franklin to Noah Webster dated Dec. 26, 1789:

In examining the English Books, that were printed between the Restoration and the Accession of George the 2d, we may observe, that all *Substantives* were begun with a capital, in which we imitated our *lish; there being such a prodigious Number of our Words, that are both Verbs and*

12/16 From a letter by Benjamin Franklin to Noah Webster dated Dec. 26, 1789:

In examining the English Books, that were printed between the Restoration and the Accession of George the 2d, we may observe, that all *Substantives* were begun with a capital, in which we imitated our Mother Tongue, the German. This was more particularly useful to *tives, and spelt in the same manner, tho' often accented differently in Pronunciation.*

ABCDEFGHIJKLMNOPQRSTUVWX
ABCDEFGHIJKLMNOPQRSTUVWX
&.,"-:;!?""'1234567890$
&.,"-:;!?""'1234567890$
abcdefghijklmnopqrstuvwxyz
abcdefghijklmnopqrstuvwxyz

ABCDEFGHIJKLMNOPQRSTUVWXYZ
ABCDEFGHIJKLMNOPQRSTUVWXYZ
&.,"-:;!?""'1234567890$
&.,"-:;!?""'1234567890$
abcdefghijklmnopqrstuvwxyz
abcdefghijklmnopqrstuvwxyz

NEW GARAMOND: SIMONCINI *This face must be set 1 pt leaded.

PICAS	6	7	8	9	10	11	12	13	14	15	16	17	18	19	20	21	22	23	24	25	26	27	28	29	30
14 POINT	11	14	16	18	21	23	25	28	30	32	34	36	38	40	42	44	47	49	51	53	55	57	59	61	63
12 POINT	14	16	19	21	24	26	28	31	33	35	38	40	43	45	47	50	52	54	57	59	62	64	66	69	71

From a letter by Benjamin Franklin to Noah Web-
$^{11}/_{12}$ ster dated Dec. 26, 1789:

In examining the English Books, that were
printed between the Restoration and the Accession
of George the 2d, we may observe, that all *Substantives* were begun with a capital, in which we
imitated our Mother Tongue, the German. This
was more particularly useful to those, who were
not well acquainted with the English; there being
such a prodigious Number of our Words, that are
both *Verbs* and *Substantives,* and spelt in the same
manner, tho' often accented differently in Pro-
nunciation.

This method has, by the Fancy of Printers, of

From a letter by Benjamin Franklin to Noah Webster
$^{10}/_{11}$ dated Dec. 26, 1789:

In examining the English Books, that were printed
between the Restoration and the Accession of George
the 2d, we may observe, that all *Substantives* were
begun with a capital, in which we imitated our Mother
Tongue, the German. This was more particularly useful to those, who were not well acquainted with the
English; there being such a prodigious Number of our
Words, that are both *Verbs* and *Substantives,* and
spelt in the same manner, tho' often accented differently in Pronunciation.

This method has, by the Fancy of Printers, of late
Years been laid aside, from an Idea, that suppressing
the Capitals shows the Character to greater Advantage;
those Letters prominent above the line distributing its

From a letter by Benjamin Franklin to Noah Web-
$^{11}/_{13}$ ster dated Dec. 26, 1789:

In examining the English Books, that were
printed between the Restoration and the Accession
of George the 2d, we may observe, that all *Substantives* were begun with a capital, in which we
imitated our Mother Tongue, the German. This
was more particularly useful to those, who were
not well acquainted with the English; there being
such a prodigious Number of our Words, that are
both *Verbs* and *Substantives,* and spelt in the same
nunciation.

This method has, by the Fancy of Printers, of

From a letter by Benjamin Franklin to Noah Webster
$^{10}/_{12}$ dated Dec. 26, 1789:

In examining the English Books, that were printed
between the Restoration and the Accession of George
the 2d, we may observe, that all *Substantives* were
begun with a capital, in which we imitated our Mother
Tongue, the German. This was more particularly useful to those, who were not well acquainted with the
English; there being such a prodigious Number of our
Words, that are both *Verbs* and *Substantives,* and
spelt in the same manner, tho' often accented differently in Pronunciation.

the Capitals shows the Character to greater Advantage;
those Letters prominent above the line distributing its

From a letter by Benjamin Franklin to Noah Web-
$^{11}/_{15}$ ster dated Dec. 26, 1789:

In examining the English Books, that were
printed between the Restoration and the Accession
of George the 2d, we may observe, that all *Substantives* were begun with a capital, in which we
imitated our Mother Tongue, the German. This
was more particularly useful to those, who were
not well acquainted with the English; there being
nunciation.

This method has, by the Fancy of Printers, of

From a letter by Benjamin Franklin to Noah Webster
$^{10}/_{14}$ dated Dec. 26, 1789:

In examining the English Books, that were printed
between the Restoration and the Accession of George
the 2d, we may observe, that all *Substantives* were
begun with a capital, in which we imitated our Mother
Tongue, the German. This was more particularly useful to those, who were not well acquainted with the
English; there being such a prodigious Number of our
Words, that are both *Verbs* and *Substantives,* and
the Capitals shows the Character to greater Advantage;
those Letters prominent above the line distributing its

ABCDEFGHIJKLMNOPQRSTUVWXYZ
ABCDEFGHIJKLMNOPQRSTUVWXYZ
&.,"-:;!?""''1234567890$
&.,"-:;!?""''1234567890$
abcdefghijklmnopqrstuvwxyz
abcdefghijklmnopqrstuvwxyz

ABCDEFGHIJKLMNOPQRSTUVWXYZ
ABCDEFGHIJKLMNOPQRSTUVWXYZ
&.,"-:;!?""''1234567890$
&.,"-:;!?""''1234567890$
abcdefghijklmnopqrstuvwxyz
abcdefghijklmnopqrstuvwxyz

NEW GARAMOND: SIMONCINI

PICAS	6	7	8	9	10	11	12	13	14	15	16	17	18	19	20	21	22	23	24	25	26	27	28	29	30
11 POINT	15	18	20	23	25	28	30	33	35	38	40	43	45	48	50	53	55	58	60	63	65	68	70	73	75
10 POINT	17	20	22	25	27	30	32	35	38	40	43	46	49	51	54	57	59	62	65	68	70	73	76	78	81

9/10

From a letter by Benjamin Franklin to Noah Webster dated Dec. 26, 1789:

In examining the English Books, that were printed between the Restoration and the Accession of George the 2d, we may observe, that all *Substantives* were begun with a capital, in which we imitated our Mother Tongue, the German. This was more particularly useful to those, who were not well acquainted with the English; there being such a prodigious Number of our Words, that are both *Verbs* and *Substantives,* and spelt in the same manner, tho' often accented differently in Pronunciation.

This method has, by the Fancy of Printers, of late Years been laid aside, from an Idea, that suppressing the Capitals shows the Character to greater Advantage; those Letters prominent above the line disturbing its even regular Ap-*pearance. The Effect of this Change is so considerable, that a learned Man of France, who used to read our Books, tho'*

8/9

From a letter by Benjamin Franklin to Noah Webster dated Dec. 26, 1789:

In examining the English Books, that were printed between the Restoration and the Accession of George the 2d, we may observe, that all *Substantives* were begun with a capital, in which we imitated our Mother Tongue, the German. This was more particularly useful to those, who were not well acquainted with the English; there being such a prodigious Number of our Words, that are both *Verbs* and *Substantives,* and spelt in the same manner, tho' often accented differently in Pronunciation.

This method has, by the Fancy of Printers, of late Years been laid aside, from an Idea, that suppressing the Capitals shows the Character to greater Advantage; those Letters prominent above the line disturbing its even regular Appearance. The Effect of this Change is so considerable, that a learned Man of France, who used to read our Books, tho' not perfectly acquainted wit our Language, in Conversation with me on the *Subject of our Authors, attributed the greater Obscurity he found in our modern Books, compared with those of the Period*

9/11

From a letter by Benjamin Franklin to Noah Webster dated Dec. 26, 1789:

In examining the English Books, that were printed between the Restoration and the Accession of George the 2d, we may observe, that all *Substantives* were begun with a capital, in which we imitated our Mother Tongue, the German. This was more particularly useful to those, who were not well acquainted with the English; there being such a prodigious Number of our Words, that are both *Verbs* and *Substantives,* and spelt in the same manner, tho' often accented differently in Pronunciation.

This method has, by the Fancy of Printers, of late Years been laid aside, from an Idea, that suppressing the Capitals *pearance. The Effect of this Change is so considerable, that a learned Man of France, who used to read our Books, tho'*

8/10

From a letter by Benjamin Franklin to Noah Webster dated Dec. 26, 1789:

In examining the English Books, that were printed between the Restoration and the Accession of George the 2d, we may observe, that all *Substantives* were begun with a capital, in which we imitated our Mother Tongue, the German. This was more particularly useful to those, who were not well acquainted with the English; there being such a prodigious Number of our Words, that are both *Verbs* and *Substantives,* and spelt in the same manner, tho' often accented differently in Pronunciation.

This method has, by the Fancy of Printers, of late Years been laid aside, from an Idea, that suppressing the Capitals shows the Character to greater Advantage; those Letters prominent above the line disturbing its even regular Appearance. The *Subject of our Authors, attributed the greater Obscurity he found in our modern Books, compared with those of the Period*

9/13

From a letter by Benjamin Franklin to Noah Webster dated Dec. 26, 1789:

In examining the English Books, that were printed between the Restoration and the Accession of George the 2d, we may observe, that all *Substantives* were begun with a capital, in which we imitated our Mother Tongue, the German. This was more particularly useful to those, who were not well acquainted with the English; there being such a prodigious Number of our Words, that are both *Verbs* and *Substantives,* and spelt in the same manner, tho' often accented differently in Pronunciation.

pearance. The Effect of this Change is so considerable, that a learned Man of France, who used to read our Books, tho'

8/12

From a letter by Benjamin Franklin to Noah Webster dated Dec. 26, 1789:

In examining the English Books, that were printed between the Restoration and the Accession of George the 2d, we may observe, that all *Substantives* were begun with a capital, in which we imitated our Mother Tongue, the German. This was more particularly useful to those, who were not well acquainted with the English; there being such a prodigious Number of our Words, that are both *Verbs* and *Substantives,* and spelt in the same manner, tho' often accented differently in Pronunciation.

This method has, by the Fancy of Printers, of late Years been laid aside, from an Idea, that suppressing the Capitals shows *Subject of our Authors, attributed the greater Obscurity he found in our modern Books, compared with those of the Period*

ABCDEFGHIJKLMNOPQRSTUVWXYZ
ABCDEFGHIJKLMNOPQRSTUVWXYZ
&.,"-:;!?""'1234567890$
&.,"-:;!?""'1234567890$
abcdefghijklmnopqrstuvwxyz
abcdefghijklmnopqrstuvwxyz

ABCDEFGHIJKLMNOPQRSTUVWXYZ
ABCDEFGHIJKLMNOPQRSTUVWXYZ
&.,"-:;!?""'1234567890$
&.,"-:;!?""'1234567890$
abcdefghijklmnopqrstuvwxyz
abcdefghijklmnopqrstuvwxyz

NEW GARAMOND: SIMONCINI

PICAS	6	7	8	9	10	11	12	13	14	15	16	17	18	19	20	21	22	23	24	25	26	27	28	29	30
9 POINT	18	22	24	27	29	32	34	37	40	43	46	49	52	54	57	60	63	66	69	72	75	77	80	83	86
8 POINT	19	23	25	28	31	34	37	40	43	46	50	53	56	59	62	65	68	71	74	78	81	84	87	90	93

ABCDEFGHIJKLMN
OPQRSTUVWXYZ&
abcdefghijklmnopqrstuv
wxyzfifffflffifffl1234567 8
90$.,'‑‑:;!?"‟

48 POINT GARAMOND LIGHT (GARAMONT, GOUDY 248) MONOTYPE

*ABCDEFGHIJKLMNO
PQRSTUVW XYZ&abc
defghijklmnopqrstuvwxyz fi
ff fl ffi ffl1234567890$.,'‑‑:;!?"‟*

48 POINT GARAMOND LIGHT ITALIC (GARAMONT, GOUDY 2481) MONOTYPE

ABCDEFGHIJKLMNOPQ
RSTUVWXYZ&abcdefghi
jklmnopqrstuvwxyzfifffflffi
ffl1234567890$.,'‑‑:;!?"‟

42 POINT GARAMOND LIGHT (GARAMONT, GOUDY 248) MONOTYPE

ABCDEFGHIJKLMNOPQ
RSTUVWXYZ&abcdefghij
klmnopqrstuvwxyz fifffffffffffffl123
4567890$.,'‹-:;.!?"‟

42 POINT GARAMOND LIGHT ITALIC (GARAMONT, GOUDY 2481) MONOTYPE

ABCDEFGHIJKLMNOPQRS
TUVWXYZ&abcdefghijklmno
pqrstuvwxyzfifffflffffiffl12345678
90$.,'‹-:;!?"‟

36 POINT GARAMOND LIGHT (GARAMONT, GOUDY 248) MONOTYPE

ABCDEFGHIJKLMNOPQRST
UVWXYZ&abcdefghijklmnopqrs
tuvwxyz fifff flffiffl1234567890$
.,'‹-:;!?"‟

36 POINT GARAMOND LIGHT ITALIC (GARAMONT, GOUDY 2481) MONOTYPE

ABCDEFGHIJKLMNOPQRSTUV
WXYZ&abcdefghijklmnopqrstuvwx
yzfiff flffiffl1234567890$.,'‹-:;!?"‟

30 POINT GARAMOND LIGHT (GARAMONT, GOUDY 248) MONOTYPE

ABCDEFGHIJKLMNOPQRSTUVW XYZ&abcdefghijklmnopqrstuvwxyz fiffflffiffl1234567890$.,'-:;!?"''

30 POINT GARAMOND LIGHT ITALIC (GARAMONT, GOUDY 2481) MONOTYPE

ABCDEFGHIJKLMNOPQRSTUVWXYZ& abcdefghijklmnopqrstuvwxyzfiffflffiffl12345678 90$.,'-:;!?"''

24 POINT GARAMOND LIGHT (GARAMONT, GOUDY 248) MONOTYPE

ABCDEFGHIJKLMNOPQRSTUVWXYZ& abcdefghijklmnopqrstuvwxyz fiffflffiffl1234567890$.,'-:;!?"''

24 POINT GARAMOND LIGHT ITALIC (GARAMONT, GOUDY 2481) MONOTYPE

ABCDEFGHIJKLMNOPQRSTUVWXYZ&abcdefghijklmn opqrstuvwxyzfiffflffiffl1234567890$.,'-:;!?"''

18 POINT GARAMOND LIGHT (GARAMONT, GOUDY 248) MONOTYPE

ABCDEFGHIJKLMNOPQRSTUVWXYZ&abcdefghijklmnopqr stuvwxyz fiffflffiffl1234567890$.,'-:;!?"''

18 POINT GARAMOND LIGHT ITALIC (GARAMONT, GOUDY 2481) MONOTYPE

14/14

From a letter by Benjamin Franklin to Noah Webster dated Dec. 26, 1789:

In examining the English Books, that were printed between the Restoration and the Accession of George the 2d, we may observe, that all *Substantives* were begun with a capital, in which we imitated our Mother Tongue, the German. This was more particularly useful to those, who were not well acquainted with the English; there being such a prodigious Num-*ber of our Words, that are both Verbs and Substantives, and spelt in the same manner, tho'*

12/12

From a letter by Benjamin Franklin to Noah Webster dated Dec. 26, 1789:

In examining the English Books, that were printed between the Restoration and the Accession of George the 2d, we may observe, that all *Substantives* were begun with a capital, in which we imitated our Mother Tongue, the German. This was more particularly useful to those, who were not well acquainted with the English; there being such a prodigious Number of our Words, that are both *Verbs* and *Substantives,* and spelt in the same manner, tho' often accented differently in Pronunciation.

This Method has, by the Fancy of Printers, of late Years been laid aside, from an Idea, that suppressing

14/16

From a letter by Benjamin Franklin to Noah Webster dated Dec. 26, 1789:

In examining the English Books, that were printed between the Restoration and the Accession of George the 2d, we may observe, that all *Substantives* were begun with a capital, in which we imitated our Mother Tongue, the German. This was more particularly useful to those, who were not well *ber of our Words, that are both Verbs and Substantives, and spelt in the same manner, tho'*

12/14

From a letter by Benjamin Franklin to Noah Webster dated Dec. 26, 1789:

In examining the English Books, that were printed between the Restoration and the Accession of George the 2d, we may observe, that all *Substantives* were begun with a capital, in which we imitated our Mother Tongue, the German. This was more particularly useful to those, who were not well acquainted with the English; there being such a pro-

This Method has, by the Fancy of Printers, of late Years been laid aside, from an Idea, that suppressing

14/18

From a letter by Benjamin Franklin to Noah Webster dated Dec. 26, 1789:

In examining the English Books, that were printed between the Restoration and the Accession of George the 2d, we may observe, that all *Substantives* were begun with a capital, in which we imitated our Mother Tongue, the *ber of our Words, that are both Verbs and Substantives, and spelt in the same manner, tho'*

12/16

From a letter by Benjamin Franklin to Noah Webster dated Dec. 26, 1789:

In examining the English Books, that were printed between the Restoration and the Accession of George the 2d, we may observe, that all *Substantives* were begun with a capital, in which we imitated our Mother Tongue, the German. This was more particularly useful to those, who were not well

This Method has, by the Fancy of Printers, of late Years been laid aside, from an Idea, that suppressing

ABCDEFGHIJKLMNOPQRSTUVWXYZ
ABCDEFGHIJKLMNOPQRSTUVWXYZ
&.,"-:;!?""''1234567890$
&.,"-:;!?""''1234567890$
abcdefghijklmnopqrstuvwxyz
abcdefghijklmnopqrstuvwxyz

ABCDEFGHIJKLMNOPQRSTUVWXYZ
ABCDEFGHIJKLMNOPQRSTUVWXYZ
&.,"-:;!?""''1234567890$
&.,"-:;!?""''1234567890$
abcdefghijklmnopqrstuvwxyz
abcdefghijklmnopqrstuvwxyz

GARAMOND: INTERTYPE

PICAS	6	7	8	9	10	11	12	13	14	15	16	17	18	19	20	21	22	23	24	25	26	27	28	29	30
14 POINT	14	16	18	21	23	25	28	30	32	34	37	39	41	44	46	48	51	53	55	57	60	62	64	66	69
12 POINT	15	18	21	23	26	28	31	34	36	39	41	44	47	49	52	54	57	59	62	65	67	70	72	75	78

From a letter by Benjamin Franklin to Noah Webster
11/11 dated Dec. 26, 1789:

In examining the English Books, that were printed between the Restoration and the Accession of George the 2d, we may observe, that all *Substantives* were begun with a capital, in which we imitated our Mother Tongue, the German. This was more particularly useful to those, who were not well acquainted with the English; there being such a prodigious Number of our Words, that are both *Verbs* and *Substantives,* and spelt in the same manner, tho' often accented differently in Pronunciation.

This Method has, by the Fancy of Printers, of late *Years been laid aside, from an Idea, that suppressing the Capitals shows the Character to greater Advantage;*

From a letter by Benjamin Franklin to Noah Webster dated
10/10 Dec. 26, 1789:

In examining the English Books, that were printed between the Restoration and the Accession of George the 2d, we may observe, that all *Substantives* were begun with a capital, in which we imitated our Mother Tongue, the German. This was more particularly useful to those, who were not well acquainted with the English; there being such a prodigious Number of our Words, that are both *Verbs* and *Substantives,* and spelt in the same manner, tho' often accented differently in Pronunciation.

This Method has, by the Fancy of Printers, of late Years been laid aside, from an Idea, that suppressing the Capitals shows the Character to greater Advantage; those Letters prominent above the line disturbing its even regular Appearance. *The Effect of this Change is so considerable, that a learned Man of France, who used to read our Books, tho'*

From a letter by Benjamin Franklin to Noah Webster
11/13 dated Dec. 26, 1789:

In examining the English Books, that were printed between the Restoration and the Accession of George the 2d, we may observe, that all *Substantives* were begun with a capital, in which we imitated our Mother Tongue, the German. This was more particularly useful to those, who were not well acquainted with the English; there being such a prodigious Number of our Words, that are both *Verbs* and *Substantives,* and spelt in the same manner, tho' often accented differ-*Years been laid aside, from an Idea, that suppressing the Capitals shows the Character to greater Advantage;*

From a letter by Benjamin Franklin to Noah Webster dated
10/12 Dec. 26, 1789:

In examining the English Books, that were printed between the Restoration and the Accession of George the 2d, we may observe, that all *Substantives* were begun with a capital, in which we imitated our Mother Tongue, the German. This was more particularly useful to those, who were not well acquainted with the English; there being such a prodigious Number of our Words, that are both *Verbs* and *Substantives,* and spelt in the same manner, tho' often accented differently in Pronunciation.

This Method has, by the Fancy of Printers, of late Years *pearance. The Effect of this Change is so considerable, that a learned Man of France, who used to read our Books, tho'*

From a letter by Benjamin Franklin to Noah Webster
11/15 dated Dec. 26, 1789:

In examining the English Books, that were printed between the Restoration and the Accession of George the 2d, we may observe, that all *Substantives* were begun with a capital, in which we imitated our Mother Tongue, the German. This was more particularly useful to those, who were not well acquainted with the English; there being such a prodigious Number of *Years been laid aside, from an Idea, that suppressing the Capitals shows the Character to greater Advantage:*

From a letter by Benjamin Franklin to Noah Webster dated
10/14 Dec. 26, 1789:

In examining the English Books, that were printed between the Restoration and the Accession of George the 2d, we may observe, that all *Substantives* were begun with a capital, in which we imitated our Mother Tongue, the German. This was more particularly useful to those, who were not well acquainted with the English; there being such a prodigious Number of our Words, that are both *Verbs* and *Substantives,* and spelt in the same manner, tho' often ac-*pearance. The Effect of this Change is so considerable, that a learned Man of France, who used to read our Books, tho'*

ABCDEFGHIJKLMNOPQRSTUVWXYZ
ABCDEFGHIJKLMNOPQRSTUVWXYZ
&.,"-:;!?''''1234567890$
&.,"-:;!?''''1234567890$
abcdefghijklmnopqrstuvwxyz
abcdefghijklmnopqrstuvwxyz

ABCDEFGHIJKLMNOPQRSTUVWXYZ
ABCDEFGHIJKLMNOPQRSTUVWXYZ
&.,"-:;!?''''1234567890$
&.,"-:;!?''''1234567890$
abcdefghijklmnopqrstuvwxyz
abcdefghijklmnopqrstuvwxyz

GARAMOND: INTERTYPE

PICAS	6	7	8	9	10	11	12	13	14	15	16	17	18	19	20	21	22	23	24	25	26	27	28	29	30
11 POINT	16	19	22	25	27	30	32	35	38	40	43	46	49	51	54	57	59	62	65	67	70	73	75	78	81
10 POINT	17	20	23	26	29	32	35	38	41	43	46	49	52	55	58	61	64	66	70	72	75	78	81	84	87

8/8 From a letter by Benjamin Franklin to Noah Webster dated Dec. 26, 1789:

In examining the English Books, that were printed between the Restoration and the Accession of George the 2d, we may observe, that all *Substantives* were begun with a capital, in which we imitated our Mother Tongue, the German. This was more particularly useful to those, who were not well acquainted with the English; there being such a prodigious Number of our Words, that are both *Verbs* and *Substantives*, and spelt in the same manner, tho' often accented differently in Pronunciation.

This Method has, by the Fancy of Printers, of late Years been laid aside, from an Idea, that suppressing the Capitals shows the Character to greater Advantage; those Letters prominent above the line disturbing its even regular Appearance. The Effect of this Change is so considerable, that a learned Man of France, who used to read our Books, tho' not perfectly acquainted with our Language, in Conversation with me on the Subject of our Authors, attributed the greater Obscurity he found in our modern Books, compared with those of the Period above mentioned, to a Change *of Style for the worse in our Writers, of which Mistake I convinced him, by marking for him each Substantive with a Capital in*

6/6 From a letter by Benjamin Franklin to Noah Webster dated Dec. 26, 1789:

In examining the English Books, that were printed between the Restoration and the Accession of George the 2d, we may observe, that all *Substantives* were begun with a capital, in which we imitated our Mother Tongue, the German. This was more particularly useful to those, who were not well acquainted with the English; there being such a prodigious Number of our Words, that are both *Verbs* and *Substantives*, and spelt in the same manner, tho' often accented differently in Pronunciation.

This Method has, by the Fancy of Printers, of late Years been laid aside, from an Idea, that suppressing the Capitals shows the Character to greater Advantage; those Letters prominent above the line disturbing its even regular Appearance. The Effect of this Change is so considerable, that a learned Man of France, who used to read our Books, tho' not perfectly acquainted with our Language, in Conversation with me on the Subject of our Authors, attributed the greater Obscurity he found in our modern Books, compared with those of the Period above mentioned, to a Change of Style for the worse in our Writers, of which Mistake I convinced him, by marking for him each *Substantive* with a Capital in a Paragraph, which he then easily understood, tho' before he could not comprehend it. This shows the Inconvenience of that pretended Improvement.

From the same Fondness for an even and uniform Appearance of Characters in the Line, the Printers have of late banished also the Italic Types, in which Words of Importance to be attended to in the Sense of the Sentence, and Words on which an Emphasis should be put in Reading, used to be printed. And lately another Fancy has induced some Printers to use the short round *s*, instead of the long one, which formerly served well to *distinguish a word readily by its varied appearance. Certainly the omitting this prominent Letter makes the Line appear more even; but renders it less imme-*

8/10 From a letter by Benjamin Franklin to Noah Webster dated Dec. 26, 1789:

In examining the English Books, that were printed between the Restoration and the Accession of George the 2d, we may observe, that all *Substantives* were begun with a capital, in which we imitated our Mother Tongue, the German. This was more particularly useful to those, who were not well acquainted with the English; there being such a prodigious Number of our Words, that are both *Verbs* and *Substantives*, and spelt in the same manner, tho' often accented differently in Pronunciation.

This Method has, by the Fancy of Printers, of late Years been laid aside, from an Idea, that suppressing the Capitals shows the Character to greater Advantage; those Letters prominent above the line disturbing its even regular Appearance. The Effect of this Change is so considerable, that a learned Man of France, who used *of Style for the worse in our Writers, of which Mistake I convinced him, by marking for him each Substantive with a Capital in*

6/8 From a letter by Benjamin Franklin to Noah Webster dated Dec. 26, 1789:

In examining the English Books, that were printed between the Restoration and the Accession of George the 2d, we may observe, that all *Substantives* were begun with a capital, in which we imitated our Mother Tongue, the German. This was more particularly useful to those, who were not well acquainted with the English; there being such a prodigious Number of our Words, that are both *Verbs* and *Substantives*, and spelt in the same manner, tho' often accented differently in Pronunciation.

This Method has, by the Fancy of Printers, of late Years been laid aside, from an Idea, that suppressing the Capitals shows the Character to greater Advantage; those Letters prominent above the line disturbing its even regular Appearance. The Effect of this Change is so considerable, that a learned Man of France, who used to read our Books, tho' not perfectly acquainted with our Language, in Conversation with me on the Subject of our Authors, attributed the greater Obscurity he found in our modern Books, compared with those of the Period above mentioned, to a Change of Style for the worse in our Writers, of which Mistake I convinced him, by marking for him each *Substantive* with a Capital in a Paragraph, which he then easily understood, tho' before he could not comprehend it. This shows the Inconvenience *guish a word readily by its varied appearance. Certainly the omitting this prominent Letter makes the Line appear more even; but renders it less imme-*

8/12 From a letter by Benjamin Franklin to Noah Webster dated Dec. 26, 1789:

In examining the English Books, that were printed between the Restoration and the Accession of George the 2d, we may observe, that all *Substantives* were begun with a capital, in which we imitated our Mother Tongue, the German. This was more particularly useful to those, who were not well acquainted with the English; there being such a prodigious Number of our Words, that are both *Verbs* and *Substantives*, and spelt in the same manner, tho' often accented differently in Pronunciation.

This Method has, by the Fancy of Printers, of late Years been laid aside, from an Idea, that suppressing the Capitals shows the *of Style for the worse in our Writers, of which Mistake I convinced him, by marking for him each Substantive with a Capital in*

6/10 From a letter by Benjamin Franklin to Noah Webster dated Dec. 26, 1789:

In examining the English Books, that were printed between the Restoration and the Accession of George the 2d, we may observe, that all *Substantives* were begun with a capital, in which we imitated our Mother Tongue, the German. This was more particularly useful to those, who were not well acquainted with the English; there being such a prodigious Number of our Words, that are both *Verbs* and *Substantives*, and spelt in the same manner, tho' often accented differently in Pronunciation.

This Method has, by the Fancy of Printers, of late Years been laid aside, from an Idea, that suppressing the Capitals shows the Character to greater Advantage; those Letters prominent above the line disturbing its even regular Appearance. The Effect of this Change is so considerable, that a learned Man of France, who used to read our Books, tho' not perfectly acquainted with our Language, in Conversation with me on the Subject of our Authors, attributed the greater Obscurity he found in our modern Books, compared *guish a word readily by its varied appearance. Certainly the omitting this prominent Letter makes the Line appear more even; but renders it less imme-*

ABCDEFGHIJKLMNOPQRSTUVWXYZ
ABCDEFGHIJKLMNOPQRSTUVWXYZ
&.,"'-:;!?""1234567890$
&.,"'-:;!?""1234567890$
abcdefghijklmnopqrstuvwxyz
abcdefghijklmnopqrstuvwxyz

ABCDEFGHIJKLMNOPQRSTUVWXYZ
ABCDEFGHIJKLMNOPQRSTUVWXYZ
&.,"'-:;!?""1234567890$
&.,"'-:;!?""1234567890$
abcdefghijklmnopqrstuvwxyz
abcdefghijklmnopqrstuvwxyz

GARAMOND: INTERTYPE

PICAS	6	7	8	9	10	11	12	13	14	15	16	17	18	19	20	21	22	23	24	25	26	27	28	29	30
8 POINT	20	24	27	31	34	37	41	44	47	51	54	57	61	64	67	71	74	78	81	85	88	91	95	98	102
6 POINT	24	27	31	35	39	43	47	51	55	59	63	67	71	75	79	83	86	90	94	98	102	106	110	114	118

ABCDEFGHIJKLMNO
PQRSTUVWXYZ&abc
defghijklmnopqrstuvwxy
zfifl1234567890$.,''-:;!?''''''

48 POINT GARAMOND BOLD, ATF

ABCDEFGHIJKLMNOP
QRSTUVWXYZ&abcdef
ghijklmnopqrstuvwxyzfifl12
34567890$.,''-:;!?''''''

48 POINT GARAMOND BOLD ITALIC, ATF

ABCDEFGHIJKLMNOPQRSTU
VWXYZ&abcdefghijklmnopqrst
uvwxyzfifl1234567890$.,''-:;!?''''''

36 POINT GARAMOND BOLD, ATF

*ABCDEFGHIJKLMNOPQRSTU
VWXYZ&abcdefghijklmnopqrstuv
wxyzfifl1234567890$.,"-:;!?""''*

36 POINT GARAMOND BOLD ITALIC, ATF

ABCDEFGHIJKLMNOPQRSTUVW
XYZ&abcdefghijklmnopqrstuvwxyzfifl
1234567890$.,"-:;!?""''

30 POINT GARAMOND BOLD, ATF

*ABCDEFGHIJKLMNOPQRSTUVWX
YZ&abcdefghijklmnopqrstuvwxyzfifl12345
67890$.,"-:;!?""''*

30 POINT GARAMOND BOLD ITALIC, ATF

ABCDEFGHIJKLMNOPQRSTUVWXYZ&abc
defghijklmnopqrstuvwxyzfifl1234567890$.,"-:;!?""''

24 POINT GARAMOND BOLD, ATF

*ABCDEFGHIJKLMNOPQRSTUVWXYZ&abcd
efghijklmnopqrstuvwxyzfifl1234567890$.,"-:;!?""''*

24 POINT GARAMOND BOLD ITALIC, ATF

ABCDEFGHIJKLMNOPQRSTUVWXYZ&abcdefghijklmnop
qrstuvwxyzfifl1234567890$.,"-:;!?""''

18 POINT GARAMOND BOLD, ATF

*ABCDEFGHIJKLMNOPQRSTUVWXYZ&abcdefghijklmopqrst
uvwxyzfifl1234567890$.,"-:;!?""''*

18 POINT GARAMOND BOLD ITALIC, ATF

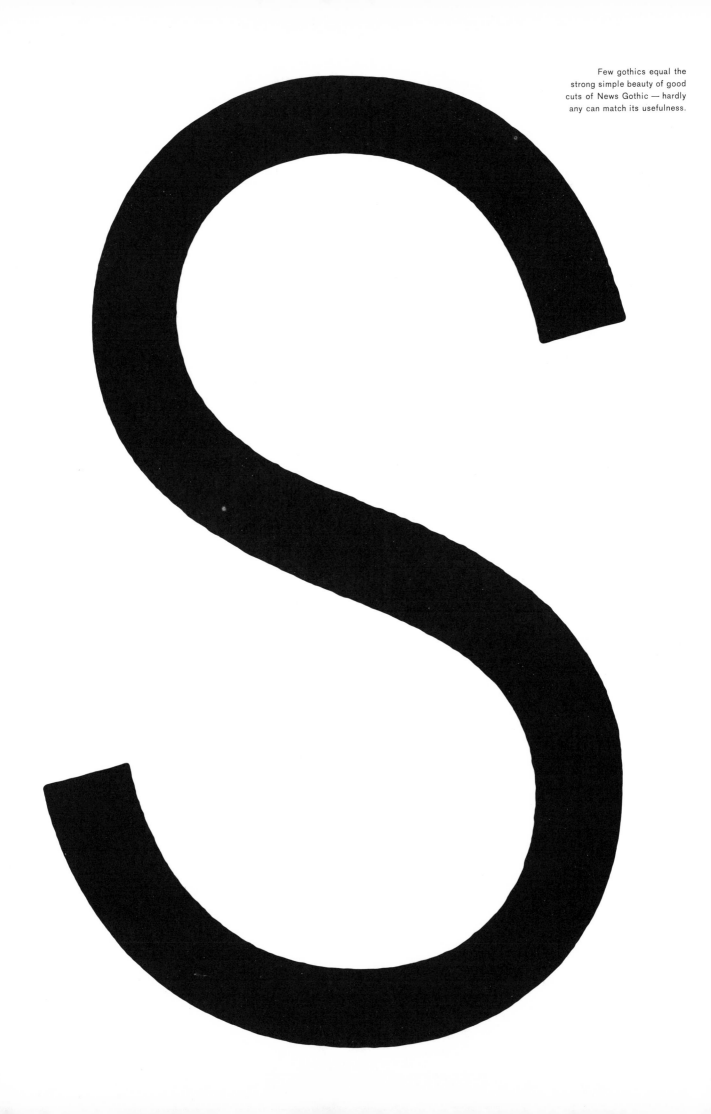

NEWS GOTHIC, ATF

ABCDEFGH abcdefg

NEWS GOTHIC 20€, MONOTYPE

ABCD abcd

RECORD GOTHIC, LUDLOW

MODERN entire plant

All comparisons are made on 24 point type.

ABCDEFGHIJK
LMNOPQRSTU
VWXYZ&abcdef
ghijklmnopqrst
uvwxyz123456
7890$.,''-·:!?''''

72 POINT NEWS GOTHIC, ATF

ABCDEFGHIJKLM
NOPQRSTUVWXY
Z&abcdefghijklmn
opqrstuvwxyz1234
567890$.,'"-:;!?'"''

60 POINT NEWS GOTHIC, ATF

ABCDEFGHIJKLMNOP
QRSTUVWXYZ&abcdef
ghijklmnopqrstuvwxyz1
234567890$.,'"-:;!?'"''

48 POINT NEWS GOTHIC, ATF

ABCDEFGHIJKLMNOPQR
STUVWXYZ&abcdefghijklm
nopqrstuvwxyz123456789
0$.,"-:;!?""''

42 POINT NEWS GOTHIC, ATF

ABCDEFGHIJKLMNOPQRSTUV
WXYZ&abcdefghijklmnopqrstuv
wxyz1234567890$.,"-:;!?""''

36 POINT NEWS GOTHIC, ATF

ABCDEFGHIJKLMNOPQRSTUVWXYZ&
abcdefghijklmnopqrstuvwxyz1234567
890$.,"-:;!?""''

30 POINT NEWS GOTHIC, ATF

ABCDEFGHIJKLMNOPQRSTUVWXYZ&abcdefg
hijklmnopqrstuvwxyz1234567890$.,"-:;!?""''

24 POINT NEWS GOTHIC, ATF

ABCDEFGHIJKLMNOPQRSTUVWXYZ&abcdefghijklmnopq
rstuvwxyz1234567890$.,"-:;!?""''

18 POINT NEWS GOTHIC, ATF

14/14 Besides the three principal proper-ties which we have mentioned, the following (like Satellites to good letter) are not undeserving the purchaser's examination, who ought to take notice, 1. Whether the letter stands even, and in line; which is the chief good quality in letter, and makes the face thereof sometimes to pass, though otherwise ill-shaped. 2. Whether it *stands parallel; and whether it drives out or gets in, either at the head, or*

12/12 Besides the three principal properties which we have mentioned, the following (like Satellites to good letter) are not undeserving the purchaser's examination, who ought to take notice, 1. Whether the letter stands even, and in line; which is the chief good quality in letter, and makes the face thereof sometimes to pass, though otherwise ill-shaped. 2. Whether it stands parallel; and whether it drives out or gets in, either at the head, or the foot, and is, as Printers call it, bottle-arsed; which is a fault that cannot be *mended but by rubbing the whole fount over again. 3. Whether the thin lower-case letter*

14/16 Besides the three principal proper-ties which we have mentioned, the following (like Satellites to good letter) are not undeserving the purchaser's examination, who ought to take notice, 1. Whether the letter stands even, and in line; which is the chief good quality in letter, and makes the face *stands parallel; and whether it drives out or gets in, either at the head, or*

12/14 Besides the three principal properties which we have mentioned, the following (like Satellites to good letter) are not undeserving the purchaser's examination, who ought to take notice, 1. Whether the letter stands even, and in line; which is the chief good quality in letter, and makes the face thereof sometimes to pass, though otherwise ill-shaped. 2. Whether it stands parallel; and *mended but by rubbing the whole fount over again. 3. Whether the thin lower-case letter*

14/18 Besides the three principal proper-ties which we have mentioned, the following (like Satellites to good letter) are not undeserving the purchaser's examination, who ought to take notice, 1. Whether the letter stands even, and in line; which is the chief good *stands parallel; and whether it drives out or gets in, either at the head, or*

12/16 Besides the three principal properties which we have mentioned, the following (like Satellites to good letter) are not undeserving the purchaser's examination, who ought to take notice, 1. Whether the letter stands even, and in line; which is the chief good quality in letter, and makes the face thereof sometimes to pass, though otherwise ill-*mended but by rubbing the whole fount over again. 3. Whether the thin lower-case letter*

ABCDEFGHIJKLMNOPQRSTUVWXY
ABCDEFGHIJKLMNOPQRSTUVWXY
&.,'"-:;!?''""1234567890$
&.,'"-:;!?''""1234567890$
abcdefghijklmnopqrstuvwxyz
abcdefghijklmnopqrstuvwxyz

ABCDEFGHIJKLMNOPQRSTUVWXYZ
ABCDEFGHIJKLMNOPQRSTUVWXYZ
&.,'"-:;!?''""1234567890$
&.,'"-:;!?''""1234567890$
abcdefghijklmnopqrstuvwxyz
abcdefghijklmnopqrstuvwxyz

NEWS GOTHIC: INTERTYPE

PICAS	6	7	8	9	10	11	12	13	14	15	16	17	18	19	20	21	22	23	24	25	26	27	28	29	30
14 POINT	10	12	14	15	17	19	20	22	24	26	29	31	32	34	36	37	39	41	43	44	46	48	49	51	53
12 POINT	12	14	16	18	20	23	26	28	30	32	34	36	38	40	42	44	46	48	50	52	54	56	58	60	62

11/11

Besides the three principal properties which we have mentioned, the following (like Satellites to good letter) are not undeserving the purchaser's examination, who ought to take notice, 1. Whether the letter stands even, and in line; which is the chief good quality in letter, and makes the face thereof sometimes to pass, though otherwise ill-shaped. 2. Whether it stands parallel; and whether it drives out or gets in, either at the head, or the foot, and is, as Printers call it, bottle-arsed; which is a fault that cannot be mended but by rubbing the whole fount over again. 3. Whether the thin lower-case letters, especially *the dots over the i and j, are come in casting. 4. Whether the break is ploughed away and*

10/10

Besides the three principal properties which we have mentioned, the following (like Satellites to good letter) are not undeserving the purchaser's examination, who ought to take notice, 1. Whether the letter stands even, and in line; which is the chief good quality in letter, and makes the face thereof sometimes to pass, though otherwise ill-shaped. 2. Whether it stands parallel; and whether it drives out or gets in, either at the head, or the foot, and is, as Printers call it, bottle-arsed; which is a fault that cannot be mended but by rubbing the whole fount over again. 3. Whether the thin lower-case letters, especially the dots over the i and j, are come in casting. 4. Whether the break is ploughed away and smoothened. 5. Whether it be well scraped, so as *not to want rubbing down by the compositor. 6. Whether each letter has a due proportion, as to*

11/13

Besides the three principal properties which we have mentioned, the following (like Satellites to good letter) are not undeserving the purchaser's examination, who ought to take notice, 1. Whether the letter stands even, and in line; which is the chief good quality in letter, and makes the face thereof sometimes to pass, though otherwise ill-shaped. 2. Whether it stands parallel; and whether it drives out or gets in, either at the head, or the foot, and is, as Printers call it, bottle-arsed; which is a fault that cannot be mended *but by rubbing the whole fount over again. 3. Whether the thin lower-case letters, especially*

10/12

Besides the three principal properties which we have mentioned, the following (like Satellites to good letter) are not undeserving the purchaser's examination, who ought to take notice, 1. Whether the letter stands even, and in line; which is the chief good quality in letter, and makes the face thereof sometimes to pass, though otherwise ill-shaped. 2. Whether it stands parallel; and whether it drives out or gets in, either at the head, or the foot, and is, as Printers call it, bottle-arsed; which is a fault that cannot be mended but by rubbing the whole fount over again. 3. Whether the thin lower-case letters, *not to want rubbing down by the compositor. 6. Whether each letter has a due proportion, as to*

11/15

Besides the three principal properties which we have mentioned, the following (like Satellites to good letter) are not undeserving the purchaser's examination, who ought to take notice, 1. Whether the letter stands even, and in line; which is the chief good quality in letter, and makes the face thereof sometimes to pass, though otherwise ill-shaped. 2. Whether it stands parallel; and whether it drives out or gets in, either at the *head, or the foot, and is, as Printers call it, bottle-arsed; which is a fault that cannot be mended*

10/14

Besides the three principal properties which we have mentioned, the following (like Satellites to good letter) are not undeserving the purchaser's examination, who ought to take notice, 1. Whether the letter stands even, and in line; which is the chief good quality in letter, and makes the face thereof sometimes to pass, though otherwise ill-shaped. 2. Whether it stands parallel; and whether it drives out or gets in, either at the head, or the foot, and is, as Printers call it, bottle-arsed; which is a fault that *not to want rubbing down by the compositor. 6. Whether each letter has a due proportion, as to*

ABCDEFGHIJKLMNOPQRSTUVWXYZ
ABCDEFGHIJKLMNOPQRSTUVWXYZ
&.,'‘-:;!?''''''1234567890$
&.,'‘-:;!?''''''1234567890$
abcdefghijklmnopqrstuvwxyz
abcdefghijklmnopqrstuvwxyz

ABCDEFGHIJKLMNOPQRSTUVWXYZ
ABCDEFGHIJKLMNOPQRSTUVWXYZ
&.,'‘-:;!?''''''1234567890$
&.,'‘-:;!?''''''1234567890$
abcdefghijklmnopqrstuvwxyz
abcdefghijklmnopqrstuvwxyz

NEWS GOTHIC: INTERTYPE

PICAS	6	7	8	9	10	11	12	13	14	15	16	17	18	19	20	21	22	23	24	25	26	27	28	29	30
11 POINT	14	16	18	21	23	25	28	30	32	35	37	40	43	46	48	51	53	55	57	60	62	64	67	69	71
10 POINT	15	17	20	22	24	27	29	32	34	36	39	42	45	48	51	53	56	58	60	63	65	68	70	72	74

9/9 Besides the three principal properties which we have mentioned, the following (like Satellites to good letter) are not undeserving the purchaser's examination, who ought to take notice, 1. Whether the letter stands even, and in line; which is the chief good quality in letter, and makes the face thereof sometimes to pass, though otherwise ill-shaped. 2. Whether it stands parallel; and whether it drives out or gets in, either at the head, or the foot, and is, as Printers call it, bottle-arsed; which is a fault that cannot be mended but by rubbing the whole fount over again. 3. Whether the thin lower-case letters, especially the dots over the i and j, are come in casting. 4. Whether the break is ploughed away and smoothened. 5. Whether it be well scraped, so as not to want rubbing down by the compositor. 6. Whether each letter has a due proportion, as to thickness; and whether they are not so thin as to hinder each other from appearing with *a full face; or so thick as to occasion a gap between letter and letter. 7. Whether it be well bearded: which*

8/8 Besides the three principal properties which we have mentioned, the following (like Satellites to good letter) are not undeserving the purchaser's examination, who ought to take notice, 1. Whether the letter stands even, and in line; which is the chief good quality in letter, and makes the face thereof sometimes to pass, though otherwise ill-shaped. 2. Whether it stands parallel; and whether it drives out or gets in, either at the head, or the foot, and is, as Printers call it, bottle-arsed; which is a fault that cannot be mended but by rubbing the whole fount over again. 3. Whether the thin lower-case letters, especially the dots over the i and j, are come in casting. 4. Whether the break is ploughed away and smoothened. 5. Whether it be well scraped, so as not to want rubbing down by the compositor. 6. Whether each letter has a due proportion, as to thickness; and whether they are not so thin as to hinder each other from appearing with a full face; or so thick as to occasion a gap between letter and letter. 7. Whether it be well bearded: which founders in France are obliged to do, to their own disadvantage, on ac- *count of their shallow letter. 8. Whether it have a deep and open, single or double nick, different from other founts of*

9/11 Besides the three principal properties which we have mentioned, the following (like Satellites to good letter) are not undeserving the purchaser's examination, who ought to take notice, 1. Whether the letter stands even, and in line; which is the chief good quality in letter, and makes the face thereof sometimes to pass, though otherwise ill-shaped. 2. Whether it stands parallel; and whether it drives out or gets in, either at the head, or the foot, and is, as Printers call it, bottle-arsed; which is a fault that cannot be mended but by rubbing the whole fount over again. 3. Whether the thin lower-case letters, especially the dots over the i and j, are come in casting. 4. Whether the break is ploughed away and smoothened. 5. Whether it be well scraped, so as not to want rubbing *down by the compositor. 6. Whether each letter has a due proportion, as to thickness; and whether they are*

8/10 Besides the three principal properties which we have mentioned, the following (like Satellites to good letter) are not undeserving the purchaser's examination, who ought to take notice, 1. Whether the letter stands even, and in line; which is the chief good quality in letter, and makes the face thereof sometimes to pass, though otherwise ill-shaped. 2. Whether it stands parallel; and whether it drives out or gets in, either at the head, or the foot, and is, as Printers call it, bottle-arsed; which is a fault that cannot be mended but by rubbing the whole fount over again. 3. Whether the thin lower-case letters, especially the dots over the i and j, are come in casting. 4. Whether the break is ploughed away and smoothened. 5. Whether it be well scraped, so as not to want rubbing down by the compositor. 6. Whether each letter has a due proportion, as to thickness; and whether they *count of their shallow letter. 8. Whether it have a deep and open, single or double nick, different from other founts of*

9/13 Besides the three principal properties which we have mentioned, the following (like Satellites to good letter) are not undeserving the purchaser's examination, who ought to take notice, 1. Whether the letter stands even, and in line; which is the chief good quality in letter, and makes the face thereof sometimes to pass, though otherwise ill-shaped. 2. Whether it stands parallel; and whether it drives out or gets in, either at the head, or the foot, and is, as Printers call it, bottle-arsed; which is a fault that cannot be mended but by rubbing the whole fount over again. 3. Whether the thin lower-case letters, *especially the dots over the i and j, are come in casting. 4. Whether the break is ploughed away and smoothened.*

8/12 Besides the three principal properties which we have mentioned, the following (like Satellites to good letter) are not undeserving the purchaser's examination, who ought to take notice, 1. Whether the letter stands even, and in line; which is the chief good quality in letter, and makes the face thereof sometimes to pass, though otherwise ill-shaped. 2. Whether it stands parallel; and whether it drives out or gets in, either at the head, or the foot, and is, as Printers call it, bottle-arsed; which is a fault that cannot be mended but by rubbing the whole fount over again. 3. Whether the thin lower-case letters, especially the dots over the i and j, are come in casting. 4. Whether the break is ploughed away *count of their shallow letter. 8. Whether it have a deep and open, single or double nick, different from other founts of*

ABCDEFGHIJKLMNOPQRSTUVWXYZ
ABCDEFGHIJKLMNOPQRSTUVWXYZ
&.,''-:;!?''''''1234567890$
&.,''-:;!?''''''1234567890$
abcdefghijklmnopqrstuvwxyz
abcdefghijklmnopqrstuvwxyz

ABCDEFGHIJKLMNOPQRSTUVWXYZ
ABCDEFGHIJKLMNOPQRSTUVWXYZ
&.,''-:;!?''''''1234567890$
&.,''-:;!?''''''1234567890$
abcdefghijklmnopqrstuvwxyz
abcdefghijklmnopqrstuvwxyz

NEWS GOTHIC: INTERTYPE

PICAS	6	7	8	9	10	11	12	13	14	15	16	17	18	19	20	21	22	23	24	25	26	27	28	29	30
9 POINT	16	19	22	24	27	30	32	35	38	41	44	47	50	53	55	57	59	62	65	68	70	73	76	78	81
8 POINT	17	20	23	26	29	32	35	38	41	44	47	49	52	55	57	59	61	64	67	70	73	75	78	81	84

7/7 Besides the three principal properties which we have mentioned, the following (like Satellites to good letter) are not undeserving the purchaser's examination, who ought to take notice, 1. Whether the letter stands even, and in line; which is the chief good quality in letter, and makes the face thereof sometimes to pass, though otherwise ill-shaped. 2. Whether it stands parallel; and whether it drives out or gets in, either at the head, or the foot, and is, as Printers call it, bottle-arsed; which is a fault that cannot be mended but by rubbing the whole fount over again. 3. Whether the thin lower-case letters, especially the dots over the i and j, are come in casting. 4. Whether the break is ploughed away and smoothened. 5. Whether it be well scraped, so as not to want rubbing down by the compositor. 6. Whether each letter has a due proportion, as to thickness; and whether they are not so thin as to hinder each other from appearing with a full face; or so thick as to occasion a gap between letter and letter. 7. Whether it be well bearded: which founders in France are obliged to do, to their own disadvantage, on account of their shallow letter. 8. Whether it have a deep and open, single or double nick, different from other founts of the same body, and in the same printing-house.

We cannot too strongly urge the advantage to be derived from letter having a deep nick, and also that the nick should differ from *other founts of that body in the same house. This may appear a trifling consideration; but in a large fount the difference in weight*

6/6 Besides the three principal properties which we have mentioned, the following (like Satellites to good letter) are not undeserving the purchaser's examination, who ought to take notice, 1. Whether the letter stands even, and in line; which is the chief good quality in letter, and makes the face thereof sometimes to pass, though otherwise ill-shaped. 2. Whether it stands parallel; and whether it drives out or gets in, either at the head, or the foot, and is, as Printers call it, bottle-arsed; which is a fault that cannot be mended but by rubbing the whole fount over again. 3. Whether the thin lower-case letters, especially the dots over the i and j, are come in casting. 4. Whether the break is ploughed away and smoothened. 5. Whether it be well scraped, so as not to want rubbing down by the compositor. 6. Whether each letter has a due proportion, as to thickness; and whether they are not so thin as to hinder each other from appearing with a full face; or so thick as to occasion a gap between letter and letter. 7. Whether it be well bearded: which founders in France are obliged to do, to their own disadvantage, on account of their shallow letter. 8. Whether it have a deep and open, single or double nick, different from other founts of the same body, and in the same printing-house.

We cannot too strongly urge the advantage to be derived from letter having a deep nick, and also that the nick should differ from other founts of that body in the same house. This may appear a trifling consideration; but in a large fount the difference in weight will be considerable, and consequently a saving to the purchaser. A deep nick is an advantage to the compositor, from its more readily *catching the eye than a shallow one, and consequently greatly facilitates him in his business.*

7/9 Besides the three principal properties which we have mentioned, the following (like Satellites to good letter) are not undeserving the purchaser's examination, who ought to take notice, 1. Whether the letter stands even, and in line; which is the chief good quality in letter, and makes the face thereof sometimes to pass, though otherwise ill-shaped. 2. Whether it stands parallel; and whether it drives out or gets in, either at the head, or the foot, and is, as Printers call it, bottle-arsed; which is a fault that cannot be mended but by rubbing the whole fount over again. 3. Whether the thin lower-case letters, especially the dots over the i and j, are come in casting. 4. Whether the break is ploughed away and smoothened. 5. Whether it be well scraped, so as not to want rubbing down by the compositor. 6. Whether each letter has a due proportion, as to thickness; and whether they are not so thin as to hinder each other from appearing with a full face; or so thick as to occasion a gap between letter and letter. 7. Whether it be well bearded: which founders in France are obliged to do, to their own disadvantage, on *account of their shallow letter. 8. Whether it have a deep and open, single or double nick, different from other founts of the same body,*

6/8 Besides the three principal properties which we have mentioned, the following (like Satellites to good letter) are not undeserving the purchaser's examination, who ought to take notice, 1. Whether the letter stands even, and in line; which is the chief good quality in letter, and makes the face thereof sometimes to pass, though otherwise ill-shaped. 2. Whether it stands parallel; and whether it drives out or gets in, either at the head, or the foot, and is, as Printers call it, bottle-arsed; which is a fault that cannot be mended but by rubbing the whole fount over again. 3. Whether the thin lower-case letters, especially the dots over the i and j, are come in casting. 4. Whether the break is ploughed away and smoothened. 5. Whether it be well scraped, so as not to want rubbing down by the compositor. 6. Whether each letter has a due proportion, as to thickness; and whether they are not so thin as to hinder each other from appearing with a full face; or so thick as to occasion a gap between letter and letter. 7. Whether it be well bearded: which founders in France are obliged to do, to their own disadvantage, on account of their shallow letter. 8. Whether it have a deep and open, single or double nick, different from other founts of the same body, and in *catching the eye than a shallow one, and consequently greatly facilitates him in his business.*

7/11 Besides the three principal properties which we have mentioned, the following (like Satellites to good letter) are not undeserving the purchaser's examination, who ought to take notice, 1. Whether the letter stands even, and in line; which is the chief good quality in letter, and makes the face thereof sometimes to pass, though otherwise ill-shaped. 2. Whether it stands parallel; and whether it drives out or gets in, either at the head, or the foot, and is, as Printers call it, bottle-arsed; which is a fault that cannot be mended but by rubbing the whole fount over again. 3. Whether the thin lower-case letters, especially the dots over the i and j, are come in casting. 4. Whether the break is ploughed away and smoothened. 5. Whether it be well scraped, so as not to want rubbing down by the compositor. 6. Whether each letter has a due proportion, as to *thickness; and whether they are not so thin as to hinder each other from appearing with a full face; or so thick as to occasion a gap*

6/10 Besides the three principal properties which we have mentioned, the following (like Satellites to good letter) are not undeserving the purchaser's examination, who ought to take notice, 1. Whether the letter stands even, and in line; which is the chief good quality in letter, and makes the face thereof sometimes to pass, though otherwise ill-shaped. 2. Whether it stands parallel; and whether it drives out or gets in, either at the head, or the foot, and is, as Printers call it, bottle-arsed; which is a fault that cannot be mended but by rubbing the whole fount over again. 3. Whether the thin lower-case letters, especially the dots over the i and j, are come in casting. 4. Whether the break is ploughed away and smoothened. 5. Whether it be well scraped, so as not to want rubbing down by the compositor. 6. Whether each letter has a due proportion, as to thickness; and whether they are not so thin as to hinder each other from appearing with a full face; or so thick as to occasion a gap between *catching the eye than a shallow one, and consequently greatly facilitates him in his business.*

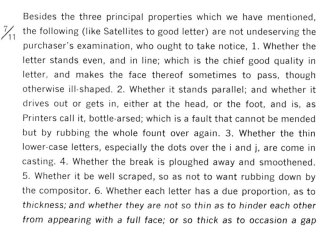

ABCDEFGHIJKLMNOPQRSTUVWXYZ
ABCDEFGHIJKLMNOPQRSTUVWXYZ
&.,''-:;!?''''1234567890$
&.,''-:;!?''''*1234567890$*
abcdefghijklmnopqrstuvwxyz
abcdefghijklmnopqrstuvwxyz

ABCDEFGHIJKLMNOPQRSTUVWXYZ
ABCDEFGHIJKLMNOPQRSTUVWXYZ
&.,''-:;!?''''1234567890$
&.,''-:;!?''''*1234567890$*
abcdefghijklmnopqrstuvwxyz
abcdefghijklmnopqrstuvwxyz

NEWS GOTHIC: INTERTYPE

PICAS	6	7	8	9	10	11	12	13	14	15	16	17	18	19	20	21	22	23	24	25	26	27	28	29	30
7 POINT	19	22	26	29	32	35	38	42	45	48	52	56	60	63	65	67	70	74	77	80	83	86	90	93	96
6 POINT	20	23	26	30	33	36	40	43	46	50	54	58	62	65	68	71	74	77	80	83	86	89	92	96	99

ABCDEFGHIJKLMNO
PQRSTUVWXYZ&ab
cdefghijklmnopqrstu
vwxyz1234567890$
"-:·!?""
·, ·,··

72 POINT NEWS GOTHIC CONDENSED, ATF

ABCDEFGHIJKLMNOPQR
STUVWXYZ&abcdefghijk
lmnopqrstuvwxyz12345
67890$.,"-:·!?""

60 POINT NEWS GOTHIC CONDENSED, ATF

ABCDEFGHIJKLMNOPQRSTUV
WXYZ&abcdefghijklmnopqrstu
vwxyz1234567890$.,"-:;!?""''

48 POINT NEWS GOTHIC CONDENSED, ATF

ABCDEFGHIJKLMNOPQRSTUVWXY
Z&abcdefghijklmnopqrstuvwxyz12
34567890$.,"-:;!?""''

42 POINT NEWS GOTHIC CONDENSED, ATF

ABCDEFGHIJKLMNOPQRSTUVWXYZ&ab
cdefghijklmnopqrstuvwxyz1234567890$
.,"-:;!?""''

36 POINT NEWS GOTHIC CONDENSED, ATF

ABCDEFGHIJKLMNOPQRSTUVWXYZ&abcdefghijkl
mnopqrstuvwxyz1234567890$.,"-:;!?""''

30 POINT NEWS GOTHIC CONDENSED, ATF

ABCDEFGHIJKLMNOPQRSTUVWXYZ&abcdefghijklmnopqrst
uvwxyz1234567890$.,"-:;!?""''

24 POINT NEWS GOTHIC CONDENSED, ATF

ABCDEFGHIJKLMNOPQRSTUVWXYZ&abcdefghijklmnopqrstuvwxyz123456
7890$.,"-:;!?""''

18 POINT NEWS GOTHIC CONDENSED, ATF

157

ABCDEFGHIJKLMNOPQRSTUVW
XYZ&abcdefghijklmnopqrstuvw
xyz1234567890$., "-:;!?""''

72 POINT NEWS GOTHIC EXTRA CONDENSED, ATF

ABCDEFGHIJKLMNOPQRSTUVWXYZ&a
bcdefghijklmnopqrstuvwxyz1234567
890$., "-:;!?""''

60 POINT NEWS GOTHIC EXTRA CONDENSED, ATF

ABCDEFGHIJKLMNOPQRSTUVWXYZ&abcdefghij
klmnopqrstuvwxyz1234567890$., "-:;!?""''

48 POINT NEWS GOTHIC EXTRA CONDENSED, ATF

ABCDEFGHIJKLMNOPQRSTUVWXYZ&abcdefghijklmnop
qrstuvwxyz1234567890$., "-:;!?""''

42 POINT NEWS GOTHIC EXTRA CONDENSED, ATF

ABCDEFGHIJKLMNOPQRSTUVWXYZ&abcdefghijklmnopqrstuvwx
yz1234567890$.,''-.;!?''''

36 POINT NEWS GOTHIC EXTRA CONDENSED, ATF

ABCDEFGHIJKLMNOPQRSTUVWXYZ&abcdefghijklmnopqrstuvwxyz1234567890
$.,''-.;!?''''

30 POINT NEWS GOTHIC EXTRA CONDENSED, ATF

ABCDEFGHIJKLMNOPQRSTUVWXYZ&abcdefghijklmnopqrstuvwxyz1234567890$.,''-.;!?''''

24 POINT NEWS GOTHIC EXTRA CONDENSED, ATF

ABCDEFGHIJKLMNOPQRSTUVWXYZ&abcdefghijklmnopqrstuvwxyz1234567890$.,''-.;!?''''

18 POINT NEWS GOTHIC EXTRA CONDENSED, ATF

ABCDEFGHIJKLMNOPQRSTUVWXYZ&abcdefghijklmnopqrstuvwxyz1234567890$.,''-.;!?''''

14 POINT NEWS GOTHIC EXTRA CONDENSED, ATF

ABCDEFGHIJKLMNOPQRSTUVWXYZ&abcdefghijklmnopqrstuvwxyz1234567890$.,''-.;!?''''

12 POINT NEWS GOTHIC EXTRA CONDENSED, ATF

ABCDEFGHIJKLMNOPQRSTUVWXYZ&abcdefghijklmnopqrstuvwxyz1234567890$.,''-.;!?''''

10 POINT NEWS GOTHIC EXTRA CONDENSED, ATF

ABCDEFGHIJKLMNOPQRSTUVWXYZ&abcdefghijklmnopqrstuvwxyz1234567890$.,''-.;!?''''

8 POINT NEWS GOTHIC EXTRA CONDENSED, ATF

ABCDEFGHIJKLMNOPQRSTUVWXYZ&abcdefghijklmnopqrstuvwxyz1234567890.,''-.;!?''''

6 POINT NEWS GOTHIC EXTRA CONDENSED, ATF

ABCDEFGHIJKL
MNOPQRSTUVW
XYZ&abcdefghij
klmnopqrstuvwx
yz1234567890
$.,'"-:;!?""""

60 POINT NEWS GOTHIC BOLD, ATF

ABCDEFGHIJKLMNO
PQRSTUVWXYZ&abc
defghijklmnopqrstuv
wxyz1234567890$
.,'"-:;!?""""

48 POINT NEWS GOTHIC BOLD, ATF

ABCDEFGHIJKLMNOPQRSTUVWXYZ&abc defghijklmnopqrstuvwxyz1234567890$., ”-:;!?”"

24 POINT NEWS GOTHIC BOLD, ATF

Engraved tablet used as a printing block. Peking, China.

14/14

Besides the three principal proper-ties which we have mentioned, the fol-lowing (like Satellites to good letter) are not undeserving the purchaser's examination, who ought to take no-tice, 1. Whether the letter stands even, and in line; which is the chief good quality in letter, and makes the face thereof sometimes to pass, though otherwise ill-shaped. 2. Whether it *stands parallel; and whether it drives out or gets in, either at the head, or*

12/12

Besides the three principal properties which we have mentioned, the following (like Sat-ellites to good letter) are not undeserving the purchaser's examination, who ought to take notice, 1. Whether the letter stands even, and in line; which is the chief good quality in letter, and makes the face thereof sometimes to pass, though otherwise ill-shaped. 2. Whether it stands parallel; and whether it drives out or gets in, either at the head, or the foot, and is, as Printers call it, bottle-arsed; which is a fault that cannot be *mended but by rubbing the whole fount over again. 3. Whether the thin lower-case letter*

14/16

Besides the three principal proper-ties which we have mentioned, the fol-lowing (like Satellites to good letter) are not undeserving the purchaser's examination, who ought to take no-tice, 1. Whether the letter stands even, and in line; which is the chief good quality in letter, and makes the face *stands parallel; and whether it drives out or gets in, either at the head, or*

12/14

Besides the three principal properties which we have mentioned, the following (like Sat-ellites to good letter) are not undeserving the purchaser's examination, who ought to take notice, 1. Whether the letter stands even, and in line; which is the chief good quality in letter, and makes the face thereof sometimes to pass, though otherwise ill-shaped. 2. Whether it stands parallel; and *mended but by rubbing the whole fount over again. 3. Whether the thin lower-case letter*

14/18

Besides the three principal proper-ties which we have mentioned, the fol-lowing (like Satellites to good letter) are not undeserving the purchaser's examination, who ought to take no-tice, 1. Whether the letter stands even, and in line; which is the chief good *stands parallel; and whether it drives out or gets in, either at the head, or*

12/16

Besides the three principal properties which we have mentioned, the following (like Sat-ellites to good letter) are not undeserving the purchaser's examination, who ought to take notice, 1. Whether the letter stands even, and in line; which is the chief good quality in letter, and makes the face thereof sometimes to pass, though otherwise ill-*mended but by rubbing the whole fount over again. 3. Whether the thin lower-case letter*

ABCDEFGHIJKLMNOPQRSTUVWXY
ABCDEFGHIJKLMNOPQRSTUVWXY
&.,''-:;!?''''1234567890$
&.,''-:;!?''''1234567890$
abcdefghijklmnopqrstuvwxyz
abcdefghijklmnopqrstuvwxyz

ABCDEFGHIJKLMNOPQRSTUVWXYZ
ABCDEFGHIJKLMNOPQRSTUVWXYZ
&.,''-:;!?''''1234567890$
&.,''-:;!?''''1234567890$
abcdefghijklmnopqrstuvwxyz
abcdefghijklmnopqrstuvwxyz

NEWS GOTHIC BOLD: INTERTYPE

PICAS	6	7	8	9	10	11	12	13	14	15	16	17	18	19	20	21	22	23	24	25	26	27	28	29	30
14 POINT	11	13	15	17	19	20	22	24	26	28	30	31	33	35	37	39	41	43	44	46	48	50	52	54	56
12 POINT	13	15	18	20	22	24	26	29	31	33	35	37	40	42	44	46	48	51	53	55	57	59	62	64	66

11/11 Besides the three principal properties which we have mentioned, the following (like Satellites to good letter) are not undeserving the purchaser's examination, who ought to take notice, 1. Whether the letter stands even, and in line; which is the chief good quality in letter, and makes the face thereof sometimes to pass, though otherwise ill-shaped. 2. Whether it stands parallel; and whether it drives out or gets in, either at the head, or the foot, and is, as Printers call it, bottle-arsed; which is a fault that cannot be mended but by rubbing the whole fount over again. 3. Whether the thin lower-case letters, especially *the dots over the i and j, are come in casting. 4. Whether the break is ploughed away and*

10/10 Besides the three principal properties which we have mentioned, the following (like Satellites to good letter) are not undeserving the purchaser's examination, who ought to take notice, 1. Whether the letter stands even, and in line; which is the chief good quality in letter, and makes the face thereof sometimes to pass, though otherwise ill-shaped. 2. Whether it stands parallel; and whether it drives out or gets in, either at the head, or the foot, and is, as Printers call it, bottle-arsed; which is a fault that cannot be mended but by rubbing the whole fount over again. 3. Whether the thin lower-case letters, especially the dots over the i and j, are come in casting. 4. Whether the break is ploughed away and smoothened. 5. Whether it be well scraped, so as *not to want rubbing down by the compositor. 6. Whether each letter has a due proportion, as to*

11/13 Besides the three principal properties which we have mentioned, the following (like Satellites to good letter) are not undeserving the purchaser's examination, who ought to take notice, 1. Whether the letter stands even, and in line; which is the chief good quality in letter, and makes the face thereof sometimes to pass, though otherwise ill-shaped. 2. Whether it stands parallel; and whether it drives out or gets in, either at the head, or the foot, and is, as Printers call it, bottle-arsed; which is a fault that cannot be mended *but by rubbing the whole fount over again. 3. Whether the thin lower-case letters, especially*

10/12 Besides the three principal properties which we have mentioned, the following (like Satellites to good letter) are not undeserving the purchaser's examination, who ought to take notice, 1. Whether the letter stands even, and in line; which is the chief good quality in letter, and makes the face thereof sometimes to pass, though otherwise ill-shaped. 2. Whether it stands parallel; and whether it drives out or gets in, either at the head, or the foot, and is, as Printers call it, bottle-arsed; which is a fault that cannot be mended but by rubbing the whole fount over again. 3. Whether the thin lower-case letters, *not to want rubbing down by the compositor. 6. Whether each letter has a due proportion, as to*

11/15 Besides the three principal properties which we have mentioned, the following (like Satellites to good letter) are not undeserving the purchaser's examination, who ought to take notice, 1. Whether the letter stands even, and in line; which is the chief good quality in letter, and makes the face thereof sometimes to pass, though otherwise ill-shaped. 2. Whether it stands parallel; and whether it drives out or gets in, either at the *head, or the foot, and is, as Printers call it, bottle-arsed; which is a fault that cannot be mended*

10/14 Besides the three principal properties which we have mentioned, the following (like Satellites to good letter) are not undeserving the purchaser's examination, who ought to take notice, 1. Whether the letter stands even, and in line; which is the chief good quality in letter, and makes the face thereof sometimes to pass, though otherwise ill-shaped. 2. Whether it stands parallel; and whether it drives out or gets in, either at the head, or the foot, and is, as Printers call it, bottle-arsed; which is a fault that *not to want rubbing down by the compositor. 6. Whether each letter has a due proportion, as to*

ABCDEFGHIJKLMNOPQRSTUVWXYZ
ABCDEFGHIJKLMNOPQRSTUVWXYZ
&.,"-:;!?""''1234567890$
&.,"-:;!?""''1234567890$
abcdefghijklmnopqrstuvwxyz
abcdefghijklmnopqrstuvwxyz

ABCDEFGHIJKLMNOPQRSTUVWXYZ
ABCDEFGHIJKLMNOPQRSTUVWXYZ
&.,"-:;!?""''1234567890$
&.,"-:;!?""''1234567890$
abcdefghijklmnopqrstuvwxyz
abcdefghijklmnopqrstuvwxyz

NEWS GOTHIC BOLD: INTERTYPE

PICAS	6	7	8	9	10	11	12	13	14	15	16	17	18	19	20	21	22	23	24	25	26	27	28	29	30
11 POINT	15	17	20	22	25	27	29	32	34	37	39	42	44	47	49	51	54	56	59	61	64	66	69	71	74
10 POINT	16	18	21	23	26	29	31	34	36	39	42	44	47	49	52	55	57	60	62	65	68	70	73	75	78

9/9 Beside the three principal properties which we have mentioned, the following (like Satellites to good letter) are not undeserving the purchaser's examination, who ought to take notice, 1. Whether the letter stands even, and in line; which is the chief good quality in letter, and makes the face thereof sometimes to pass, though otherwise ill-shaped. 2. Whether it stands parallel; and whether it drives out or gets in, either at the head, or the foot, and is, as Printers call it, bottle-arsed; which is a fault that cannot be mended but by rubbing the whole fount over again. 3. Whether the thin lower-case letters, especially the dots over the i and j, are come in casting. 4. Whether the break is ploughed away and smoothened. 5. Whether it be well scraped, so as not to want rubbing down by the compositor. 6. Whether each letter has a due proportion, as to thickness; and whether they are not so thin as to hinder each other from appearing with *a full face; or so thick as to occasion a gap between letter and letter. 7. Whether it be well bearded: which*

8/8 Besides the three principal properties which we have mentioned, the following (like Satellites to good letter) are not undeserving the purchaser's examination, who ought to take notice, 1. Whether the letter stands even, and in line; which is the chief good quality in letter, and makes the face thereof sometimes to pass, though otherwise ill-shaped. 2. Whether it stands parallel; and whether it drives out or gets in, either at the head, or the foot, and is, as Printers call it, bottle-arsed; which is a fault that cannot be mended but by rubbing the whole fount over again. 3. Whether the thin lower-case letters, especially the dots over the i and j, are come in casting. 4. Whether the break is ploughed away and smoothened. 5. Whether it be well scraped, so as not to want rubbing down by the compositor. 6. Whether each letter has a due proportion, as to thickness; and whether they are not so thin as to hinder each other from appearing with a full face; or so thick as to occasion a gap between letter and letter. 7. Whether it be well bearded: which founders in France are obliged to do, to their own disadvantage, on ac*count of their shallow letter. 8. Whether it have a deep and open, single or double nick, different from other founts of*

9/11 Beside the three principal properties which we have mentioned, the following (like Satellites to good letter) are not undeserving the purchaser's examination, who ought to take notice, 1. Whether the letter stands even, and in line; which is the chief good quality in letter, and makes the face thereof sometimes to pass, though otherwise ill-shaped. 2. Whether it stands parallel; and whether it drives out or gets in, either at the head, or the foot, and is, as Printers call it, bottle-arsed; which is a fault that cannot be mended but by rubbing the whole fount over again. 3. Whether the thin lower-case letters, especially the dots over the i and j, are come in casting. 4. Whether the break is ploughed away and smoothened. *5. Whether it will be scraped, so as not to want rubbing down by the compositor. 6. Whether each letter has a*

8/10 Besides the three principal properties which we have mentioned, the following (like Satellites to good letter) are not undeserving the purchaser's examination, who ought to take notice, 1. Whether the letter stands even, and in line; which is the chief good quality in letter, and makes the face thereof sometimes to pass, though otherwise ill-shaped. 2. Whether it stands parallel; and whether it drives out or gets in, either at the head, or the foot, and is, as Printers call it, bottle-arsed; which is a fault that cannot be mended but by rubbing the whole fount over again. 3. Whether the thin lower-case letters, especially the dots over the i and j, are come in casting. 4. Whether the break is ploughed away and smoothened. 5. Whether it be well scraped, so as not to want rubbing down by the compositor. 6. Whether each letter has a due proportion, as to thickness; and whether they *count of their shallow letter. 8. Whether it have a deep and open, single or double nick, different from other founts of*

9/13 Beside the three principal properties which we have mentioned, the following (like Satellites to good letter) are not undeserving the purchaser's examination, who ought to take notice, 1. Whether the letter stands even, and in line; which is the chief good quality in letter, and makes the face thereof sometimes to pass, though otherwise ill-shaped. 2. Whether it stands parallel; and whether it drives out or gets in, either at the head, or the foot, and is, as Printers call it, bottle-arsed; which is a fault that cannot be mended but by rubbing the whole fount over again. 3. Whether the thin lower-case letters, *especially the dots over the i and j, are come in casting. 4. Whether the break is ploughed away and smoothened.*

8/12 Besides the three principal properties which we have mentioned, the following (like Satellites to good letter) are not undeserving the purchaser's examination, who ought to take notice, 1. Whether the letter stands even, and in line; which is the chief good quality in letter, and makes the face thereof sometimes to pass, though otherwise ill-shaped. 2. Whether it stands parallel; and whether it drives out or gets in, either at the head, or the foot, and is, as Printers call it, bottle-arsed; which is a fault that cannot be mended but by rubbing the whole fount over again. 3. Whether the thin lower-case letters, especially the dots over the i and j, are come in casting. 4. Whether the break is ploughed away *count of their shallow letter. 8. Whether it have a deep and open, single or double nick, different from other founts of*

ABCDEFGHIJKLMNOPQRSTUVWXYZ
ABCDEFGHIJKLMNOPQRSTUVWXYZ
&.,.:;!?'' 1234567890$
&.,''-:;!?''''1234567890$
abcdefghijklmnopqrstuvwxyz
abcdefghijklmnopqrstuvwxyz

ABCDEFGHIJKLMNOPQRSTUVWXYZ
ABCDEFGHIJKLMNOPQRSTUVWXYZ
&.,''-:;!?''''1234567890$
&.,''-:;!?''''1234567890$
abcdefghijklmnopqrstuvwxyz
abcdefghijklmnopqrstuvwxyz

NEWS GOTHIC BOLD: INTERTYPE

PICAS	6	7	8	9	10	11	12	13	14	15	16	17	18	19	20	21	22	23	24	25	26	27	28	29	30
9 POINT	17	20	23	26	29	31	34	37	40	43	46	48	51	54	57	60	63	66	68	71	74	77	80	83	86
8 POINT	18	21	24	27	30	33	36	39	42	45	48	51	54	57	60	63	66	69	72	75	78	81	84	87	90

7/7

Besides the three principal properties which we have mentioned, the following (like Satellites to good letter) are not undeserving the purchaser's examination, who ought to take notice, 1. Whether the letter stands even, and in line; which is the chief good quality in letter, and makes the face thereof sometimes to pass, though otherwise ill-shaped. 2. Whether it stands parallel; and whether it drives out or gets in, either at the head, or the foot, and is, as Printers call it, bottle-arsed; which is a fault that cannot be mended but by rubbing the whole fount over again. 3. Whether the thin lower-case letters, especially the dots over the i and j, are come in casting. 4. Whether the break is ploughed away and smoothened. 5. Whether it be well scraped, so as not to want rubbing down by the compositor. 6. Whether each letter has a due proportion, as to thickness; and whether they are not so thin as to hinder each other from appearing with a full face; or so thick as to occasion a gap between letter and letter. 7. Whether it be well bearded: which founders in France are obliged to do, to their own disadvantage, on account of their shallow letter. 8. Whether it have a deep and open, single or double nick, different from other founts of the same body, and in the same printing-house.

We cannot too strongly urge the advantage to be derived from letter having a deep nick, and also that the nick should differ from *other founts of that body in the same house. This may appear a trifling consideration; but in a large fount the difference in weight*

6/6

Besides the three principal properties which we have mentioned, the following (like Satellites to good letter) are not undeserving the purchaser's examination, who ought to take notice, 1. Whether the letter stands even, and in line; which is the chief good quality in letter, and makes the face thereof sometimes to pass, through otherwise ill-shaped. 2. Whether it stands parallel; and whether it drives out or gets in, either at the head, or the foot, and is, as Printers call it, bottle-arsed; which is a fault that cannot be mended but by rubbing the whole fount over again. 3. Whether the thin lower-case letters, especially the dots over the i and j, are come in casting. 4. Whether the break is ploughed away and smoothened. 5. Whether it be well scraped, so as not to want rubbing down by the compositor. 6. Whether each letter has a due proportion, as to thickness; and whether they are not so thin as to hinder each other from appearing with a full face; or so thick as to occasion a gap between letter and letter. 7. Whether it be well bearded: which founders in France are obliged to do, to their own disadvantage, on account of their shallow letter. 8. Whether it have a deep and open, single or double nick, different from other founts of the same body, and in the same printing-house.

We cannot too strongly urge the advantage to be derived from letter having a deep nick, and also that the nick should differ from other founts of that body in the same house. This may appear a trifling consideration; but in a large fount the difference in weight will be considerable, and consequently a saving to the purchaser. A deep nick is an advantage to the compositor, from its more readily *catching the eye than a shallow one, and consequently greatly facilitates him in his business.*

7/9

Besides the three principal properties which we have mentioned, the following (like Satellites to good letter) are not undeserving the purchaser's examination, who ought to take notice, 1. Whether the letter stands even, and in line; which is the chief good quality in letter, and makes the face thereof sometimes to pass, though otherwise ill-shaped. 2. Whether it stands parallel; and whether it drives out or gets in, either at the head, or the foot, and is, as Printers call it, bottle-arsed; which is a fault that cannot be mended but by rubbing the whole fount over again. 3. Whether the thin lower-case letters, especially the dots over the i and j, are come in casting. 4. Whether the break is ploughed away and smoothened. 5. Whether it be well scraped, so as not to want rubbing down by the compositor. 6. Whether each letter has a due proportion, as to thickness; and whether they are not so thin as to hinder each other from appearing with a full face; or so thick as to occasion a gap between letter and letter. 7. Whether it be well bearded: which founders in France are obliged to do, to their own disadvantage, on *account of their shallow letter. 8. Whether it have a deep and open, single or double nick, different from other founts of the same body,*

6/8

Besides the three principal properties which we have mentioned, the following (like Satellites to good letter) are not undeserving the purchaser's examination, who ought to take notice, 1. Whether the letter stands even, and in line; which is the chief good quality in letter, and makes the face thereof sometimes to pass, through otherwise ill-shaped. 2. Whether it stands parallel; and whether it drives out or gets in, either at the head, or the foot, and is, as Printers call it, bottle-arsed; which is a fault that cannot be mended but by rubbing the whole fount over again. 3. Whether the thin lower-case letters, especially the dots over the i and j, are come in casting. 4. Whether the break is ploughed away and smoothened. 5. Whether it be well scraped, so as not to want rubbing down by the compositor. 6. Whether each letter has a due proportion, as to thickness; and whether they are not so thin as to hinder each other from appearing with a full face; or so thick as to occasion a gap between letter and letter. 7. Whether it be well bearded: which founders in France are obliged to do, to their own disadvantage, on account of their shallow letter. 8. Whether it have a deep and open, single or double nick, different from other founts of the same body, and in *catching the eye than a shallow one, and consequently greatly facilitates him in his business.*

7/11

Besides the three principal properties which we have mentioned, the following (like Satellites to good letter) are not undeserving the purchaser's examination, who ought to take notice, 1. Whether the letter stands even, and in line; which is the chief good quality in letter, and makes the face thereof sometimes to pass, though otherwise ill-shaped. 2. Whether it stands parallel; and whether it drives out or gets in, either at the head, or the foot, and is, as Printers call it, bottle-arsed; which is a fault that cannot be mended but by rubbing the whole fount over again. 3. Whether the thin lower-case letters, especially the dots over the i and j, are come in casting. 4. Whether the break is ploughed away and smoothened. 5. Whether it be well scraped, so as not to want rubbing down by the compositor. 6. Whether each letter has a due proportion, as to *thickness; and whether they are not so thin as to hinder each other from appearing with a full face; or so thick as to occasion a gap*

6/10

Besides the three principal properties which we have mentioned, the following (like Satellites to good letter) are not undeserving the purchaser's examination, who ought to take notice, 1. Whether the letter stands even, and in line; which is the chief good quality in letter, and makes the face thereof sometimes to pass, through otherwise ill-shaped. 2. Whether it stands parallel; and whether it drives out or gets in, either at the head, or the foot, and is, as Printers call it, bottle-arsed; which is a fault that cannot be mended but by rubbing the whole fount over again. 3. Whether the thin lower-case letters, especially the dots over the i and j, are come in casting. 4. Whether the break is ploughed away and smoothened. 5. Whether it be well scraped, so as not to want rubbing down by the compositor. 6. Whether each letter has a due proportion, as to thickness; and whether they are not so thin as to hinder each other from appearing with a full face; or so thick as to occasion a gap between *catching the eye than a shallow one, and consequently greatly facilitates him in his business.*

ABCDEFGHIJKLMNOPQRSTUVWXYZ
ABCDEFGHIJKLMNOPQRSTUVWXYZ
&.,"'-:;!?''""1234567890$
&.,"'-:;!?''""1234567890$
abcdefghijklmnopqrstuvwxyz
abcdefghijklmnopqrstuvwxyz

ABCDEFGHIJKLMNOPQRSTUVWXYZ
ABCDEFGHIJKLMNOPQRSTUVWXYZ
&.,"'-:;!?''""1234567890$
&.,"'-:;!?''""1234567890$
abcdefghijklmnopqrstuvwxyz
abcdefghijklmnopqrstuvwxyz

NEWS GOTHIC BOLD: INTERTYPE

PICAS	6	7	8	9	10	11	12	13	14	15	16	17	18	19	20	21	22	23	24	25	26	27	28	29	30
7 POINT	18	22	26	29	32	35	38	42	45	48	50	54	58	61	64	67	70	74	77	80	82	86	90	93	96
6 POINT	21	25	28	32	35	39	42	46	49	53	56	60	63	67	70	74	77	81	84	88	91	95	98	102	105

STANDARD, AMSTERDAM CONTINENTAL

BICYCLE name

VENUS MEDIUM, BAUER

ANTHOLOGY scheme

UNIVERS 55, ATF

ABCDEF abcdefgh

RECORD GOTHIC, LUDLOW

METHODS production

All comparisons are made on 24 point type.

ABCDEFGHIJK
LMNOPQRSTU
VWXYZ&abcd
efghijklmnopq
rstuvwxyz123
4567890$.,"-:;!
?"""

72 POINT STANDARD MEDIUM, AMSTERDAM CONTINENTAL

ABCDEFGHIJKLM
NOPQRSTUVWXY
Z&abcdefghijklmn
opqrstuvwxyz123
4567890$.,"-:;!?""""

60 POINT STANDARD MEDIUM, AMSTERDAM CONTINENTAL

ABCDEFGHIJKLMNOPQ
RSTUVWXYZ&abcdefgh
ijklmnopqrstuvwxyz1234
567890$.,"-:;!?""""

42 POINT STANDARD MEDIUM, AMSTERDAM CONTINENTAL

ABCDEFGHIJKLMNOPQRSTUV
WXYZ&abcdefghijklmnopqrstu
vwxyz1234567890$.,"-:;!?""""

30 POINT STANDARD MEDIUM, AMSTERDAM CONTINENTAL

ABCDEFGHIJKLMNOPQRSTUVWXY
Z&abcdefghijklmnopqrstuvwxyz1234
567890$.,"-:;!?""

24 POINT (large) STANDARD MEDIUM, AMSTERDAM CONTINENTAL

ABCDEFGHIJKLMNOPQRSTUVWXYZ&abcde
fghijklmnopqrstuvwxyz1234567890$.,"-:;!?""

24 POINT (small) STANDARD MEDIUM, AMSTERDAM CONTINENTAL

ABCDEFGHIJKLMNOPQRSTUVWXYZ&abcdefghijklmno
pqrstuvwxyz1234567890$.,"-:;!?""

18 POINT STANDARD MEDIUM, AMSTERDAM CONTINENTAL

ABCDEFGHIJKLMNOPQRSTUVWXYZ&abcdefghijklmnopqrstuvwxyz1234
567890$.,"-:;!?""

14 POINT STANDARD MEDIUM, AMSTERDAM CONTINENTAL

*ABCDEFGHIJKLMNO
PQRSTUVWXYZ&ab
cdefghijklmnopqrstuv
wxyz1234567890$.,"-:
;!?""*

42 POINT STANDARD MEDIUM ITALIC, AMSTERDAM CONTINENTAL

*ABCDEFGHIJKLMNOPQRSTUVWXY
Z&abcdefghijklmnopqrstuvwxyz123456
7890$.,"-:;!?""*

24 POINT (small) STANDARD MEDIUM ITALIC, AMSTERDAM CONTINENTAL

*ABCDEFGHIJKLMNOPQRSTUVWXYZ&abcdefghijklmnopqrstuvwxyz1234567890$
.,"-:;!?""*

12 POINT STANDARD MEDIUM ITALIC, AMSTERDAM CONTINENTAL

10/10

OBSERVATONS ON COMPOSING. Although this essential point has been passed over with little notice by most writers upon this subject, still (so great are the evils resulting from ill-contracted habits, which naturally keep pace with our growth), we cannot avoid pointing out a few instances of the sure consequences attendant on them. There are many persons now employed in the art, who frequently, with great justice, inveigh in strong terms against the conduct of those unto whose care they were first entrusted, for suffering them to contract those ill-becoming postures which are productive of knock knees, round shoulders, and other deformities. It is deeply to be regretted, that those who undertake so important a

9/9

OBSERVATIONS ON COMPOSING. Although this essential point has been passed over with little notice by most writers upon this subject, still (so great are the evils resulting from ill-contracted habits, which naturally keep pace with our growth), we cannot avoid pointing out a few instances of the sure consequences attendant on them. There are many persons now employed in the art, who frequently, with great justice, inveigh in strong terms against the conduct of those unto whose care they were first entrusted, for suffering them to contract those ill-becoming postures which are productive of knock knees, round shoulders, and other deformities. It is deeply to be regretted, that those who undertake so important a charge, are not better qualified to fulfil that duty: instead of suffering the tender shoot to grow wild and uncultivated, when the pruning-knife, in a gentle hand, with a little admo-

10/12

OBSERVATONS ON COMPOSING. Although this essential point has been passed over with little notice by most writers upon this subject, still (so great are the evils resulting from ill-contracted habits, which naturally keep pace with our growth), we cannot avoid pointing out a few instances of the sure consequences attendant on them. There are many persons now employed in the art, who frequently, with great justice, inveigh in strong terms against the conduct of those unto whose care they were first entrusted, for suffering them to contract those ill-becoming postures which are productive of knock knees, round shoul-

9/11

OBSERVATIONS ON COMPOSING. Although this essential point has been passed over with little notice by most writers upon this subject, still (so great are the evils resulting from ill-contracted habits, which naturally keep pace with our growth), we cannot avoid pointing out a few instances of the sure consequences attendant on them. There are many persons now employed in the art, who frequently, with great justice, inveigh in strong terms against the conduct of those unto whose care they were first entrusted, for suffering them to contract those ill-becoming postures which are productive of knock knees, round shoulders, and other deformities. It is deeply to be regretted, that those who undertake so important a charge, are not

10/14

OBSERVATONS ON COMPOSING. Although this essential point has been passed over with little notice by most writers upon this subject, still (so great are the evils resulting from ill-contracted habits, which naturally keep pace with our growth), we cannot avoid pointing out a few instances of the sure consequences attendant on them. There are many persons now employed in the art, who frequently, with great justice, inveigh in strong terms against the conduct of those unto whose care they were first entrusted, for suffer-

9/13

OBSERVATIONS ON COMPOSING. Although this essential point has been passed over with little notice by most writers upon this subject, still (so great are the evils resulting from ill-contracted habits, which naturally keep pace with our growth), we cannot avoid pointing out a few instances of the sure consequences attendant on them. There are many persons now employed in the art, who frequently, with great justice, inveigh in strong terms against the conduct of those unto whose care they were first entrusted, for suffering them to contract those ill-becoming postures which are productive of knock knees, round shoulders, and

ABCDEFGHIJKLMNOPQRSTUVWXYZ
&.,"-:;!?""1234567890$
abcdefghijklmnopqrstuvwxyz

ABCDEFGHIJKLMNOPQRSTUVWXYZ
&.,"-:;!?""1234567890$
abcdefghijklmnopqrstuvwxyz

AKZIDENZ GROTESK, MEDIUM: LINOTYPE

PICAS	6	7	8	9	10	11	12	13	14	15	16	17	18	19	20	21	22	23	24	25	26	27	28	29	30
10 POINT	14	16	18	21	23	25	28	30	32	35	37	40	43	46	48	51	53	55	58	60	64	67	69	71	73
9 POINT	15	18	20	23	25	28	30	33	35	38	40	43	45	48	50	53	55	58	60	63	65	68	70	73	75

8/8

OBSERVATIONS ON COMPOSING. Although this essential point has been passed over with little notice by most writers upon this subject, still (so great are the evils resulting from ill-contracted habits, which naturally keep pace with our growth), we cannot avoid pointing out a few instances of the sure consequences attendant on them. There are many persons now employed in the art, who frequently, with great justice, inveigh in strong terms against the conduct of those unto whose care they were first entrusted, for suffering them to contract those ill-becoming postures which are productive of knock knees, round shoulders, and other deformities. It is deeply to be regretted, that those who undertake so important a charge, are not better qualified to fulfil that duty: instead of suffering the tender shoot to grow wild and uncultivated, when the pruning-knife, in a gentle hand, with a little admonition, would have checked its improper growth, and trained it in a right course.

What to a learner may appear fatiguing, time and habit

6/6

OBSERVATIONS ON COMPOSING. Although this essential point has been passed over with little notice by most writers upon this subject, still (so great are the evils resulting from ill-contracted habits, which naturally keep pace with our growth), we cannot avoid pointing out a few instances of the sure consequences attendant on them. There are many persons now employed·in the art, who frequently, with great justice, inveigh in strong terms against the conduct of those unto whose care they were first entrusted, for suffering them to contract those ill-becoming postures which are productive of knock knees, round shoulders, and other deformities. It is deeply to be regretted, that those who undertake so important a charge, are not better qualified to fulfil that duty: instead of suffering the tender shoot to grow wild and uncultivated, when the pruning-knife, in a gentle hand, with a little admonition, would have checked its improper growth, and trained it in a right course.

What to a learner may appear fatiguing, time and habit will render easy and familiar; and though to work with his cases on a level with his breast, may at first tire his arms, yet use will so inure him to it, that it will become afterwards equally unpleasant to work at a low frame. His perseverance in this mode must be strengthened by the reflection, that it will most effectually prevent his becoming round shouldered, a distinguishing mark by which compositors are in general known, especially if they are above the common stature. This method will likewise keep the body in an erect position, and prevent those effects which result from pressure on the stomach.

8/10

OBSERVATIONS ON COMPOSING. Although this essential point has been passed over with little notice by most writers upon this subject, still (so great are the evils resulting from ill-contracted habits, which naturally keep pace with our growth), we cannot avoid pointing out a few instances of the sure consequences attendant on them. There are many persons now employed in the art, who frequently, with great justice, inveigh in strong terms against the conduct of those unto whose care they were first entrusted, for suffering them to contract those ill-becoming postures which are productive of knock knees, round shoulders, and other deformities. It is deeply to be regretted, that those who undertake so important a charge, are not better qualified to fulfil that duty: instead of suffering the tender shoot to grow wild and uncultivated,

6/8

OBSERVATIONS ON COMPOSING. Although this essential point has been passed over with little notice by most writers upon this subject, still (so great are the evils resulting from ,ill-contracted habits, which naturally keep pace with our growth), we cannot avoid pointing out a few instances of the sure consequences attendant on them. There are many persons now employed in the art, who frequently, with great justice, inveigh in strong terms against the conduct of those unto whose care they were first entrusted, for suffering them to contract those ill-becoming postures which are productive of knock knees, round shoulders, and other deformities. It is deeply to be regretted, that those who undertake so important a charge, are not better qualified to fulfil that duty: instead of suffering the tender shoot to grow wild and uncultivated, when the pruning-knife, in a gentle hand, with a little admonition, would have checked its improper growth, and trained it in a right course.

What to a learner may appear fatiguing, time and habit will render easy and familiar; and though to work with his cases on a level with his breast, may at first tire his arms, yet use will so inure him to it, that it will become afterwards equally unpleasant to work at a low frame. His perseverance in this mode must be strengthened by the reflection, that it will

8/12

OBSERVATIONS ON COMPOSING. Although this essential point has been passed over with little notice by most writers upon this subject, still (so great are the evils resulting from ill-contracted habits, which naturally keep pace with our growth), we cannot avoid pointing out a few instances of the sure consequences attendant on them. There are many persons now employed in the art, who frequently, with great justice, inveigh in strong terms against the conduct of those unto whose care they were first entrusted, for suffering them to contract those ill-becoming postures which are productive of knock knees, round shoulders, and other deformities. It is deeply to be regretted, that those who undertake so important a charge,

6/10

OBSERVATIONS ON COMPOSING. Although this essential point has been passed over with little notice by most writers upon this subject, still (so great are the evils resulting from ill-contracted habits, which naturally keep pace with our growth), we cannot avoid pointing out a few instances of the sure consequences attendant on them. There are many persons now employed in the art, who frequently, with great justice, inveigh in strong terms against the conduct of those unto whose care they were first entrusted, for suffering them to contract those ill-becoming postures which are productive of knock knees, round shoulders, and other deformities. It is deeply to be regretted, that those who undertake so important a charge, are not better qualified to fulfil that duty: instead of suffering the tender shoot to grow wild and uncultivated, when the pruning-knife, in a gentle hand, with a little admonition, would have checked its improper growth, and trained it in a right course.

What to a learner may appear fatiguing, time and habit will render easy and familiar; and though to work with his cases on a level with his breast,

ABCDEFGHIJKLMNOPQRSTUVWXYZ
&.,''-:;!?''''"1234567890$
abcdefghijklmnopqrstuvwxyz

ABCDEFGHIJKLMNOPQRSTUVWXYZ
&.,''-:;!?''''"1234567890$
abcdefghijklmnopqrstuvwxyz

AKZIDENZ GROTESK, MEDIUM LINOTYPE

PICAS	6	7	8	9	10	11	12	13	14	15	16	17	18	19	20	21	22	23	24	25	26	27	28	29	30
8 POINT	16	19	22	24	27	30	32	35	38	41	43	46	49	51	54	57	59	62	65	68	70	73	76	78	81
6 POINT	21	25	28	32	35	39	42	46	49	53	56	60	63	67	70	74	77	81	84	88	91	95	98	102	105

ABCDEFGHIJKLMN
OPQRSTUVWXYZ&
abcdefghijklmnopqrstu
vwxyz1234567980$.,
"-:;!?""''

48 POINT STANDARD REGULAR, AMSTERDAM CONTINENTAL

ABCDEFGHIJKLMNOPQR
STUVWXYZ&abcdefghijklmn
opqrstuvwxyz1234567890$.,
"-:;!?""''

36 POINT STANDARD REGULAR, AMSTERDAM CONTINENTAL

ABCDEFGHIJKLMNOPQRSTUVW
XYZ&abcdefghijklmnopqrstuvwxyz12
34567890$.,"-:;!?""''

30 POINT STANDARD REGULAR, AMSTERDAM CONTINENTAL

ABCDEFGHIJKLMNOPQRSTUVWXYZ&
abcdefghijklmnopqrstuvwxyz1234567890
$.,"-:;!?""''

24 POINT (large) STANDARD REGULAR, AMSTERDAM CONTINENTAL

ABCDEFGHIJKLMNOPQRSTUVWXYZ&abcdefghij
klmnopqrstuvwxyz1234567890$.,"-:;!?""''

24 POINT (small) STANDARD REGULAR, AMSTERDAM CONTINENTAL

ABCDEFGHIJKLMNOPQRSTUVWXYZ&abcdefghijklmnopq
rstuvwxyz1234567890$.,"-:;!?""''

18 POINT STANDARD REGULAR, AMSTERDAM CONTINENTAL

ABCDEFGHIJKLMNOPQRSTUVWXYZ&abcdefghijklmnopqrstuvwxyz123456
7890$.,"-:;!?""''

14 POINT STANDARD REGULAR, AMSTERDAM CONTINENTAL

ABCDEFGHIJKLMNOPQR
STUVWXYZ&abcdefghijkl
mnopqrstuvwxyz123456789
0$.,"-:;!?""''

36 POINT STANDARD REGULAR ITALIC, AMSTERDAM CONTINENTAL

ABCDEFGHIJKLMNOPQRSTUVWXYZ&abcdefg
hijklmnopqrstuvwxyz1234567890$.,"-:;!?""''

24 POINT (small) STANDARD REGULAR ITALIC, AMSTERDAM CONTINENTAL

ABCDEFGHIJKLMNOPQRSTUVWXYZ&abcdefghijklmnopqrstuvwxyz1234567890$.,"-:;!?""''

12 POINT STANDARD REGULAR ITALIC, AMSTERDAM CONTINENTAL.

10/10 OBSERVATONS ON COMPOSING. Although this essential point has been passed over with little notice by most writers upon this subject, still (so great are the evils resulting from ill-contracted habits, which naturally keep pace with our growth), we cannot avoid pointing out a few instances of the sure consequences attendant on them. There are many persons now employed in the art, who frequently, with great justice, inveigh in strong terms against the conduct of those unto whose care they were first entrusted, for suffering them to contract those ill-becoming postures which are productive of knock knees, round shoulders, and other deformities. It is deeply to be regretted, that those who undertake so important a

9/9 OBSERVATIONS ON COMPOSING. Although this essential point has been passed over with little notice by most writers upon this subject, still (so great are the evils resulting from ill-contracted habits, which naturally keep pace with our growth), we cannot avoid pointing out a few instances of the sure consequences attendant on them. There are many persons now employed in the art, who frequently, with great justice, inveigh in strong terms against the conduct of those unto whose care they were first entrusted, for suffering them to contract those ill-becoming postures which are productive of knock knees, round shoulders, and other deformities. It is deeply to be regretted, that those who undertake so important a charge, are not better qualified to fulfil that duty: instead of suffering the tender shoot to grow wild and uncultivated, when the pruning-knife, in a gentle hand, with a little admo-

10/12 OBSERVATONS ON COMPOSING. Although this essential point has been passed over with little notice by most writers upon this subject, still (so great are the evils resulting from ill-contracted habits, which naturally keep pace with our growth), we cannot avoid pointing out a few instances of the sure consequences attendant on them. There are many persons now employed in the art, who frequently, with great justice, inveigh in strong terms against the conduct of those unto whose care they were first entrusted, for suffering them to contract those ill-becoming postures which are productive of knock knees, round shoul-

9/11 OBSERVATIONS ON COMPOSING. Although this essential point has been passed over with little notice by most writers upon this subject, still (so great are the evils resulting from ill-contracted habits, which naturally keep pace with our growth), we cannot avoid pointing out a few instances of the sure consequences attendant on them. There are many persons now employed in the art, who frequently, with great justice, inveigh in strong terms against the conduct of those unto whose care they were first entrusted, for suffering them to contract those ill-becoming postures which are productive of knock knees, round shoulders, and other deformities. It is deeply to be regretted, that those who undertake so important a charge, are not

10/14 OBSERVATONS ON COMPOSING. Although this essential point has been passed over with little notice by most writers upon this subject, still (so great are the evils resulting from ill-contracted habits, which naturally keep pace with our growth), we cannot avoid pointing out a few instances of the sure consequences attendant on them. There are many persons now employed in the art, who frequently, with great justice, inveigh in strong terms against the conduct of those unto whose care they were first entrusted, for suffer-

9/13 OBSERVATIONS ON COMPOSING. Although this essential point has been passed over with little notice by most writers upon this subject, still (so great are the evils resulting from ill-contracted habits, which naturally keep pace with our growth), we cannot avoid pointing out a few instances of the sure consequences attendant on them. There are many persons now employed in the art, who frequently, with great justice, inveigh in strong terms against the conduct of those unto whose care they were first entrusted, for suffering them to contract those ill-becoming postures which are productive of knock knees, round shoulders, and

ABCDEFGHIJKLMNOPQRSTUVWXYZ
&.,'‘-:;!?’''“1234567890$
abcdefghijklmnopqrstuvwxyz

ABCDEFGHIJKLMNOPQRSTUVWXYZ
&.,'‘-:;!?’''“1234567890$
abcdefghijklmnopqrstuvwxyz

AKZIDENZ GROTESK, REGULAR: LINOTYPE

	PICAS	6	7	8	9	10	11	12	13	14	15	16	17	18	19	20	21	22	23	24	25	26	27	28	29	30
10 POINT		14	16	18	21	23	25	28	30	32	35	37	40	43	46	48	51	53	55	58	60	64	67	69	71	73
9 POINT		15	18	20	23	25	28	30	33	35	38	40	43	45	48	50	53	55	58	60	63	65	68	70	73	75

8/8

OBSERVATIONS ON COMPOSING. Although this essential point has been passed over with little notice by most writers upon this subject, still (so great are the evils resulting from ill-contracted habits, which naturally keep pace with our growth), we cannot avoid pointing out a few instances of the sure consequences attendant on them. There are many persons now employed in the art, who frequently, with great justice, inveigh in strong terms against the conduct of those unto whose care they were first entrusted, for suffering them to contract those ill-becoming postures which are productive of knock knees, round shoulders, and other deformities. It is deeply to be regretted, that those who undertake so important a charge, are not better qualified to fulfil that duty: instead of suffering the tender shoot to grow wild and uncultivated, when the pruning-knife, in a gentle hand, with a little admonition, would have checked its improper growth, and trained it in a right course.

What to a learner may appear fatiguing, time and habit

6/6

OBSERVATIONS ON COMPOSING. Although this essential point has been passed over with little notice by most writers upon this subject, still (so great are the evils resulting from ill-contracted habits, which naturally keep pace with our growth), we cannot avoid pointing out a few instances of the sure consequences attendant on them. There are many persons now employed in the art, who frequently, with great justice, inveigh in strong terms against the conduct of those unto whose care they were first entrusted, for suffering them to contract those ill-becoming postures which are productive of knock knees, round shoulders, and other deformities. It is deeply to be regretted, that those who undertake so important a charge, are not better qualified to fulfil that duty: instead of suffering the tender shoot to grow wild and uncultivated, when the pruning-knife, in a gentle hand, with a little admonition, would have checked its improper growth, and trained it in a right course.

What to a learner may appear fatiguing, time and habit will render easy and familiar; and though to work with his cases on a level with his breast, may at first tire his arms, yet use will so inure him to it, that it will become afterwards equally unpleasant to work at a low frame. His perseverance in this mode must be strengthened by the reflection, that it will most effactually prevent his becoming round shouldered, a distinguishing mark by which compositors are in general known, especially if they are above the common stature. This method will likewise keep the body in an erect position, and prevent those effects which result from pressure on the stomach.

8/10

OBSERVATIONS ON COMPOSING. Although this essential point has been passed over with little notice by most writers upon this subject, still (so great are the evils resulting from ill-contracted habits, which naturally keep pace with our growth), we cannot avoid pointing out a few instances of the sure·consequences attendant on them. There are many persons now employed in the art, who frequently, with great justice, inveigh in strong terms against the conduct of those unto whose care they were first entrusted, for suffering them to contract those ill-becoming postures which are productive of knock knees, round shoulders, and other deformities. It is deeply to be regretted, that those who undertake so important a charge, are not better qualified to fulfil that duty: instead of suffering the tender shoot to grow wild and uncultivated,

6/8

OBSERVATIONS ON COMPOSING. Although this essential point has been passed over with little notice by most writers upon this subject, still (so great are the evils resulting from ill-contracted habits, which naturally keep pace with our growth), we cannot avoid pointing out a few instances of the sure consequences attendant on them. There are many persons now employed in the art, who frequently, with great justice, inveigh in strong terms against the conduct of those unto whose care they were first entrusted, for suffering them to contract those ill-becoming postures which are productive of knock knees, round shoulders, and other deformities. It is deeply to be regretted, that those who undertake so important a charge, are not better qualified to fulfil that duty: instead of suffering the tender shoot to grow wild and uncultivated, when the pruning-knife, in a gentle hand, with a little admonition, would have checked its improper growth, and trained it in a right course.

What to a learner may appear fatiguing, time and habit will render easy and familiar; and though to work with his cases on a level with his breast, may at first tire his arms, yet use will so inure him to it, that it will become afterwards equally unpleasant to work at a low frame. His perseverance in this mode must be strengthened by the reflection, that it will

3/12

OBSERVATIONS ON COMPOSING. Although this essential point has been passed over with little notice by most writers upon this subject, still (so great are the evils resulting from ill-contracted habits, which naturally keep pace with our growth), we cannot avoid pointing out a few instances of the sure consequences attendant on them. There are many persons now employed in the art, who frequently, with great justice, inveigh in strong terms against the conduct of those unto whose care they were first entrusted, for suffering them to contract those ill-becoming postures which are productive of knock knees, round shoulders, and other deformities. It is deeply to be regretted, that those who undertake so important a charge,

6/10

OBSERVATIONS ON COMPOSING. Although this essential point has been passed over with little notice by most writers upon this subject, still (so great are the evils resulting from ill-contracted habits, which naturally keep pace with our growth), we cannot avoid pointing out a few instances of the sure consequences attendant on them. There are many persons now employed in the art, who frequently, with great justice, inveigh in strong terms against the conduct of those unto whose care they were first entrusted, for suffering them to contract those ill-becoming postures which are productive of knock knees, round shoulders, and other deformities. It is deeply to be regretted, that those who undertake so important a charge, are not better qualified to fulfil that duty: instead of suffering the tender shoot to grow wild and uncultivated, when the pruning-knife, in a gentle hand, with a little admonition, would have checked its improper growth, and trained it in a right course.

What to a learner may appear fatiguing, time and habit will render easy and familiar; and though to work with his cases on a level with his breast,

ABCDEFGHIJKLMNOPQRSTUVWXYZ
&.,"-:;!?'"“”1234567890$
abcdefghijklmnopqrstuvwxyz

ABCDEFGHIJKLMNOPQRSTUVWXYZ
&.,"-:;!?'"“”1234567890$
abcdefghijklmnopqrstuvwxyz

AKZIDENZ GROTESK, REGULAR: LINOTYPE

PICAS	6	7	8	9	10	11	12	13	14	15	16	17	18	19	20	21	22	23	24	25	26	27	28	29	30
8 POINT	16	19	22	24	27	30	32	35	38	41	43	46	49	51	54	57	59	62	65	68	70	73	76	78	81
6 POINT	21	25	28	32	35	39	42	46	49	53	56	60	63	67	70	74	77	81	84	88	91	95	98	102	105

ABCDEFGHIJKL
MNOPQRSTUV
WXYZ&abcdefgh
ijklmnopqrstuvw
xyz123456789
0$.,"-:;!?"""

60 POINT STANDARD BOLD, AMSTERDAM CONTINENTAL

ABCDEFGHIJKLMNOP
QRSTUVWXYZ&abcdef
ghijklmnopqrstuvwxyz1
234567890$.,"-:;!?"""

42 POINT STANDARD BOLD, AMSTERDAM CONTINENTAL

ABCDEFGHIJKLMNOPQRSTUVWXYZ&a
bcdefghijklmnopqrstuvwxyz123456789
0$.,"-:;!?"""

24 POINT (small) STANDARD BOLD, AMSTERDAM CONTINENTAL

ABCDEFGHIJKLMNOPQRSTUVWXYZ&abcdefghijklm
nopqrstuvwxyz1234567890$.,"-:;!?""''

24 POINT STANDARD LIGHT, AMSTERDAM CONTINENTAL

ABCDEFGHIJKLMNOPQRSTUVWXYZ&abcdefghijklmnopqrstuv
wxyz1234567890$.,"-:;!?""''

18 POINT STANDARD LIGHT, AMSTERDAM CONTINENTAL

ABCDEFGHIJKLMNOPQRSTUVWXYZ&abcdefghijklmnopqrstuvwxyz1234567890$
.,"-:;!?""''

14 POINT STANDARD LIGHT, AMSTERDAM CONTINENTAL

ABCDEFGHIJKLMNOPQRSTUVWXYZ&abcdefghijklmnopqrstuvwxyz1234567890$.,"-:;!?""''

12 POINT STANDARD LIGHT, AMSTERDAM CONTINENTAL

ABCDEFGHIJKLMNOPQRSTUVWXYZ&abcdefghijklmnopqrstuvwxyz1234567890$.,"-:;!?""''

10 POINT STANDARD LIGHT, AMSTERDAM CONTINENTAL

ABCDEFGHIJKLMNOPQRSTUVWXYZ&abcdefghijklmnopqrstuvwxyz1234567890$.,"-:;!?""''

8 POINT STANDARD LIGHT, AMSTERDAM CONTINENTAL

ABCDEFGHIJKLMNOPQRSTUVWXYZ&abcdefghijklmnopqrstuvwxyz1234567890$.,"-:;!?""''

6 POINT STANDARD LIGHT, AMSTERDAM CONTINENTAL

ABCDEFGHIJKLMNOPQRSTUVWXYZ&abcdefghijklmnopqrstuv
wxyz1234567890$.,"-:;!?""''

24 POINT (large) STANDARD LIGHT CONDENSED, AMSTERDAM CONTINENTAL

ABCDEFGHIJKLMNOPQRSTUVWXYZ&abcdefghijklmnopqrstuvwxyz&123
4567890$.,"-:;!?""''

24 POINT (small) STANDARD LIGHT CONDENSED, AMSTERDAM CONTINENTAL

ABCDEFGHIJKLMNOPQRSTUVWXYZ&abcdefghijklmnopqrstuvwxyz1234567890$.,"-:;!?""''

18 POINT STANDARD LIGHT CONDENSED, AMSTERDAM CONTINENTAL

ABCDEFGHIJKLMNOPQRSTUVWXYZ&abcdefghijklmnopqrstuvwxyz1234567890$.,"-:;!?""''

14 POINT STANDARD LIGHT CONDENSED, AMSTERDAM CONTINENTAL

ABCDEFGHIJKLMNOPQRSTUVWXYZ&abcdefghijklmnopqrstuvwxyz1234567890$.,"-:;!?""

12 POINT STANDARD LIGHT CONDENSED, AMSTERDAM CONTINENTAL

ABCDEFGHIJKLMNOPQRSTUVWXYZ&abcdefghijklmnopqrstuvwxyz1234567890$.,"-:;!?""

10 POINT STANDARD LIGHT CONDENSED, AMSTERDAM CONTINENTAL

ABCDEFGHIJKLMNOPQRSTUVWXYZ&abcdefghijklmnopqrstuvwxyz1234567890$.,"-:;!?""

8 POINT STANDARD LIGHT CONDENSED, AMSTERDAM CONTINENTAL

ABCDEFGHIJKLMNOPQRSTUVWXYZ&abcdefghijklmnopqrstuvwxyz1234567890$.,"-:;!?""

6 POINT STANDARD LIGHT CONDENSED, AMSTERDAM CONTINENTAL

ABCDEFGHIJKLMNOPQRS TUVWXYZ&abcdefghijklm nopqrstuvwxyz123456789 0$., "-:;!?""""

60 POINT STANDARD CONDENSED, AMSTERDAM CONTINENTAL

ABCDEFGHIJKLMNOPQRSTUVWXYZ&abc defghijklmnopqrstuvwxyz1234567890$.,"-:;!?""""

42 POINT STANDARD CONDENSED, AMSTERDAM CONTINENTAL

ABCDEFGHIJKLMNOPQRSTUVWXYZ&abcdefghijklmnopqrstuvwxyz12 34567890$.,"-:;!?""

24 POINT (small) STANDARD CONDENSED, AMSTERDAM CONTINENTAL

178

ABCDEFGHIJKLMNOPQRSTUVWX YZ&abcdefghijklmnopqrstuvwxyz1 234567890$.,"-:;!?"""

60 POINT STANDARD MEDIUM CONDENSED, AMSTERDAM CONTINENTAL

ABCDEFGHIJKLMNOPQRSTUVWXYZ&abcd efghijklmnopqrstuvwxyz1234567890$.,"-: .!?"""
;,!"

42 POINT STANDARD MEDIUM CONDENSED, AMSTERDAM CONTINENTAL

ABCDEFGHIJKLMNOPQRSTUVWXYZ&abcdefghijklmnopqrstuvwxyz1234567
890$.,"-:;!?"""

24 POINT STANDARD MEDIUM CONDENSED, AMSTERDAM CONTINENTAL

ABCDEFGHIJKLMNOPQRS TUVWXYZ&abcdefghijklm nopqrstuvwxyz123456789 0$.,"-:;!?"""

60 POINT STANDARD BOLD CONDENSED, AMSTERDAM CONTINENTAL

ABCDEFGHIJKLMNOPQRSTUVWXY
Z&abcdefghijklmnopqrstuvwxyz12
34567890$.,"-:;!?""

42 POINT STANDARD BOLD CONDENSED, AMSTERDAM CONTINENTAL

ABCDEFGHIJKLMNOPQRSTUVWXYZ&abcdefghijklmnopqr
stuvwxyz1234567890$.,"-:;!?""

24 POINT (small) STANDARD BOLD CONDENSED, AMSTERDAM CONTINENTAL

ABCDEFGHIJKLMNO
PQRSTUVWXYZ&ab
cdefghijklmnopqrs
tuvwxyz12345678
90$.,"-:;!?""

60 POINT STANDARD EXTRA BOLD CONDENSED, AMSTERDAM CONTINENTAL

ABCDEFGHIJKLMNOPQRSTUVWX
YZ&abcdefghijklmnopqrstuvwx
yz1234567890$.,"-:;!?""

42 POINT STANDARD EXTRA BOLD CONDENSED, AMSTERDAM CONTINENTAL

ABCDEFGHIJKLMNOPQRSTUVWXYZ&abcdefghijklmnopqrstuv
wxyz1234567890$.,"-:;!?""

24 POINT (small) STANDARD EXTRA BOLD CONDENSED, AMSTERDAM CONTINENTAL

ABCDEFGHIJKLMNOPQR
STUVWXYZ&abcdefghijkl
mnopqrstuvwxyz12345678
90$.,"-:;!?""

30 POINT STANDARD EXTRA LIGHT EXTENDED, AMSTERDAM CONTINENTAL

ABCDEFGHIJKLMNOPQRSTUVWXYZ
&abcdefghijklmnopqrstuvwxyz1234567
890$.,"-:;!?""

24 POINT STANDARD EXTRA LIGHT EXTENDED, AMSTERDAM CONTINENTAL

ABCDEFGHIJKLMNOPQRSTUVWXYZ&abcdefghijklmnopqrstuvwxyz123
4567890$.,"-:;!?""

12 POINT STANDARD EXTRA LIGHT EXTENDED, AMSTERDAM CONTINENTAL

ABCDEFGHIJKLMN
OPQRSTUVWXYZ&
abcdefghijklmnopqr
stuvwxyz123456789
0$.,"-:;!?""

42 POINT STANDARD LIGHT EXTENDED, AMSTERDAM CONTINENTAL

ABCDEFGHIJKLMNOPQRSTUVWX
YZ&abcdefghijklmnopqrstuvwxyz12
34567890$.,"-:;!?""''

24 POINT STANDARD LIGHT EXTENDED, AMSTERDAM CONTINENTAL

ABCDEFGHIJKLMNOPQRSTUVWXYZ&abcdefghijklmnopqrstuvwx
yz1234567890$.,"-:;!?""''

12 POINT STANDARD LIGHT EXTENDED, AMSTERDAM CONTINENTAL

ABCDEFGHIJKLMN
OPQRSTUVWXYZ&
abcdefghijklmnopq
rstuvwxyz12345678
90$.,"-:;!?""

42 POINT STANDARD EXTENDED, AMSTERDAM CONTINENTAL

ABCDEFGHIJKLMNOPQRSTUV
WXYZ&abcdefghijklmnopqrstuvw
xyz1234567890$.,"-:;!?""

24 POINT (small) STANDARD EXTENDED, AMSTERDAM CONTINENTAL

ABCDEFGHIJKLMNOPQRSTUVWXYZ&abcdefghijklmnopqrstuv
wxyz1234567890$.,"-:;!?""''

12 POINT STANDARD EXTENDED, AMSTERDAM CONTINENTAL

ABCDEFG HIJKLMNO PQRSTUV WXYZ&ab cdefghijkl mnopqrstu vwxyz123 4567890$.,'"-:;!?'"''

60 POINT STANDARD EXTRA BOLD EXTENDED, AMSTERDAM CONTINENTAL

ABCDEFGHIJKLM
NOPQRSTUVWXY
Z&abcdefghijklm
nopqrstuvwxyz12
34567890$.,"-:;!
?""""

42 POINT STANDARD EXTRA BOLD EXTENDED, AMSTERDAM CONTINENTAL

ABCDEFGHIJKLMNOPQRSTUVWX
YZ&abcdefghijklmnopqrstuvwxy
z1234567890$.,"-:;!?""""

24 POINT (small) STANDARD EXTRA BOLD EXTENDED, AMSTERDAM CONTINENTAL

ABCDEFGHIJKLMNOPQRSTUVWXYZ&abcdefghijklmno
pqrstuvwxyz1234567890$.,"-:;!?""""

12 POINT STANDARD EXTRA BOLD EXTENDED, AMSTERDAM CONTINENTAL

First edition of the Hebrew Bible, Solomon Soncino, 1488.

ABCDEFGH
IJKLMNOP
QRSTUVWX
YZ&abcdefgh
ijklmnopqrstu
vwxyzfifffflffiffl
1234567890$.,
,"–.·!?"'"
.;··

ABCDEFGHIJ
KLMNOPQRS
TUVWXYZ&ab
cdefghijklmnopq
rstuvwxyzfifffflffi
ffl1234567890$.,"
-.;!?""''

60 POINT TIMES ROMAN, MOULDTYPE FOUNDRY LTD.

ABCDEFGHIJKL
MNOPQRSTUVWX
YZ&abcdefghijklmno
pqrstuvwxyzfifffflffifffl
1234567890$.,"-:;!?""''

48 POINT TIMES ROMAN, MONOTYPE

ABCDEFGHIJKLM
NOPQRSTUVWXY
Z&abcdefghijklmnop
qrstuvwxyzffffiflffifffl12
34567890$.,'-:;!?

48 POINT TIMES ROMAN ITALIC, MONOTYPE

ABCDEFGHIJKLMNOPQ
RSTUVWXYZ&abcdefghij
klmnopqrstuvwxyzfifffflffifffl12
34567890$.,"-:;!?""''

36 POINT TIMES ROMAN, MONOTYPE

ABCDEFGHIJKLMNOPQ
RSTUVWXYZ&abcdefghijk
lmnopqrstuvwxyzfffiflffiffl123
4567890$.,'-:;!?

36 POINT TIMES ROMAN ITALIC, MONOTYPE

ABCDEFGHIJKLMNOPQRSTU
VWXYZ&abcdefghijklmnopqrstuv
wxyzfifffflffiffl1234567890$.,"-:;!?""

30 POINT TIMES ROMAN, MONOTYPE

ABCDEFGHIJKLMNOPQRSTU
VWXYZ&abcdefghijklmnopqrstuvw
xyzfffifflffiffl1234567890$.,'-:;!?

30 POINT TIMES ROMAN ITALIC, MONOTYPE

ABCDEFGHIJKLMNOPQRSTUVWXY
Z&abcdefghijklmnopqrstuvwxyzfifffflffiffl123
4567890$.,"-:;!?""

24 POINT TIMES ROMAN, MONOTYPE

ABCDEFGHIJKLMNOPQRSTUVWXYZ
&abcdefghijklmnopqrstuvwxyzfiffflffiffl1234
567890$.,"-:;!?""

24 POINT TIMES ROMAN ITALIC, MONOTYPE

ABCDEFGHIJKLMNOPQRSTUVWXYZ&abcdefghijkl
mnopqrstuvwxyzfifffflffiffl1234567890$.,"-:;!?""

18 POINT TIMES ROMAN, MONOTYPE

190

ABCDEFGHIJKLMNOPQRSTUVWXYZ&abcdefghijkl
mnopqrstuvwxyzfifflffffffffl1234567890$.,"-:,!?""''

18 POINT TIMES ROMAN ITALIC, MONOTYPE

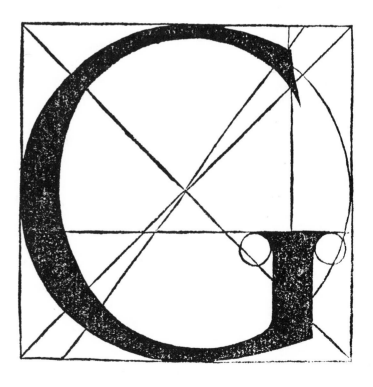

Leonardo drawing of the letter G
from "Divina Proportione." Venice, 1509.

Queſta letera G. ſe forma cõmel .C. del ſuo tondo e qua
dro. La gamba deritta de ſotto uol eſſer alta un terzo del
ſuo quadro : e'groſſa dele noue parti luna de lalteza del
ſuo quadrato.

14/14 To cast off manuscript with accuracy and precision, is a task of a disagreeable nature, which requires great attention and mature deliberation. The trouble and difficulty is much encreased, when the copy is not only irregularly written (which is too frequently the case), but also abounds with interlineations, erasures, and variations in the sizes of paper. To surmount these defects the closest application and attention is re-*quired; yet, at times, so numerous are the alterations and additions, that they not un-*

12/12 To cast off manuscript with accuracy and pre-cision, is a task of a disagreeable nature, which requires great attention and mature delibera-tion. The trouble and difficulty is much en-creased, when the copy is not only irregularly written (which is too frequently the case), but also abounds with interlineations, erasures, and variations in the sizes of paper. To sur-mount these defects the closest application and attention is required; yet, at times, so numer-ous are the alterations and additions, that they not unfrequently baffle the skill and judgment *of the most experienced calculators of copy. Such an imperfect and slovenly mode of send-*

14/16 To cast off manuscript with accuracy and precision, is a task of a disagreeable nature, which requires great attention and mature deliberation. The trouble and difficulty is much encreased, when the copy is not only irregularly written (which is too frequently the case), but also abounds with interlineations, erasures, and variations in the sizes *quired; yet, at times, so numerous are the alterations and additions, that they not un-*

12/14 To cast off manuscript with accuracy and pre-cision, is a task of a disagreeable nature, which requires great attention and mature delibera-tion. The trouble and difficulty is much en-creased, when the copy is not only irregularly written (which is too frequently the case), but also abounds with interlineations, erasures, and variations in the sizes of paper. To sur-mount these defects the closest application and *of the most experienced calculators of copy. Such an imperfect and slovenly mode of send-*

14/18 To cast off manuscript with accuracy and precision, is a task of a disagreeable nature, which requires great attention and mature deliberation. The trouble and difficulty is much encreased, when the copy is not only irregularly written (which is too frequently the case), but also abounds with interlinea-*quired; yet, at times, so numerous are the alterations and additions, that they not un-*

12/16 To cast off manuscript with accuracy and pre-cision, is a task of a disagreeable nature, which requires great attention and mature delibera-tion. The trouble and difficulty is much en-creased, when the copy is not only irregularly written (which is too frequently the case), but also abounds with interlineations, erasures, and variations in the sizes of paper. To sur-*of the most experienced calculators of copy. Such an imperfect and slovenly mode of send-*

ABCDEFGHIJKLMNOPQRSTUVW
ABCDEFGHIJKLMNOPQRSTUVW
&.,":;!?""1234567890$
&.,":;!?""1234567890$
abcdefghijklmnopqrstuvwxyz
abcdefghijklmnopqrstuvwxyz

ABCDEFGHIJKLMNOPQRSTUVWXYZ
ABCDEFGHIJKLMNOPQRSTUVWXYZ
&.,"-:;!?""1234567890$
&.,"-:;!?""1234567890$
abcdefghijklmnopqrstuvwxyz
abcdefghijklmnopqrstuvwxyz

TIMES ROMAN: LINOTYPE

PICAS	6	7	8	9	10	11	12	13	14	15	16	17	18	19	20	21	22	23	24	25	26	27	28	29	30
14 POINT	14	16	18	20	22	24	26	28	30	32	34	36	38	40	42	44	46	48	50	52	54	56	58	60	62
12 POINT	13	16	18	20	23	25	27	29	32	34	36	39	41	43	46	48	50	53	55	57	59	62	64	66	69

11/11

To cast off manuscript with accuracy and precision, is a task of a disagreeable nature, which requires great attention and mature deliberation. The trouble and difficulty is much encreased, when the copy is not only irregularly written (which is too frequently the case), but also abounds with interlineations, erasures, and variations in the sizes of paper. To surmount these defects the closest application and attention is required; yet, at times, so numerous are the alterations and additions, that they not unfrequently baffle the skill and judgment of the most experienced calculators of copy. Such an imperfect and slovenly mode of sending works to the *press (which is generally attended with unpleasant consequences to all parties) cannot be too strongly*

10/10

To cast off manuscript with accuracy and precision, is a task of a disagreeable nature, which requires great attention and mature deliberation. The trouble and difficulty is much encreased, when the copy is not only irregularly written (which is too frequently the case), but also abounds with interlineations, erasures, and variations in the sizes of paper. To surmount these defects the closest application and attention is required; yet, at times, so numerous are the alterations and additions, that they not unfrequently baffle the skill and judgment of the most experienced calculators of copy. Such an imperfect and slovenly mode of sending works to the press (which is generally attended with unpleasant consequences to all parties) cannot be too strongly deprecated by all admirers of the art. *The first thing necessary is to take a comprehensive view of the copy, and to notice whether it is written*

11/13

To cast off manuscript with accuracy and precision, is a task of a disagreeable nature, which requires great attention and mature deliberation. The trouble and difficulty is much encreased, when the copy is not only irregularly written (which is too frequently the case), but also abounds with interlineations, erasures, and variations in the sizes of paper. To surmount these defects the closest application and attention is required; yet, at times, so numerous are the alterations and additions, that they not unfrequently baffle the skill and judgment of the *press (which is generally attended with unpleasant consequences to all parties) cannot be too strongly*

10/12

To cast off manuscript with accuracy and precision, is a task of a disagreeable nature, which requires great attention and mature deliberation. The trouble and difficulty is much encreased, when the copy is not only irregularly written (which is too frequently the case), but also abounds with interlineations, erasures, and variations in the sizes of paper. To surmount these defects the closest application and attention is required; yet, at times, so numerous are the alterations and additions, that they not unfrequently baffle the skill and judgment of the most experienced calculators of copy. Such an imperfect and slovenly mode of sending works *The first thing necessary is to take a comprehensive view of the copy, and to notice whether it is written*

11/15

To cast off manuscript with accuracy and precision, is a task of a disagreeable nature, which requires great attention and mature deliberation. The trouble and difficulty is much encreased, when the copy is not only irregularly written (which is too frequently the case), but also abounds with interlineations, erasures, and variations in the sizes of paper. To surmount these defects the closest application and attention is required; yet, at times, so numer- *press (which is generally attended with unpleasant consequences to all parties) cannot be too strongly*

10/14

To cast off manuscript with accuracy and precision, is a task of a disagreeable nature, which requires great attention and mature deliberation. The trouble and difficulty is much encreased, when the copy is not only irregularly written (which is too frequently the case), but also abounds with interlineations, erasures, and variations in the sizes of paper. To surmount these defects the closest application and attention is required; yet, at times, so numerous are the alterations and additions, that they not unfrequently baffle the skill and *The first thing necessary is to take a comprehensive view of the copy, and to notice whether it is written*

ABCDEFGHIJKLMNOPQRSTUVWXYZ
ABCDEFGHIJKLMNOPQRSTUVWXYZ
&.,'‑:;!?'""1234567890$
&.,'‑:;!?'""1234567890$
abcdefghijklmnopqrstuvwxyz
abcdefghijklmnopqrstuvwxyz

ABCDEFGHIJKLMNOPQRSTUVWXYZ
ABCDEFGHIJKLMNOPQRSTUVWXYZ
&.,'‑:;!?'""1234567890$
&.,'‑:;!?'""1234567890$
abcdefghijklmnopqrstuvwxyz
abcdefghijklmnopqrstuvwxyz

TIMES ROMAN: LINOTYPE

PICAS	6	7	8	9	10	11	12	13	14	15	16	17	18	19	20	21	22	23	24	25	26	27	28	29	30
11 POINT	15	17	20	22	25	27	30	32	35	37	40	43	46	49	51	53	55	57	60	62	65	67	70	72	75
10 POINT	16	18	21	24	27	29	32	35	37	40	43	45	48	51	54	56	59	62	64	67	70	72	75	78	81

9/9 To cast off manuscript with accuracy and precision, is a task of a disagreeable nature, which requires great attention and mature deliberation. The trouble and difficulty is much encreased, when the copy is not only irregularly written (which is too frequently the case), but also abounds with interlineations, erasures, and variations in the sizes of paper. To surmount these defects the closest application and attention is required; yet, at times, so numerous are the alterations and additions, that they not unfrequently baffle the skill and judgment of the most experienced calculators of copy. Such an imperfect and slovenly mode of sending works to the press (which is generally attended with unpleasant consequences to all parties) cannot be too strongly deprecated by all admirers of the art.

The first thing necessary is to take a comprehensive view of the copy, and to notice whether it is written even, if it has many interlineations, &c. also the number of break *lines, and whether divided into chapters and sub-heads, in order that allowance may be made for them in the calcu-*

8/8 To cast off manuscript with accuracy and precision, is a task of a disagreeable nature, which requires great attention and mature deliberation. The trouble and difficulty is much encreased, when the copy is not only irregularly written (which is too frequently the case), but also abounds with interlineations, erasures, and variations in the sizes of paper. To surmount these defects the closest application and attention is required; yet, at times, so numerous are the alterations and additions, that they not unfrequently baffle the skill and judgment of the most experienced calculators of copy, Such an imperfect and slovenly mode of sending works to the press (which is generally attended with unpleasant consequences to all parties) cannot be too strongly deprecated by all admirers of the art.

The first thing necessary is to take a comprehensive view of the copy, and to notice whether it is written even, if it has many interlineations, &c. also the number of break lines, and whether divided into chapters and sub-heads, in order that allowance may be made for them in the calculation, so that the *plan of the work may not afterwards be infringed on. These observations should be entered as a memorandum, on a sep-*

9/11 To cast off manuscript with accuracy and precision, is a task of a disagreeable nature, which requires great attention and mature deliberation. The trouble and difficulty is much encreased, when the copy is not only irregularly written (which is too frequently the case), but also abounds with interlineations, erasures, and variations in the sizes of paper. To surmount these defects the closest application and attention is required; yet, at times, so numerous are the alterations and additions, that they not unfrequently baffle the skill and judgment of the most experienced calculators of copy. Such an imperfect and slovenly mode of sending works to the press (which is generally attended with unpleasant consequences to all parties) cannot be too *lines, and whether divided into chapters and sub-heads, in order that allowance may be made for them in the calcu-*

8/10 To cast off manuscript with accuracy and precision, is a task of a disagreeable nature, which requires great attention and mature deliberation. The trouble and difficulty is much encreased, when the copy is not only irregularly written (which is too frequently the case), but also abounds with interlineations, erasures, and variations in the sizes of paper. To surmount these defects the closest application and attention is required; yet, at times, so numerous are the alterations and additions, that they not unfrequently baffle the skill and judgment of the most experienced calculators of copy. Such an imperfect and slovenly mode of sending works to the press (which is generally attended with unpleasant consequences to all parties) cannot be too strongly deprecated by all admirers of the art.

The first thing necessary is to take a comprehensive view of *plan of the work may not afterwards be infringed on. These observations should be entered as a memorandum, on a sep-*

9/13 To cast off manuscript with accuracy and precision, is a task of a disagreeable nature, which requires great attention and mature deliberation. The trouble and difficulty is much encreased, when the copy is not only irregularly written (which is too frequently the case), but also abounds with interlineations, erasures, and variations in the sizes of paper. To surmount these defects the closest application and attention is required; yet, at times, so numerous are the alterations and additions, that they not unfrequently baffle the skill and judgment of the most experienced calculators of copy. Such an imperfect and slovenly mode of *lines, and whether divided into chapters and sub-heads, in order that allowance may be made for them in the calcu-*

8/12 To cast off manuscript with accuracy and precision, is a task of a disagreeable nature, which requires great attention and mature deliberation. The trouble and difficulty is much encreased, when the copy is not only irregularly written (which is too frequently the case), but also abounds with interlineations, erasures, and variations in the sizes of paper. To surmount these defects the closest application and attention is required; yet, at times, so numerous are the alterations and additions, that they not unfrequently baffle the skill and judgment of the most experienced calculators of copy. Such an imperfect and slovenly mode of sending works to the press (which is generally attended with unpleasant consequences to *plan of the work may not afterwards be infringed on. These observations should be entered as a memorandum, on a sep-*

ABCDEFGHIJKLMNOPQRSTUVWXYZ
ABCDEFGHIJKLMNOPQRSTUVWXYZ
&.,"-:;!?""'1234567890$
&.,"-:;!?""'1234567890$
abcdefghijklmnopqrstuvwxyz
abcdefghijklmnopqrstuvwxyz

ABCDEFGHIJKLMNOPQRSTUVWXYZ
ABCDEFGHIJKLMNOPQRSTUVWXYZ
&.,"-:;!?""'1234567890$
&.,"-:;!?""'1234567890$
abcdefghijklmnopqrstuvwxyz
abcdefghijklmnopqrstuvwxyz

TIMES ROMAN: LINOTYPE

PICAS	6	7	8	9	10	11	12	13	14	15	16	17	18	19	20	21	22	23	24	25	26	27	28	29	30
9 POINT	17	20	23	26	29	31	34	37	40	43	46	49	52	55	58	60	63	66	69	72	75	78	81	84	87
8 POINT	18	21	24	27	31	34	37	40	43	46	49	52	56	59	62	65	68	71	74	77	80	83	86	89	93

7/7

To cast off manuscript with accuracy and precision, is a task of a disagreeable nature, which requires great attention and mature deliberation. The trouble and difficulty is much encreased, when the copy is not only irregularly written (which is too frequently the case), but also abounds with interlineations, erasures, and variations in the sizes of paper. To surmount these defects the closest application and attention is required; yet, at times, so numerous are the alterations and additions, that they not unfrequently baffle the skill and judgment of the most experienced calculators of copy. Such an imperfect and slovenly mode of sending works to the press (which is generally attended with unpleasant consequences to all parties) cannot be too strongly deprecated by all admirers of the art.

The first thing necessary is to take a comprehensive view of the copy, and to notice whether it is written even, if it has many interlineations, &c. also the number of break lines, and whether divided into chapters and sub-heads, in order that allowance may be made for them in the calculation, so that the plan of the work may not afterwards be infringed on. These observations should be entered as a memorandum, on a separate piece of paper, to assist the memory, and save the trouble of re-examining the manuscript.

This preparation being made, we then take that part of the copy for our calculation which comes nearest to the general tendency of *the writing, and reckon the number of words contained in one line, previously counting a number of separate lines, so that the one we*

6/6

To cast off manuscript with accuracy and precision, is a task of a disagreeable nature, which requires great attention and mature deliberation. The trouble and difficulty is much encreased, when the copy is not only irregularly written (which is too frequently the case), but also abounds with interlineations, erasures, and variations in the sizes of paper. To surmount these defects the closest application and attention is required; yet, at times, so numerous are the alterations and additions, that they not unfrequently baffle the skill and judgment of the most experienced calculators of copy. Such an imperfect and slovenly mode of sending works to the press (which is generally attended with unpleasant consequences to all parties) cannot be too strongly deprecated by all admirers of the art.

The first thing necessary is to take a comprehensive view of the copy, and to notice whether it is written even, if it has many interlineations, &c. also the number of break lines, and whether divided into chapters and sub-heads, in order that allowance may be made for them in the calculation, so that the plan of the work may not afterwards be infringed on. These observations should be entered as a memorandum, on a separate piece of paper, to assist the memory, and save the trouble of re-examining the manuscript.

This preparation being made, we then take that part of the copy for our calculation which comes nearest to the general tendency of the writing, and reckon the number of words contained in one line, previously counting a number of separate lines, so that the one we adopt may be a fair average; we then take the number of lines in a page, and multiply the one by the other, which we again multiply by the quantity of folios the manuscript copy may contain, and thus we are put in possession of *the amount of the words contained in the work, with as little loss of time, and as much accuracy as circumstances will admit; the necessary allow-*

7/9

To cast off manuscript with accuracy and precision, is a task of a disagreeable nature, which requires great attention and mature deliberation. The trouble and difficulty is much encreased, when the copy is not only irregularly written (which is too frequently the case), but also abounds with interlineations, erasures, and variations in the sizes of paper. To surmount these defects the closest application and attention is required; yet, at times, so numerous are the alterations and additions, that they not unfrequently baffle the skill and judgment of the most experienced calculators of copy. Such an imperfect and slovenly mode of sending works to the press (which is generally attended with unpleasant consequences to all parties) cannot be too strongly deprecated by all admirers of the art.

The first thing necessary is to take a comprehensive view of the copy, and to notice whether it is written even, if it has many interlineations, &c. also the number of break lines, and whether divided into chapters and sub-heads, in order that allowance may be made for them in the calculation, so that the plan of the work may not *the writing, and reckon the number of words contained in one line, previously counting a number of separate lines, so that the one we*

6/8

To cast off manuscript with accuracy and precision, is a task of a disagreeable nature, which requires great attention and mature deliberation. The trouble and difficulty is much encreased, when the copy is not only irregularly written (which is too frequently the case), but also abounds with interlineations, erasures, and variations in the sizes of paper. To surmount these defects the closest application and attention is required; yet, at times, so numerous are the alterations and additions, that they not unfrequently baffle the skill and judgment of the most experienced calculators of copy. Such an imperfect and slovenly mode of sending works to the press (which is generally attended with unpleasant consequences to all parties) cannot be too strongly deprecated by all admirers of the art.

The first thing necessary is to take a comprehensive view of the copy, and to notice whether it is written even, if it has many interlineations, &c. also the number of break lines, and whether divided into chapters and sub-heads, in order that allowance may be made for them in the calculation, so that the plan of the work may not afterwards be infringed on. These observations should be entered as a memorandum, on a separate piece of paper, to assist the memory, and save the trouble of re-examining the manuscript.
the amount of the words contained in the work, with as little loss of time, and as much accuracy as circumstances will admit; the necessary allow-

7/11

To cast off manuscript with accuracy and precision, is a task of a disagreeable nature, which requires great attention and mature deliberation. The trouble and difficulty is much encreased, when the copy is not only irregularly written (which is too frequently the case), but also abounds with interlineations, erasures, and variations in the sizes of paper. To surmount these defects the closest application and attention is required; yet, at times, so numerous are the alterations and additions, that they not unfrequently baffle the skill and judgment of the most experienced calculators of copy. Such an imperfect and slovenly mode of sending works to the press (which is generally attended with unpleasant consequences to all parties) cannot be too strongly deprecated by all admirers of the art.

The first thing necessary is to take a comprehensive view of the *the writing, and reckon the number of words contained in one line, previously counting a number of separate lines, so that the one we*

6/10

To cast off manuscript with accuracy and precision, is a task of a disagreeable nature, which requires great attention and mature deliberation. The trouble and difficulty is much encreased, when the copy is not only irregularly written (which is too frequently the case), but also abounds with interlineations, erasures, and variations in the sizes of paper. To surmount these defects the closest application and attention is required; yet, at times, so numerous are the alterations and additions, that they not unfrequently baffle the skill and judgment of the most experienced calculators of copy. Such an imperfect and slovenly mode of sending works to the press (which is generally attended with unpleasant consequences to all parties) cannot be too strongly deprecated by all admirers of the art.

The first thing necessary is to take a comprehensive view of the copy, and to notice whether it is written even, if it has many interlineations, &c. also the number of break lines, and whether divided into chapters and sub-heads, in order that allowance may be made for them in the calcula-
the amount of the words contained in the work, with as little loss of time, and as much accuracy as circumstances will admit; the necessary allow-

ABCDEFGHIJKLMNOPQRSTUVWXYZ
ABCDEFGHIJKLMNOPQRSTUVWXYZ
&.,"-:;!?""1234567890$
&.,"-:;!?""1234567890$
abcdefghijklmnopqrstuvwxyz
abcdefghijklmnopqrstuvwxyz

ABCDEFGHIJKLMNOPQRSTUVWXYZ
ABCDEFGHIJKLMNOPQRSTUVWXYZ
&.,"-:;!?""1234567890$
&.,"-:;!?""1234567890$
abcdefghijklmnopqrstuvwxyz
abcdefghijklmnopqrstuvwxyz

TIMES ROMAN: LINOTYPE

PICAS	6	7	8	9	10	11	12	13	14	15	16	17	18	19	20	21	22	23	24	25	26	27	28	29	30
7 POINT	20	23	27	30	33	37	40	43	46	50	53	56	59	63	66	70	73	76	79	83	86	89	92	96	99
6 POINT	22	25	29	32	36	39	43	47	50	54	58	62	65	69	72	76	79	83	86	90	94	98	101	105	108

ABCDEFGH
IJKLMNOP
QRSTUVWX
YZ&abcdefgh
ijklmnopqrstu
vwxyzfiffffflffffffffl
1234567890$.,
''—.:!?''''
.;:

72 POINT TIMES ROMAN BOLD, MOULDTYPE FOUNDRY LTD.

ABCDEFGHIJKLM
NOPQRSTUVWXY
Z&abcdefghijklmnop
qrstuvwxyzfifffflffffiffl12
34567890$.,"-:;!?""''

48 POINT TIMES ROMAN BOLD, MOULDTYPE FOUNDRY LTD.

ABCDEFGHIJKLMNOPQRSTUVWXYZ
&abcdefghijklmnopqrstuvwxyzfiffflffffi12345
67890$.,"-:;!?""''

24 POINT TIMES ROMAN BOLD, MOULDTYPE FOUNDRY LTD.

Weiss displays classical
characteristics — lending
dignity and suggesting elegance.

WEISS ROMAN, BAUER
INDUSTRY fireworks

ELIZABETH, BAUER
WORKMEN excursions

EUSEBIUS, LUDLOW
LINES display

DE ROOS ROMAN, ATF
COUNTRIES doubtful

All comparisons are made on 24 point type.

ABCDEFGHIJKLMN OPQRSTUVWXYZ& abcdefghijklmnopqrstu vwxyzfiffffl1234567890$.,'' -:;!?""''

48 POINT WEISS ROMAN, BAUER

ABCDEFGHIJKLMNOPQR STUVWXYZ&abcdefghijkl mnopqrstuvwxyzfiffffl1234567 890$.,'' -:;!?""''

36 POINT WEISS ROMAN, BAUER

ABCDEFGHIJKLMNOPQRST
UVWXYZ&abcdefghijklmnopqrstu
vwxyzfifffl1234567890$.,"'-:;!?""

36 POINT WEISS ITALIC, BAUER

ABCDEFGHIJKLMNOPQRSTUV
WXYZ&abcdefghijklmnopqrstuvwxy
zfifffl1234567890$.,"'-:;!?""

30 POINT WEISS ROMAN, BAUER

ABCDEFGHIJKLMNOPQRSTUVWXY
Z&abcdefghijklmnopqrstuvwxyzfifffl1234567890
$.,"-:;!?""

30 POINT WEISS ITALIC, BAUER

ABCDEFGHIJKLMNOPQRSTUVWXYZ&abcdefgh
ijklmnopqrstuvwxyzfifffl1234567890$.,"-:;!?""

24 POINT WEISS ROMAN, BAUER

ABCDEFGHIJKLMNOPQRSTUVWXYZ&abcdefghijklm
nopqrstuvwxyzfifffl1234567890$.,"-:;!?""

24 POINT WEISS ITALIC, BAUER

ABCDEFGHIJKLMNOPQRSTUVWXYZ&abcdefghijklmnopqrst
uvwxyzfifffl1234567890$.,"-:;!?""

18 POINT WEISS ROMAN, BAUER

ABCDEFGHIJKLMNOPQRSTUVWXYZ&abcdefghijklmnopqrstuvwxyz
fifffl1234567890$.,"-:;!?""

18 POINT WEISS ITALIC, BAUER

ABCDEFGHIJKLMNOPQRSTUVWXYZ&abcdefghijklmnopqrstuvwxyz
fifffl1234567890$.,'′-:;!?""
16 POINT WEISS ROMAN, BAUER

*ABCDEFGHIJKLMNOPQRSTUVWXYZ&abcdefghijklmnopqrstuvwxyzfifffl1234567
890$.,''-:;!?""*
16 POINT WEISS ITALIC, BAUER

14/14

Many years ago a cynical Frenchman sneered at England as the country of a dozen religions and of one sauce. Yet Frenchmen and Englishmen, and Americans too, persist in a simplicity of taste concerning letters which some may regard as equally narrow. The calligrapher of the middle ages, who delighted to show his skill in new forms of letters, would despise the plainness of our printed books. There are modern readers, also, who admire the freedom of the *letters made by engravers; others, again, who like the quaintness of the letters of mediæval*

12/12

Many years ago a cynical Frenchman sneered at England as the country of a dozen religions and of one sauce. Yet Frenchmen and Englishmen, and Americans too, persist in a simplicity of taste concerning letters which some may regard as equally narrow. The calligrapher of the middle ages, who delighted to show his skill in new forms of letters, would despise the plainness of our printed books. There are modern readers, also, who admire the freedom of the letters made by engravers; others, again, who like the quaintness of the letters of mediæval books, compared with which Roman and Italic letters seem stiff, ungraceful, *and incapable of pleasing combinations. To please these tastes, and others not so severe, modern type-*

14/16

Many years ago a cynical Frenchman sneered at England as the country of a dozen religions and of one sauce. Yet Frenchmen and Englishmen, and Americans too, persist in a simplicity of taste concerning letters which some may regard as equally narrow. The calligrapher of the middle ages, who delighted to show his skill in new forms of letters, would despise the plain-*letters made by engravers; others, again, who like the quaintness of the letters of mediæval*

12/14

Many years ago a cynical Frenchman sneered at England as the country of a dozen religions and of one sauce. Yet Frenchmen and Englishmen, and Americans too, persist in a simplicity of taste concerning letters which some may regard as equally narrow. The calligrapher of the middle ages, who delighted to show his skill in new forms of letters, would despise the plainness of our printed books. There are modern readers, also, who admire the freedom of the letters *and incapable of pleasing combinations. To please these tastes, and others not so severe, modern type-*

14/18

Many years ago a cynical Frenchman sneered at England as the country of a dozen religions and of one sauce. Yet Frenchmen and Englishmen, and Americans too, persist in a simplicity of taste concerning letters which some may regard as equally narrow. The calligrapher of the middle ages, who delighted to show his skill in *letters made by engravers; others, again, who like the quaintness of the letters of mediæval*

12/16

Many years ago a cynical Frenchman sneered at England as the country of a dozen religions and of one sauce. Yet Frenchmen and Englishmen, and Americans too, persist in a simplicity of taste concerning letters which some may regard as equally narrow. The calligrapher of the middle ages, who delighted to show his skill in new forms of letters, would despise the plainness of our printed books. There are modern *and incapable of pleasing combinations. To please these tastes, and others not so severe, modern type-*

ABCDEFGHIJKLMNOPQRSTUVWXY
ABCDEFGHIJKLMNOPQRSTUVWXY
&.":;!?'""1234567890$
&." :;!?'"" 1234567890$
abcdefghijklmnopqrstuvwxyz
abcdefghijklmnopqrstuvwxyz

ABCDEFGHIJKLMNOPQRSTUVWXYZ
ABCDEFGHIJKLMNOPQRSTUVWXYZ
&.,"-:;!?'""1234567890$
&.,"-:;!?'"" 1234567890$
abcdefghijklmnopqrstuvwxyz
abcdefghijklmnopqrstuvwxyz

WEISS: INTERTYPE

PICAS	6	7	8	9	10	11	12	13	14	15	16	17	18	19	20	21	22	23	24	25	26	27	28	29	30
14 POINT	14	16	19	21	23	25	28	30	32	35	37	40	42	44	47	49	51	53	56	58	60	62	65	67	70
12 POINT	16	18	21	24	26	29	31	34	36	39	42	44	47	50	52	55	57	60	62	65	68	70	73	75	78

11/11

Many years ago a cynical Frenchman sneered at England as the country of a dozen religions and of one sauce. Yet Frenchmen and Englishmen, and Americans too, persist in a simplicity of taste concerning letters which some may regard as equally narrow. The calligrapher of the middle ages, who delighted to show his skill in new forms of letters, would despise the plainness of our printed books. There are modern readers, also, who admire the freedom of the letters made by engravers; others, again, who like the quaintness of the letters of mediæval books, compared with which Roman and Italic letters seem stiff, ungraceful, and incapable of pleasing combinations. To please these tastes, and others not so severe, modern type-founders make many *forms of ornamental types; engravers and lithographers are daily devising other forms of more or less ingenuity and*

10/10

Many years ago a cynical Frenchman sneered at England as the country of a dozen religions and of one sauce. Yet Frenchmen and Englishmen, and Americans too, persist in a simplicity of taste concerning letters which some may regard as equally narrow. The calligrapher of the middle ages, who delighted to show his skill in new forms of letters, would despise the plainness of our printed books. There are modern readers, also, who admire the freedom of the letters made by engravers; others, again, who like the quaintness of the letters of mediæval books, compared with which Roman and Italic letters seem stiff, ungraceful, and incapable of pleasing combinations. To please these tastes, and others not so severe, modern type-founders make many forms of ornamental types; engravers and lithographers are daily devising other forms of more or less ingenuity and merit. All of them have admirers; but, though all may be useful, at least in the broad field *of job printing, they are not permitted in the standard book. The world of letters is full of alphabets, and there are many of them*

11/13

Many years ago a cynical Frenchman sneered at England as the country of a dozen religions and of one sauce. Yet Frenchmen and Englishmen, and Americans too, persist in a simplicity of taste concerning letters which some may regard as equally narrow. The calligrapher of the middle ages, who delighted to show his skill in new forms of letters, would despise the plainness of our printed books. There are modern readers, also, who admire the freedom of the letters made by engravers; others, again, who like the quaintness of the letters of mediæval books, compared with which Roman and Italic letters seem stiff, ungraceful, and incapa-*forms of ornamental types; engravers and lithographers are daily devising other forms of more or less ingenuity and*

10/12

Many years ago a cynical Frenchman sneered at England as the country of a dozen religions and of one sauce. Yet Frenchmen and Englishmen, and Americans too, persist in a simplicity of taste concerning letters which some may regard as equally narrow. The calligrapher of the middle ages, who delighted to show his skill in new forms of letters, would despise the plainness of our printed books. There are modern readers, also, who admire the freedom of the letters made by engravers; others, again, who like the quaintness of the letters of mediæval books, compared with which Roman and Italic letters seem stiff, ungraceful, and incapable of pleasing combinations. To please these tastes, and others not so severe, modern type-founders make many forms of *of job printing, they are not permitted in the standard book. The world of letters is full of alphabets, and there are many of them*

11/15

Many years ago a cynical Frenchman sneered at England as the country of a dozen religions and of one sauce. Yet Frenchmen and Englishmen, and Americans too, persist in a simplicity of taste concerning letters which some may regard as equally narrow. The calligrapher of the middle ages, who delighted to show his skill in new forms of letters, would despise the plainness of our printed books. There are modern readers, also, who admire the freedom of the letters made by engravers; others, again, who like the quaintness *forms of ornamental types; engravers and lithographers are daily devising other forms of more or less ingenuity and*

10/14

Many years ago a cynical Frenchman sneered at England as the country of a dozen religions and of one sauce. Yet Frenchmen and Englishmen, and Americans too, persist in a simplicity of taste concerning letters which some may regard as equally narrow. The calligrapher of the middle ages, who delighted to show his skill in new forms of letters, would despise the plainness of our printed books. There are modern readers, also, who admire the freedom of the letters made by engravers; others, again, who like the quaintness of the letters of mediæval books, compared with which Roman and Italic letters seem stiff, ungraceful, and *of job printing, they are not permitted in the standard book. The world of letters is full of alphabets, and there are many of them*

ABCDEFGHIJKLMNOPQRSTUVWXYZ
ABCDEFGHIJKLMNOPQRSTUVWXYZ
&.,'"-:;!?""1234567890$
&.,'"-:;!?""1234567890$
abcdefghijklmnopqrstuvwxyz
abcdefghijklmnopqrstuvwxyz

ABCDEFGHIJKLMNOPQRSTUVWXYZ
ABCDEFGHIJKLMNOPQRSTUVWXYZ
&.,'"-:;!?""1234567890$
&.,'"-:;!?""1234567890$
abcdefghijklmnopqrstuvwxyz
abcdefghijklmnopqrstuvwxyz

WEISS: INTERTYPE

PICAS	6	7	8	9	10	11	12	13	14	15	16	17	18	19	20	21	22	23	24	25	26	27	28	29	30
11 POINT	18	21	24	27	30	33	36	39	42	45	48	51	54	56	60	62	65	68	71	74	77	80	83	86	89
10 POINT	19	22	26	29	32	36	39	42	45	49	52	55	58	61	65	68	71	74	78	81	84	87	91	94	97

9/9 Many years ago a cynical Frenchman sneered at England as the country of a dozen religions and of one sauce. Yet Frenchmen and Englishmen, and Americans too, persist in a simplicity of taste concerning letters which some may regard as equally narrow. The calligrapher of the middle ages, who delighted to show his skill in new forms of letters, would despise the plainness of our printed books. There are modern readers, also, who admire the freedom of the letters made by engravers; others, again, who like the quaintness of the letters of mediæval books, compared with which Roman and Italic letters seem stiff, ungraceful, and incapable of pleasing combinations. To please these tastes, and others not so severe, modern type-founders make many forms of ornamental types; engravers and lithographers are daily devising other forms of more or less ingenuity and merit. All of them have admirers; but, though all may be useful, at least in the broad field of job printing, they are not permitted in the standard book. The world of letters is full of alphabets, and there are many of them that can be easily read, but *printers and publishers and readers are fully agreed that all standard works shall be in Roman. No publisher dares print magazines*

8/8 Many years ago a cynical Frenchman sneered at England as the country of a dozen religions and of one sauce. Yet Frenchmen and Englishmen, and Americans too, persist in a simplicity of taste concerning letters which some may regard as equally narrow. The calligrapher of the middle ages, who delighted to show his skill in new forms of letters, would despise the plainness of our printed books. There are modern readers, also, who admire the freedom of the letters made by engravers; others, again, who like the quaintness of the letters of mediæval books, compared with which Roman and Italic letters seem stiff, ungraceful, and incapable of pleasing combinations. To please these tastes, and others not so severe, modern type-founders make many forms of ornamental types; engravers and lithographers are daily devising other forms of more or less ingenuity and merit. All of them have admirers; but, though all may be useful, at least in the broad field of job printing, they are not permitted in the standard book. The world of letters is full of alphabets, and there are many of them that can be easily read, but printers and publishers and readers are fully agreed that all standard works shall be in Roman. No publisher dares print magazines or important volumes in types that deviate from the Roman model. Whatever the subject-matter, whether for the child in his nursery or for the wise man in his *study, the book must be in Roman; for it is with types as with dress—at proper times man may wear any style of dress that pleases his fancy, but*

9/11 Many years ago a cynical Frenchman sneered at England as the country of a dozen religions and of one sauce. Yet Frenchmen and Englishmen, and Americans too, persist in a simplicity of taste concerning letters which some may regard as equally narrow. The calligrapher of the middle ages, who delighted to show his skill in new forms of letters, would despise the plainness of our printed books. There are modern readers, also, who admire the freedom of the letters made by engravers; others, again, who like the quaintness of the letters of mediæval books, compared with which Roman and Italic letters seem stiff, ungraceful, and incapable of pleasing combinations. To please these tastes, and others not so severe, modern type-founders make many forms of ornamental types; engravers and lithographers are daily devising other forms of more or less *printers and publishers and readers are fully agreed that all standard works shall be in Roman. No publisher dares print magazines*

8/10 Many years ago a cynical Frenchman sneered at England as the country of a dozen religions and of one sauce. Yet Frenchmen and Englishmen, and Americans too, persist in a simplicity of taste concerning letters which some may regard as equally narrow. The calligrapher of the middle ages, who delighted to show his skill in new forms of letters, would despise the plainness of our printed books. There are modern readers, also, who admire the freedom of the letters made by engravers; others, again, who like the quaintness of the letters of mediæval books, compared with which Roman and Italic letters seem stiff, ungraceful, and incapable of pleasing combinations. To please these tastes, and others not so severe, modern type-founders make many forms of ornamental types; engravers and lithographers are daily devising other forms of more or less ingenuity and merit. All of them have admirers; but, though all may be useful, at least in the broad field of job printing, they are not permitted in the standard book. The world of letters is full of alphabets, and there are many of them that can be easily read, but *study, the book must be in Roman; for it is with types as with dress—at proper times man may wear any style of dress that pleases his fancy, but*

9/13 Many years ago a cynical Frenchman sneered at England as the country of a dozen religions and of one sauce. Yet Frenchmen and Englishmen, and Americans too, persist in a simplicity of taste concerning letters which some may regard as equally narrow. The calligrapher of the middle ages, who delighted to show his skill in new forms of letters, would despise the plainness of our printed books. There are modern readers, also, who admire the freedom of the letters made by engravers; others, again, who like the quaintness of the letters of mediæval books, compared with which Roman and Italic letters seem stiff, ungraceful, and incapable of pleasing combinations. To please these tastes, and others not so severe, mod-*printers and publishers and readers are fully agreed that all standard works shall be in Roman. No publisher dares print magazines*

8/12 Many years ago a cynical Frenchman sneered at England as the country of a dozen religions and of one sauce. Yet Frenchmen and Englishmen, and Americans too, persist in a simplicity of taste concerning letters which some may regard as equally narrow. The calligrapher of the middle ages, who delighted to show his skill in new forms of letters, would despise the plainness of our printed books. There are modern readers, also, who admire the freedom of the letters made by engravers; others, again, who like the quaintness of the letters of mediæval books, compared with which Roman and Italic letters seem stiff, ungraceful, and incapable of pleasing combinations. To please these tastes, and others not so severe, modern type-founders make many forms of ornamental types; engravers and lithographers are daily devising other forms of more or less ingenuity and merit. All of them have *study, the book must be in Roman; for it is with types as with dress—at proper times man may wear any style of dress that pleases his fancy, but*

ABCDEFGHIJKLMNOPQRSTUVWXYZ
ABCDEFGHIJKLMNOPQRSTUVWXYZ
&.,''-:;!?''''1234567890$
&.,''-:;!?''''1234567890$
abcdefghijklmnopqrstuvwxyz
abcdefghijklmnopqrstuvwxyz

ABCDEFGHIJKLMNOPQRSTUVWXYZ
ABCDEFGHIJKLMNOPQRSTUVWXYZ
&.,''-:;!?''''1234567890$
&.,''-:;!?''''1234567890$
abcdefghijklmnopqrstuvwxyz
abcdefghijklmnopqrstuvwxyz

WEISS: INTERTYPE

PICAS	6	7	8	9	10	11	12	13	14	15	16	17	18	19	20	21	22	23	24	25	26	27	28	29	30
9 POINT	21	24	28	31	34	38	41	45	48	52	55	59	62	65	69	73	76	79	83	86	90	93	97	100	104
8 POINT	23	27	31	35	39	43	49	50	54	58	62	66	70	74	77	81	85	89	93	97	100	105	108	112	116

ABCDEFGHIJKLMN
OPQRSTUVWXYZ
&abcdefghijklmnopqr
stuvwxyzfiffffl12345678
90$.,'-:;!?""

48 POINT WEISS ROMAN BOLD, BAUER

ABCDEFGHIJKLMNOPQRSTUVWXYZ&abcdef
ghijklmnopqrstuvwxyzfiffffl1234567890$.,'-:;!?""

24 POINT WEISS ROMAN BOLD, BAUER

ABCDEFGHIJKLMNOPQRSTUVWXYZ&abcdefghijklmnopqrstuvwxyzfiffffl1234567890$.,'-:;!?""

12 POINT WEISS ROMAN BOLD, BAUER

ABCDEFGHIJKLM
NOPQRSTUVWXY
Z&abcdefghijklmno
pqrstuvwxyzfiffffl123
4567890$.,'-:;!?""

48 POINT WEISS ROMAN EXTRA BOLD, BAUER

ABCDEFGHIJKLMNOPQRSTUVWXYZ&abcde
fghijklmnopqrstuvwxyzfifffl1234567890$.,''-:;!?""

24 POINT WEISS ROMAN EXTRA BOLD, BAUER

ABCDEFGHIJKLMNOPQRSTUVWXYZ&abcdefghijklmnopqrstuvwxyzfifffl1234567890$.,''-:;!?""

12 POINT WEISS ROMAN EXTRA BOLD, BAUER

ABCDEFGHIJK
LMNOPQRST
UVWXYZ&1
234567890$.,"
-.,!?""
.;.'

66 POINT WEISS INITIALS 1, BAUER

ABCDEFGHIJKLMNOP
QRSTUVWXYZ&1234
567890$.,"-:,!?""""

42 POINT WEISS INITIALS 1, BAUER

ABCDEFGHIJKLMNOPQRSTUVWXYZ&
1234567890$.,"-:;!?""""

24 POINT WEISS INITIALS 1, BAUER

ABCDEFGHIJK
LMNOPQRST
UVWXYZ&12
34567890$.,"-
.:!?""""
.:;.:. .

66 POINT WEISS INITIALS 2, BAUER

ABCDEFGHIJKLMNOPQ
RSTUVWXYZ&123456
7890$.,"-:;!?""""

42 POINT WEISS INITIALS 2, BAUER

ABCDEFGHIJKLMNOPQRSTUVWXYZ&12
34567890$.,"-:;!?""""

24 POINT WEISS INITIALS 2, BAUER

ABCDEFGHIJ
KLMNOPQR
STUVWXYZ
&123456789
O$.,"-:;!?"''

66 POINT WEISS INITIALS 3, BAUER

ABCDEFGHIJKLMNO
PQRSTUVWXYZ&12
34567890$.,"-:;!?"''

42 POINT WEISS INITIALS 3, BAUER

ABCDEFGHIJKLMNOPQRSTUVWXY
Z&1234567890$.,"-:;!?"''

24 POINT WEISS INITIALS 3, BAUER

SUPPLEMENTARY FACES

12/12 THE HISTORY OF PRINTING BY PHILIP LUCKOMBE, 1770. Having given a list of the places where, and by whom first introduced, in Europe, we shall now observe that it extended itself to Africa and America, not indeed at the invitation of the natives, especially of America, but by means of the Europeans, and particularly of the Spanish missionaries; who carried it to the latter for their ends, where it has made some progress. Printing houses being set up in the cities of Goa, Rachol, &c. in the country of Salsetta; *Manilla, the metropolis of the Philippine islands, &c. from whence there have been sev-*

11/11 THE HISTORY OF PRINTING BY PHILIP LUCKOMBE, 1770. Having given a list of the places where, and by whom first introduced, in Europe, we shall now observe that it extended itself to Africa and America, not indeed at the invitation of the natives, especially of America, but by means of the Europeans, and particularly of the Spanish missionaries; who carried it to the latter for their ends, where it has made some progress. Printing houses being set up in the cities of Goa, Rachol, &c. in the country of Salsetta; Manilla, the metropolis of the Philippine islands, &c. from whence there have been sev-*eral productions that have found their way to Europe. We find also that several Printing-houses*

12/14 THE HISTORY OF PRINTING BY PHILIP LUCKOMBE, 1770. Having given a list of the places where, and by whom first introduced, in Europe, we shall now observe that it extended itself to Africa and America, not indeed at the invitation of the natives, especially of America, but by means of the Europeans, and particularly of the Spanish missionaries; who carried it to the latter for their ends, where it has made some progress. *Manilla, the metropolis of the Philippine islands, &c. from whence there have been sev-*

11/13 THE HISTORY OF PRINTING BY PHILIP LUCKOMBE, 1770. Having given a list of the places where, and by whom first introduced, in Europe, we shall now observe that it extended itself to Africa and America, not indeed at the invitation of the natives, especially of America, but by means of the Europeans, and particularly of the Spanish missionaries; who carried it to the latter for their ends, where it has made some progress. Printing houses being set up in the cities of Goa, Rachol, &c. in the country of Sal-*eral productions that have found their way to Europe. We find also that several Printing-houses*

12/16 THE HISTORY OF PRINTING BY PHILIP LUCKOMBE, 1770. Having given a list of the places where, and by whom first introduced, in Europe, we shall now observe that it extended itself to Africa and America, not indeed at the invitation of the natives, especially of America, but by means of the Europeans, and particularly of the Spanish *Manilla, the metropolis of the Philippine islands, &c. from whence there have been sev-*

11/15 THE HISTORY OF PRINTING BY PHILIP LUCKOMBE, 1770. Having given a list of the places where, and by whom first introduced, in Europe, we shall now observe that it extended itself to Africa and America, not indeed at the invitation of the natives, especially of America, but by means of the Europeans, and particularly of the Spanish missionaries; who carried it to the latter for their ends, where it has made some *eral productions that have found their way to Europe. We find also that several Printing-houses*

ABCDEFGHIJKLMNOPQRSTUVWXYZ
ABCDEFGHIJKLMNOPQRSTUVWXYZ
&.,"-:;!?""1234567890$
&.,"-:;!?""1234567890$
abcdefghijklmnopqrstuvwxyz
abcdefghijklmnopqrstuvwxyz

ABCDEFGHIJKLMNOPQRSTUVWXYZ
ABCDEFGHIJKLMNOPQRSTUVWXYZ
&.,"-:;!?""1234567890$
&.,"-:;!?""1234567890$
abcdefghijklmnopqrstuvwxyz
abcdefghijklmnopqrstuvwxyz

CALEDONIA: LINOTYPE

PICAS	6	7	8	9	10	11	12	13	14	15	16	17	18	19	20	21	22	23	24	25	26	27	28	29	30
12 POINT	13	15	17	19	22	24	26	28	30	33	35	37	39	41	44	46	48	50	52	55	57	59	61	63	66
11 POINT	14	16	19	21	24	26	28	31	33	36	38	40	43	45	48	50	52	55	57	60	62	64	67	69	72

10/10

THE HISTORY OF PRINTING BY PHILIP LUCKOMBE, 1770. Having given a list of the places where, and by whom first introduced, in Europe, we shall now observe that it extended itself to Africa and America, not indeed at the invitation of the natives, especially of America, but by means of the Europeans, and particularly of the Spanish missionaries; who carried it to the latter for their ends, where it has made some progress. Printing houses being set up in the cities of Goa, Rachol, &c. in the country of Salsetta; Manilla, the metropolis of the Philippine islands, &c. from whence there have been several productions that have found their way to Europe. We find also that several Printing-houses were erected very early in the city of Lima, capital *of the empire of Peru, and in several cities of the kingdom of Mexico. We shall only add, that some*

9/9

THE HISTORY OF PRINTING BY PHILIP LUCKOMBE, 1770. Having given a list of the places where, and by whom first introduced, in Europe, we shall now observe that it extended itself to Africa and America, not indeed at the invitation of the natives, especially of America, but by means of the Europeans, and particularly of the Spanish missionaries; who carried it to the latter for their ends, where it has made some progress. Printing houses being set up in the cities of Goa, Rachol, &c. in the country of Salsetta; Manilla, the metropolis of the Philippine islands, &c. from whence there have been several productions that have found their way to Europe. We find also that several Printing-houses were erected very early in the city of Lima, capital of the empire of Peru, and in several cities of the kingdom of Mexico. We shall only add, that some Danish missionaries, sent to *the coast of Tanquebar, who had good success there in converting a great number of the natives, had sent to*

10/12

THE HISTORY OF PRINTING BY PHILIP LUCKOMBE, 1770. Having given a list of the places where, and by whom first introduced, in Europe, we shall now observe that it extended itself to Africa and America, not indeed at the invitation of the natives, especially of America, but by means of the Europeans, and particularly of the Spanish missionaries; who carried it to the latter for their ends, where it has made some progress. Printing houses being set up in the cities of Goa, Rachol, &c. in the country of Salsetta; Manilla, the metropolis of the Philippine islands, &c. from whence there have *of the empire of Peru, and in several cities of the kingdom of Mexico. We shall only add, that some*

9/11

THE HISTORY OF PRINTING BY PHILIP LUCKOMBE, 1770. Having given a list of the places where, and by whom first introduced, in Europe, we shall now observe that it extended itself to Africa and America, not indeed at the invitation of the natives, especially of America, but by means of the Europeans, and particularly of the Spanish missionaries; who carried it to the latter for their ends, where it has made some progress. Printing houses being set up in the cities of Goa, Rachol, &c. in the country of Salsetta; Manilla, the metropolis of the Philippine islands, &c. from whence there have been several productions that have found their way to Europe. We find also that several Printing-houses were erected *the coast of Tanquebar, who had good success there in converting a great number of the natives, had sent to*

10/14

THE HISTORY OF PRINTING BY PHILIP LUCKOMBE, 1770. Having given a list of the places where, and by whom first introduced, in Europe, we shall now observe that it extended itself to Africa and America, not indeed at the invitation of the natives, especially of America, but by means of the Europeans, and particularly of the Spanish missionaries; who carried it to the latter for their ends, where it has made some progress. Printing houses being set up in the cities of Goa, Rachol, &c. *of the empire of Peru, and in several cities of the kingdom of Mexico. We shall only add, that some*

9/13

THE HISTORY OF PRINTING BY PHILIP LUCKOMBE, 1770. Having given a list of the places where, and by whom first introduced, in Europe, we shall now observe that it extended itself to Africa and America, not indeed at the invitation of the natives, especially of America, but by means of the Europeans, and particularly of the Spanish missionaries; who carried it to the latter for their ends, where it has made some progress. Printing houses being set up in the cities of Goa, Rachol, &c. in the country of Salsetta; Manilla, the metropolis of the Philippine islands, &c. from whence there have been *the coast of Tanquebar, who had good success there in converting a great number of the natives, had sent to*

ABCDEFGHIJKLMNOPQRSTUVWXYZ
ABCDEFGHIJKLMNOPQRSTUVWXYZ
&.,"-:;!?""1234567890$
&.,"-:;!?""1234567890$
abcdefghijklmnopqrstuvwxyz
abcdefghijklmnopqrstuvwxyz

ABCDEFGHIJKLMNOPQRSTUVWXYZ
ABCDEFGHIJKLMNOPQRSTUVWXYZ
&.,"-:;!?""1234567890$
&.,"-:;!?""1234567890$
abcdefghijklmnopqrstuvwxyz
abcdefghijklmnopqrstuvwxyz

CALEDONIA: LINOTYPE

PICAS	6	7	8	9	10	11	12	13	14	15	16	17	18	19	20	21	22	23	24	25	26	27	28	29	30
10 POINT	15	18	20	23	26	28	31	33	36	39	41	44	46	49	52	54	57	59	62	65	67	69	72	75	78
9 POINT	16	19	22	25	28	30	33	36	39	42	44	47	50	53	56	58	61	64	67	70	72	75	78	81	84

THE HISTORY OF PRINTING BY PHILIP LUCKOMBE, 1770. Having given a list of the places where, and by whom first introduced, in Europe, we shall now observe that it extended itself to Africa and America, not indeed at the invitation of the natives, especially of America, but by means of the Europeans, and particularly of the Spanish missionaries; who carried it to the latter for their ends, where it has made some progress. Printing houses being set up in the cities of *Goa, Rachol, &c. in the country of Salsetta; Manilla, the metropolis of the Philippine is-*

12/13

THE HISTORY OF PRINTING BY PHILIP LUCKOMBE, 1770. Having given a list of the places where, and by whom first introduced, in Europe, we shall now observe that it extended itself to Africa and America, not indeed at the invitation of the natives, especially of America, but by means of the Europeans, and particularly of the Spanish missionaries; who carried it to the latter for their ends, where it has made some progress. *Goa, Rachol, &c. in the country of Salsetta; Manilla, the metropolis of the Philippine is-*

12/14

THE HISTORY OF PRINTING BY PHILIP LUCKOMBE, 1770. Having given a list of the places where, and by whom first introduced, in Europe, we shall now observe that it extended itself to Africa and America, not indeed at the invitation of the natives, especially of America, but by means of the Europeans, and particularly of the Spanish *Goa, Rachol, &c. in the country of Salsetta; Manilla, the metropolis of the Philippine is-*

12/16

THE HISTORY OF PRINTING BY PHILIP LUCKOMBE, 1770. Having given a list of the places where, and by whom first introduced, in Europe, we shall now observe that it extended itself to Africa and America, not indeed at the invitation of the natives, especially of America, but by means of the Europeans, and particularly of the Spanish missionaries; who carried it to the latter for their ends, where it has made some progress. Printing houses being set up in the cities of Goa, Rachol, &c. in the country of Salsetta; Manilla, the metropolis of the Philippine islands, &c. from whence there have been several productions that have found their way *to Europe. We find also that several Printing-houses were erected very early in the city of Lima, capital*

10/11

THE HISTORY OF PRINTING BY PHILIP LUCKOMBE, 1770. Having given a list of the places where, and by whom first introduced, in Europe, we shall now observe that it extended itself to Africa and America, not indeed at the invitation of the natives, especially of America, but by means of the Europeans, and particularly of the Spanish missionaries; who carried it to the latter for their ends, where it has made some progress. Printing houses being set up in the cities of Goa, Rachol, &c. in the country of Salsetta; Manilla, the metropolis of the Philippine islands, &c. from whence there have *to Europe. We find also that several Printing-houses were erected very early in the city of Lima, capital*

10/12

THE HISTORY OF PRINTING BY PHILIP LUCKOMBE, 1770. Having given a list of the places where, and by whom first introduced, in Europe, we shall now observe that it extended itself to Africa and America, not indeed at the invitation of the natives, especially of America, but by means of the Europeans, and particularly of the Spanish missionaries; who carried it to the latter for their ends, where it has made some progress. Printing houses being set up in the cities of Goa, Rachol, &c. *to Europe. We find also that several Printing-houses were erected very early in the city of Lima, capital*

10/14

ABCDEFGHIJKLMNOPQRSTUVWXYZ
ABCDEFGHIJKLMNOPQRSTUVWXYZ
.,"'-:;!?""&1234567890$1234567890$
.,"'-:;!?""&1234567890$1234567890$
abcdefghijklmnopqrstuvwxyz
abcdefghijklmnopqrstuvwxyz

ABCDEFGHIJKLMNOPQRSTUVWXYZ
ABCDEFGHIJKLMNOPQRSTUVWXYZ
.,"'-:;!?""&1234567890$1234567890$
.,"'-:;!?""&1234567890$1234567890$
abcdefghijklmnopqrstuvwxyz
abcdefghijklmnopqrstuvwxyz

CALEDONIA BOLD: LINOTYPE   *When long descenders are used (as shown) type must be set on a slug one point greater than specified size.

PICAS	6	7	8	9	10	11	12	13	14	15	16	17	18	19	20	21	22	23	24	25	26	27	28	29	30
12 POINT	14	16	18	20	23	25	27	29	32	34	36	38	41	43	45	47	50	52	54	56	59	61	63	65	68
10 POINT	15	18	20	23	26	28	31	33	36	38	41	43	46	48	51	54	56	59	61	64	66	69	71	74	77

14/14

Type is defined as a right-angled, prism-shaped piece of metal, having for its face a letter or character, usually in high relief, adapted for use in letter-press printing; and type in the aggregate is described as an assemblage of the characters used for printing. In a single type the chief points to be described are the face, counter, stem, hair-line, serif, beard or neck, shoulder, body or shank, pin-mark, nick, feet, and groove.

The accompanying diagram of a piece of type (fig. 2) shows its face, body, nick,

12/12

Type is defined as a right-angled, prism-shaped piece of metal, having for its face a letter or character, usually in high relief, adapted for use in letter-press printing; and type in the aggregate is described as an assemblage of the characters used for printing. In a single type the chief points to be described are the face, counter, stem, hair-line, serif, beard or neck, shoulder, body or shank, pin-mark, nick, feet, and groove.

The accompanying diagram of a piece of type (fig. 2) shows its face, body, nick, groove, feet, and pin-mark; and the plan of the face (fig. 3) *shows the stem, hair-line, serif, counter, beard, and shoulder.*

14/16

Type is defined as a right-angled, prism-shaped piece of metal, having for its face a letter or character, usually in high relief, adapted for use in letter-press printing; and type in the aggregate is described as an assemblage of the characters used for printing. In a single type the chief points to be described are the face, counter, stem, hair-line,

The accompanying diagram of a piece of type (fig. 2) shows its face, body, nick,

12/14

Type is defined as a right-angled, prism-shaped piece of metal, having for its face a letter or character, usually in high relief, adapted for use in letter-press printing; and type in the aggregate is described as an assemblage of the characters used for printing. In a single type the chief points to be described are the face, counter, stem, hair-line, serif, beard or neck, shoulder, body or shank, pin-mark, nick, feet, and groove.

The accompanying diagram of a piece of type *shows the stem, hair-line, serif, counter, beard, and shoulder.*

14/18

Type is defined as a right-angled, prism-shaped piece of metal, having for its face a letter or character, usually in high relief, adapted for use in letter-press printing; and type in the aggregate is described as an assemblage of the characters used for printing. In a single type the chief points to be described are the face, counter, stem, hair-line,

The accompanying diagram of a piece of type (fig. 2) shows its face, body, nick,

12/16

Type is defined as a right-angled, prism-shaped piece of metal, having for its face a letter or character, usually in high relief, adapted for use in letter-press printing; and type in the aggregate is described as an assemblage of the characters used for printing. In a single type the chief points to be described are the face, counter, stem, hair-line, serif, beard or neck, shoulder, body or shank, pin-mark, nick, feet, and groove.

shows the stem, hair-line, serif, counter, beard, and shoulder.

ABCDEFGHIJKLMNOPQRSTUV
ABCDEFGHIJKLMNOPQRSTUV
WXYZ.,"-:;!?""&1234567890$
WXYZ.,"-:;!?""&1234567890$
abcdefghijklmnopqrstuvwxyz
abcdefghijklmnopqrstuvwxyz

ABCDEFGHIJKLMNOPQRSTUVWXYZ
ABCDEFGHIJKLMNOPQRSTUVWXYZ
.,"-:;!?""&1234567890$
.,"-:;!?""&1234567890$
abcdefghijklmnopqrstuvwxyz
abcdefghijklmnopqrstuvwxyz

CHELTENHAM: LINOTYPE

PICAS	6	7	8	9	10	11	12	13	14	15	16	17	18	19	20	21	22	23	24	25	26	27	28	29	30
14 POINT	12	14	16	18	21	23	25	27	29	31	33	35	37	39	42	44	46	48	50	52	54	56	58	60	63
12 POINT	15	17	20	22	25	27	30	32	35	37	40	42	45	47	50	52	55	57	60	62	65	67	70	72	75

10/10

Type is defined as a right-angled, prism-shaped piece of metal, having for its face a letter or character, usually in high relief, adapted for use in letter-press printing; and type in the aggregate is described as an assemblage of the characters used for printing. In a single type the chief points to be described are the face, counter, stem, hair-line, serif, beard or neck, shoulder, body or shank, pin-mark, nick, feet, and groove.

The accompanying diagram of a piece of type (fig. 2) shows its face, body, nick, groove, feet, and pin-mark; and the plan of the face (fig. 3) shows the stem, hair-line, serif, counter, beard, and shoulder.

The body (or shank) of a piece of type is the metal between the shoulder and the feet (described later), and the term "body" is also used to denote the size or thickness of *types, leads, etc. The pin-mark is an indentation on the upper part of the body, made by the pin in casting. The nick is*

8/8

Type is defined as a right-angled, prism-shaped piece of metal, having for its face a letter or character, usually in high relief, adapted for use in letter-press printing; and type in the aggregate is described as an assemblage of the characters used for printing. In a single type the chief points to be described are the face, counter, stem, hair-line, serif, beard or neck, shoulder, body or shank, pin-mark, nick, feet, and groove.

The accompanying diagram of a piece of type (fig. 2) shows its face, body, nick, groove, feet, and pin-mark; and the plan of the face (fig. 3) shows the stem, hair-line, serif, counter, beard, and shoulder.

The body (or shank) of a piece of type is the metal between the shoulder and the feet (described later), and the term "body" is also used to denote the size or thickness of types, leads, etc. The pin-mark is an indentation on the upper part of the body, made by the pin in casting. The nick is the groove across the lower part of the body of the type, and is a guide to the position in which it is to be set up. The feet are the projections on each side of the groove on which the type stands, the groove being the hollow left between the feet where formerly was the jet.

The face of a type is the letter on its upper end which carries the ink *to be impressed upon the paper; the counter is the cavity left by the surrounding lines of the face. The stem is the thick stroke or line of the*

10/12

Type is defined as a right-angled, prism-shaped piece of metal, having for its face a letter or character, usually in high relief, adapted for use in letter-press printing; and type in the aggregate is described as an assemblage of the characters used for printing. In a single type the chief points to be described are the face, counter, stem, hair-line, serif, beard or neck, shoulder, body or shank, pin-mark, nick, feet, and groove.

The accompanying diagram of a piece of type (fig. 2) shows its face, body, nick, groove, feet, and pin-mark; and the plan of the face (fig. 3) shows the stem, hair-line, serif, counter, beard, and shoulder.

types, leads, etc. The pin-mark is an indentation on the upper part of the body, made by the pin in casting. The nick is

8/10

Type is defined as a right-angled, prism-shaped piece of metal, having for its face a letter or character, usually in high relief, adapted for use in letter-press printing; and type in the aggregate is described as an assemblage of the characters used for printing. In a single type the chief points to be described are the face, counter, stem, hair-line, serif, beard or neck, shoulder, body or shank, pin-mark, nick, feet, and groove.

The accompanying diagram of a piece of type (fig. 2) shows its face, body, nick, groove, feet, and pin-mark; and the plan of the face (fig. 3) shows the stem, hair-line, serif, counter, beard, and shoulder.

The body (or shank) of a piece of type is the metal between the shoulder and the feet (described later), and the term "body" is also used to denote the size or thickness of types, leads, etc. The pin-mark is an indentation on the upper part of the body, made by the pin in casting. The nick is the groove across the lower part of the body of the

The face of a type is the letter on its upper end which carries the ink *to be impressed upon the paper; the counter is the cavity left by the surrounding lines of the face. The stem is the thick stroke or line of the*

10/14

Type is defined as a right-angled, prism-shaped piece of metal, having for its face a letter or character, usually in high relief, adapted for use in letter-press printing; and type in the aggregate is described as an assemblage of the characters used for printing. In a single type the chief points to be described are the face, counter, stem, hair-line, serif, beard or neck, shoulder, body or shank, pin-mark, nick, feet, and groove.

The accompanying diagram of a piece of type (fig. 2) shows its face, body, nick, groove, feet, and pin-mark; and *types, leads, etc. The pin-mark is an indentation on the upper part of the body, made by the pin in casting. The nick is*

8/12

Type is defined as a right-angled, prism-shaped piece of metal, having for its face a letter or character, usually in high relief, adapted for use in letter-press printing; and type in the aggregate is described as an assemblage of the characters used for printing. In a single type the chief points to be described are the face, counter, stem, hair-line, serif, beard or neck, shoulder, body or shank, pin-mark, nick, feet, and groove.

The accompanying diagram of a piece of type (fig. 2) shows its face, body, nick, groove, feet, and pin-mark; and the plan of the face (fig. 3) shows the stem, hair-line, serif, counter, beard, and shoulder.

The body (or shank) of a piece of type is the metal between the shoulder and the feet (described later), and the term "body" is also used to denote the size or thickness of types, leads, etc. The pin-mark *to be impressed upon the paper; the counter is the cavity left by the surrounding lines of the face. The stem is the thick stroke or line of the*

ABCDEFGHIJKLMNOPQRSTUVWXYZ
ABCDEFGHIJKLMNOPQRSTUVWXYZ
.,"-:;!?""''&1234567890$
.,"-:;!?""''&1234567890$
abcdefghijklmnopqrstuvwxyz
abcdefghijklmnopqrstuvwxyz

ABCDEFGHIJKLMNOPQRSTUVWXYZ
ABCDEFGHIJKLMNOPQRSTUVWXYZ
.,"-:;!?""''&1234567890$
.,"-:;!?""''&1234567890$
abcdefghijklmnopqrstuvwxyz
abcdefghijklmnopqrstuvwxyz

CHELTENHAM: LINOTYPE

PICAS	6	7	8	9	10	11	12	13	14	15	16	17	18	19	20	21	22	23	24	25	26	27	28	29	30
10 POINT	17	20	23	26	29	31	34	37	40	43	46	49	52	55	58	60	63	66	69	72	75	78	81	84	87
8 POINT	21	24	28	31	35	38	42	45	49	52	56	59	63	66	70	73	77	80	84	87	91	94	98	101	105

14/14

Type is defined as a right-angled, prism-shaped piece of metal, having for its face a letter or character, usually in high relief, adapted for use in letter-press printing; and type in the aggregate is described as an assemblage of the characters used for printing. In a single type the chief points to be described are the face, counter, stem, hair-line, *serif, beard or neck, shoulder, body or shank, pin-mark, nick, feet, and*

14/16

Type is defined as a right-angled, prism-shaped piece of metal, having for its face a letter or character, usually in high relief, adapted for use in letter-press printing; and type in the aggregate is described as an assemblage of the characters used for printing. In a single type the chief points to be described are *serif, beard or neck, shoulder, body or shank, pin-mark, nick, feet, and*

14/18

Type is defined as a right-angled, prism-shaped piece of metal, having for its face a letter or character, usually in high relief, adapted for use in letter-press printing; and type in the aggregate is described as an assemblage of the characters used for printing. In a single type *serif, beard or neck, shoulder, body or shank, pin-mark, nick, feet, and*

12/12

Type is defined as a right-angled, prism-shaped piece of metal, having for its face a letter or character, usually in high relief, adapted for use in letter-press printing; and type in the aggregate is described as an assemblage of the characters used for printing. In a single type the chief points to be described are the face, counter, stem, hair-line, serif, beard or neck, shoulder, body or shank, pin-mark, nick, feet, and groove.

The accompanying diagram of a piece *of type (fig. 2) shows its face, body, nick, groove, feet, and pin-mark; and the plan of*

12/14

Type is defined as a right-angled, prism-shaped piece of metal, having for its face a letter or character, usually in high relief, adapted for use in letter-press printing; and type in the aggregate is described as an assemblage of the characters used for printing. In a single type the chief points to be described are the face, counter, stem, hair-line, serif, beard or neck, shoulder, body or shank, pin-mark, nick, feet, and *of type (fig. 2) shows its face, body, nick, groove, feet, and pin-mark; and the plan of*

12/16

Type is defined as a right-angled, prism-shaped piece of metal, having for its face a letter or character, usually in high relief, adapted for use in letter-press printing; and type in the aggregate is described as an assemblage of the characters used for printing. In a single type the chief points to be described are the face, counter, stem, hair-line, serif, beard or neck, shoulder, *of type (fig. 2) shows its face, body, nick, groove, feet, and pin-mark; and the plan of*

ABCDEFGHIJKLMNOPQRSTU
ABCDEFGHIJKLMNOPQRSTU
VWXYZ.,"-:;!?""&1234567890$
VWXYZ.,"-:;!?""&1234567890$
abcdefghijklmnopqrstuvwxyz
abcdefghijklmnopqrstuvwxyz

ABCDEFGHIJKLMNOPQRSTUVWXY
ABCDEFGHIJKLMNOPQRSTUVWXY
Z.,"-:;!?""&1234567890$
Z.,"-:;!?""&1234567890$
abcdefghijklmnopqrstuvwxyz
abcdefghijklmnopqrstuvwxyz

CHELTENHAM BOLD: LINOTYPE

PICAS	6	7	8	9	10	11	12	13	14	15	16	17	18	19	20	21	22	23	24	25	26	27	28	29	30
14 POINT	10	11	13	15	17	18	20	22	23	25	27	28	30	32	34	35	37	39	40	42	44	45	47	49	51
12 POINT	12	14	16	18	20	22	24	26	28	30	32	34	36	38	40	42	44	46	48	50	52	54	56	58	60

10/10

Type is defined as a right-angled, prism-shaped piece of metal, having for its face a letter or character, usually in high relief, adapted for use in letter-press printing; and type in the aggregate is described as an assemblage of the characters used for printing. In a single type the chief points to be described are the face, counter, stem, hair-line, serif, beard or neck, shoulder, body or shank, pin-mark, nick, feet, and groove.

The accompanying diagram of a piece of type (fig. 2) shows its face, body, nick, groove, feet, and pin-mark; and the plan of the face (fig. 3) shows the stem, hair-line, serif, counter, beard, and shoulder.

The body (or shank) of a piece of type is the metal between the shoulder and the feet (de-

8/8

Type is defined as a right-angled, prism-shaped piece of metal, having for its face a letter or character, usually in high relief, adapted for use in letter-press printing; and type in the aggregate is described as an assemblage of the characters used for printing. In a single type the chief points to be described are the face, counter, stem, hair-line, serif, beard or neck, shoulder, body or shank, pin-mark, nick, feet, and groove.

The accompanying diagram of a piece of type (fig. 2) shows its face, body, nick, groove, feet, and pin-mark; and the plan of the face (fig. 3) shows the stem, hair-line, serif, counter, beard, and shoulder.

The body (or shank) of a piece of type is the metal between the shoulder and the feet (described later), and the term "body" is also used to denote the size or thickness of types, leads, etc. The pin-mark is an indentation on the upper part of the body, made by the pin in casting. The nick is the groove across the lower part of the body of the type, and is a guide to the position in which it is to *be set up. The feet are the projections on each side of the groove on which the type stands, the groove being the hol-*

10/12

Type is defined as a right-angled, prism-shaped piece of metal, having for its face a letter or character, usually in high relief, adapted for use in letter-press printing; and type in the aggregate is described as an assemblage of the characters used for printing. In a single type the chief points to be described are the face, counter, stem, hair-line, serif, beard or neck, shoulder, body or shank, pin-mark, nick, feet, and groove.

The accompanying diagram of a piece of type (fig. 2) shows its face, body, nick, groove,

The body (or shank) of a piece of type is the metal between the shoulder and the feet (de-

8/10

Type is defined as a right-angled, prism-shaped piece of metal, having for its face a letter or character, usually in high relief, adapted for use in letter-press printing; and type in the aggregate is described as an assemblage of the characters used for printing. In a single type the chief points to be described are the face, counter, stem, hair-line, serif, beard or neck, shoulder, body or shank, pin-mark, nick, feet, and groove.

The accompanying diagram of a piece of type (fig. 2) shows its face, body, nick, groove, feet, and pin-mark; and the plan of the face (fig. 3) shows the stem, hair-line, serif, counter, beard, and shoulder.

The body (or shank) of a piece of type is the metal between the shoulder and the feet (described later), and of the type, and is a guide to the position in which it is to *be set up. The feet are the projections on each side of the groove on which the type stands, the groove being the hol-*

10/14

Type is defined as a right-angled, prism-shaped piece of metal, having for its face a letter or character, usually in high relief, adapted for use in letter-press printing; and type in the aggregate is described as an assemblage of the characters used for printing. In a single type the chief points to be described are the face, counter, stem, hair-line, serif, beard or neck, shoulder, body or shank, pin-mark, nick, feet, and groove.

The body (or shank) of a piece of type is the metal between the shoulder and the feet (de-

8/12

Type is defined as a right-angled, prism-shaped piece of metal, having for its face a letter or character, usually in high relief, adapted for use in letter-press printing; and type in the aggregate is described as an assemblage of the characters used for printing. In a single type the chief points to be described are the face, counter, stem, hair-line, serif, beard or neck, shoulder, body or shank, pin-mark, nick, feet, and groove.

The accompanying diagram of a piece of type (fig. 2) shows its face, body, nick, groove, feet, and pin-mark; and the plan of the face (fig. 3) shows the stem, hair-line, serif, counter, beard, and shoulder.

be set up. The feet are the projections on each side of the groove on which the type stands, the groove being the hol-

ABCDEFGHIJKLMNOPQRSTUVWXYZ
ABCDEFGHIJKLMNOPQRSTUVWXYZ
.,"-:;!?""&1234567890$
.,"-:;!?""&1234567890$
abcdefghijklmnopqrstuvwxyz
abcdefghijklmnopqrstuvwxyz

ABCDEFGHIJKLMNOPQRSTUVWXYZ
ABCDEFGHIJKLMNOPQRSTUVWXYZ
.,"-:;!?""&1234567890$
.,"-:;!?""&1234567890$
abcdefghijklmnopqrstuvwxyz
abcdefghijklmnopqrstuvwxyz

CHELTENHAM BOLD: LINOTYPE

PICAS	6	7	8	9	10	11	12	13	14	15	16	17	18	19	20	21	22	23	24	25	26	27	28	29	30
10 POINT	13	15	17	19	22	24	26	28	30	33	35	37	39	41	44	46	48	50	52	55	57	59	61	63	66
8 POINT	16	19	22	25	28	30	33	36	39	42	44	47	50	53	56	58	61	64	67	70	72	75	78	81	84

10/11
GIAMBATTISTA BODONI, "TO THE READER," 1818. This essay is the fruit of many years' assiduous labour—a real labour of love—in the service of the art of printing. Printing is the final outcome of man's most beautiful, ingenious and useful invention: that I mean, of writing: and its most valuable form where it is required to turn out many copies of the same text. This applies still more where it is important to ensure uniformity, and most of all where the work in question is one which deserves transmission in clearer and more readable form for the enjoyment of posterity. When we consider the range of usefulness of printing, together with the long series of devices which have brought us from

8/9
GIAMBATTISTA BODONI, "TO THE READER," 1818. This essay is the fruit of many years' assiduous labour—a real labour of love—in the service of the art of printing. Printing is the final outcome of man's most beautiful, ingenious and useful invention: that I mean, of writing: and its most valuable form where it is required to turn out many copies of the same text. This applies still more where it is important to ensure uniformity, and most of all where the work in question is one which deserves transmission in clearer and more readable form for the enjoyment of posterity. When we consider the range of usefulness of printing, together with the long series of devices which have brought us from the first discovery of letters to our present power of printing on thousands of sheets of fine laid paper words no longer evanescent but fixed and preserved with sharper outlines than the articulation of lips can give them, the thought of such surpassing achievement compels

10/12
GIAMBATTISTA BODONI, "TO THE READER," 1818. This essay is the fruit of many years' assiduous labour—a real labour of love—in the service of the art of printing. Printing is the final outcome of man's most beautiful, ingenious and useful invention: that I mean, of writing: and its most valuable form where it is required to turn out many copies of the same text. This applies still more where it is important to ensure uniformity, and most of all where the work in question is one which deserves transmission in clearer and more readable form for the enjoyment of posterity. When we consider the range of

8/10
GIAMBATTISTA BODONI, "TO THE READER," 1818. This essay is the fruit of many years' assiduous labour—a real labour of love—in the service of the art of printing. Printing is the final outcome of man's most beautiful, ingenious and useful invention: that I mean, of writing: and its most valuable form where it is required to turn out many copies of the same text. This applies still more where it is important to ensure uniformity, and most of all where the work in question is one which deserves transmission in clearer and more readable form for the enjoyment of posterity. When we consider the range of usefulness of printing, together with the long series of devices which have brought us from the first discovery of letters to our present power of printing on thousands of sheets of fine laid paper words no longer evanescent but fixed and preserved with sharper out-

10/14
GIAMBATTISTA BODONI, "TO THE READER," 1818. This essay is the fruit of many years' assiduous labour—a real labour of love—in the service of the art of printing. Printing is the final outcome of man's most beautiful, ingenious and useful invention: that I mean, of writing: and its most valuable form where it is required to turn out many copies of the same text. This applies still more where it is important to ensure uniformity, and most of all where the work in question is one which deserves transmission in clearer

8/12
GIAMBATTISTA BODONI, "TO THE READER," 1818. This essay is the fruit of many years' assiduous labour—a real labour of love—in the service of the art of printing. Printing is the final outcome of man's most beautiful, ingenious and useful invention: that I mean, of writing: and its most valuable form where it is required to turn out many copies of the same text. This applies still more where it is important to ensure uniformity, and most of all where the work in question is one which deserves transmission in clearer and more readable form for the enjoyment of posterity. When we consider the range of usefulness of printing, together with the long series of devices which have brought us from the first discovery

ABCDEFGHIJKLMNOPQRSTUVWXYZ
.,"-:;!?""&1234567890$
abcdefghijklmnopqrstuvwxyz

ABCDEFGHIJKLMNOPQRSTUVWXYZ
.,"-:;!?""&1234567890$
abcdefghijklmnopqrstuvwxyz

CLARENDON: LINOTYPE *This face must be set 1 pt leaded.

PICAS	6	7	8	9	10	11	12	13	14	15	16	17	18	19	20	21	22	23	24	25	26	27	28	29	30
10 POINT	13	15	17	20	22	24	26	29	31	33	35	38	40	42	44	47	49	51	53	56	58	60	62	65	67
8 POINT	16	18	21	23	26	29	31	33	36	38	40	43	46	49	51	54	56	59	61	64	67	70	72	75	77

14/15

Ever since the sixteenth century, elaborate diagrams have been published to show how letters should be drawn, as we shall learn from some accounts given of men who suggested new methods of designing them. Generally a diagram of minute squares was first made, and on this the design and dimension of each letter were determined. Jaugeon, who was ap-*pointed by the Académie des Sciences of Paris in the last years of the seven-*

12/13

Ever since the sixteenth century, elaborate diagrams have been published to show how letters should be drawn, as we shall learn from some accounts given of men who suggested new methods of designing them. Generally a diagram of minute squares was first made, and on this the design and dimension of each letter were determined. Jaugeon, who was appointed by the Académie des Sciences of Paris in the last years of the seventeenth century to supply a *type should be cut, began by stating that "the eye is the sovereign ruler of taste."*

14/16

Ever since the sixteenth century, elaborate diagrams have been published to show how letters should be drawn, as we shall learn from some accounts given of men who suggested new methods of designing them. Generally a diagram of minute squares was first made, and on this the design *pointed by the Académie des Sciences of Paris in the last years of the seven-*

12/14

Ever since the sixteenth century, elaborate diagrams have been published to show how letters should be drawn, as we shall learn from some accounts given of men who suggested new methods of designing them. Generally a diagram of minute squares was first made, and on this the design and dimension of each letter were determined. Jaugeon, who was appointed by the Académie des Sciences of Paris in the last years *type should be cut, began by stating that "the eye is the sovereign ruler of taste."*

14/18

Ever since the sixteenth century, elaborate diagrams have been published to show how letters should be drawn, as we shall learn from some accounts given of men who suggested new methods of designing them. Generally a diagram of minute squares *pointed by the Académie des Sciences of Paris in the last years of the seven-*

12/16

Ever since the sixteenth century, elaborate diagrams have been published to show how letters should be drawn, as we shall learn from some accounts given of men who suggested new methods of designing them. Generally a diagram of minute squares was first made, and on this the design and dimension of each letter were determined. *type should be cut, began by stating that "the eye is the sovereign ruler of taste."*

ABCDEFGHIJKLMNOPQRSTU
ABCDEFGHIJKLMNOPQRSTU
VWXYZ.,"-:;!?""&1234567890$
VWXYZ.,"-:;!?""&1234567890$
abcdefghijklmnopqrstuvwxyz
abcdefghijklmnopqrstuvwxyz

ABCDEFGHIJKLMNOPQRSTUVWX
ABCDEFGHIJKLMNOPQRSTUVWX
YZ.,"-:;!?""&1234567890$
YZ.,"-:;!?""&1234567890$
abcdefghijklmnopqrstuvwxyz
abcdefghijklmnopqrstuvwxyz

DEVINNE: LINOTYPE *When long descenders are used (as shown) type must be set on a slug one point greater than specified size.

PICAS	6	7	8	9	10	11	12	13	14	15	16	17	18	19	20	21	22	23	24	25	26	27	28	29	30
14 POINT	10	12	14	16	18	19	21	23	25	27	28	30	32	34	36	37	39	41	43	45	46	48	50	52	54
12 POINT	12	14	16	18	21	23	25	27	29	31	33	35	37	39	42	44	46	48	50	52	54	56	58	60	63

11/12

Ever since the sixteenth century, elaborate diagrams have been published to show how letters should be drawn, as we shall learn from some accounts given of men who suggested new methods of designing them. Generally a diagram of minute squares was first made, and on this the design and dimension of each letter were determined. Jaugeon, who was appointed by the Académie des Sciences of Paris in the last years of the seventeenth century to supply a scheme or series of directions by which type should be cut, began by stating that "the eye is *he set forth were extremely complicated— every Roman capital was to be designed on a*

10/11

Ever since the sixteenth century, elaborate diagrams have been published to show how letters should be drawn, as we shall learn from some accounts given of men who suggested new methods of designing them. Generally a diagram of minute squares was first made, and on this the design and dimension of each letter were determined. Jaugeon, who was appointed by the Académie des Sciences of Paris in the last years of the seventeenth century to supply a scheme or series of directions by which type should be cut, began by stating that "the eye is the sovereign ruler of taste.'' The rules which he set forth were extremely complicated—every Roman capital was to *follow them, is said to have observed sarcastically, that he should certainly accept Jaugeon's dictum*

11/13

Ever since the sixteenth century, elaborate diagrams have been published to show how letters should be drawn, as we shall learn from some accounts given of men who suggested new methods of designing them. Generally a diagram of minute squares was first made, and on this the design and dimension of each letter were determined. Jaugeon, who was appointed by the Académie des Sciences of Paris in the last years of the seventeenth century to supply a scheme or series of directions by which type *he set forth were extremely complicated— every Roman capital was to be designed on a*

10/12

Ever since the sixteenth century, elaborate diagrams have been published to show how letters should be drawn, as we shall learn from some accounts given of men who suggested new methods of designing them. Generally a diagram of minute squares was first made, and on this the design and dimension of each letter were determined. Jaugeon, who was appointed by the Académie des Sciences of Paris in the last years of the seventeenth century to supply a scheme or series of directions by which type should be cut, began by stating that "the eye is the sovereign ruler of taste.'' The rules which he set forth were ex- *follow them, is said to have observed sarcastically, that he should certainly accept Jaugeon's dictum*

11/15

Ever since the sixteenth century, elaborate diagrams have been published to show how letters should be drawn, as we shall learn from some accounts given of men who suggested new methods of designing them. Generally a diagram of minute squares was first made, and on this the design and dimension of each letter were determined. Jaugeon, who was appointed by the Académie des Sciences of Paris in the *he set forth were extremely complicated— every Roman capital was to be designed on a*

10/14

Ever since the sixteenth century, elaborate diagrams have been published to show how letters should be drawn, as we shall learn from some accounts given of men who suggested new methods of designing them. Generally a diagram of minute squares was first made, and on this the design and dimension of each letter were determined. Jaugeon, who was appointed by the Académie des Sciences of Paris in the last years of the seventeenth century to supply a scheme or series of directions by which type should be cut, *follow them, is said to have observed sarcastically, that he should certainly accept Jaugeon's dictum*

ABCDEFGHIJKLMNOPQRSTUVWXYZ
ABCDEFGHIJKLMNOPQRSTUVWXYZ
.,"-:;!?''""&1234567890$
.,"-:;!?''""&1234567890$
abcdefghijklmnopqrstuvwxyz
abcdefghijklmnopqrstuvwxyz

ABCDEFGHIJKLMNOPQRSTUVWXYZ
ABCDEFGHIJKLMNOPQRSTUVWXYZ
.,"-:;!?''""&1234567890$
.,"-:;!?''""&1234567890$
abcdefghijklmnopqrstuvwxyz
abcdefghijklmnopqrstuvwxyz

DEVINNE: LINOTYPE *When long descenders are used (as shown) type must be set on a slug one point greater than specified size.

PICAS	6	7	8	9	10	11	12	13	14	15	16	17	18	19	20	21	22	23	24	25	26	27	28	29	30
11 POINT	13	16	18	20	23	25	27	29	32	34	36	39	41	43	46	48	50	53	55	57	59	62	64	66	69
10 POINT	15	18	20	23	26	28	31	33	36	39	41	44	46	49	52	54	57	59	62	65	67	69	72	75	78

9/10

Ever since the sixteenth century, elaborate diagrams have been published to show how letters should be drawn, as we shall learn from some accounts given of men who suggested new methods of designing them. Generally a diagram of minute squares was first made, and on this the design and dimension of each letter were determined. Jaugeon, who was appointed by the Académie des Sciences of Paris in the last years of the seventeenth century to supply a scheme or series of directions by which type should be cut, began by stating that "the eye is the sovereign ruler of taste." The rules which he set forth were extremely complicated—every Roman capital was to be designed on a framework of 2304 little squares. Grandjean, the first type-cutter who attempted to follow them, is said to have observed sarcastically, that he should certainly accept Jaugeon's dictum that

In casting type the two schools of typography spoken of on an earlier page—one experimental and crude, the other

8/9

Ever since the sixteenth century, elaborate diagrams have been published to show how letters should be drawn, as we shall learn from some accounts given of men who suggested new methods of designing them. Generally a diagram of minute squares was first made, and on this the design and dimension of each letter were determined. Jaugeon, who was appointed by the Académie des Sciences of Paris in the last years of the seventeenth century to supply a scheme or series of directions by which type should be cut, began by stating that "the eye is the sovereign ruler of taste." The rules which he set forth were extremely complicated—every Roman capital was to be designed on a framework of 2304 little squares. Grandjean, the first type-cutter who attempted to follow them, is said to have observed sarcastically, that he should certainly accept Jaugeon's dictum that "the eye is the sovereign ruler of taste," and accepting this, should throw the rest of his rules over—*and perfected—had probably different methods. One cast letters in moulds of clay or sand; the other understood something*

9/11

Ever since the sixteenth century, elaborate diagrams have been published to show how letters should be drawn, as we shall learn from some accounts given of men who suggested new methods of designing them. Generally a diagram of minute squares was first made, and on this the design and dimension of each letter were determined. Jaugeon, who was appointed by the Académie des Sciences of Paris in the last years of the seventeenth century to supply a scheme or series of directions by which type should be cut, began by stating that "the eye is the sovereign ruler of taste." The rules which he set forth were extremely complicated—every Roman capital was to be designed on a framework of 2304 little squares. Grandjean, the first type-cutter who at-

In casting type the two schools of typography spoken of on an earlier page—one experimental and crude, the other

8/10

Ever since the sixteenth century, elaborate diagrams have been published to show how letters should be drawn, as we shall learn from some accounts given of men who suggested new methods of designing them. Generally a diagram of minute squares was first made, and on this the design and dimension of each letter were determined. Jaugeon, who was appointed by the Académie des Sciences of Paris in the last years of the seventeenth century to supply a scheme or series of directions by which type should be cut, began by stating that "the eye is the sovereign ruler of taste." The rules which he set forth were extremely complicated—every Roman capital was to be designed on a framework of 2304 little squares. Grandjean, the first type-cutter who attempted to follow them, is said to have observed sarcastically, that he should certainly accept Jaugeon's dictum that "the eye is the sovereign ruler of taste," *and perfected—had probably different methods. One cast letters in moulds of clay or sand; the other understood something*

9/13

Ever since the sixteenth century, elaborate diagrams have been published to show how letters should be drawn, as we shall learn from some accounts given of men who suggested new methods of designing them. Generally a diagram of minute squares was first made, and on this the design and dimension of each letter were determined. Jaugeon, who was appointed by the Académie des Sciences of Paris in the last years of the seventeenth century to supply a scheme or series of directions by which type should be cut, began by stating that "the eye is the sovereign ruler of taste." The rules which he set forth were extremely complicated—every

In casting type the two schools of typography spoken of on an earlier page—one experimental and crude, the other

8/12

Ever since the sixteenth century, elaborate diagrams have been published to show how letters should be drawn, as we shall learn from some accounts given of men who suggested new methods of designing them. Generally a diagram of minute squares was first made, and on this the design and dimension of each letter were determined. Jaugeon, who was appointed by the Académie des Sciences of Paris in the last years of the seventeenth century to supply a scheme or series of directions by which type should be cut, began by stating that "the eye is the sovereign ruler of taste." The rules which he set forth were extremely complicated—every Roman capital was to be designed on a framework of 2304 little squares. Grandjean, the *and perfected—had probably different methods. One cast letters in moulds of clay or sand; the other understood something*

ABCDEFGHIJKLMNOPQRSTUVWXYZ
ABCDEFGHIJKLMNOPQRSTUVWXYZ
.,"-:;!?""&1234567890$
.,"-:;!?""&1234567890$
abcdefghijklmnopqrstuvwxyz
abcdefghijklmnopqrstuvwxyz

ABCDEFGHIJKLMNOPQRSTUVWXYZ
ABCDEFGHIJKLMNOPQRSTUVWXYZ
.,"-:;!?""&1234567890$
.,"-:;!?""&1234567890$
abcdefghijklmnopqrstuvwxyz
abcdefghijklmnopqrstuvwxyz

DEVINNE: LINOTYPE *When long descenders are used (as shown) type must be set on a slug one point greater than specified size.

PICAS	6	7	8	9	10	11	12	13	14	15	16	17	18	19	20	21	22	23	24	25	26	27	28	29	30
9 POINT	17	20	23	26	29	31	34	37	40	43	46	49	52	55	58	60	63	66	69	72	75	78	81	84	87
8 POINT	18	21	24	27	31	34	37	40	43	46	49	52	56	59	62	65	68	71	74	77	80	83	86	89	93

9/9

The Greek alphabet had a close relation to the Phœnician, or (as perhaps it is more properly called) the Semitic alphabet. In the first place, the forms were in many cases very much alike. The word "alphabet," which gives a clue to the connection, is derived from alpha and beta, the names of the first and second letters of the Greek alphabet. "The names of the Semitic letters," Sir Edward Maunde Thompson tells us, "are Semitic words, each describing the letter from its resemblance to some particular object, as, aleph, an ox, beth, a house. When the Greeks took over their Semitic letters, they also took over their Semitic names." Both the names of the letters and their order in the two alphabets are the same. This alphabet was employed by the Phœnicians, by the Jews, and by the Moabites, and from early inscriptions, the primitive Phœnician alphabet, consisting of twenty-two letters, can be made up.

The Greeks learned the art of writing in the ninth

8/8

The Greek alphabet had a close relation to the Phœnician, or (as perhaps it is more properly called) the Semitic alphabet. In the first place, the forms were in many cases very much alike. The word "alphabet," which gives a clue to the connection, is derived from alpha and beta, the names of the first and second letters of the Greek alphabet. "The names of the Semitic letters," Sir Edward Maunde Thompson tells us, "are Semitic words, each describing the letter from its resemblance to some particular object, as, aleph, an ox, beth, a house. When the Greeks took over their Semitic letters, they also took over their Semitic names." Both the names of the letters and their order in the two alphabets are the same. This alphabet was employed by the Phœnicians, by the Jews, and by the Moabites, and from early inscriptions, the primitive Phœnician alphabet, consisting of twenty-two letters, can be made up.

The Greeks learned the art of writing in the ninth century B.C.—perhaps earlier. The primitive Greek alphabet was generally known as the Cadmean alphabet, and it had many varieties. The alphabets first in use were written from right to left; then the boustrophedon method of writing came into

9/11

The Greek alphabet had a close relation to the Phœnician, or (as perhaps it is more properly called) the Semitic alphabet. In the first place, the forms were in many cases very much alike. The word "alphabet," which gives a clue to the connection, is derived from alpha and beta, the names of the first and second letters of the Greek alphabet. "The names of the Semitic letters," Sir Edward Maunde Thompson tells us, "are Semitic words, each describing the letter from its resemblance to some particular object, as, aleph, an ox, beth, a house. When the Greeks took over their Semitic letters, they also took over their Semitic names." Both the names of the letters and their order in the two alphabets are the same. This alphabet was employed by the Phœnicians, by the Jews, and by the

8/10

The Greek alphabet had a close relation to the Phœnician, or (as perhaps it is more properly called) the Semitic alphabet. In the first place, the forms were in many cases very much alike. The word "alphabet," which gives a clue to the connection, is derived from alpha and beta, the names of the first and second letters of the Greek alphabet. "The names of the Semitic letters," Sir Edward Maunde Thompson tells us, "are Semitic words, each describing the letter from its resemblance to some particular object, as, aleph, an ox, beth, a house. When the Greeks took over their Semitic letters, they also took over their Semitic names." Both the names of the letters and their order in the two alphabets are the same. This alphabet was employed by the Phœnicians, by the Jews, and by the Moabites, and from early inscriptions, the primitive Phœnician alphabet, consisting of twenty-two letters, can be made up.

The Greeks learned the art of writing in the ninth century

9/13

The Greek alphabet had a close relation to the Phœnician, or (as perhaps it is more properly called) the Semitic alphabet. In the first place, the forms were in many cases very much alike. The word "alphabet," which gives a clue to the connection, is derived from alpha and beta, the names of the first and second letters of the Greek alphabet. "The names of the Semitic letters," Sir Edward Maunde Thompson tells us, "are Semitic words, each describing the letter from its resemblance to some particular object, as, aleph, an ox, beth, a house. When the Greeks took over their Semitic letters, they also took over their Semitic names." Both the names of the letters and their order in the

8/12

The Greek alphabet had a close relation to the Phœnician, or (as perhaps it is more properly called) the Semitic alphabet. In the first place, the forms were in many cases very much alike. The word "alphabet," which gives a clue to the connection, is derived from alpha and beta, the names of the first and second letters of the Greek alphabet. "The names of the Semitic letters," Sir Edward Maunde Thompson tells us, "are Semitic words, each describing the letter from its resemblance to some particular object, as, aleph, an ox, beth, a house. When the Greeks took over their Semitic letters, they also took over their Semitic names." Both the names of the letters and their order in the two alphabets are the same. This alphabet was employed by the Phœnicians, by the Jews, and by the Moabites,

ABCDEFGHIJKLMNOPQRSTUVWXYZ
.,"-:;!?""''&1234567890$
abcdefghijklmnopqrstuvwxyz

ABCDEFGHIJKLMNOPQRSTUVWXYZ
.,"-:;!?""''&1234567890$
abcdefghijklmnopqrstuvwxyz

DOMINANTE: SIMONCINI

PICAS	6	7	8	9	10	11	12	13	14	15	16	17	18	19	20	21	22	23	24	25	26	27	28	29	30
9 POINT	14	17	20	23	26	29	31	34	37	39	42	44	47	50	52	55	58	60	63	65	68	71	73	76	78
8 POINT	17	20	23	26	29	32	35	37	40	43	46	49	52	55	58	61	63	66	69	72	75	78	81	84	86

14/15 In cutting type by hand to-day, the first thing a type-cutter does in following his design, or that supplied him, is to make a counter-punch. This consists in cutting out the spaces inside of certain letters, such as O, or the upper part of an A. This counter-punch is sunk into the end of a bar of steel, and when this is done the inside of the model letter is finished. The outlines of *the model letter are then cut until it assumes its proper shape, numerous "smoke-*

12/13 In cutting type by hand to-day, the first thing a type-cutter does in following his design, or that supplied him, is to make a counter-punch. This consists in cutting out the spaces inside of certain letters, such as O, or the upper part of an A. This counter-punch is sunk into the end of a bar of steel, and when this is done the inside of the model letter is finished. The outlines of the model letter are then cut until it assumes its proper shape, numerous "smoke-proofs" meanwhile having been examined to see that the let-*ter follows the form which the designer intends. After the punch is completed, the steel is hard-*

14/16 In cutting type by hand to-day, the first thing a type-cutter does in following his design, or that supplied him, is to make a counter-punch. This consists in cutting out the spaces inside of certain letters, such as O, or the upper part of an A. This counter-punch is sunk into the end of a bar of steel, and when this is done the inside of the *the model letter are then cut until it assumes its proper shape, numerous "smoke-*

12/14 In cutting type by hand to-day, the first thing a type-cutter does in following his design, or that supplied him, is to make a counter-punch. This consists in cutting out the spaces inside of certain letters, such as O, or the upper part of an A. This counter-punch is sunk into the end of a bar of steel, and when this is done the inside of the model letter is finished. The outlines of the model letter are then cut until it assumes its proper shape, numerous "smoke-proofs" meanwhile having been examined to see that the let-*After the punch is completed, the steel is hard-*

14/18 In cutting type by hand to-day, the first thing a type-cutter does in following his design, or that supplied him, is to make a counter-punch. This consists in cutting out the spaces inside of certain letters, such as O, or the upper part of an A. This counter-punch is sunk into the end of a bar of steel, *the model letter are then cut until it assumes its proper shape, numerous "smoke-*

12/16 In cutting type by hand to-day, the first thing a type-cutter does in following his design, or that supplied him, is to make a counter-punch. This consists in cutting out the spaces inside of certain letters, such as O, or the upper part of an A. This counter-punch is sunk into the end of a bar of steel, and when this is done the inside of the model letter is finished. The outlines of the *ter follows the form which the designer intends. After the punch is completed, the steel is hard-*

ABCDEFGHIJKLMNOPQRSTUVWX
ABCDEFGHIJKLMNOPQRSTUVWX
YZ.,'"-:;!?""&1234567890$1234567890$
YZ.,'"-:;!?""&1234567890$1234567890$
abcdefghijklmnopqrstuvwxyz
abcdefghijklmnopqrstuvwxyz

ABCDEFGHIJKLMNOPQRSTUVWXYZ
ABCDEFGHIJKLMNOPQRSTUVWXYZ
.,'"-:;!?""&1234567890$1234567890$
.,'"-:;!?""&1234567890$1234567890$
abcdefghijklmnopqrstuvwxyz
abcdefghijklmnopqrstuvwxyz

ELECTRA: LINOTYPE   *When long descenders are used (as shown) type must be set on a slug one point greater than specified size.

PICAS	6	7	8	9	10	11	12	13	14	15	16	17	18	19	20	21	22	23	24	25	26	27	28	29	30
14 POINT	12	14	16	18	21	23	25	27	29	31	33	35	37	39	42	44	46	48	50	52	54	56	58	60	63
12 POINT	14	16	19	21	24	26	28	31	33	36	38	40	43	45	48	50	52	55	57	60	62	64	67	69	72

11/12

In cutting type by hand to-day, the first thing a type-cutter does in following his design, or that supplied him, is to make a counter-punch. This consists in cutting out the spaces inside of certain letters, such as O, or the upper part of an A. This counter-punch is sunk into the end of a bar of steel, and when this is done the inside of the model letter is finished. The outlines of the model letter are then cut until it assumes its proper shape, numerous "smoke-proofs" meanwhile having been examined to see that the letter follows the form which the designer intends. After the punch is completed, *the steel is hardened, and it is then punched into a bar of cold rolled copper, producing what is called*

10/11

In cutting type by hand to-day, the first thing a type-cutter does in following his design, or that supplied him, is to make a counter-punch. This consists in cutting out the spaces inside of certain letters, such as O, or the upper part of an A. This counter-punch is sunk into the end of a bar of steel, and when this is done the inside of the model letter is finished. The outlines of the model letter are then cut until it assumes its proper shape, numerous "smoke-proofs" meanwhile having been examined to see that the letter follows the form which the designer intends. After the punch is completed, the steel is hardened, and it is then punched into a bar of cold rolled copper, producing *what is called a "strike." In this state it is really an unfinished matrix. It is then "fitted" so that it will cast*

11/13

In cutting type by hand to-day, the first thing a type-cutter does in following his design, or that supplied him, is to make a counter-punch. This consists in cutting out the spaces inside of certain letters, such as O, or the upper part of an A. This counter-punch is sunk into the end of a bar of steel, and when this is done the inside of the model letter is finished. The outlines of the model letter are then cut until it assumes its proper shape, numerous "smoke-proofs" meanwhile having been examined to see that the letter follows the form which the designer intends. After the punch is completed, *bar of cold rolled copper, producing what is called*

10/12

In cutting type by hand to-day, the first thing a type-cutter does in following his design, or that supplied him, is to make a counter-punch. This consists in cutting out the spaces inside of certain letters, such as O, or the upper part of an A. This counter-punch is sunk into the end of a bar of steel, and when this is done the inside of the model letter is finished. The outlines of the model letter are then cut until it assumes its proper shape, numerous "smoke-proofs" meanwhile having been examined to see that the letter follows the form which the designer intends. After the punch is completed, the steel is hardened, and it is then *what is called a "strike." In this state it is really an unfinished matrix. It is then "fitted" so that it will cast*

11/15

In cutting type by hand to-day, the first thing a type-cutter does in following his design, or that supplied him, is to make a counter-punch. This consists in cutting out the spaces inside of certain letters, such as O, or the upper part of an A. This counter-punch is sunk into the end of a bar of steel, and when this is done the inside of the model letter is finished. The outlines of the model letter are then cut until it assumes its proper shape, numer-*the steel is hardened, and it is then punched into a bar of cold rolled copper, producing what is called*

10/14

In cutting type by hand to-day, the first thing a type-cutter does in following his design, or that supplied him, is to make a counter-punch. This consists in cutting out the spaces inside of certain letters, such as O, or the upper part of an A. This counter-punch is sunk into the end of a bar of steel, and when this is done the inside of the model letter is finished. The outlines of the model letter are then cut until it assumes its proper shape, numerous "smoke-proofs" meanwhile having been examined to see that the letter follows the *what is called a "strike." In this state it is really an unfinished matrix. It is then "fitted" so that it will cast*

ABCDEFGHIJKLMNOPQRSTUVWXYZ
ABCDEFGHIJKLMNOPQRSTUVWXYZ
.,"'-:;!?""&1234567890$1234567890$
.,"'-:;!?""&1234567890$1234567890$
abcdefghijklmnopqrstuvwxyz
abcdefghijklmnopqrstuvwxyz

ABCDEFGHIJKLMNOPQRSTUVWXYZ
ABCDEFGHIJKLMNOPQRSTUVWXYZ
.,"'-:;!?""&1234567890$1234567890$
.,"'-:;!?""&1234567890$1234567890$
abcdefghijklmnopqrstuvwxyz
abcdefghijklmnopqrstuvwxyz

ELECTRA: LINOTYPE   *When long descenders are used (as shown) type must be set on a slug one point greater than specified size.

PICAS	6	7	8	9	10	11	12	13	14	15	16	17	18	19	20	21	22	23	24	25	26	27	28	29	30
11 POINT	15	17	20	22	25	27	30	32	35	37	40	42	45	47	50	52	55	57	60	62	65	67	70	72	75
10 POINT	16	18	21	24	27	29	32	35	37	40	43	45	48	51	54	56	59	62	64	67	70	72	75	78	81

9/10

In cutting type by hand to-day, the first thing a type-cutter does in following his design, or that supplied him, is to make a counter-punch. This consists in cutting out the spaces inside of certain letters, such as O, or the upper part of an A. This counter-punch is sunk into the end of a bar of steel, and when this is done the inside of the model letter is finished. The outlines of the model letter are then cut until it assumes its proper shape, numerous "smoke-proofs" meanwhile having been examined to see that the letter follows the form which the designer intends. After the punch is completed, the steel is hardened, and it is then punched into a bar of cold rolled copper, producing what is called a "strike." In this state it is really an unfinished matrix. It is then "fitted" so that it will cast in the proper position on its body. When this matrix is square on *its sides, holds its letter in the same position as do the matrices of other letters of the new alphabet, and has the same*

8/9

In cutting type by hand to-day, the first thing a type-cutter does in following his design, or that supplied him, is to make a counter-punch. This consists in cutting out the spaces inside of certain letters, such as O, or the upper part of an A. This counter-punch is sunk into the end of a bar of steel, and when this is done the inside of the model letter is finished. The outlines of the model letter are then cut until it assumes its proper shape, numerous "smoke-proofs" meanwhile having been examined to see that the letter follows the form which the designer intends. After the punch is completed, the steel is hardened, and it is then punched into a bar of cold rolled copper, producing what is called a "strike." In this state it is really an unfinished matrix. It is then "fitted" so that it will cast in the proper position on its body. When this matrix is square on its sides, holds its letter in the same position as do the matrices of other letters of the new alphabet, and has the same depth throughout from the surface of the bar, it is finished. This is, roughly speaking, the process by which hand-cut punches and their matrices are produced.

But all type is not cut by hand to-day; in fact, quite the con-

9/11

In cutting type by hand to-day, the first thing a type-cutter does in following his design, or that supplied him, is to make a counter-punch. This consists in cutting out the spaces inside of certain letters, such as O, or the upper part of an A. This counter-punch is sunk into the end of a bar of steel, and when this is done the inside of the model letter is finished. The outlines of the model letter are then cut until it assumes its proper shape, numerous "smoke-proofs" meanwhile having been examined to see that the letter follows the form which the designer intends. After the punch is completed, the steel is hardened, and it is then punched into a bar of cold rolled copper, producing what is called a "strike." In this state it is really an unfin-*its sides, holds its letter in the same position as do the matrices of other letters of the new alphabet, and has the same*

8/10

In cutting type by hand to-day, the first thing a type-cutter does in following his design, or that supplied him, is to make a counter-punch. This consists in cutting out the spaces inside of certain letters, such as O, or the upper part of an A. This counter-punch is sunk into the end of a bar of steel, and when this is done the inside of the model letter is finished. The outlines of the model letter are then cut until it assumes its proper shape, numerous "smoke-proofs" meanwhile having been examined to see that the letter follows the form which the designer intends. After the punch is completed, the steel is hardened, and it is then punched into a bar of cold rolled copper, producing what is called a "strike." In this state it is really an unfinished matrix. It is then "fitted" so that it will cast in the proper position on its body. When this matrix is square on its sides, holds its letter in the same position as do the matrices of other letters of the ess by which hand-cut punches and their matrices are produced.

But all type is not cut by hand to-day; in fact, quite the con-

9/13

In cutting type by hand to-day, the first thing a type-cutter does in following his design, or that supplied him, is to make a counter-punch. This consists in cutting out the spaces inside of certain letters, such as O, or the upper part of an A. This counter-punch is sunk into the end of a bar of steel, and when this is done the inside of the model letter is finished. The outlines of the model letter are then cut until it assumes its proper shape, numerous "smoke-proofs" meanwhile having been examined to see that the letter follows the form which the designer intends. After the punch is completed, the steel is hardened, and it is *its sides, holds its letter in the same position as do the matrices of other letters of the new alphabet, and has the same*

8/12

In cutting type by hand to-day, the first thing a type-cutter does in following his design, or that supplied him, is to make a counter-punch. This consists in cutting out the spaces inside of certain letters, such as O, or the upper part of an A. This counter-punch is sunk into the end of a bar of steel, and when this is done the inside of the model letter is finished. The outlines of the model letter are then cut until it assumes its proper shape, numerous "smoke-proofs" meanwhile having been examined to see that the letter follows the form which the designer intends. After the punch is completed, the steel is hardened, and it is then punched into a bar of cold rolled copper, producing what is called a "strike." In this state it is really an unfinished matrix. ess by which hand-cut punches and their matrices are produced.

But all type is not cut by hand to-day; in fact, quite the con-

ABCDEFGHIJKLMNOPQRSTUVWXYZ
ABCDEFGHIJKLMNOPQRSTUVWXYZ
.,"'-:;!?""&1234567890$1234567890$
.,"'-:;!?""&1234567890$1234567890$
abcdefghijklmnopqrstuvwxyz
abcdefghijklmnopqrstuvwxyz

ABCDEFGHIJKLMNOPQRSTUVWXYZ
ABCDEFGHIJKLMNOPQRSTUVWXYZ
.,"'-:;!?""&1234567890$1234567890$
.,"'-:;!?""&1234567890$1234567890$
abcdefghijklmnopqrstuvwxyz
abcdefghijklmnopqrstuvwxyz

ELECTRA: LINOTYPE   *When long descenders are used (as shown) type must be set on a slug one point greater than specified size.

PICAS	6	7	8	9	10	11	12	13	14	15	16	17	18	19	20	21	22	23	24	25	26	27	28	29	30
9 POINT	17	20	23	26	29	31	34	37	40	43	46	49	52	55	58	60	63	66	69	72	75	78	81	84	87
8 POINT	19	23	26	29	33	36	39	42	46	49	52	56	60	63	66	69	72	76	79	82	85	89	92	95	99

14/15 Nowadays all type is cast by machine. The difference, however, between early hand type-casting and modern mechanical type-casting is not so great as one would suppose, and is nothing more than the substitution of the movement of a machine for manual dexterity. The modern type-casting machine has the advantage of infinitely greater production; and as much more more care is *taken in examining the types produced and discarding those with imperfections, its*

12/13 Nowadays all type is cast by machine. The difference, however, between early hand type-casting and modern mechanical type-casting is not so great as one would suppose, and is nothing more than the substitution of the movement of a machine for manual dexterity. The modern type-casting machine has the advantage of infinitely greater production; and as much more care is taken in examining the types produced and discarding those with imperfections, its product is more uniform and perfect than in earlier fonts cast by hand. *The use of hand-moulds survived for a time for*

14/16 Nowadays all type is cast by machine. The difference, however, between early hand type-casting and modern mechanical type-casting is not so great as one would suppose, and is nothing more than the substitution of the movement of a machine for manual dexterity. The modern type-casting machine has the advantage of infinitely greater pro-*taken in examining the types produced and discarding those with imperfections, its*

12/14 Nowadays all type is cast by machine. The difference, however, between early hand type-casting and modern mechanical type-casting is not so great as one would suppose, and is nothing more than the substitution of the movement of a machine for manual dexterity. The modern type-casting machine has the advantage of infinitely greater production; and as much more care is taken in examining the types produced and discarding those with imperfections, its product is more uniform and perfect than in earlier fonts cast by hand. *The use of hand-moulds survived for a time for*

14/18 Nowadays all type is cast by machine. The difference, however, between early hand type-casting and modern mechanical type-casting is not so great as one would suppose, and is nothing more than the substitution of the movement of a machine for manual dexterity. The modern type-casting machine *taken in examining the types produced and discarding those with imperfections, its*

12/16 Nowadays all type is cast by machine. The difference, however, between early hand type-casting and modern mechanical type-casting is not so great as one would suppose, and is nothing more than the substitution of the movement of a machine for manual dexterity. The modern type-casting machine has the advantage of infinitely greater production; and as much more care is taken in *form and perfect than in earlier fonts cast by hand.* *The use of hand-moulds survived for a time for*

ABCDEFGHIJKLMNOPQRSTUVWX
ABCDEFGHIJKLMNOPQRSTUVWX
YZ.,"-:;!?""&1234567890$1234567890$
YZ.,"-:;!?""&1234567890$1234567890$
abcdefghijklmnopqrstuvwxyz
abcdefghijklmnopqrstuvwxyz

ABCDEFGHIJKLMNOPQRSTUVWXYZ
ABCDEFGHIJKLMNOPQRSTUVWXYZ
.,"-:;!?""&1234567890$1234567890$
.,"-:;!?""&1234567890$1234567890$
abcdefghijklmnopqrstuvwxyz
abcdefghijklmnopqrstuvwxyz

FAIRFIELD: LINOTYPE   *When long descenders are used (as shown) type must be set on a slug one point greater than specified size.

PICAS	6	7	8	9	10	11	12	13	14	15	16	17	18	19	20	21	22	23	24	25	26	27	28	29	30
14 POINT	12	14	16	18	21	23	25	27	29	31	33	35	37	39	42	44	46	48	50	52	54	56	58	60	63
12 POINT	14	16	19	21	24	26	28	31	33	36	38	40	43	45	48	50	52	55	57	60	62	64	67	69	72

11/12

Nowadays all type is cast by machine. The difference, however, between early hand type-casting and
modern mechanical type-casting is not so great as one
would suppose, and is nothing more than the substitution of the movement of a machine for manual dexterity. The modern type-casting machine has the advantage of infinitely greater production; and as much
more care is taken in examining the types produced
and discarding those with imperfections, its product
is more uniform and perfect than in earlier fonts cast
by hand.

The use of hand-moulds survived for a time for
casting small and special sorts, kerned letters and
script types. The modern type-casting machine is

10/11

Nowadays all type is cast by machine. The difference,
however, between early hand type-casting and modern
mechanical type-casting is not so great as one would
suppose, and is nothing more than the substitution of
the movement of a machine for manual dexterity. The
modern type-casting machine has the advantage of infinitely greater production; and as much more care is
taken in examining the types produced and discarding
those with imperfections, its product is more uniform
and perfect than in earlier fonts cast by hand.

The use of hand-moulds survived for a time for casting small and special sorts, kerned letters and script
types. The modern type-casting machine is now, how-
ever, employed in the United States for everything.

The ingredients of modern printing types are, roughly

11/13

Nowadays all type is cast by machine. The difference, however, between early hand type-casting and
modern mechanical type-casting is not so great as one
would suppose, and is nothing more than the substitution of the movement of a machine for manual dexterity. The modern type-casting machine has the advantage of infinitely greater production; and as much
more care is taken in examining the types produced
and discarding those with imperfections, its product
is more uniform and perfect than in earlier fonts cast
by hand.

casting small and special sorts, kerned letters and
script types. The modern type-casting machine is

10/12

Nowadays all type is cast by machine. The difference,
however, between early hand type-casting and modern
mechanical type-casting is not so great as one would
suppose, and is nothing more than the substitution of
the movement of a machine for manual dexterity. The
modern type-casting machine has the advantage of infinitely greater production; and as much more care is
taken in examining the types produced and discarding
those with imperfections, its product is more uniform
and perfect than in earlier fonts cast by hand.

The use of hand-moulds survived for a time for casting small and special sorts, kerned letters and script
ever, employed in the United States for everything.

The ingredients of modern printing types are, roughly

11/15

Nowadays all type is cast by machine. The difference, however, between early hand type-casting and
modern mechanical type-casting is not so great as one
would suppose, and is nothing more than the substitution of the movement of a machine for manual dexterity. The modern type-casting machine has the advantage of infinitely greater production; and as much
more care is taken in examining the types produced
and discarding those with imperfections, its product
casting small and special sorts, kerned letters and
script types. The modern type-casting machine is

10/14

Nowadays all type is cast by machine. The difference,
however, between early hand type-casting and modern
mechanical type-casting is not so great as one would
suppose, and is nothing more than the substitution of
the movement of a machine for manual dexterity. The
modern type-casting machine has the advantage of infinitely greater production; and as much more care is
taken in examining the types produced and discarding
those with imperfections, its product is more uniform
and perfect than in earlier fonts cast by hand.
ever, employed in the United States for everything.

The ingredients of modern printing types are, roughly

ABCDEFGHIJKLMNOPQRSTUVWXYZ
ABCDEFGHIJKLMNOPQRSTUVWXYZ
.,"-:;!?""&1234567890$1234567890$
.,"-:;!?""&1234567890$1234567890$
abcdefghijklmnopqrstuvwxyz .
abcdefghijklmnopqrstuvwxyz .

ABCDEFGHIJKLMNOPQRSTUVWXYZ
ABCDEFGHIJKLMNOPQRSTUVWXYZ
.,"-:;!?""&1234567890$1234567890$
.,"-:;!?""&1234567890$1234567890$
abcdefghijklmnopqrstuvwxyz
abcdefghijklmnopqrstuvwxyz

FAIRFIELD: LINOTYPE   *When long descenders are used (as shown) type must be set on a slug one point greater than specified size.

PICAS	6	7	8	9	10	11	12	13	14	15	16	17	18	19	20	21	22	23	24	25	26	27	28	29	30
11 POINT	15	18	20	23	26	28	31	33	36	39	41	44	46	49	52	54	57	59	62	65	67	69	72	75	78
10 POINT	16	19	22	25	28	30	33	36	39	42	44	47	50	53	56	58	61	64	67	70	72	75	78	81	84

9/10

Nowadays all type is cast by machine. The difference, however, between early hand type-casting and modern mechanical type-casting is not so great as one would suppose, and is nothing more than the substitution of the movement of a machine for manual dexterity. The modern type-casting machine has the advantage of infinitely greater production; and as much more care is taken in examining the types produced and discarding those with imperfections, its product is more uniform and perfect than in earlier fonts cast by hand.

The use of hand-moulds survived for a time for casting small and special sorts, kerned letters and script types. The modern type-casting machine is now, however, employed in the United States for everything.

speaking, lead, tin, antimony, and sometimes a little copper; these vary in proportion, according to the size of the type be-

8/9

Nowadays all type is cast by machine. The difference, however, between early hand type-casting and modern mechanical type-casting is not so great as one would suppose, and is nothing more than the substitution of the movement of a machine for manual dexterity. The modern type-casting machine has the advantage of infinitely greater production; and as much more care is taken in examining the types produced and discarding those with imperfections, its product is more uniform and perfect than in earlier fonts cast by hand.

The use of hand-moulds survived for a time for casting small and special sorts, kerned letters and script types. The modern type-casting machine is now, however, employed in the United States for everything.

The ingredients of modern printing types are, roughly speaking, lead, tin, antimony, and sometimes a little copper; these vary in proportion, according to the size of the type being cast. The *dense, ductile, and fusible at a low temperature. Lead is too soft to be used alone; antimony is therefore introduced to give it hard-*

9/11

Nowadays all type is cast by machine. The difference, however, between early hand type-casting and modern mechanical type-casting is not so great as one would suppose, and is nothing more than the substitution of the movement of a machine for manual dexterity. The modern type-casting machine has the advantage of infinitely greater production; and as much more care is taken in examining the types produced and discarding those with imperfections, its product is more uniform and perfect than in earlier fonts cast by hand.

The use of hand-moulds survived for a time for casting small and special sorts, kerned letters and script types. The modern type-casting machine is now, however, employed

speaking, lead, tin, antimony, and sometimes a little copper; these vary in proportion, according to the size of the type be-

8/10

Nowadays all type is cast by machine. The difference, however, between early hand type-casting and modern mechanical type-casting is not so great as one would suppose, and is nothing more than the substitution of the movement of a machine for manual dexterity. The modern type-casting machine has the advantage of infinitely greater production; and as much more care is taken in examining the types produced and discarding those with imperfections, its product is more uniform and perfect than in earlier fonts cast by hand.

The use of hand-moulds survived for a time for casting small and special sorts, kerned letters and script types. The modern type-casting machine is now, however, employed in the United States for everything.

The ingredients of modern printing types are, roughly speaking, lead, tin, antimony, and sometimes a little copper; these vary *dense, ductile, and fusible at a low temperature. Lead is too soft to be used alone; antimony is therefore introduced to give it hard-*

9/13

Nowadays all type is cast by machine. The difference, however, between early hand type-casting and modern mechanical type-casting is not so great as one would suppose, and is nothing more than the substitution of the movement of a machine for manual dexterity. The modern type-casting machine has the advantage of infinitely greater production; and as much more care is taken in examining the types produced and discarding those with imperfections, its product is more uniform and perfect than in earlier fonts cast by hand.

The use of hand-moulds survived for a time for casting

speaking, lead, tin, antimony, and sometimes a little copper; these vary in proportion, according to the size of the type be-

8/12

Nowadays all type is cast by machine. The difference, however, between early hand type-casting and modern mechanical type-casting is not so great as one would suppose, and is nothing more than the substitution of the movement of a machine for manual dexterity. The modern type-casting machine has the advantage of infinitely greater production; and as much more care is taken in examining the types produced and discarding those with imperfections, its product is more uniform and perfect than in earlier fonts cast by hand.

The use of hand-moulds survived for a time for casting small and special sorts, kerned letters and script types. The modern type-casting machine is now, however, employed in the United *dense, ductile, and fusible at a low temperature. Lead is too soft to be used alone; antimony is therefore introduced to give it hard-*

ABCDEFGHIJKLMNOPQRSTUVWXYZ
ABCDEFGHIJKLMNOPQRSTUVWXYZ
.,"-:;!?""&1234567890$1234567890$
.,"-:;!?""&1234567890$1234567890$
abcdefghijklmnopqrstuvwxyz
abcdefghijklmnopqrstuvwxyz

ABCDEFGHIJKLMNOPQRSTUVWXYZ
ABCDEFGHIJKLMNOPQRSTUVWXYZ
.,"-:;!?""&1234567890$1234567890$
.,"-:;!?""&1234567890$1234567890$
abcdefghijklmnopqrstuvwxyz
abcdefghijklmnopqrstuvwxyz

FAIRFIELD: LINOTYPE   *When long descenders are used (as shown) type must be set on a slug one point greater than specified size.

PICAS	6	7	8	9	10	11	12	13	14	15	16	17	18	19	20	21	22	23	24	25	26	27	28	29	30
9 POINT	18	21	24	27	30	33	36	39	42	45	48	51	54	57	60	63	66	69	72	75	78	81	84	87	90
8 POINT	19	22	25	28	32	35	38	41	44	48	51	54	58	61	64	67	70	73	76	80	83	86	89	92	96

12/13 Amongst the several mechanic Arts that have engaged my attention, there is no one which I have pursued with so much steadiness and pleasure, as that of Letter-Founding. Having been an early admirer of the beauty of Letters, I became insensibly desirous of contributing to the perfection of them. I formed to my self Ideas of greater accuracy than had yet appeared, and have endeavoured to produce a Sett of Types according to what I conceived to be their true proportion.

10/11 Among the several mechanic Arts that have engaged my attention, there is no one which I have pursued with so much steadiness and pleasure, as that of Letter-Founding. Having been an early admirer of the beauty of Letters, I became insensibly desirous of contributing to the perfection of them. I formed to my self Ideas of greater accuracy than had yet appeared, and have endeavoured to produce a Sett of Types according to what I conceived to be their true proportion.

Mr. Caslon is an Artist, to whom the Republic of Learning has great obligations; his ingenuity has left a fairer copy for my emulation, than any other master. In his great variety of Characters I

12/14 Amongst the several mechanic Arts that have engaged my attention, there is no one which I have pursued with so much steadiness and pleasure, as that of Letter-Founding. Having been an early admirer of the beauty of Letters, I became insensibly desirous of contributing to the perfection of them. I formed to my self Ideas of greater accuracy than had yet appeared, and have endeavoured to produce a Sett of Types according to what I

10/12 Among the several mechanic Arts that have engaged my attention, there is no one which I have pursued with so much steadiness and pleasure, as that of Letter-Founding. Having been an early admirer of the beauty of Letters, I became insensibly desirous of contributing to the perfection of them. I formed to my self Ideas of greater accuracy than had yet appeared, and have endeavoured to produce a Sett of Types according to what I conceived to be their true proportion.

Mr. Caslon is an Artist, to whom the Republic of Learning has great obligations; his ingenuity has left a fairer copy for my emulation, than any

12/16 Amongst the several mechanic Arts that have engaged my attention, there is no one which I have pursued with so much steadiness and pleasure, as that of Letter-Founding. Having been an early admirer of the beauty of Letters, I became insensibly desirous of contributing to the perfection of them. I formed to my self Ideas of greater accuracy than had yet appeared, and have endeavoured to pro-

10/14 Among the several mechanic Arts that have engaged my attention, there is no one which I have pursued with so much steadiness and pleasure, as that of Letter-Founding. Having been an early admirer of the beauty of Letters, I became insensibly desirous of contributing to the perfection of them. I formed to my self Ideas of greater accuracy than had yet appeared, and have endeavoured to produce a Sett of Types according to what I conceived to be their true proportion.

Mr. Caslon is an Artist, to whom the Republic of Learning has great obligations; his ingenuity

ABCDEFGHIJKLMNOPQRSTUVWXYZ
ABCDEFGHIJKLMNOPQRSTUVWXYZ
.,''-:;!?''''&1234567890$
.,''-:;!?''''&1234567890$
abcdefghijklmnopqrstuvwxyz
abcdefghijklmnopqrstuvwxyz

ABCDEFGHIJKLMNOPQRSTUVWXYZ
ABCDEFGHIJKLMNOPQRSTUVWXYZ
.,''-:;!?''''&1234567890$
.,''-:;!?''''&1234567890$
abcdefghijklmnopqrstuvwxyz
abcdefghijklmnopqrstuvwxyz

FOLIO GROTESQUE LIGHT: INTERTYPE *This face must be set 1 pt leaded.

PICAS	6	7	8	9	10	11	12	13	14	15	16	17	18	19	20	21	22	23	24	25	26	27	28	29	30
12 POINT	15	18	20	23	25	27	30	32	35	37	40	42	45	47	50	52	55	57	60	62	65	67	70	72	75
10 POINT	18	21	24	28	32	35	38	41	44	47	50	53	57	60	63	66	69	72	76	79	82	85	88	91	95

9/10 Amongst the several mechanic Arts that have engaged my attention, there is no one which I have pursued with so much steadiness and pleasure, as that of Letter-Founding. Having been an early admirer of the beauty of Letters, I became insensibly desirous of contributing to the perfection of them. I formed to my self Ideas of greater accuracy than had yet appeared, and have endeavoured to produce a Sett of Types according to what I conceived to be their true proportion.

Mr. Caslon is an Artist, to whom the Republic of Learning has great obligations; his ingenuity has left a fairer copy for my emulation, than any other master. In his great variety of Characters I intend not to follow him; The Roman and Italic are all I have hitherto attempted; if in these he has left room for improvement, it is probably more owing to that variety which divided

8/9 Amongst the several mechanic Arts that have engaged my attention, there is no one which I have pursued with so much steadiness and pleasure, as that of Letter-Founding. Having been an early admirer of the beauty of Letters, I became insensibly desirous of contributing to the perfection of them. I formed to my self Ideas of greater accuracy than had yet appeared, and have endeavoured to produce a Sett of Types according to what I conceived to be their true proportion.

Mr. Caslon is an Artist, to whom the Republic of Learning has great obligations; his ingenuity has left a fairer copy for my emulation, than any other master. In his great variety of Characters I intend not to follow him; the Roman and Italic are all I have hitherto attempted; if in these he has left room for improvement, it is probably more owing to that variety which divided his attention, than to any other cause. I honor his merit, and only wish to derive some small share of Reputation, from an Art which proves accidentally to have been the object of our mutual pursuit.

9/11 Amongst the several mechanic Arts that have engaged my attention, there is no one which I have pursued with so much steadiness and pleasure, as that of Letter-Founding. Having been an early admirer of the beauty of Letters, I became insensibly desirous of contributing to the perfection of them. I formed to my self Ideas of greater accuracy than had yet appeared, and have endeavoured to produce a Sett of Types according to what I conceived to be their true proportion.

Mr. Caslon is an Artist, to whom the Republic of Learning has great obligations; his ingenuity has left a fairer copy for my emulation, than any other master. In his great variety of Characters I intend not to follow him; The Roman and Italic are all I have hitherto attempted; if in these he has left room for improvement,

8/10 Amongst the several mechanic Arts that have engaged my attention, there is no one which I have pursued with so much steadiness and pleasure, as that of Letter-Founding. Having been an early admirer of the beauty of Letters, I became insensibly desirous of contributing to the perfection of them. I formed to my self Ideas of greater accuracy than had yet appeared, and have endeavoured to produce a Sett of Types according to what I conceived to be their true proportion.

Mr. Caslon is an Artist, to whom the Republic of Learning has great obligations; his ingenuity has left a fairer copy for my emulation, than any other master. In his great variety of Characters I intend not to follow him; the Roman and Italic are all I have hitherto attempted; if in these he has left room for improvement, it is probably more owing to that variety which divided his attention, than to any other cause. I honor his merit, and only wish to derive some small share of Reputation, from an Art which proves accidentally to have been the

9/13 Amongst the several mechanic Arts that have engaged my attention, there is no one which I have pursued with so much steadiness and pleasure, as that of Letter-Founding. Having been an early admirer of the beauty of Letters, I became insensibly desirous of contributing to the perfection of them. I formed to my self Ideas of greater accuracy than had yet appeared, and have endeavoured to produce a Sett of Types according to what I conceived to be their true proportion.

Mr. Caslon is an Artist, to whom the Republic of Learning has great obligations; his ingenuity has left a fairer copy for my emulation, than any other master. In his great variety of Characters I intend not to follow

8/12 Amongst the several mechanic Arts that have engaged my attention, there is no one which I have pursued with so much steadiness and pleasure, as that of Letter-Founding. Having been an early admirer of the beauty of Letters, I became insensibly desirous of contributing to the perfection of them. I formed to my self Ideas of greater accuracy than had yet appeared, and have endeavoured to produce a Sett of Types according to what I conceived to be their true proportion.

Mr. Caslon is an Artist, to whom the Republic of Learning has great obligations; his ingenuity has left a fairer copy for my emulation, than any other master. In his great variety of Characters I intend not to follow him; the Roman and Italic are all I have hitherto attempted; if in these he has left room for improvement, it is probably more owing to that variety

ABCDEFGHIJKLMNOPQRSTUVWXYZ
ABCDEFGHIJKLMNOPQRSTUVWXYZ
.,''-:;!?''''&1234567890$
.,''-:;!?''''&1234567890$
abcdefghijklmnopqrstuvwxyz
abcdefghijklmnopqrstuvwxyz

ABCDEFGHIJKLMNOPQRSTUVWXYZ
ABCDEFGHIJKLMNOPQRSTUVWXYZ
.,''-:;!?''''&1234567890$
.,''-:;!?''''&1234567890$
abcdefghijklmnopqrstuvwxyz
abcdefghijklmnopqrstuvwxyz

FOLIO GROTESQUE LIGHT: INTERTYPE *This face must be set 1 pt leaded.

PICAS	6	7	8	9	10	11	12	13	14	15	16	17	18	19	20	21	22	23	24	25	26	27	28	29	30
9 POINT	19	22	26	30	33	36	40	43	46	49	53	56	59	62	66	69	73	76	79	82	86	89	92	95	99
8 POINT	20	24	28	32	36	39	43	46	50	54	58	61	65	68	72	75	79	82	86	90	94	97	101	104	108

14/14

From a letter by Benjamin Franklin to B. Vaughan Esq. dated Apr. 21, 1785:

If the Irish can manufacture cottons, stuffs and silks, and linens, and cutlery, and toys, and books etc. etc. etc., so as to sell them cheaper in England than the *manufacturers* of England sell them, is not this good *for the people of England who are not manufacturers? and will*

14/16

From a letter by Benjamin Franklin to B. Vaughan Esq. dated Apr. 21, 1785:

If the Irish can manufacture cottons, stuffs and silks, and linens, and cutlery, and toys, and books etc. etc. etc., so as to sell them cheaper in England than the *manufacturers* of England sell them, is not this good for the people of England who

14/18

From a letter by Benjamin Franklin to B. Vaughan Esq. dated Apr. 21, 1785:

If the Irish can manufacture cottons, stuffs and silks, and linens, and cutlery, and toys, and books etc. etc. etc., so as to sell them cheaper in England *than the manufacturers of England sell them, is not this good*

ABCDEFGHIJKLMNOPQRSTU
ABCDEFGHIJKLMNOPQRSTU
VWXYZ &.,''-:;!?''''1234567890$
VWXYZ &.,''-:;!?''''1234567890$
abcdefghijklmnopqrstuvwxyz
abcdefghijklmnopqrstuvwxyz

12/12

From a letter by Benjamin Franklin to B. Vaughan Esq. dated April 21, 1785:

If the Irish can manufacture cottons, stuffs and silks, and linens, and cutlery, and toys, and books etc. etc. etc., so as to sell them cheaper in England than the *manufacturers* of England sell them, is not this good for the *people* of England who are not *manufacturers?* and will not even the manufacturers themselves share the benefit? Since if cottons are cheaper, *all the other manufacturers who wear cottons will save in that article, as so*

12/14

From a letter by Benjamin Franklin to B. Vaughan Esq. dated April 21, 1785:

If the Irish can manufacture cottons, stuffs and silks, and linens, and cutlery, and toys, and books etc. etc. etc., so as to sell them cheaper in England than the *manufacturers* of England sell them, is not this good for the *people* of England who are not *manufacturers?* and will not even the *manufacturers themselves share the benefit? Since if cottons are cheaper,*

12/16

From a letter by Benjamin Franklin to B. Vaughan Esq. dated April 21, 1785:

If the Irish can manufacture cottons, stuffs and silks, and linens, and cutlery, and toys, and books etc. etc. etc., so as to sell them cheaper in England than the *manufacturers* of England sell them, is not this good for the people of England who are not *manufacturers? and will not even the* manufacturers themselves share the

ABCDEFGHIJKLMNOPQRSTUVWXYZ
ABCDEFGHIJKLMNOPQRSTUVWXYZ
&,.''-:;!?''''1234567890$
&,.''-:;!?''''1234567890$
abcdefghijklmnopqrstuvwxyz
abcdefghijklmnopqrstuvwxyz

FRANKLIN GOTHIC: INTERTYPE

PICAS	6	7	8	9	10	11	12	13	14	15	16	17	18	19	20	21	22	23	24	25	26	27	28	29	30
14 POINT	9	10	12	14	15	17	18	20	21	23	24	26	28	29	31	32	34	35	37	38	40	41	43	44	46
12 POINT	10	12	14	16	19	21	23	25	27	28	30	32	34	36	38	40	42	44	46	47	49	51	53	55	57

10/10

From a letter by Benjamin Franklin to B. Vaughan Esq. dated April 21, 1785:

If the Irish can manufacture cottons, stuffs and silks, and linens, and cutlery, and toys, and books etc. etc. etc., so as to sell them cheaper in England than the *manufacturers* of England sell them, is not this good for the *people* of England who are not *manufacturers*? and will not even the manufacturers themselves share the benefit? Since if cottons are cheaper, all the other manufacturers who wear cottons will save in that article, and so of the rest. If books can be had much cheaper from *Ireland, (which I believe for I bought Blackstone there for 24/- when it was sold*

10/12

From a letter by Benjamin Franklin to B. Vaughan Esq. dated April 21, 1785:

If the Irish can manufacture cottons, stuffs and silks, and linens, and cutlery, and toys, and books etc. etc. etc., so as to sell them cheaper in England than the *manufacturers* of England sell them, is not this good for the *people* of England who are not *manufacturers*? and will not even the manufacturers themselves share the benefit? Since if cottons are cheaper, all the other manufacturers who wear cottons *will save in that article, and so of the rest. If books can be had much cheaper from*

10/14

From a letter by Benjamin Franklin to B. Vaughan Esq. dated April 21, 1785:

If the Irish can manufacture cottons, stuffs and silks, and linens, and cutlery, and toys, and books etc. etc. etc., so as to sell them cheaper in England than the *manufacturers* of England sell them, is not this good for the *people* of England who are not *manufacturers*? and will not even the manufacturers themselves share the *benefit? Since if cottons are cheaper, all the other manufacturers who wear cottons*

8/8

From a letter by Benjamin Franklin to B. Vaughan Esq. dated April 21, 1785:

If the Irish can manufacture cottons, stuffs and silks, and linens, and cutlery, and toys, and books etc. etc. etc., so as to sell them cheaper in England than the *manufacturers* of England sell them, is not this good for the *people* of England who are not *manu*facturers? and will not even the manufacturers themselves share the benefit? Since if cottons are cheaper, all the other manufacturers who wear cottons will save in that article, and so of the rest. If books can be had much cheaper from Ireland, (which I believe for I bought Blackstone there for 24/- when it was sold in England at four guineas) is not this an advantage not to English booksellers indeed, but to English readers and to learning. And of all the complainants perhaps these booksellers are least worthy of considera*tion. The catalogue you last sent me amazes me by the high prices (said to be the lowest) affixed to*

8/10

From a letter by Benjamin Franklin to B. Vaughan Esq. dated April 21, 1785:

If the Irish can manufacture cottons, stuffs and silks, and linens, and cutlery, and toys, and books etc. etc. etc., so as to sell them cheaper in England than the *manufacturers* of England sell them, is not this good for the *people* of England who are not *manu*facturers? and will not even the manufacturers themselves share the benefit? Since if cottons are cheaper, all the other manufacturers who wear cottons will save in that article, and so of the rest. If books can be had much cheaper from Ireland, (which I believe for I bought Blackstone there for 24/- when it was sold in England at four guineas) is not this an advantage not to English *booksellers indeed, but to English readers and to learning. And of all the complainants perhaps*

8/12

From a letter by Benjamin Franklin to B. Vaughan Esq. dated April 21, 1785:

If the Irish can manufacture cottons, stuffs and silks, and linens, and cutlery, and toys, and books etc. etc. etc., so as to sell them cheaper in England than the *manufacturers* of England sell them, is not this good for the *people* of England who are not *manufacturers*? and will not even the manufacturers themselves share the benefit? Since if cottons are cheaper, all the other manufacturers who wear cottons will save in that article, and so of the rest. If books can be had much cheaper from Ire*land, (which I believe for I bought Blackstone there for 24/- when it was sold in England at four*

ABCDEFGHIJKLMNOPQRSTUVWXYZ
ABCDEFGHIJKLMNOPQRSTUVWXYZ
&.,"'-:;!?"''"1234567890$
&.,"'-:;!?"''"1234567890$
abcdefghijklmnopqrstuvwxyz
abcdefghijklmnopqrstuvwxyz

ABCDEFGHIJKLMNOPQRSTUVWXYZ
ABCDEFGHIJKLMNOPQRSTUVWXYZ
&.,"'-:;!?"''"1234567890$
&.,"'-:;!?"''"1234567890$
abcdefghijklmnopqrstuvwxyz
abcdefghijklmnopqrstuvwxyz

FRANKLIN GOTHIC: INTERTYPE

PICAS	6	7	8	9	10	11	12	13	14	15	16	17	18	19	20	21	22	23	24	25	26	27	28	29	30
10 POINT	12	14	16	18	21	23	25	27	29	31	34	36	38	40	42	44	46	48	50	52	55	57	59	61	63
8 POINT	15	18	21	23	25	27	30	32	35	37	40	42	45	47	50	52	55	57	60	62	65	67	70	72	75

6/6

From a letter by Benjamin Franklin to B. Vaughan Esq. dated April 21, 1785:
If the Irish can manufacture cottons, stuffs and silks, and linens, and cutlery, and toys, and books etc. etc., so as to sell them cheaper in England than the *manufacturers* of England sell them, is not this good for the *people* of England who are not *manufacturers?* and will not even the manufacturers themselves share the benefit? Since if cottons are cheaper, all the other manufacturers who wear cottons will save in that article, and so of the rest. If books can be had much cheaper from Ireland, (which I believe for I bought Blackstone there for 24/- when it was sold in England at four guineas) is not this an advantage not to English booksellers indeed, but to English readers and to learning. And of all the complainants perhaps these booksellers are least worthy of consideration. The catalogue you last sent me amazes me by the high prices (said to be the lowest) affixed to each article. And one can scarce see a new book, without observing the excessive artifices may use of to puff up a paper of verses into a pamphlet, a pamphlet into an octavo, and an octavo into a quarto, with scab boardings, white lines, sparse titles of chapters, and exorbitant margins, to such a degree, that the selling of paper seems now the object and printing on it only the pretence. I inclose the copy of a page in a late comedy. Between every two lines there is a white space equal to another line. You have a law, I think, against butchers blowing of veal *to make it look fatter; why not one against booksellers blowing of books to make them look bigger. All this to yourself; you can*

6/8

From a letter by Benjamin Franklin to B. Vaughan Esq. dated April 21, 1785:
If the Irish can manufacture cottons, stuffs and silks, and linens, and cutlery, and toys, and books etc. etc., so as to sell them cheaper in England than the *manufacturers* of England sell them, is not this good for the *people* of England who are not *manufacturers?* and will not even the manufacturers themselves share the benefit? Since if cottons are cheaper, all the other manufacturers who wear cottons will save in that article, and so of the rest. If books can be had much cheaper from Ireland, (which I believe for I bought Blackstone there for 24/- when it was sold in England at four guineas) is not this an advantage not to English booksellers indeed, but to English readers and to learning. And of all the complainants perhaps these booksellers are least worthy of consideration. The catalogue you last sent me amazes me by the high prices (said to be the lowest) affixed to each article. And one can scarce see a new book, without observing the excessive artifices may use of to puff up a paper of verses into a pamphlet, a pamphlet into an octavo, and an *octavo into a quarto, with scab boardings, white lines, sparse titles of chapters, and exorbitant margins, to such a degree, that*

6/10

From a letter by Benjamin Franklin to B. Vaughan Esq. dated April 21, 1785:
If the Irish can manufacture cottons, stuffs and silks, and linens, and cutlery, and toys, and books etc. etc., so as to sell them cheaper in England than the *manufacturers* of England sell them, is not this good for the *people* of England who are not *manufacturers?* and will not even the manufacturers themselves share the benefit? Since if cottons are cheaper, all the other manufacturers who wear cottons will save in that article, and so of the rest. If books can be had much cheaper from Ireland, (which I believe for I bought Blackstone there for 24/- when it was sold in England at four guineas) is not this an advantage not to English booksellers indeed, but to English readers and to learning. And of all the complainants perhaps these booksellers are least worthy of consideration. The catalogue you last sent *me amazes me by the high prices (said to be the lowest) affixed to each article. And one can scarce see a new book, without*

ABCDEFGHIJKLMNOPQRSTUVWXYZ
ABCDEFGHIJKLMNOPQRSTUVWXYZ
&..,''-:;!?''''1234567890$
&..,''-:;!?''''1234567890$
abcdefghijklmnopqrstuvwxyz
abcdefghijklmnopqrstuvwxyz

 4/5

From a letter by Benjamin Franklin to B. Vaughan Esq. dated April 21, 1785:
If the Irish can manufacture cottons, stuffs and silks, and linens, and cutlery, and toys, and books etc. etc., so as to sell them cheaper in England than the manufacturers of England sell them, is not this good for the people of England who are not manufacturers? and will not even the manufacturers themselves share the benefit? Since if cottons are cheaper, all the other manufacturers who wear cottons will save in that article, and so of the rest. If books can be had much cheaper from Ireland, (which I believe for I bought Blackstone there for 24/- when it was sold in England at four guineas) is not this an advantage not to English booksellers indeed, but to English readers and to learning. And of all the complainants perhaps these booksellers are least worthy of consideration. The catalogue you last sent me amazes me by the high prices (said to be the lowest) affixed to each article. And one can scarce see a new book, without observing the excessive artifices may use of to puff up a paper of verses into a pamphlet, a pamphlet into an octavo, and an octavo into a quarto, with scab boardings, white lines, sparse titles of chapters, and exorbitant margins, to such a degree, that the selling of paper seems now the object and printing on it only the pretence. I inclose the copy of a page in a late comedy. Between every two lines there is a white space equal to another line. You have a law, I think, against butchers blowing of veal to make it look fatter; why not one against booksellers blowing of books to make them look bigger. All this to yourself; you can easily guess the reason.
My grandson is a little indisposed, but sends you two pamphlets, Figaro and Le Roy Voyageux. The first is a play of Beaumarchais, which has had a great run here. If books can be had much cheaper from Ireland, (which I believe for I bought Blackstone there for 24/- when it was sold in England at four guineas) is not this an advantage not to English booksellers indeed, but to English readers and to learning. And of all the complainants perhaps these booksellers are least worthy of consideration. The catalogue you last sent me amazes me by the high prices (said to be the lowest) affixed to each article. And one can scarce see a new book, without observing the excessive artifices may use of to puff up a paper of verses into a pamphlet, a pamphlet into an octavo, and an octavo into a quarto, with scab boardings, white lines, sparse titles of chapters, and exorbitant margins, to such a degree, that the selling of paper seems now the object and printing on it only the

4/6

From a letter by Benjamin Franklin to B. Vaughan Esq. dated April 21, 1785:
If the Irish can manufacture cottons, stuffs and silks, and linens, and cutlery, and toys, and books etc. etc., so as to sell them cheaper in England than the manufacturers of England sell them, is not this good for the people of England who are not manufacturers? and will not even the manufacturers themselves share the benefit? Since if cottons are cheaper, all the other manufacturers who wear cottons will save in that article, and so of the rest. If books can be had much cheaper from Ireland, (which I believe for I bought Blackstone there for 24/- when it was sold in England at four guineas) is not this an advantage not to English booksellers indeed, but to English readers and to learning. And of all the complainants perhaps these booksellers are least worthy of consideration. The catalogue you last sent me amazes me by the high prices (said to be the lowest) affixed to each article. And one can scarce see a new book, without observing the excessive artifices may use of to puff up a paper of verses into a pamphlet, a pamphlet into an octavo, and an octavo into a quarto, with scab boardings, white lines, sparse titles of chapters, and exorbitant margins, to such a degree, that the selling of paper seems now the object and printing on it only the pretence. I inclose the copy of a page in a late comedy. Between every two lines there is a white space equal to another line. You have a law, I think, against butchers blowing of veal to make it look fatter; why not one against booksellers blowing of books to make them look bigger. All this to yourself; you can easily guess the reason.
My grandson is a little indisposed, but sends you two pamphlets, Figaro and Le Roy Voyageux. The first is a play of Beaumarchais, which has had a great run here. If books can be had much cheaper from Ireland, (which I believe for I bought Blackstone there for 24/- when it was sold in England at four guineas) is not this an advantage not to English booksellers indeed, but to English readers and to learning. And of all the complainants perhaps these booksellers are least worthy of consideration. The catalogue you last sent me amazes me by the high prices (said

4/8

From a letter by Benjamin Franklin to B. Vaughan Esq. dated April 21, 1785:
If the Irish can manufacture cottons, stuffs and silks, and linens, and cutlery, and toys, and books etc. etc., so as to sell them cheaper in England than the manufacturers of England sell them, is not this good for the people of England who are not manufacturers? and will not even the manufacturers themselves share the benefit? Since if cottons are cheaper, all the other manufacturers who wear cottons will save in that article, and so of the rest. If books can be had much cheaper from Ireland, (which I believe for I bought Blackstone there for 24/- when it was sold in England at four guineas) is not this an advantage not to English booksellers indeed, but to English readers and to learning. And of all the complainants perhaps these booksellers are least worthy of consideration. The catalogue you last sent me amazes me by the high prices (said to be the lowest) affixed to each article. And one can scarce see a new book, without observing the excessive artifices may use of to puff up a paper of verses into a pamphlet, a pamphlet into an octavo, and an octavo into a quarto, with scab boardings, white lines, sparse titles of chapters, and exorbitant margins, to such a degree, that the selling of paper seems now the object and printing on it only the pretence. I inclose the copy of a page in a late comedy. Between every two lines there is a white space equal to another line. You have a law, I think, against butchers blowing of veal to make it look fatter; why not one against booksellers blowing of books to make them look bigger. All this to yourself; you can easily guess the reason.

ABCDEFGHIJKLMNOPQRSTUVWXYZ
&..,''-:;!?''''1234567890$
abcdefghijklmnopqrstuvwxyz

FRANKLIN GOTHIC: INTERTYPE   *This face set 1 pt leaded.

PICAS	6	7	8	9	10	11	12	13	14	15	16	17	18	19	20	21	22	23	24	25	26	27	28	29	30
6 POINT	20	23	26	29	32	35	38	41	44	47	50	53	57	60	63	66	69	72	76	79	82	85	88	91	95
4 POINT	25	30	34	38	41	45	49	53	57	61	65	69	73	77	81	85	89	93	97	101	105	109	113	117	122

12/13 Typography is closely allied to the fine arts, and types have always reflected the taste or feeling of their time. The charm of the early Italian types has perhaps never been equalled; and the like is true of the Renaissance manuscripts on which they were based—and of many other departments of art in that same wonderful time. Note, too, the relation of the French manuscripts and types of a slightly later date to the manuscripts and the types of the Italian Renaissance.

In spite of the increasing interest in the

10/11 Typography is closely allied to the fine arts, and types have always reflected the taste or feeling of their time. The charm of the early Italian types has perhaps never been equalled; and the like is true of the Renaissance manuscripts on which they were based—and of many other departments of art in that same wonderful time. Note, too, the relation of the French manuscripts and types of a slightly later date to the manuscripts and the types of the Italian Renaissance.

In spite of the increasing interest in the history of printing, and the attention paid in many quarters to the work of famous typographers, a knowl-*edge of standards among the rank and file of printers is still greatly lacking. To the average*

12/14 Typography is closely allied to the fine arts, and types have always reflected the taste or feeling of their time. The charm of the early Italian types has perhaps never been equalled; and the like is true of the Renaissance manuscripts on which they were based—and of many other departments of art in that same wonderful time. Note, too, the relation of the French manuscripts and types of a slightly later date to the manuscripts and the types of

10/12 Typography is closely allied to the fine arts, and types have always reflected the taste or feeling of their time. The charm of the early Italian types has perhaps never been equalled; and the like is true of the Renaissance manuscripts on which they were based—and of many other departments of art in that same wonderful time. Note, too, the relation of the French manuscripts and types of a slightly later date to the manuscripts and the types of the Italian Renaissance.

In spite of the increasing interest in the history *edge of standards among the rank and file of printers is still greatly lacking. To the average*

12/16 Typography is closely allied to the fine arts, and types have always reflected the taste or feeling of their time. The charm of the early Italian types has perhaps never been equalled; and the like is true of the Renaissance manuscripts on which they were based—and of many other departments of art in that same wonderful time. Note, too, the relation of the French manuscripts and types of a slightly later

10/14 Typography is closely allied to the fine arts, and types have always reflected the taste or feeling of their time. The charm of the early Italian types has perhaps never been equalled; and the like is true of the Renaissance manuscripts on which they were based—and of many other departments of art in that same wonderful time. Note, too, the relation of the French manuscripts and types of a slightly later date to the manuscripts and the *edge of standards among the rank and file of printers is still greatly lacking. To the average*

ABCDEFGHIJKLMNOPQRSTUVWXYZ
.,''-:;!?''''&1234567890
abcdefghijklmnopqrstuvwxyz

ABCDEFGHIJKLMNOPQRSTUVWXYZ
ABCDEFGHIJKLMNOPQRSTUVWXYZ
abcdefghijklmnopqrstuvwxyz
abcdefghijklmnopqrstuvwxyz
.,''-:;!?''''&1234567890
.,''-:;!?''''&1234567890

HELVETICA: LINOTYPE *Helvetica must be set on a slug one point greater than specified size.

PICAS	6	7	8	9	10	11	12	13	14	15	16	17	18	19	20	21	22	23	24	25	26	27	28	29	30
12 POINT	13	15	17	19	21	23	25	27	29	32	34	36	38	40	42	44	46	48	50	53	55	57	59	61	63
10 POINT	15	17	20	22	25	27	29	32	34	37	39	42	44	47	49	51	54	56	59	61	64	66	69	71	74

9/10 Typography is closely allied to the fine arts, and types have always reflected the taste or feeling of their time. The charm of the early Italian types has perhaps never been equalled; and the like is true of the Renaissance manuscripts on which they were based—and of many other departments of art in that same wonderful time. Note, too, the relation of the French manuscripts and types of a slightly later date to the manuscripts and the types of the Italian Renaissance.

In spite of the increasing interest in the history of printing, and the attention paid in many quarters to the work of famous typographers, a knowledge of standards among the rank and file of printers is still greatly lacking. To the average printer of to-day, type *is type, printing is printing—it is all about alike; and he concerns himself only with alleged labour-saving*

8/9 Typography is closely allied to the fine arts, and types have always reflected the taste or feeling of their time. The charm of the early Italian types has perhaps never been equalled; and the like is true of the Renaissance manuscripts on which they were based—and of many other departments of art in that same wonderful time. Note, too, the relation of the French manuscripts and types of a slightly later date to the manuscripts and the types of the Italian Renaissance.

In spite of the increasing interest in the history of printing, and the attention paid in many quarters to the work of famous typographers, a knowledge of standards among the rank and file of printers is still greatly lacking. To the average printer of to-day, type is type, printing is printing—it is all about alike; and he concerns himself only with alleged labour-saving contrivances, or new type-faces that ensure convenience at the expense of proper design. In a more *advanced class is to be found the printer who, knowing something of the historical side of printing and realizing*

9/11 Typography is closely allied to the fine arts, and types have always reflected the taste or feeling of their time. The charm of the early Italian types has perhaps never been equalled; and the like is true of the Renaissance manuscripts on which they were based—and of many other departments of art in that same wonderful time. Note, too, the relation of the French manuscripts and types of a slightly later date to the manuscripts and the types of the Italian Renaissance.

In spite of the increasing interest in the history of printing, and the attention paid in many quarters to the work of famous typographers, a knowledge of *is type, printing is printing—it is all about alike; and he concerns himself only with alleged labour-saving*

8/10 Typography is closely allied to the fine arts, and types have always reflected the taste or feeling of their time. The charm of the early Italian types has perhaps never been equalled; and the like is true of the Renaissance manuscripts on which they were based—and of many other departments of art in that same wonderful time. Note, too, the relation of the French manuscripts and types of a slightly later date to the manuscripts and the types of the Italian Renaissance.

In spite of the increasing interest in the history of printing, and the attention paid in many quarters to the work of famous typographers, a knowledge of standards among the rank and file of printers is still greatly lacking. To the average printer of to-day, type is type, printing is printing—it is *advanced class is to be found the printer who, knowing something of the historical side of printing and realizing*

9/13 Typography is closely allied to the fine arts, and types have always reflected the taste or feeling of their time. The charm of the early Italian types has perhaps never been equalled; and the like is true of the Renaissance manuscripts on which they were based—and of many other departments of art in that same wonderful time. Note, too, the relation of the French manuscripts and types of a slightly later date to the manuscripts and the types of the Italian Renaissance.

In spite of the increasing interest in the history of *is type, printing is printing—it is all about alike; and he concerns himself only with alleged labour-saving*

8/12 Typography is closely allied to the fine arts, and types have always reflected the taste or feeling of their time. The charm of the early Italian types has perhaps never been equalled; and the like is true of the Renaissance manuscripts on which they were based—and of many other departments of art in that same wonderful time. Note, too, the relation of the French manuscripts and types of a slightly later date to the manuscripts and the types of the Italian Renaissance.

In spite of the increasing interest in the history of printing, and the attention paid in many quarters to the work of famous typographers, a knowledge of standards among the *advanced class is to be found the printer who, knowing something of the historical side of printing and realizing*

ABCDEFGHIJKLMNOPQRSTUVWXYZ
ABCDEFGHIJKLMNOPQRSTUVWXYZ
.,''-:;!?''''&1234567890
.,''-:;!?''''&1234567890
abcdefghijklmnopqrstuvwxyz
abcdefghijklmnopqrstuvwxyz

ABCDEFGHIJKLMNOPQRSTUVWXYZ
ABCDEFGHIJKLMNOPQRSTUVWXYZ
.,''-:;!?''''&1234567890
.,''-:;!?''''&1234567890
abcdefghijklmnopqrstuvwxyz
abcdefghijklmnopqrstuvwxyz

HELVETICA: LINOTYPE *Helvetica must be set on a slug one point greater than specified size.

PICAS	6	7	8	9	10	11	12	13	14	15	16	17	18	19	20	21	22	23	24	25	26	27	28	29	30
9 POINT	16	19	22	24	27	30	32	35	38	41	43	46	49	51	54	57	59	62	65	68	70	73	76	78	81
8 POINT	18	21	24	27	31	34	37	40	43	46	49	52	55	58	61	64	67	70	73	76	79	82	85	88	92

7/8

Typography is closely allied to the fine arts, and types have always reflected the taste or feeling of their time. The charm of the early Italian types has perhaps never been equalled; and the like is true of the Renaissance manuscripts on which they were based—and of many other departments of art in that same wonderful time. Note, too, the relation of the French manuscripts and types of a slightly later date to the manuscripts and the types of the Italian Renaissance.

In spite of the increasing interest in the history of printing, and the attention paid in many quarters to the work of famous typographers, a knowledge of standards among the rank and file of printers is still greatly lacking. To the average printer of to-day, type is type, printing is printing—it is all about alike; and he concerns himself only with alleged labour-saving contrivances, or new type-faces that ensure convenience at the expense of proper design. In a more advanced class is to be found the printer who, knowing something of the historical side of printing and realizing intellectually that there is a standard of excellence, yet has never considered the question as applying in any practical way to him-

Typography is closely allied to the fine arts, and types have always reflected the taste or feeling of their time. The charm of

6/7

Typography is closely allied to the fine arts, and types have always reflected the taste or feeling of their time. The charm of the early Italian types has perhaps never been equalled; and the like is true of the Renaissance manuscripts on which they were based—and of many other departments of art in that same wonderful time. Note, too, the relation of the French manuscripts and types of a slightly later date to the manuscripts and the types of the Italian Renaissance.

In spite of the increasing interest in the history of printing, and the attention paid in many quarters to the work of famous typographers, a knowledge of standards among the rank and file of printers is still greatly lacking. To the average printer of to-day, type is type, printing is printing—it is all about alike; and he concerns himself only with alleged labour-saving contrivances, or new type-faces that ensure convenience at the expense of proper design. In a more advanced class is to be found the printer who, knowing something of the historical side of printing and realizing intellectually that there is a standard of excellence, yet has never considered the question as applying in any practical way to himself or his work.

Typography is closely allied to the fine arts, and types have always reflected the taste or feeling of their time. The charm of the early Italian types has perhaps never been equalled; and the like is true of the Renaissance manuscripts on which they were based—and of many other departments of art in that same wonderful time. Note, too, the *relation of the French manuscripts and types of a slightly later date*

7/9

Typography is closely allied to the fine arts, and types have always reflected the taste or feeling of their time. The charm of the early Italian types has perhaps never been equalled; and the like is true of the Renaissance manuscripts on which they were based—and of many other departments of art in that same wonderful time. Note, too, the relation of the French manuscripts and types of a slightly later date to the manuscripts and the types of the Italian Renaissance.

In spite of the increasing interest in the history of printing, and the attention paid in many quarters to the work of famous typographers, a knowledge of standards among the rank and file of printers is still greatly lacking. To the average printer of to-day, type is type, printing is printing—it is all about alike; and he concerns himself only with alleged labour-saving contrivances, or new type-faces that ensure convenience at the expense of proper

Typography is closely allied to the fine arts, and types have always reflected the taste or feeling of their time. The charm of

6/8

Typography is closely allied to the fine arts, and types have always reflected the taste or feeling of their time. The charm of the early Italian types has perhaps never been equalled; and the like is true of the Renaissance manuscripts on which they were based—and of many other departments of art in that same wonderful time. Note, too, the relation of the French manuscripts and types of a slightly later date to the manuscripts and the types of the Italian Renaissance.

In spite of the increasing interest in the history of printing, and the attention paid in many quarters to the work of famous typographers, a knowledge of standards among the rank and file of printers is still greatly lacking. To the average printer of to-day, type is type, printing is printing—it is all about alike; and he concerns himself only with alleged labour-saving contrivances, or new type-faces that ensure convenience at the expense of proper design. In a more advanced class is to be found the printer who, knowing something of the historical side of printing and realizing intellectually that there is a standard of excellence, yet has never considered the question as *other departments of art in that same wonderful time. Note, too, the relation of the French manuscripts and types of a slightly later date*

7/11

Typography is closely allied to the fine arts, and types have always reflected the taste or feeling of their time. The charm of the early Italian types has perhaps never been equalled; and the like is true of the Renaissance manuscripts on which they were based—and of many other departments of art in that same wonderful time. Note, too, the relation of the French manuscripts and types of a slightly later date to the manuscripts and the types of the Italian Renaissance.

In spite of the increasing interest in the history of printing, and the attention paid in many quarters to the work of famous typographers, a knowledge of standards among the rank and file of printers is still greatly lacking. To the average printer of to-day,

Typography is closely allied to the fine arts, and types have always reflected the taste or feeling of their time. The charm of

6/10

Typography is closely allied to the fine arts, and types have always reflected the taste or feeling of their time. The charm of the early Italian types has perhaps never been equalled; and the like is true of the Renaissance manuscripts on which they were based—and of many other departments of art in that same wonderful time. Note, too, the relation of the French manuscripts and types of a slightly later date to the manuscripts and the types of the Italian Renaissance.

In spite of the increasing interest in the history of printing, and the attention paid in many quarters to the work of famous typographers, a knowledge of standards among the rank and file of printers is still greatly lacking. To the average printer of to-day, type is type, printing is printing—it is all about alike; and he concerns himself only with alleged labour-saving contrivances, or new type-faces that ensure *other departments of art in that same wonderful time. Note, too, the relation of the French manuscripts and types of a slightly later date*

ABCDEFGHIJKLMNOPQRSTUVWXYZ
ABCDEFGHIJKLMNOPQRSTUVWXYZ
.,'':;!?''''&1234567890
.,'':;!?''''&1234567890
abcdefghijklmnopqrstuvwxyz
abcdefghijklmnopqrstuvwxyz

ABCDEFGHIJKLMNOPQRSTUVWXYZ
ABCDEFGHIJKLMNOPQRSTUVWXYZ
.,'':;!?''''&1234567890$
.,'':;!?''''&1234567890$
abcdefghijklmnopqrstuvwxyz
abcdefghijklmnopqrstuvwxyz

HELVETICA: LINOTYPE   *Helvetica must be set on a slug one point greater than specified size.

PICAS	6	7	8	9	10	11	12	13	14	15	16	17	18	19	20	21	22	23	24	25	26	27	28	29	30
7 POINT	19	23	26	30	33	36	40	43	46	50	53	56	59	63	66	69	73	76	79	83	86	89	92	96	99
6 POINT	21	25	28	32	35	39	42	46	49	53	56	60	63	67	70	74	77	81	84	88	91	95	98	102	105

10/10

Ever since the sixteenth century, elaborate diagrams have been published to show how letters should be drawn, as we shall learn from some accounts given of men who suggested new methods of designing them. Generally a diagram of minute squares was first made, and on this the design and dimension of each letter were determined. Jaugeon, who was appointed by the Académie des Sciences of Paris in the last years of the seventeenth century to supply a scheme or series of directions by which type should be cut, began by stating that "the eye is the sovereign ruler of taste." The rules which he set forth were extremely complicated—every Roman capital was to be designed on a framework of 2304 little *squares. Grandjean, the first type-cutter who attempted to follow them, is said to have observed*

8/8

Ever since the sixteenth century, elaborate diagrams have been published to show how letters should be drawn, as we shall learn from some accounts given of men who suggested new methods of designing them. Generally a diagram of minute squares was first made, and on this the design and dimension of each letter were determined. Jaugeon, who was appointed by the Académie des Sciences of Paris in the last years of the seventeenth century to supply a scheme or series of directions by which type should be cut, began by stating that "the eye is the sovereign ruler of taste." The rules which he set forth were extremely complicated—every Roman capital was to be designed on a framework of 2304 little squares. Grandjean, the first type-cutter who attempted to follow them, is said to have observed sarcastically, that he should certainly accept Jaugeon's dictum that "the eye is the sovereign ruler of taste," and accepting this, should throw the rest of his rules overboard. This then is the only consideration, many other type cutters tried until they had it simplified *and perfected—had probably different methods. One cast letters in moulds of clay or sand; the other understood*

10/12

Ever since the sixteenth century, elaborate diagrams have been published to show how letters should be drawn, as we shall learn from some accounts given of men who suggested new methods of designing them. Generally a diagram of minute squares was first made, and on this the design and dimension of each letter were determined. Jaugeon, who was appointed by the Académie des Sciences of Paris in the last years of the seventeenth century to supply a scheme or series of directions by which type should be cut, began by stating that "the eye is the sovereign *squares. Grandjean, the first type-cutter who attempted to follow them, is said to have observed*

8/10

Ever since the sixteenth century, elaborate diagrams have been published to show how letters should be drawn, as we shall learn from some accounts given of men who suggested new methods of designing them. Generally a diagram of minute squares was first made, and on this the design and dimension of each letter were determined. Jaugeon, who was appointed by the Académie des Sciences of Paris in the last years of the seventeenth century to supply a scheme or series of directions by which type should be cut, began by stating that "the eye is the sovereign ruler of taste." The rules which he set forth were extremely complicated—every Roman capital was to be designed on a framework of 2304 little squares. Grandjean, the first type-cutter who attempted to follow them, is said *and perfected—had probably different methods. One cast letters in moulds of clay or sand; the other understood*

10/14

Ever since the sixteenth century, elaborate diagrams have been published to show how letters should be drawn, as we shall learn from some accounts given of men who suggested new methods of designing them. Generally a diagram of minute squares was first made, and on this the design and dimension of each letter were determined. Jaugeon, who was appointed by the Académie des Sciences of Paris in the last years of the seventeenth century to supply a scheme or *squares. Grandjean, the first type-cutter who at-*

8/12

Ever since the sixteenth century, elaborate diagrams have been published to show how letters should be drawn, as we shall learn from some accounts given of men who suggested new methods of designing them. Generally a diagram of minute squares was first made, and on this the design and dimension of each letter were determined. Jaugeon, who was appointed by the Académie des Sciences of Paris in the last years of the seventeenth century to supply a scheme or series of directions by which type to have observed sarcastically, that he should certainly accept Jaugeon's dictum that "the eye is the sovereign ruler of taste," and accepting this, should throw the rest of *and perfected—had probably different methods. One cast*

ABCDEFGHIJKLMNOPQRSTUVWXYZ
ABCDEFGHIJKLMNOPQRSTUVWXYZ
.,"-:;!?""&1234567890$
.,"-:;!?""&1234567890$
abcdefghijklmnopqrstuvwxyz
abcdefghijklmnopqrstuvwxyz

ABCDEFGHIJKLMNOPQRSTUVWXYZ
ABCDEFGHIJKLMNOPQRSTUVWXYZ
.,"-:;!?""1234567890
.,"-:;!?""1234567890
abcdefghijklmnopqrstuvwxyz
abcdefghijklmnopqrstuvwxyz

HELVETICA BOLD: LINOTYPE

PICAS	6	7	8	9	10	11	12	13	14	15	16	17	18	19	20	21	22	23	24	25	26	27	28	29	30
10 POINT	15	17	20	22	25	27	29	32	34	37	39	42	44	47	49	51	54	56	59	61	64	66	69	71	74
8 POINT	18	21	24	27	31	34	37	40	43	46	49	52	55	58	61	64	67	70	73	76	79	82	85	88	92

14/15 Whence are derived the shapes of the characters in which you read the sentence before you; and whence comes the type in which this sentence is printed? The type of this book is a font transitional between the "old style" types of the school of Caslon and the English equivalent of the pseudo-classic types made at the beginning of the nineteenth century under the *influence of Didot of Paris, Bodoni of Parma, and Unger of Berlin. These pseu-*

12/13 Whence are derived the shapes of the characters in which you read the sentence before you; and whence comes the type in which this sentence is printed? The type of this book is a font transitional between the "old style" types of the school of Caslon and the English equivalent of the pseudo-classic types made at the beginning of the nineteenth century under the influence of Didot of Paris, Bodoni of Parma, and Unger of Berlin. These pseudo-classic types were modifications of that old style type (as *we should now call it) which was in use in England and throughout Europe in the middle*

14/16 Whence are derived the shapes of the characters in which you read the sentence before you; and whence comes the type in which this sentence is printed? The type of this book is a font transitional between the "old style" types of the school of Caslon and the English equivalent of the pseudo-classic types made at the begin-*influence of Didot of Paris, Bodoni of Parma, and Unger of Berlin. These pseu-*

12/14 Whence are derived the shapes of the characters in which you read the sentence before you; and whence comes the type in which this sentence is printed? The type of this book is a font transitional between the "old style" types of the school of Caslon and the English equivalent of the pseudo-classic types made at the beginning of the nineteenth century under the influence of Didot of Paris, Bodoni of Parma, and Unger of Berlin. These pseudo-classic types *we should now call it) which was in use in England and throughout Europe in the middle*

14/18 Whence are derived the shapes of the characters in which you read the sentence before you; and whence comes the type in which this sentence is printed? The type of this book is a font transitional between the "old style" types of the school of Caslon and the English equivalent of the pseudo-classic types made at the beginning of the *influence of Didot of Paris, Bodoni of Parma, and Unger of Berlin. These pseu-*

12/16 Whence are derived the shapes of the characters in which you read the sentence before you; and whence comes the type in which this sentence is printed? The type of this book is a font transitional between the "old style" types of the school of Caslon and the English equivalent of the pseudo-classic types made at the beginning of the nineteenth century under the in-*we should now call it) which was in use in England and throughout Europe in the middle*

ABCDEFGHIJKLMNOPQRSTUVW
ABCDEFGHIJKLMNOPQRSTUVW
XYZ.,"-:;!?""&1234567890$1234567890$
XYZ.,"-:;!?""&1234567890$1234567890$
abcdefghijklmnopqrstuvwxyz
abcdefghijklmnopqrstuvwxyz

ABCDEFGHIJKLMNOPQRSTUVWXYZ
ABCDEFGHIJKLMNOPQRSTUVWXYZ
.,"-:;!?""&1234567890$1234567890$
.,"-:;!?""&1234567890$1234567890$
abcdefghijklmnopqrstuvwxyz
abcdefghijklmnopqrstuvwxyz

JANSON: LINOTYPE   *When long descenders are used (as shown) type must be set on a slug one point greater than specified size.

PICAS	6	7	8	9	10	11	12	13	14	15	16	17	18	19	20	21	22	23	24	25	26	27	28	29	30
14 POINT	12	14	16	18	20	22	24	26	28	30	32	34	36	38	40	42	44	46	48	50	52	54	56	58	60
12 POINT	13	16	18	20	23	25	27	29	32	34	36	39	41	43	46	48	50	53	55	57	59	62	64	66	69

11/12 Whence are derived the shapes of the characters in which you read the sentence before you; and whence comes the type in which this sentence is printed? The type of this book is a font transitional between the "old style" types of the school of Caslon and the English equivalent of the pesudo-classic types made at the beginning of the nineteenth century under the influence of Didot of Paris, Bodoni of Parma, and Unger of Berlin. These pseudo-classic types were modifications of that old style type (as we should now call it) which was in use in England and throughout Europe in the middle of the eighteenth century. *The English old style types of the seventeenth and*

10/11 Whence are derived the shapes of the characters in which you read the sentence before you; and whence comes the type in which this sentence is printed? The type of this book is a font transitional between the "old style" types of the school of Caslon and the English equivalent of the pseudo-classic types made at the beginning of the nineteenth century under the influence of Didot of Paris, Bodoni of Parma, and Unger of Berlin. These pseudo-classic types were modifications of that old style type (as we should now call it) which was in use in England and throughout Europe in the middle of the eighteenth century. The English old style types of the seven-*teenth and eighteenth centuries were chiefly derived from Dutch models of the middle of the seventeenth*

11/13 Whence are derived the shapes of the characters in which you read the sentence before you; and whence comes the type in which this sentence is printed? The type of this book is a font transitional between the "old style" types of the school of Caslon and the English equivalent of the pesudo-classic types made at the beginning of the nineteenth century under the influence of Didot of Paris, Bodoni of Parma, and Unger of Berlin. These pseudo-classic types were modifications of that old style type (as we should now call it) *rope in the middle of the eighteenth century. The English old style types of the seventeenth and*

10/12 Whence are derived the shapes of the characters in which you read the sentence before you; and whence comes the type in which this sentence is printed? The type of this book is a font transitional between the "old style" types of the school of Caslon and the English equivalent of the pseudo-classic types made at the beginning of the nineteenth century under the influence of Didot of Paris, Bodoni of Parma, and Unger of Berlin. These pseudo-classic types were modifications of that old style type (as we should now call it) which was in use in England and throughout Europe in the middle of the eighteenth *teenth and eighteenth centuries were chiefly derived from Dutch models of the middle of the seventeenth*

11/15 Whence are derived the shapes of the characters in which you read the sentence before you; and whence comes the type in which this sentence is printed? The type of this book is a font transitional between the "old style" types of the school of Caslon and the English equivalent of the pesudo-classic types made at the beginning of the nineteenth century under the influence of Didot of Paris, Bodoni of Parma, and Unger of Berlin. *rope in the middle of the eighteenth century. The English old style types of the seventeenth and*

10/14 Whence are derived the shapes of the characters in which you read the sentence before you; and whence comes the type in which this sentence is printed? The type of this book is a font transitional between the "old style" types of the school of Caslon and the English equivalent of the pseudo-classic types made at the beginning of the nineteenth century under the influence of Didot of Paris, Bodoni of Parma, and Unger of Berlin. These pseudo-classic types were modifications of that old style type (as we should *teenth and eighteenth centuries were chiefly derived from Dutch models of the middle of the seventeenth*

ABCDEFGHIJKLMNOPQRSTUVWXYZ
ABCDEFGHIJKLMNOPQRSTUVWXYZ
.,"-:;!?""&1234567890$1234567890$
.,"-:;!?""&1234567890$1234567890$
abcdefghijklmnopqrstuvwxyz
abcdefghijklmnopqrstuvwxyz

ABCDEFGHIJKLMNOPQRSTUVWXYZ
ABCDEFGHIJKLMNOPQRSTUVWXYZ
.,"-:;!?""&1234567890$1234567890$
.,"-:;!?""&1234567890$1234567890$
abcdefghijklmnopqrstuvwxyz
abcdefghijklmnopqrstuvwxyz

JANSON: LINOTYPE *When long descenders are used (as shown) type must be set on a slug one point greater than specified size.

PICAS	6	7	8	9	10	11	12	13	14	15	16	17	18	19	20	21	22	23	24	25	26	27	28	29	30
11 POINT	14	16	19	21	24	26	28	31	33	36	38	40	43	45	48	50	52	55	57	60	62	64	67	69	72
10 POINT	15	18	20	23	26	28	31	33	36	39	41	44	46	49	52	54	57	59	62	65	67	69	72	75	78

9/10

Whence are derived the shapes of the characters in which you read the sentence before you; and whence comes the type in which this sentence is printed? The type of this book is a font transitional between the "old style" types of the school of Caslon and the English equivalent of the pseudo-classic types made at the beginning of the nineteenth century under the influence of Didot of Paris, Bodoni of Parma, and Unger of Berlin. These pseudo-classic types were modifications of that old style type (as we should now call it) which was in use in England and throughout Europe in the middle of the eighteenth century. The English old style types of the seventeenth and eighteenth centuries were chiefly derived from Dutch models of the middle of the seventeenth century; and these seventeenth century types in turn were modelled on *earlier roman types common in Europe which were introduced into Italy at the time of the Renaissance. Any*

8/9

Whence are derived the shapes of the characters in which you read the sentence before you; and whence comes the type in which this sentence is printed? The type of this book is a font transitional between the "old style" types of the school of Caslon and the English equivalent of the pseudo-classic types made at the beginning of the nineteenth century under the influence of Didot of Paris, Bodoni of Parma, and Unger of Berlin. These pseudo-classic types were modifications of that old style type (as we should now call it) which was in use in England and throughout Europe in the middle of the eighteenth century. The English old style types of the seventeenth and eighteenth centuries were chiefly derived from Dutch models of the middle of the seventeenth century; and these seventeenth century types in turn were modelled on earlier roman types common in Europe which were introduced into Italy at the time of the Renaissance. Any one familiar with the earliest printing will note that many of the early types were black-let-*ter characters derived from manuscripts, and at first sight it is a little perplexing to know where Roman characters come*

9/11

Whence are derived the shapes of the characters in which you read the sentence before you; and whence comes the type in which this sentence is printed? The type of this book is a font transitional between the "old style" types of the school of Caslon and the English equivalent of the pseudo-classic types made at the beginning of the nineteenth century under the influence of Didot of Paris, Bodoni of Parma, and Unger of Berlin. These pseudo-classic types were modifications of that old style type (as we should now call it) which was in use in England and throughout Europe in the middle of the eighteenth century. The English old style types of the seventeenth and eighteenth centuries were chiefly derived from Dutch *earlier roman types common in Europe which were introduced into Italy at the time of the Renaissance. Any*

8/10

Whence are derived the shapes of the characters in which you read the sentence before you; and whence comes the type in which this sentence is printed? The type of this book is a font transitional between the "old style" types of the school of Caslon and the English equivalent of the pseudo-classic types made at the beginning of the nineteenth century under the influence of Didot of Paris, Bodoni of Parma, and Unger of Berlin. These pseudo-classic types were modifications of that old style type (as we should now call it) which was in use in England and throughout Europe in the middle of the eighteenth century. The English old style types of the seventeenth and eighteenth centuries were chiefly derived from Dutch models of the middle of the seventeenth century; and these seventeenth century types in turn were modelled on earlier roman types common in Europe which were introduced into Italy at *ter characters derived from manuscripts, and at first sight it is a little perplexing to know where Roman characters come*

9/13

Whence are derived the shapes of the characters in which you read the sentence before you; and whence comes the type in which this sentence is printed? The type of this book is a font transitional between the "old style" types of the school of Caslon and the English equivalent of the pseudo-classic types made at the beginning of the nineteenth century under the influence of Didot of Paris, Bodoni of Parma, and Unger of Berlin. These pseudo-classic types were modifications of that old style type (as we should now call it) which was in use in England and throughout Europe in the middle of the eighteenth cen-*earlier roman types common in Europe which were introduced into Italy at the time of the Renaissance. Any*

8/12

Whence are derived the shapes of the characters in which you read the sentence before you; and whence comes the type in which this sentence is printed? The type of this book is a font transitional between the "old style" types of the school of Caslon and the English equivalent of the pseudo-classic types made at the beginning of the nineteenth century under the influence of Didot of Paris, Bodoni of Parma, and Unger of Berlin. These pseudo-classic types were modifications of that old style type (as we should now call it) which was in use in England and throughout Europe in the middle of the eighteenth century. The English old style types of the seventeenth and eighteenth centuries were chiefly derived from Dutch models *ter characters derived from manuscripts, and at first sight it is a little perplexing to know where Roman characters come*

ABCDEFGHIJKLMNOPQRSTUVWXYZ
ABCDEFGHIJKLMNOPQRSTUVWXYZ
.,"-:;!?""&1234567890$1234567890$
.,"-:;!?""&1234567890$1234567890$
abcdefghijklmnopqrstuvwxyz
abcdefghijklmnopqrstuvwxyz

ABCDEFGHIJKLMNOPQRSTUVWXYZ
ABCDEFGHIJKLMNOPQRSTUVWXYZ
.,"-:;!?""&1234567890$1234567890$
.,"-:;!?""&1234567890$1234567890$
abcdefghijklmnopqrstuvwxyz
abcdefghijklmnopqrstuvwxyz

JANSON: LINOTYPE *When long descenders are used (as shown) type must be set on a slug one point greater than specified size.

PICAS	6	7	8	9	10	11	12	13	14	15	16	17	18	19	20	21	22	23	24	25	26	27	28	29	30
9 POINT	16	19	22	25	28	30	33	36	39	42	44	47	50	53	56	58	61	64	67	70	72	75	78	81	84
8 POINT	18	21	24	27	30	33	36	39	42	45	48	51	54	57	60	63	66	69	72	75	78	81	84	87	90

10/11

Ever since the sixteenth century, elaborate dia-grams have been published to show how letters should be drawn, as we shall learn from some ac-counts given of men who suggested new methods of designing them. Generally a diagram of minute squares was first made, and on this the design and dimension of each letter were determined. Jaugeon, who was appointed by the Académie des Sciences of Paris in the last years of the sev-enteenth century to supply a scheme or series of directions by which type should be cut, began by stating that "the eye is the sovereign ruler of taste." The rules which he set forth were ex-tremely complicated—every Roman capital was *to be designed on a framework of 2304 little squares. Grandjean, the first type-cutter who*

8/9

Ever since the sixteenth century, elaborate diagrams have been published to show how letters should be drawn, as we shall learn from some accounts given of men who suggested new methods of designing them. Generally a diagram of minute squares was first made, and on this the design and dimension of each letter were determined. Jaugeon, who was appointed by the Acadé-mie des Sciences of Paris in the last years of the seven-tenth century to supply a scheme or series of directions by which type should be cut, began by stating that "the eye is the sovereign ruler of taste." The rules which he set forth were extremely complicated—every Roman cap-ital was to be designed on a framework of 2304 little squares. Grandjean, the first type-cutter who attempted to follow them, is said to have observed sarcastically, that he should certainly accept Jaugeon's dictum that "the eye is the sovereign ruler of taste," and accepting *this, should throw the rest of his rules overboard and perfected—had probably different methods. One cast*

10/12

Ever since the sixteenth century, elaborate dia-grams have been published to show how letters should be drawn, as we shall learn from some ac-counts given of men who suggested new methods of designing them. Generally a diagram of minute squares was first made, and on this the design and dimension of each letter were determined. Jaugeon, who was appointed by the Académie des Sciences of Paris in the last years of the sev-enteenth century to supply a scheme or series of directions by which type should be cut, began by stating that "the eye is the sovereign ruler of *to be designed on a framework of 2304 little squares. Grandjean, the first type-cutter who*

8/10

Ever since the sixteenth century, elaborate diagrams have been published to show how letters should be drawn, as we shall learn from some accounts given of men who suggested new methods of designing them. Generally a diagram of minute squares was first made, and on this the design and dimension of each letter were determined. Jaugeon, who was appointed by the Acadé-mie des Sciences of Paris in the last years of the seven-tenth century to supply a scheme or series of directions by which type should be cut, began by stating that "the eye is the sovereign ruler of taste." The rules which he set forth were extremely complicated—every Roman capital was to be designed on a framework of 2304 little squares. Grandjean, the first type-cutter who attempted to follow them, is said to have observed sarcastically, *this, should throw the rest of his rules overboard and perfected—had probably different methods. One cast*

10/14

Ever since the sixteenth century, elaborate dia-grams have been published to show how letters should be drawn, as we shall learn from some ac-counts given of men who suggested new methods of designing them. Generally a diagram of minute squares was first made, and on this the design and dimension of each letter were determined. Jaugeon, who was appointed by the Académie des Sciences of Paris in the last years of the sev-enteenth century to supply a scheme or series of *to be designed on a framework of 2304 little squares. Grandjean, the first type-cutter who*

8/12

Ever since the sixteenth century, elaborate diagrams have been published to show how letters should be drawn, as we shall learn from some accounts given of men who suggested new methods of designing them. Generally a diagram of minute squares was first made, and on this the design and dimension of each letter were determined. Jaugeon, who was appointed by the Acadé-mie des Sciences of Paris in the last years of the seven-tenth century to supply a scheme or series of directions by which type should be cut, began by stating that "the eye is the sovereign ruler of taste." The rules which he set forth were extremely complicated—every Roman cap-*this, should throw the rest of his rules overboard and perfected—had probably different methods. One cast*

ABCDEFGHIJKLMNOPQRSTUVWXYZ
ABCDEFGHIJKLMNOPQRSTUVWXYZ
.,''-:;!?''''&1234567890$
.,''-:;!?''''&1234567890$
abcdefghijklmnopqrstuvwxyz
abcdefghijklmnopqrstuvwxyz

ABCDEFGHIJKLMNOPQRSTUVWXYZ
ABCDEFGHIJKLMNOPQRSTUVWXYZ
.,''-:;!?''''1234567890
.,''-:;!?''''1234567890
abcdefghijklmnopqrstuvwxyz
abcdefghijklmnopqrstuvwxyz

MELIOR: LINOTYPE   *This face must be set 1 pt leaded.

PICAS	6	7	8	9	10	11	12	13	14	15	16	17	18	19	20	21	22	23	24	25	26	27	28	29	30
9 POINT	15	18	21	23	26	28	31	33	36	39	42	44	47	49	52	54	57	59	62	65	68	70	73	75	78
8 POINT	18	21	24	27	29	31	34	37	40	43	46	48	51	54	57	60	63	65	68	71	74	77	80	83	86

14/14

Besides the three principal properties which we have mentioned, the following (like Satellites to good letter) are not undeserving the purchaser's examination, who ought to take notice, 1. Whether the letter stands even, and in line; which is the chief good quality in letter, and makes the face thereof sometimes to pass, though otherwise ill-shaped. 2. Whether it stands parallel; and whether it drives out or gets in, either at the head, or the foot, and is, as Printers call it, bottle-arsed; **which is a fault that cannot be mended but by rubbing the whole fount over again. 3. Whether**

12/12

Besides the three principal properties which we have mentioned, the following (like Satellites to good letter) are not undeserving the purchaser's examination, who ought to take notice, 1. Whether the letter stands even, and in line which is the chief good quality in letter, and makes the face thereof sometimes to pass, though otherwise ill-shaped. 2. Whether it stands parallel; and whether it drives out or gets in, either at the head, or the foot, and is, as Printers call it, bottle-arsed; which is a fault that cannot be mended but by rubbing the whole fount over again. 3. Whether the thin lower-case letters, especially the dots over the i and j, are come in **casting. 4. Whether the break is ploughed away and smoothened. 5. Whether it be well scraped, so as not to**

14/16

Besides the three principal properties which we have mentioned, the following (like Satellites to good letter) are not undeserving the purchaser's examination, who ought to take notice, 1. Whether the letter stands even, and in line; which is the chief good quality in letter, and makes the face thereof sometimes to pass, though otherwise ill-shaped. 2. Whether it stands parallel; and whether **it drives out or gets in, either at the head, or the foot, and is, as Printers call it, bottle-arsed;**

12/14

Besides the three principal properties which we have mentioned, the following (like Satellites to good letter) are not undeserving the purchaser's examination, who ought to take notice, 1. Whether the letter stands even, and in line which is the chief good quality in letter, and makes the face thereof sometimes to pass, though otherwise ill-shaped. 2. Whether it stands parallel; and whether it drives out or gets in, either at the head, or the foot, and is, as Printers call it, bottle-arsed; which **is a fault that cannot be mended but by rubbing the whole fount over again. 3. Whether the thin lower-case**

14/18

Besides the three principal properties which we have mentioned, the following (like Satellites to good letter) are not undeserving the purchaser's examination, who ought to take notice, 1. Whether the letter stands even, and in line; which is the chief good quality in letter, and makes the face thereof sometimes to pass, though otherwise ill-shaped. **2. Whether it stands parallel; and whether it drives out or gets in, either at the head, or**

12/16

Besides the three principal properties which we have mentioned, the following (like Satellites to good letter) are not undeserving the purchaser's examination, who ought to take notice, 1. Whether the letter stands even, and in line which is the chief good quality in letter, and makes the face thereof sometimes to pass, though otherwise ill-shaped. 2. Whether it stands parallel; and whether it drives out or gets in, either at the head, or **the foot, and is, as Printers call it, bottle-arsed; which is a fault that cannot be mended but by rubbing the**

ABCDEFGHIJKLMNOPQRSTUVWXYZ
ABCDEFGHIJKLMNOPQRSTUVWXYZ
&.,"-:;!?""1234567890$
&.,"-:;!?""1234567890$
abcdefghijklmnopqrstuvwxyz
abcdefghijklmnopqrstuvwxyz

ABCDEFGHIJKLMNOPQRSTUVWXYZ
ABCDEFGHIJKLMNOPQRSTUVWXYZ
&.,"-:;!?""1234567890$
&.,"-:;!?""1234567890$
abcdefghijklmnopqrstuvwxyz
abcdefghijklmnopqrstuvwxyz

NEWS GOTHIC CONDENSED: INTERTYPE

PICAS	6	7	8	9	10	11	12	13	14	15	16	17	18	19	20	21	22	23	24	25	26	27	28	29	30
14 POINT	14	16	19	21	24	26	29	31	34	36	38	40	43	45	48	50	53	55	58	60	62	64	67	69	72
12 POINT	17	20	23	25	28	31	34	36	38	42	45	47	50	53	56	59	62	64	67	70	73	75	78	81	84

10/10 Besides the three principal properties which we have mentioned, the following (like Satellites to good letter) are not undeserving the purchaser's examination, who ought to take notice, 1. Whether the letter stands even, and in line; which is the chief good quality in letter, and makes the face thereof sometimes to pass, though otherwise ill-shaped. 2. Whether it stands parallel; and whether it drives out or gets in, either at the head, or the foot, and is, as Printers call it, bottle-arsed; which is a fault that cannot be mended but by rubbing the whole fount over again. 3. Whether the thin lower-case letters, especially the dots over the i and j, are come in casting. 4. Whether the break is ploughed away and smoothened. 5. Whether it be well scraped, so as not to want rubbing down by the compositor. 6. Whether each letter has a due proportion, as to thickness; and whether they are not so thin as to hinder each other from appearing with a full face; or so thick as to occasion a gap between letter and letter. 7. Whether it be **well bearded: which founders in France are obliged to do, to their**

9/9 Besides the three principal properties which we have mentioned, the following (like Satellites to good letter) are not undeserving the purchaser's examination, who ought to take notice, 1. Whether the letter stands even, and in line; which is the chief good quality in letter, and makes the face thereof sometimes to pass, though otherwise ill-shaped. 2. Whether it stands parallel; and whether it drives out or gets in, either at the head, or the foot, and is, as Printers call it, bottle-arsed; which is a fault that cannot be mended but by rubbing the whole fount over again. 3. Whether the thin lower-case letters, especially the dots over the i and j, are come in casting. 4. Whether the break is ploughed away and smoothened. 5. Whether it be well scraped, so as not to want rubbing down by the compositor. 6. Whether each letter has a due proportion, as to thickness; and whether they are not so thin as to hinder each other from appearing with a full face; or so thick as to occasion a gap between letter and letter. 7. Whether it be well bearded: which founders in France are obliged to do, to their own disadvantage, on account of their shallow letter. 8. Whether it have a deep and open, **single or double nick, different from other founts to the same body, and in the same printing-house.**

10/12 Besides the three principal properties which we have mentioned, the following (like Satellites to good letter) are not undeserving the purchaser's examination, who ought to take notice, 1. Whether the letter stands even, and in line; which is the chief good quality in letter, and makes the face thereof sometimes to pass, though otherwise ill-shaped. 2. Whether it stands parallel; and whether it drives out or gets in, either at the head, or the foot, and is, as Printers call it, bottle-arsed; which is a fault that cannot be mended but by rubbing the whole fount over again. 3. Whether the thin lower-case letters, especially the dots over the i and j, are come in casting. 4. Whether the break is ploughed away and smoothened. 5. Whether it be well scraped, so as not to want **rubbing down by the compositor. 6. Whether each letter has a due proportion, as to thickness; and whether they are not so thin as**

9/11 Besides the three principal properties which we have mentioned, the following (like Satellites to good letter) are not undeserving the purchaser's examination, who ought to take notice, 1. Whether the letter stands even, and in line; which is the chief good quality in letter, and makes the face thereof sometimes to pass, though otherwise ill-shaped. 2. Whether it stands parallel; and whether it drives out or gets in, either at the head, or the foot, and is, as Printers call it, bottle-arsed; which is a fault that cannot be mended but by rubbing the whole fount over again. 3. Whether the thin lower-case letters, especially the dots over the i and j, are come in casting. 4. Whether the break is ploughed away and smoothened. 5. Whether it be well scraped, so as not to want rubbing down by the compositor. 6. Whether each letter has a due proportion, as to thickness; and whether they are not so thin as to **hinder each other from appearing with a full face; or so thick as to occasion a gap between letter and letter. 7. Whether it be well bearded:**

10/14 Besides the three principal properties which we have mentioned, the following (like Satellites to good letter) are not undeserving the purchaser's examination, who ought to take notice, 1. Whether the letter stands even, and in line; which is the chief good quality in letter, and makes the face thereof sometimes to pass, though otherwise ill-shaped. 2. Whether it stands parallel; and whether it drives out or gets in, either at the head, or the foot, and is, as Printers call it, bottle-arsed; which is a fault that cannot be mended but by rubbing the whole fount over again. 3. Whether the thin lower-case letters, especially the dots over the i and j, are **come in casting. 4. Whether the break is ploughed away and smoothened. 5. Whether it be well scraped, so as not to want**

9/13 Besides the three principal properties which we have mentioned, the following (like Satellites to good letter) are not undeserving the purchaser's examination, who ought to take notice, 1. Whether the letter stands even, and in line; which is the chief good quality in letter, and makes the face thereof sometimes to pass, though otherwise ill-shaped. 2. Whether it stands parallel; and whether it drives out or gets in, either at the head, or the foot, and is, as Printers call it, bottle-arsed; which is a fault that cannot be mended but by rubbing the whole fount over again. 3. Whether the thin lower-case letters, especially the dots over the i and j, are come in casting. 4. Whether the break is ploughed away and smoothened. 5. Whether it be well scraped, so as not to want **rubbing down by the compositor. 6. Whether each letter has a due proportion, as to thickness; and whether they are not so thin as to**

ABCDEFGHIJKLMNOPQRSTUVWXYZ
ABCDEFGHIJKLMNOPQRSTUVWXYZ
&.,"-:;!?"""1234567890$
&.,"-:;!?"""1234567890$
abcdefghijklmnopqrstuvwxyz
abcdefghijklmnopqrstuvwxyz

ABCDEFGHIJKLMNOPQRSTUVWXYZ
ABCDEFGHIJKLMNOPQRSTUVWXYZ
&.,"-:;!?"""1234567890$
&.,"-:;!?"""1234567890$
abcdefghijklmnopqrstuvwxyz
abcdefghijklmnopqrstuvwxyz

NEWS GOTHIC CONDENSED INTERTYPE

PICAS	6	7	8	9	10	11	12	13	14	15	16	17	18	19	20	21	22	23	24	25	26	27	28	29	30
10 POINT	18	21	25	28	31	34	37	40	43	46	50	53	56	59	62	65	68	71	74	77	81	84	87	90	93
9 POINT	20	22	26	29	32	35	38	41	45	48	51	54	58	61	64	67	70	73	77	80	83	86	90	93	96

8/8

Besides the three principal properties which we have mentioned, the following (like Satellites to good letter) are not undeserving the purchaser's examination, who ought to take notice, 1. Whether the letter stands even, and in line; which is the chief good quality in letter, and makes the face thereof sometimes to pass, though otherwise ill-shaped. 2. Whether it stands parallel; and whether it drives out or gets in, either at the head, or the foot, and is, as Printers call it, bottle-arsed; which is a fault that cannot be mended but by rubbing the whole fount over again. 3. Whether the thin lower-case letters, especially the dots over the i and j, are come in casting. 4. Whether the break is ploughed away and smoothened. 5. Whether it be well scraped, so as not to want rubbing down by the compositor. 6. Whether each letter has a due proportion, as to thickness; and whether they are not so thin as to hinder each other from appearing with a full face; or so thick as to occasion a gap between letter and letter. 7. Whether it be well bearded: which founders in France are obliged to do, to their own disadvantage, on account of their shallow letters. 8. Whether it have a deep and open, single or double nick, different from other founts of the same body, and in the same printing-house.

We cannot to strongly urge the advantage to be derived from letter having a deep nick, and also that the nick should differ from other

6/6

Besides the three principal properties which we have mentioned, the following (like Satellites to good letter) are not undeserving the purchaser's examination, who ought to take notice. 1. Whether the letter stands even, and in line; which is the chief good quality in letter, and makes the face thereof sometimes to pass, though otherwise ill-shaped. 2. Whether it stands parallel; and whether it drives out or gets in, either at the head, or the foot, and is, as Printers call it, bottle-arsed; which is a fault that cannot be mended but by rubbing the whole fount over again. 3. Whether the thin lower-case letters, especially the dots over the i and j, are come in casting. 4. Whether the break is ploughed away and smoothened. 5. Whether it be well scraped, so as not to want rubbing down by the compositor. 6. Whether each letter has a due proportion, as to thickness; and whether they are not so thin as to hinder each other from appearing with a full face; or so thick as to occasion a gap between letter and letter. 7. Whether it be well bearded: which founders in France are obliged to do, to their own disadvantage, on account of their shallow letter. 8. Whether it have a deep and open, single or double nick, different from other founts to the same body, and in the same printing-house.

We cannot too strongly urge the advantage to be derived from letter having a deep nick, and also that the nick should differ from other founts of that body in the same house. This may appear a trifling consideration; but in a large fount the difference in weight will be considerable, and consequently a saving to the purchaser. A deep nick is an advantage to the compositor, from its more readily catching the eye than a shallow one, and consequently greatly facilitates him in his business.

Besides the three principal properties which we have mentioned, the following (like Satellites to good letter) are not undeserving the purchaser's examination, **who ought to take notice, 1. Whether the letter stands even, and in line; which is the chief good quality in letter, and makes the face thereof something to pass,**

8/10

Besides the three principal properties which we have mentioned, the following (like Satellites to good letter) are not undeserving the purchaser's examination, who ought to take notice, 1. Whether the letter stands even, and in line; which is the chief good quality in letter, and makes the face thereof sometimes to pass, though otherwise ill-shaped. 2. Whether it stands parallel; and whether it drives out or gets in, either at the head, or the foot, and is, as Printers call it, bottle-arsed; which is a fault that cannot be mended but by rubbing the whole fount over again. 3. Whether the thin lower-case letters, especially the dots over the i and j, are come in casting. 4. Whether the break is ploughed away and smoothened. 5. Whether it be well scraped, so as not to want rubbing down by the compositor. 6. Whether each letter has a due proportion, as to thickness; and whether they are not so thin as to hinder each other from appearing with a full face; or so thick as to occasion a gap between letter and letter. 7. Whether it be well bearded: which **founders in France are obliged to do, to their own disadvantage, on account of their shallow letters. 8. Whether it have a deep and open,**

6/8

Besides the three principal properties which we have mentioned, the following (like Satellites to good letter) are not undeserving the purchaser's examination, who ought to take notice. 1. Whether the letter stands even, and in line; which is the chief good quality in letter, and makes the face thereof sometimes to pass, though otherwise ill-shaped. 2. Whether it stands parallel; and whether it drives out or gets in, either at the head, or the foot, and is, as Printers call it, bottle-arsed; which is a fault that cannot be mended but by rubbing the whole fount over again. 3. Whether the thin lower-case letters, especially the dots over the i and j, are come in casting. 4. Whether the break is ploughed away and smoothened. 5. Whether it be well scraped, so as not to want rubbing down by the compositor. 6. Whether each letter has a due proportion, as to thickness; and whether they are not so thin as to hinder each other from appearing with a full face; or so thick as to occasion a gap between letter and letter. 7. Whether it be well bearded: which founders in France are obliged to do, to their own disadvantage, on account of their shallow letter. 8. Whether it have a deep and open, single or double nick, different from other founts to the same body, and in the same printing-house.

We cannot too strongly urge the advantage to be derived from letter having a deep nick, and also that the nick should differ from other founts of that body **in the same house. This may appear a trifling consideration; but in a large fount the difference in weight will be considerable, and consequently a saving to the**

8/12

Besides the three principal properties which we have mentioned, the following (like Satellites to good letter) are not undeserving the purchaser's examination, who ought to take notice, 1. Whether the letter stands even, and in line; which is the chief good quality in letter, and makes the face thereof sometimes to pass, though otherwise ill-shaped. 2. Whether it stands parallel; and whether it drives out or gets in, either at the head, or the foot, and is, as Printers call it, bottle-arsed; which is a fault that cannot be mended but by rubbing the whole fount over again. 3. Whether the thin lower-case letters, especially the dots over the i and j, are come in casting. 4. Whether the break is ploughed away and smoothened. 5. Whether it be well scraped, so as not to want rubbing down by the compositor. 6. Whether each letter has a due propor**tion, as to thickness; and whether they are not so thin as to hinder each other from appearing with a full face; or so thick as to occasion**

6/10

Besides the three principal properties which we have mentioned, the following (like Satellites to good letter) are not undeserving the purchaser's examination, who ought to take notice. 1. Whether the letter stands even, and in line; which is the chief good quality in letter, and makes the face thereof sometimes to pass, though otherwise ill-shaped. 2. Whether it stands parallel; and whether it drives out or gets in, either at the head, or the foot, and is, as Printers call it, bottle-arsed; which is a fault that cannot be mended but by rubbing the whole fount over again. 3. Whether the thin lower-case letters, especially the dots over the i and j, are come in casting. 4. Whether the break is ploughed away and smoothened. 5. Whether it be well scraped, so as not to want rubbing down by the compositor. 6. Whether each letter has a due proportion, as to thickness; and whether they are not so thin as to hinder each other from appearing with a full face; or so thick as to occasion a gap between letter and letter. 7. Whether it be well bearded: which founders in France are obliged to do, to their own disadvantage, on account of their shallow letter. 8. Whether it have a deep and open, **single or double nick, different from other founts to the same body, and in the same printing-house.**

ABCDEFGHIJKLMNOPQRSTUVWXYZ
ABCDEFGHIJKLMNOPQRSTUVWXYZ
&.,''-:;!?''""1234567890$
&.,''-:;!?''""1234567890$
abcdefghijklmnopqrstuvwxyz
abcdefghijklmnopqrstuvwxyz

ABCDEFGHIJKLMNOPQRSTUVWXYZ
ABCDEFGHIJKLMNOPQRSTUVWXYZ
&.,''-:;!?''""1234567890$
&.,''-:;!?''""1234567890$
abcdefghijklmnopqrstuvwxyz
abcdefghijklmnopqrstuvwxyz

NEWS GOTHIC CONDENSED: INTERTYPE

PICAS	6	7	8	9	10	11	12	13	14	15	16	17	18	19	20	21	22	23	24	25	26	27	28	29	30
8 POINT	22	25	28	32	35	38	42	45	49	52	56	59	63	66	70	73	77	80	84	87	91	94	98	101	105
6 POINT	23	27	30	34	39	42	46	50	54	58	62	65	69	73	77	81	85	88	92	96	100	104	108	112	116

10/11

From a letter to John Baskerville by Benjamin Franklin dated London, 1760:

Let me give you a pleasant Instance of the Prejudice some have entertained against your Work. Soon after I returned, discoursing with a Gentleman concerning the Artists of Birmingham, he said you would [be] a Means of blinding all the Readers in the Nation; for the Strokes of your Letters, being too thin and narrow, hurt the Eye, and he could never read a Line of them without Pain. "I thought," said I, "you were going to complain of the Gloss of the Paper, some object to." "No, no," says he, "I have heard that mentioned, but it is not that; it Is in the Form and Cut of the Letters themselves; they have not that Height and Thickness of the Stroke which make the common Printing so

9/10

From a letter to John Baskerville by Benjamin Franklin dated London, 1760:

Let me give you a pleasant Instance of the Prejudice some have entertained against your Work. Soon after I returned, discoursing with a Gentleman concerning the Artists of Birmingham, he said you would [be] a Means of blinding all the Readers in the Nation; for the Strokes of your Letters, being too thin and narrow, hurt the Eye, and he could never read a Line of them without Pain. "I thought," said I, "you were going to complain of the Gloss of the Paper, some object to." "No, no," says he, "I have heard that mentioned, but it is not that; it Is in the Form and Cut of the Letters themselves; they have not that Height and Thickness of the Stroke, which make the common Printing so much the more comfortable to the Eye." You see this Gentleman was a Connoisseur. In vain I endeavored to support your character

10/12

From a letter to John Baskerville by Benjamin Franklin dated London, 1760:

Let me give you a pleasant Instance of the Prejudice some have entertained against your Work. Soon after I returned, discoursing with a Gentleman concerning the Artists of Birmingham, he said you would [be] a Means of blinding all the Readers in the Nation; for the Strokes of your Letters, being too thin and narrow, hurt the Eye, and he could never read a Line of them without Pain. "I thought," said I, "you were going to complain of the Gloss of the Paper, some object to." "No, no," selves; they have not that Height and Thickness of the Stroke which make the common Printing so

9/11

From a letter to John Baskerville by Benjamin Franklin dated London, 1760:

Let me give you a pleasant Instance of the Prejudice some have entertained against your Work. Soon after I returned, discoursing with a Gentleman concerning the Artists of Birmingham, he said you would [be] a Means of blinding all the Readers in the Nation; for the Strokes of your Letters, being too thin and narrow, hurt the Eye, and he could never read a Line of them without Pain. "I thought," said I, "you were going to complain of the Gloss of the Paper, some object to." "No, no," says he, "I have heard that mentioned, but it is not that; it Is in the Form and Cut of the Letters themselves; they have able to the Eye." You see this Gentleman was a Connoisseur. In vain I endeavored to support your character

10/14

From a letter to John Baskerville by Benjamin Franklin dated London, 1760:

Let me give you a pleasant Instance of the Prejudice some have entertained against your Work. Soon after I returned, discoursing with a Gentleman concerning the Artists of Birmingham, he said you would [be] a Means of blinding all the Readers in the Nation; for the Strokes of your Letters, being too thin and narrow, hurt the Eye, and he could never read a Line of them without Pain. "I selves; they have not that Height and Thickness of the Stroke which make the common Printing so

9/13

From a letter to John Baskerville by Benjamin Franklin dated London, 1760:

Let me give you a pleasant Instance of the Prejudice some have entertained against your Work. Soon after I returned, discoursing with a Gentleman concerning the Artists of Birmingham, he said you would [be] a Means of blinding all the Readers in the Nation; for the Strokes of your Letters, being too thin and narrow, hurt the Eye, and he could never read a Line of them without Pain. "I thought," said I, "you were going to complain of the Gloss of the Paper, some object to." "No, no," says he, able to the Eye." You see this Gentleman was a Connoisseur. In vain I endeavored to support your character

ABCDEFGHIJKLMNOPQRSTUVWXYZ
ABCDEFGHIJKLMNOPQRSTUVWXYZ
&.,"-:;!?""'1234567890$
&.,"-:;!?""'1234567890$
abcdefghijklmnopqrstuvwxyz
abcdefghijklmnopqrstuvwxyz

ABCDEFGHIJKLMNOPQRSTUVWXYZ
ABCDEFGHIJKLMNOPQRSTUVWXYZ
&.,"-:;!?""'1234567890$
&.,"-:;!?""'1234567890$
abcdefghijklmnopqrstuvwxyz
abcdefghijklmnopqrstuvwxyz

OPTIMA: LINOTYPE   *This face must be set 1 pt leaded.

PICAS	6	7	8	9	10	11	12	13	14	15	16	17	18	19	20	21	22	23	24	25	26	27	28	29	30
10 POINT	16	18	20	23	25	27	30	32	35	37	40	42	45	47	50	52	55	57	60	62	65	67	70	72	75
9 POINT	17	20	23	26	28	31	34	36	39	42	45	47	50	53	56	59	62	64	67	70	73	75	78	81	84

From a letter to John Baskerville by Benjamin Franklin dated London, 1760:

8/9

Let me give you a pleasant Instance of the Prejudice some have entertained against your Work. Soon after I returned, discoursing with a Gentleman concerning the Artists of Birmingham, he said you would [be] a Means of blinding all the Readers in the Nation; for the Strokes of your Letters, being too thin and narrow, hurt the Eye, and he could never read a Line of them without Pain. "I thought," said I, "you were going to complain of the Gloss of the Paper, some object to." "No, no," says he, "I have heard that mentioned, but it is not that; it Is in the Form and Cut of the Letters themselves; they have not that Height and Thickness of the Stroke, which make the common Printing so much the more comfortable to the Eye." You see this Gentleman was a Connoisseur. In vain I endeavoured to support your character against the Charge; he knew what he felt, and could see the Reason of it, and *several other Gentlemen among his Friends had made the same Observation, &c.*

From a letter to John Baskerville by Benjamin Franklin dated London, 1760:

6/7

Let me give you a pleasant Instance of the Prejudice some have entertained against your Work. Soon after I returned, discoursing with a Gentleman concerning the Artists of Birmingham, he said you would [be] a Means of blinding all the Readers in the Nation; for the Strokes of your Letters, being too thin and narrow, hurt the Eye, and he could never read a Line of them without Pain. "I thought," said I, "you were going to complain of the Gloss of the Paper, some object to." "No, no," says he, "I have heard that mentioned, but it is not that; it Is in the Form and Cut of the Letters themselves; they have not that Height and Thickness of the Stroke, which make the common Printing so much the more comfortable to the Eye." You see this Gentleman was a *Connoisseur.* In vain I endeavoured to support your character against the Charge; he knew what he felt, and could see the Reason of it, and several other Gentlemen among his Friends had made the same Observation, &c.

This Method has, by the Fancy of Printers, of late Years been laid aside, from an Idea, that suppressing the Capitals shows the Character to greater Advantage; those Letters prominent above the line disturbing its even regular Appearance. The Effect of this Change is so considerable, that a learned Man of France, who used to read our Books, tho' not perfectly acquainted with our Language, in Conversation with me on the *Subject of our Authors, attributed the greater Obscurity he found in our modern Books, compared with those of the period above mentioned, to*

From a letter to John Baskerville by Benjamin Franklin dated London, 1760:

8/10

Let me give you a pleasant Instance of the Prejudice some have entertained against your Work. Soon after I returned, discoursing with a Gentleman concerning the Artists of Birmingham, he said you would [be] a Means of blinding all the Readers in the Nation; for the Strokes of your Letters, being too thin and narrow, hurt the Eye, and he could never read a Line of them without Pain. "I thought," said I, "you were going to complain of the Gloss of the Paper, some object to." "No, no," says he, "I have heard that mentioned, but it is not that; it Is in the Form and Cut of the Letters themselves; they have not that Height and Thickness of the Stroke, which make the common Printing so much the more comfortable to the Eye." You see this Gentleman was a Connoisseur. In vain I *several other Gentlemen among his Friends had made the same Observation, &c.*

From a letter to John Baskerville by Benjamin Franklin dated London, 1760:

6/8

Let me give you a pleasant Instance of the Prejudice some have entertained against your Work. Soon after I returned, discoursing with a Gentleman concerning the Artists of Birmingham, he said you would [be] a Means of blinding all the Readers in the Nation; for the Strokes of your Letters, being too thin and narrow, hurt the Eye, and he could never read a Line of them without Pain. "I thought," said I, "you were going to complain of the Gloss of the Paper, some object to." "No, no," says he, "I have heard that mentioned, but it is not that; it Is in the Form and Cut of the Letters themselves; they have not that Height and Thickness of the Stroke, which make the common Printing so much the more comfortable to the Eye." You see this Gentleman was a *Connoisseur.* In vain I endeavoured to support your character against the Charge; he knew what he felt, and could see the Reason of it, and several other Gentlemen among his Friends had made the same Observation, &c.

This Method has, by the Fancy of Printers, of late Years been laid aside, from an Idea, that suppressing the Capitals shows the Character to greater Advantage; those Letters prominent above the line disturbing *Subject of our Authors, attributed the greater Obscurity he found in our modern Books, compared with those of the period above mentioned, to*

From a letter to John Baskerville by Benjamin Franklin dated London, 1760:

8/12

Let me give you a pleasant Instance of the Prejudice some have entertained against your Work. Soon after I returned, discoursing with a Gentleman concerning the Artists of Birmingham, he said you would [be] a Means of blinding all the Readers in the Nation; for the Strokes of your Letters, being too thin and narrow, hurt the Eye, and he could never read a Line of them without Pain. "I thought," said I, "you were going to complain of the Gloss of the Paper, some object to." "No, no," says he, "I have heard that mentioned, but it is not that; it Is in the Form and Cut of the Letters themselves; they *several other Gentlemen among his Friends had made the same Observation, &c.*

From a letter to John Baskerville by Benjamin Franklin dated London, 1760:

6/10

Let me give you a pleasant Instance of the Prejudice some have entertained against your Work. Soon after I returned, discoursing with a Gentleman concerning the Artists of Birmingham, he said you would [be] a Means of blinding all the Readers in the Nation; for the Strokes of your Letters, being too thin and narrow, hurt the Eye, and he could never read a Line of them without Pain. "I thought," said I, "you were going to complain of the Gloss of the Paper, some object to." "No, no," says he, "I have heard that mentioned, but it is not that; it Is in the Form and Cut of the Letters themselves; they have not that Height and Thickness of the Stroke, which make the common Printing so much the more comfortable to the Eye." You see this Gentleman was a *Connoisseur.* In vain I endeavoured to support your character against the Charge; he knew what he felt, and could see the Reason of it, and several other *Subject of our Authors, attributed the greater Obscurity he found in our*

ABCDEFGHIJKLMNOPQRSTUVWXYZ
ABCDEFGHIJKLMNOPQRSTUVWXYZ
&.,"-:;!?""''1234567890$
&.,"-:;!?""''1234567890$
abcdefghijklmnopqrstuvwxyz
abcdefghijklmnopqrstuvwxyz

ABCDEFGHIJKLMNOPQRSTUVWXYZ
ABCDEFGHIJKLMNOPQRSTUVWXYZ
&.,"-:;!?""''1234567890$
&.,"-:;!?""''1234567890$
abcdefghijklmnopqrstuvwxyz
abcdefghijklmnopqrstuvwxyz

OPTIMA: LINOTYPE   *This face must be set 1 pt leaded.

PICAS	6	7	8	9	10	11	12	13	14	15	16	17	18	19	20	21	22	23	24	25	26	27	28	29	30
8 POINT	19	22	25	28	31	34	37	40	43	46	50	53	56	59	62	65	68	71	74	77	81	84	87	91	93
6 POINT	23	27	30	34	37	40	44	47	51	54	58	62	66	69	73	76	80	84	88	91	95	98	102	106	110

12/13 From a letter by Benjamin Franklin to B. Vaughan Esq. dated April 21, 1785:

If the Irish can manufacture cottons, stuffs and silks, and linens, and cutlery, and toys, and books etc. etc. etc., so as to sell them cheaper in England than the *manufacturers* of England sell them, is not this good for the *people* of England who are not *manufactur-ers*? and will not even the manufacturers themselves share the benefit? Since if cottons are cheaper, all the other manufac-*turers who wear cottons will save in that article, and so of the rest. If books can be had*

10/11 From a letter by Benjamin Franklin to B. Vaughan Esq. dated April 21, 1785:

If the Irish can manufacture cottons, stuffs and silks, and linens, and cutlery, and toys, and books etc. etc. etc., so as to sell them cheaper in England than the *manufacturers* of England sell them, is not this good for the *people* of England who are not *manufacturers*? and will not even the manufacturers themselves share the benefit? Since if cottons are cheaper, all the other manufacturers who wear cottons will save in that article, and so of the rest. If books can be had much cheaper from Ireland, (which I believe for I bought Blackstone there for 24/- when it was sold in England for four guineas) *is not this an advantage not to English booksellers indeed, but to English readers and to learning. And*

12/14 From a letter by Benjamin Franklin to B. Vaughan Esq. dated April 21, 1785:

If the Irish can manufacture cottons, stuffs and silks, and linens, and cutlery, and toys, and books etc. etc. etc., so as to sell them cheaper in England than the *manufacturers* of England sell them, is not this good for the *people* of England who are not *manufactur-ers*? and will not even the manufacturers themselves share the benefit? Since if cot-*turers who wear cottons will save in that article, and so of the rest. If books can be had*

10/12 From a letter by Benjamin Franklin to B. Vaughan Esq. dated April 21, 1785:

If the Irish can manufacture cottons, stuffs and silks, and linens, and cutlery, and toys, and books etc. etc. etc., so as to sell them cheaper in England than the *manufacturers* of England sell them, is not this good for the *people* of England who are not *manufacturers*? and will not even the manufacturers themselves share the benefit? Since if cottons are cheaper, all the other manufacturers who wear cottons will save in that article, and so of the rest. If books can be had much cheaper from Ireland, *is not this an advantage not to English booksellers indeed, but to English readers and to learning. And*

12/16 From a letter by Benjamin Franklin to B. Vaughan Esq. dated April 21, 1785:

If the Irish can manufacture cottons, stuffs and silks, and linens, and cutlery, and toys, and books etc. etc. etc., so as to sell them cheaper in England than the *manufacturers* of England sell them, is not this good for the *people* of England who are not *manufactur-turers who wear cottons will save in that article, and so of the rest. If books can be had*

10/14 From a letter by Benjamin Franklin to B. Vaughan Esq. dated April 21, 1785:

If the Irish can manufacture cottons, stuffs and silks, and linens, and cutlery, and toys, and books etc. etc. etc., so as to sell them cheaper in England than the *manufacturers* of England sell them, is not this good for the *people* of England who are not *manufacturers*? and will not even the manufacturers themselves share the benefit? Since if cottons are cheaper, all the other manufacturers who wear *is not this an advantage not to English booksellers indeed, but to English readers and to learning. And*

ABCDEFGHIJKLMNOPQRSTUVWXYZ
ABCDEFGHIJKLMNOPQRSTUVWXYZ
&.,"-:;!?""''1234567890$
&.,"-:;!?""''1234567890$
abcdefghijklmnopqrstuvwxyz
abcdefghijklmnopqrstuvwxyz

ABCDEFGHIJKLMNOPQRSTUVWXYZ
ABCDEFGHIJKLMNOPQRSTUVWXYZ
&.,"-:;!?""''1234567890$
&.,"-:;!?""''1234567890$
abcdefghijklmnopqrstuvwxyz
abcdefghijklmnopqrstuvwxyz

PALATINO: LINOTYPE *This face must be set 1 pt leaded.

PICAS	6	7	8	9	10	11	12	13	14	15	16	17	18	19	20	21	22	23	24	25	26	27	28	29	30
12 POINT	12	15	17	19	22	24	26	28	31	33	35	37	40	42	44	46	48	50	53	55	57	59	62	64	66
10 POINT	16	19	22	24	26	28	31	33	36	38	41	43	46	48	51	53	56	58	61	63	66	68	71	74	77

From a letter by Benjamin Franklin to B. Vaughan Esq. dated
April 21, 1785:

8/9

If the Irish can manufacture cottons, stuffs and silks, and
linens, and cutlery, and toys, and books etc. etc. etc., so as
to sell them cheaper in England than the *manufacturers* of
England sell them, is not this good for the *people* of England
who are not *manu*facturers? and will not even the manufacturers themselves share the benefit? Since if cottons are
cheaper, all the other manufacturers who wear cottons will
save in that article, and so of the rest. If books can be had
much cheaper from Ireland, (which I believe for I bought
Blackstone there for 24/- when it was sold in England at
four guineas) is not this an advantage not to English booksellers indeed, but to English readers and to learning. And
of all the complainants perhaps these booksellers are least
worthy of consideration. The catalogue you last sent me
amazes me by the high prices (said to be the lowest) affixed
*to each article. And one can scarce see a new book, without
observing the excessive artifices may use of to puff up a*

From a letter by Benjamin Franklin to B. Vaughan Esq. dated April
21, 1785:

6/7

If the Irish can manufacture cottons, stuffs and silks, and linens, and
cutlery, and toys, and books etc. etc. etc., so as to sell them cheaper in
England than the *manufacturers* of England sell them, is not this good
for the *people* of England who are not *manufacturers*? and will not
even the manufacturers themselves share the benefit? Since if cottons
are cheaper, all the other manufacturers who wear cottons will save in
that article, and so of the rest. If books can be had much cheaper from
Ireland, (which I believe for I bought Blackstone there for 24/- when
it was sold in England at four guineas) is not this an advantage not to
English booksellers indeed, but to English readers and to learning. And
of all the complainants perhaps these booksellers are least worthy of
consideration. The catalogue you last sent me amazes me by the high
prices (said to be the lowest) affixed to each article. And one can scarce
see a new book, without observing the excessive artifices may use of
to puff up a paper of verses into a pamphlet, a pamphlet into an
octavo, and an octavo into a quarto, with scab boardings, white lines,
sparse titles of chapters, and exorbitant margins, to such a degree, that
the selling of paper seems now the object and printing on it only the
pretence. I inclose the copy of a page in a late comedy. Between every
two lines there is a white space equal to another line. You have a law, I
think, against butchers blowing of veal to make it look fatter; why not
one against booksellers blowing of books to make them look bigger. All*

From a letter by Benjamin Franklin to B. Vaughan Esq. dated
April 21, 1785:

8/10

If the Irish can manufacture cottons, stuffs and silks, and
linens, and cutlery, and toys, and books etc. etc. etc., so as
to sell them cheaper in England than the *manufacturers* of
England sell them, is not this good for the *people* of England
who are not *manu*facturers? and will not even the manufacturers themselves share the benefit? Since if cottons are
cheaper, all the other manufacturers who wear cottons will
save in that article, and so of the rest. If books can be had
much cheaper from Ireland, (which I believe for I bought
Blackstone there for 24/- when it was sold in England at
four guineas) is not this an advantage not to English booksellers indeed, but to English readers and to learning. And
of all the complainants perhaps these booksellers are least
*to each article. And one can scarce see a new book, without
observing the excessive artifices may use of to puff up a*

From a letter by Benjamin Franklin to B. Vaughan Esq. dated April
21, 1785:

6/8

If the Irish can manufacture cottons, stuffs and silks, and linens, and
cutlery, and toys, and books etc. etc. etc., so as to sell them cheaper in
England than the *manufacturers* of England sell them, is not this good
for the *people* of England who are not *manufacturers*? and will not
even the manufacturers themselves share the benefit? Since if cottons
are cheaper, all the other manufacturers who wear cottons will save in
that article, and so of the rest. If books can be had much cheaper from
Ireland, (which I believe for I bought Blackstone there for 24/- when
it was sold in England at four guineas) is not this an advantage not to
English booksellers indeed, but to English readers and to learning. And
of all the complainants perhaps these booksellers are least worthy of
consideration. The catalogue you last sent me amazes me by the high
prices (said to be the lowest) affixed to each article. And one can scarce
see a new book, without observing the excessive artifices may use of
to puff up a paper of verses into a pamphlet, a pamphlet into an
octavo, and an octavo into a quarto, with scab boardings, white lines,
sparse titles of chapters, and exorbitant margins, to such a degree, that
*think, against butchers blowing of veal to make it look fatter; why not
one against booksellers blowing of books to make them look bigger. All*

From a letter by Benjamin Franklin to B. Vaughan Esq. dated
April 21, 1785:

8/12

If the Irish can manufacture cottons, stuffs and silks, and
linens, and cutlery, and toys, and books etc. etc. etc., so as
to sell them cheaper in England than the *manufacturers* of
England sell them, is not this good for the *people* of England
who are not *manu*facturers? and will not even the manufacturers themselves share the benefit? Since if cottons are
cheaper, all the other manufacturers who wear cottons will
save in that article, and so of the rest. If books can be had
much cheaper from Ireland, (which I believe for I bought
Blackstone there for 24/- when it was sold in England at
*to each article. And one can scarce see a new book, without
observing the excessive artifices may use of to puff up a*

From a letter by Benjamin Franklin to B. Vaughan Esq. dated April
21, 1785:

6/10

If the Irish can manufacture cottons, stuffs and silks, and linens, and
cutlery, and toys, and books etc. etc. etc., so as to sell them cheaper in
England than the *manufacturers* of England sell them, is not this good
for the *people* of England who are not *manufacturers*? and will not
even the manufacturers themselves share the benefit? Since if cottons
are cheaper, all the other manufacturers who wear cottons will save in
that article, and so of the rest. If books can be had much cheaper from
Ireland, (which I believe for I bought Blackstone there for 24/- when
it was sold in England at four guineas) is not this an advantage not to
English booksellers indeed, but to English readers and to learning. And
of all the complainants perhaps these booksellers are least worthy of
consideration. The catalogue you last sent me amazes me by the high
prices (said to be the lowest) affixed to each article. And one can scarce
*think, against butchers blowing of veal to make it look fatter; why not
one against booksellers blowing of books to make them look bigger. All*

ABCDEFGHIJKLMNOPQRSTUVWXYZ
ABCDEFGHIJKLMNOPQRSTUVWXYZ
&.,"-:;!?""''1234567890$
&.,"-:;!?""''1234567890$
abcdefghijklmnopqrstuvwxyz
abcdefghijklmnopqrstuvwxyz

ABCDEFGHIJKLMNOPQRSTUVWXYZ
ABCDEFGHIJKLMNOPQRSTUVWXYZ
&.,"-:;!?""''1234567890$
&.,"-:;!?""''1234567890$
abcdefghijklmnopqrstuvwxyz
abcdefghijklmnopqrstuvwxyz

PALATINO: LINOTYPE *This face must be set 1 pt leaded.

PICAS	6	7	8	9	10	11	12	13	14	15	16	17	18	19	20	21	22	23	24	25	26	27	28	29	30
8 POINT	18	21	24	27	30	33	36	39	42	45	48	51	54	57	60	63	66	68	72	75	78	81	84	87	90
6 POINT	22	26	30	33	36	39	43	46	50	53	57	60	64	67	71	74	78	81	85	88	92	95	99	103	107

12/13 The Greek alphabet had a close relation to the Phœnician, or (as perhaps it is more properly called) the Semitic alphabet. In the first place, the forms were in many cases very much alike. The word "alphabet," which gives a clue to the connection, is derived from alpha and beta, the names of the first and second letters of the Greek alphabet. "The names of the Semitic letters," Sir Edward Maunde Thompson tells us, "are Semitic words, each describing the letter from its resemblance to some particular *object, as, aleph, an ox, beth, a house. When the Greeks took over their Semitic letters,*

11/12 The Greek alphabet had a close relation to the Phœnician, or (as perhaps it is more properly called) the Semitic alphabet. In the first place, the forms were in many cases very much alike. The word "alphabet," which gives a clue to the connection, is derived from alpha and beta, the names of the first and second letters of the Greek alphabet. "The names of the Semitic letters," Sir Edward Maunde Thompson tells us, "are Semitic words, each describing the letter from its resemblance to some particular object, as, aleph, an ox, beth, a house. When the Greeks took over their Semitic *letters, they also took over their Semitic names." Both the names of the letters and their order in*

12/14 The Greek alphabet had a close relation to the Phœnician, or (as perhaps it is more properly called) the Semitic alphabet. In the first place, the forms were in many cases very much alike. The word "alphabet," which gives a clue to the connection, is derived from alpha and beta, the names of the first and second letters of the Greek alphabet. "The names of the Semitic letters," Sir Edward Maunde Thompson tells us, "are Semitic words, each describing the *object, as, aleph, an ox, beth, a house. When the Greeks took over their Semitic letters,*

11/13 The Greek alphabet had a close relation to the Phœnician, or (as perhaps it is more properly called) the Semitic alphabet. In the first place, the forms were in many cases very much alike. The word "alphabet," which gives a clue to the connection, is derived from alpha and beta, the names of the first and second letters of the Greek alphabet. "The names of the Semitic letters," Sir Edward Maunde Thompson tells us, "are Semitic words, each describing the letter from its resemblance to some particular object, as, aleph, an ox, beth, a *letters, they also took over their Semitic names." Both the names of the letters and their order in*

12/16 The Greek alphabet had a close relation to the Phœnician, or (as perhaps it is more properly called) the Semitic alphabet. In the first place, the forms were in many cases very much alike. The word "alphabet," which gives a clue to the connection, is derived from alpha and beta, the names of the first and second letters of the Greek alphabet. "The names of the Semitic *object, as, aleph, an ox, beth, a house. When the Greeks took over their Semitic letters,*

11/15 The Greek alphabet had a close relation to the Phœnician, or (as perhaps it is more properly called) the Semitic alphabet. In the first place, the forms were in many cases very much alike. The word "alphabet," which gives a clue to the connection, is derived from alpha and beta, the names of the first and second letters of the Greek alphabet. "The names of the Semitic letters," Sir Edward Maunde Thompson tells us, "are Semitic words, *letters, they also took over their Semitic names." Both the names of the letters and their order in*

ABCDEFGHIJKLMNOPQRSTUVWXYZ
ABCDEFGHIJKLMNOPQRSTUVWXYZ
.,"-:;!?""&1234567890$
.,"-:;!?""&1234567890$
abcdefghijklmnopqrstuvwxyz
abcdefghijklmnopqrstuvwxyz

ABCDEFGHIJKLMNOPQRSTUVWXYZ
ABCDEFGHIJKLMNOPQRSTUVWXYZ
.,"-:;!?""&1234567890$
.,"-:;!?""&1234567890$
abcdefghijklmnopqrstuvwxyz
abcdefghijklmnopqrstuvwxyz

SCOTCH 2: LINOTYPE   *When long descenders are used (as shown) type must be set on a slug one point greater than specified size.

PICAS	6	7	8	9	10	11	12	13	14	15	16	17	18	19	20	21	22	23	24	25	26	27	28	29	30
12 POINT	14	16	18	20	23	25	27	29	32	34	36	38	41	43	45	47	50	52	54	56	59	61	63	65	68
11 POINT	14	17	19	22	24	26	29	31	34	36	38	41	43	46	48	50	53	55	58	60	62	65	67	69	72

10/11

The Greek alphabet had a close relation to the Phœnician, or (as perhaps it is more properly called) the Semitic alphabet. In the first place, the forms were in many cases very much alike. The word "alphabet," which gives a clue to the connection, is derived from alpha and beta, the names of the first and second letters of the Greek alphabet. "The names of the Semitic letters," Sir Edward Maunde Thompson tells us, "are Semitic words, each describing the letter from its resemblance to some particular object, as, aleph, an ox, beth, a house. When the Greeks took over their Semitic letters, they also took over their Semitic names." Both the names of the letters and their order in the *two alphabets are the same. This alphabet was employed by the Phœnicians, by the Jews, and by the*

8/8

The Greek alphabet had a close relation to the Phœnician, or (as perhaps it is more properly called) the Semitic alphabet. In the first place, the forms were in many cases very much alike. The word "alphabet," which gives a clue to the connection, is derived from alpha and beta, the names of the first and second letters of the Greek alphabet. "The names of the Semitic letters," Sir Edward Maunde Thompson tells us, "are Semitic words, each describing the letter from its resemblance to some particular object, as, aleph, an ox, beth, a house. When the Greeks took over their Semitic letters, they also took over their Semitic names." Both the names of the letters and their order in the two alphabets are the same. This alphabet was employed by the Phœnicians, by the Jews, and by the Moabites, and from early inscriptions, the primitive Phœnician alphabet, consisting of twenty-two letters, can be made up.

The Greeks learned the art of writing in the ninth century B.C.— perhaps earlier. The primitive Greek alphabet was generally known as the Cadmean alphabet, and it had many varieties. The alphabets first in use were written from right to left; then the boustrophedon method of writing came into vogue, in which the lines ran *alternately from right to left and from left to right, like the furrows of a plough; and finally writing all ran from left to right as it does*

10/12

The Greek alphabet had a close relation to the Phœnician, or (as perhaps it is more properly called) the Semitic alphabet. In the first place, the forms were in many cases very much alike. The word "alphabet," which gives a clue to the connection, is derived from alpha and beta, the names of the first and second letters of the Greek alphabet. "The names of the Semitic letters," Sir Edward Maunde Thompson tells us, "are Semitic words, each describing the letter from its resemblance to some particular object, as, aleph, an ox, beth, a house. When the Greeks took over their Semitic letters, they also took over their Semitic names." *two alphabets are the same. This alphabet was employed by the Phœnicians, by the Jews, and by the*

8/10

The Greek alphabet had a close relation to the Phœnician, or (as perhaps it is more properly called) the Semitic alphabet. In the first place, the forms were in many cases very much alike. The word "alphabet," which gives a clue to the connection, is derived from alpha and beta, the names of the first and second letters of the Greek alphabet. "The names of the Semitic letters," Sir Edward Maunde Thompson tells us, "are Semitic words, each describing the letter from its resemblance to some particular object, as, aleph, an ox, beth, a house. When the Greeks took over their Semitic letters, they also took over their Semitic names." Both the names of the letters and their order in the two alphabets are the same. This alphabet was employed by the Phœnicians, by the Jews, and by the Moabites, and from early inscriptions, the primitive Phœnician alphabet, consisting of twenty-two letters, can be made up.

The Greeks learned the art of writing in the ninth century B.C.— *alternately from right to left and from left to right, like the furrows of a plough; and finally writing all ran from left to right as it does*

10/14

The Greek alphabet had a close relation to the Phœnician, or (as perhaps it is more properly called) the Semitic alphabet. In the first place, the forms were in many cases very much alike. The word "alphabet," which gives a clue to the connection, is derived from alpha and beta, the names of the first and second letters of the Greek alphabet. "The names of the Semitic letters," Sir Edward Maunde Thompson tells us, "are Semitic words, each describing the letter from its resemblance to some particular object, as, aleph, an ox, *two alphabets are the same. This alphabet was employed by the Phœnicians, by the Jews, and by the*

8/12

The Greek alphabet had a close relation to the Phœnician, or (as perhaps it is more properly called) the Semitic alphabet. In the first place, the forms were in many cases very much alike. The word "alphabet," which gives a clue to the connection, is derived from alpha and beta, the names of the first and second letters of the Greek alphabet. "The names of the Semitic letters," Sir Edward Maunde Thompson tells us, "are Semitic words, each describing the letter from its resemblance to some particular object, as, aleph, an ox, beth, a house. When the Greeks took over their Semitic letters, they also took over their Semitic names." Both the names of the letters and their order in the two alphabets are the same. This alphabet was employed by the Phœnicians, by the Jews, and by *alternately from right to left and from left to right, like the furrows of a plough; and finally writing all ran from left to right as it does*

ABCDEFGHIJKLMNOPQRSTUVWXYZ
ABCDEFGHIJKLMNOPQRSTUVWXYZ
.,"-:;!?""&1234567890$
.,"-:;!?""&1234567890$
abcdefghijklmnopqrstuvwxyz
abcdefghijklmnopqrstuvwxyz

ABCDEFGHIJKLMNOPQRSTUVWXYZ
ABCDEFGHIJKLMNOPQRSTUVWXYZ
.,"-:;!?""&1234567890$
.,"-:;!?""&1234567890$
abcdefghijklmnopqrstuvwxyz
abcdefghijklmnopqrstuvwxyz

SCOTCH 2: LINOTYPE   *When long descenders are used (as shown) type must be set on a slug one point greater than specified size.

PICAS	6	7	8	9	10	11	12	13	14	15	16	17	18	19	20	21	22	23	24	25	26	27	28	29	30
10 POINT	15	18	20	23	26	28	31	33	36	39	41	44	46	49	52	54	57	59	62	65	67	69	72	75	78
8 POINT	19	23	26	29	33	36	39	42	46	49	52	56	60	63	66	69	72	76	79	82	85	89	92	95	99

GIAMBATTISTA BODONI, "TO THE READER," 1818. This essay is the fruit of many years' assiduous labour—a real labour of love—in the service of the art of printing. Printing is the final outcome of man's most beautiful, ingenious and useful invention: that I mean, of writing: and its most valuable form where it is required to turn out many copies of the same text. This *applies still more where it is important to ensure uniformity, and most of all*

14/14

GIAMBATTISTA BODONI, "TO THE READER," 1818. This essay is the fruit of many years' assiduous labour—a real labour of love—in the service of the art of printing. Printing is the final outcome of man's most beautiful, ingenious and useful invention: that I mean, of writing: and its most valuable form where it is required to turn out *applies still more where it is important to ensure uniformity, and most of all*

14/16

GIAMBATTISTA BODONI, "TO THE READER," 1818. This essay is the fruit of many years' assiduous labour—a real labour of love—in the service of the art of printing. Printing is the final outcome of man's most beautiful, ingenious and useful invention: that I mean, of writing: and its most valuable *applies still more where it is important to ensure uniformity, and most of all*

14/18

ABCDEFGHIJKLMNOPQRSTUVWXYZ
ABCDEFGHIJKLMNOPQRSTUVWXYZ
.,"-:;!?""&1234567890$
.,"-:;!?""&1234567890$
abcdefghijklmnopqrstuvwxyz
abcdefghijklmnopqrstuvwxyz

GIAMBATTISTA BODONI, "TO THE READER," 1818. This essay is the fruit of many years' assiduous labour—a real labour of love—in the service of the art of printing. Printing is the final outcome of man's most beautiful, ingenious and useful invention: that I mean, of writing: and its most valuable form where it is required to turn out many copies of the same text. This applies still more where it is important to ensure uniformity, and most of all where the work in question is one which deserves transmission in clearer *and more readable form for the enjoyment of of posterity. When we consider the range of*

12/12

GIAMBATTISTA BODONI, "TO THE READER," 1818. This essay is the fruit of many years' assiduous labour—a real labour of love—in the service of the art of printing. Printing is the final outcome of man's most beautiful, ingenious and useful invention: that I mean, of writing: and its most valuable form where it is required to turn out many copies of the same text. This applies still more where it is important to ensure uniformity, *and more readable form for the enjoyment of of posterity. When we consider the range of*

12/14

GIAMBATTISTA BODONI, "TO THE READER," 1818. This essay is the fruit of many years' assiduous labour—a real labour of love—in the service of the art of printing. Printing is the final outcome of man's most beautiful, ingenious and useful invention: that I mean, of writing: and its most valuable form where it is required to turn out many copies of the same text. This applies still more *and more readable form for the enjoyment of of posterity. When we consider the range of*

12/16

ABCDEFGHIJKLMNOPQRSTUVWXYZ
ABCDEFGHIJKLMNOPQRSTUVWXYZ
.,"-:;!?""&1234567890$
.,"-:;!?""&1234567890$
abcdefghijklmnopqrstuvwxyz
abcdefghijklmnopqrstuvwxyz

TRADE GOTHIC LIGHT: LINOTYPE

PICAS	6	7	8	9	10	11	12	13	14	15	16	17	18	19	20	21	22	23	24	25	26	27	28	29	30
14 POINT	12	14	16	18	20	21	23	25	27	29	31	33	35	37	39	41	43	45	47	49	51	53	55	57	59
12 POINT	14	16	18	21	23	25	28	30	32	35	37	39	41	44	46	48	51	53	55	58	60	62	64	67	69

10/10

GIAMBATTISTA BODONI, "TO THE READER," 1818. This essay is the fruit of many years' assiduous labour—a real labour of love—in the service of the art of printing. Printing is the final outcome of man's most beautiful, ingenious and useful invention: that I mean, of writing: and its most valuable form where it is required to turn out many copies of the same text. This applies still more where it is important to ensure uniformity, and most of all where the work in question is one which deserves transmission in clearer and more readable form for the enjoyment of posterity. When we consider the range of use-fulness of printing, together with the long series of devices which have brought us from the first dis-*covery of letters to our present power of printing on thousands of sheets of fine laid paper words no*

8/8

GIAMBATTISTA BODONI, "TO THE READER," 1818. This essay is the fruit of many years' assiduous labour—a real labour of love—in the service of the art of printing. Printing is the final outcome of man's most beautiful, ingenious and useful invention: that I mean, of writing: and its most valuable form where it is required to turn out many copies of the same text. This applies still more where it is important to ensure uniformity, and most of all where the work in question is one which deserves transmission in clearer and more readable form for the enjoyment of posterity. When we consider the range of usefulness of printing, together with the long series of devices which have brought us from the first discovery of letters to our present power of printing on thousands of sheets of fine laid paper words no longer evanescent but fixed and preserved with sharper outlines than the articulation of lips can give them, the thought of such sur-passing achievement compels admiration at the force of the human intellect. But it would be superfluous to enlarge on *the merits of an invention which has already been the sub-ject of many elaborate treatises and of much eloquent*

10/12

GIAMBATTISTA BODONI, "TO THE READER," 1818. This essay is the fruit of many years' assiduous labour—a real labour of love—in the service of the art of printing. Printing is the final outcome of man's most beautiful, ingenious and useful invention: that I mean, of writing: and its most valuable form where it is required to turn out many copies of the same text. This applies still more where it is important to ensure uniformity, and most of all where the work in question is one which deserves transmission in clearer and more readable form for the enjoyment of posterity. When we consider the range of use-*covery of letters to our present power of printing on thousands of sheets of fine laid paper words no*

8/10

GIAMBATTISTA BODONI, "TO THE READER," 1818. This essay is the fruit of many years' assiduous labour—a real labour of love—in the service of the art of printing. Printing is the final outcome of man's most beautiful, ingenious and useful invention: that I mean, of writing: and its most valu-able form where it is required to turn out many copies of the same text. This applies still more where it is important to ensure uniformity, and most of all where the work in ques-tion is one which deserves transmission in clearer and more readable form for the enjoyment of posterity. When we con-sider the range of usefulness of printing, together with the long series of devices which have brought us from the first discovery of letters to our present power of printing on thou-sands of sheets of fine laid paper words no longer evanes-cent but fixed and preserved with sharper outlines than the *the merits of an invention which has already been the sub-ject of many elaborate treatises and of much eloquent*

10/14

GIAMBATTISTA BODONI, "TO THE READER," 1818. This essay is the fruit of many years' assiduous labour—a real labour of love—in the service of the art of printing. Printing is the final outcome of man's most beautiful, ingenious and useful invention: that I mean, of writing: and its most valuable form where it is required to turn out many copies of the same text. This applies still more where it·is important to ensure uniformity, and most of all where the work in question is one which deserves transmission in *covery of letters to our present power of printing on thousands of sheets of fine laid paper words no*

8/12

GIAMBATTISTA BODONI, "TO THE READER," 1818. This essay is the fruit of many years' assiduous labour—a real labour of love—in the service of the art of printing. Printing is the final outcome of man's most beautiful, ingenious and useful invention: that I mean, of writing: and its most valu-able form where it is required to turn out many copies of the same text. This applies still more where it is important to ensure uniformity, and most of all where the work in ques-tion is one which deserves transmission in clearer and more readable form for the enjoyment of posterity. When we con-sider the range of usefulness of printing, together with the long series of devices which have brought us from the first *the merits of an invention which has already been the sub-ject of many elaborate treatises and of much eloquent*

ABCDEFGHIJKLMNOPQRSTUVWXYZ
ABCDEFGHIJKLMNOPQRSTUVWXYZ
.,"-:;!?""&1234567890$
.,"-:;!?""&1234567890$
abcdefghijklmnopqrstuvwxyz
abcdefghijklmnopqrstuvwxyz

ABCDEFGHIJKLMNOPQRSTUVWXYZ
ABCDEFGHIJKLMNOPQRSTUVWXYZ
.,"-:;!?""&1234567890$
.,"-:;!?""&1234567890$
abcdefghijklmnopqrstuvwxyz
abcdefghijklmnopqrstuvwxyz

TRADE GOTHIC LIGHT: LINOTYPE

PICAS	6	7	8	9	10	11	12	13	14	15	16	17	18	19	20	21	22	23	24	25	26	27	28	29	30
10 POINT	15	18	20	23	26	28	31	33	36	38	41	43	46	48	51	54	56	59	61	64	66	69	71	74	77
8 POINT	18	21	24	27	30	33	36	39	42	45	48	51	54	57	60	63	66	69	72	75	78	81	84	87	90

12/12

Besides the three principal properties which we have mentioned, the following (like Satellites to good letter) are not undeserving the purchaser's examination, who ought to take notice, 1. Whether the letter stands even, and in line; which is the chief good quality in letter, and makes the face thereof sometimes to pass, though otherwise ill-shaped. 2. Whether it stands parallel; and whether it drives out **or gets in, either at the head, or the foot, and is, as Printers call it, bot-**

10/10

Besides the three principal properties which we have mentioned, the following (like Satellites to good letter) are not undeserving the purchaser's examination, who ought to take notice, 1. Whether the letter stands even, and in line; which is the chief good quality in letter, and makes the face thereof sometimes to pass, though otherwise ill-shaped. 2. Whether it stands parallel; and whether it drives out or gets in, either at the head, or the foot, and is, as Printers call it, bottle-arsed; which is a fault that cannot be mended but by rubbing the whole fount over again. 3. Whether the thin **lower-case letters, especially the dots over the i and j, are come in casting. 4.**

12/14

Besides the three principal properties which we have mentioned, the following (like Satellites to good letter) are not undeserving the purchaser's examination, who ought to take notice, 1. Whether the letter stands even, and in line; which is the chief good quality in letter, and makes the face thereof sometimes to pass, though otherwise **or gets in, either at the head, or the foot, and is, as Printers call it, bot-**

10/12

Besides the three principal properties which we have mentioned, the following (like Satellites to good letter) are not undeserving the purchaser's examination, who ought to take notice, 1. Whether the letter stands even, and in line; which is the chief good quality in letter, and makes the face thereof sometimes to pass, though otherwise ill-shaped. 2. Whether it stands parallel; and whether it drives out or gets in, either at the head, or the foot, and is, as Printers call it, **lower-case letters, especially the dots over the i and j, are come in casting. 4.**

12/16

Besides the three principal properties which we have mentioned, the following (like Satellites to good letter) are not undeserving the purchaser's examination, who ought to take notice, 1. Whether the letter stands even, and in line; which is the chief good quality in letter, **or gets in, either at the head, or the foot, and is, as Printers call it, bot-**

10/14

Besides the three principal properties which we have mentioned, the following (like Satellites to good letter) are not undeserving the purchaser's examination, who ought to take notice, 1. Whether the letter stands even, and in line; which is the chief good quality in letter, and makes the face thereof sometimes to pass, though otherwise ill-shaped. 2. Whether it stands parallel; and whether **lower-case letters, especially the dots over the i and j, are come in casting. 4.**

ABCDEFGHIJKLMNOPQRSTU
ABCDEFGHIJKLMNOPQRSTU
&.,"-;:!?""1234567890$
&.,"-;:!?""1234567890$
abcdefghijklmnopqrstuvwxyz
abcdefghijklmnopqrstuvwxyz

ABCDEFGHIJKLMNOPQRSTUVWXY
ABCDEFGHIJKLMNOPQRSTUVWXY
&.,"-:;!?""1234567890$
&.,"-:;!?""1234567890$
abcdefghijklmnopqrstuvwxyz
abcdefghijklmnopqrstuvwxyz

TRADE GOTHIC EXTENDED: LINOTYPE

PICAS	6	7	8	9	10	11	12	13	14	15	16	17	18	19	20	21	22	23	24	25	26	27	28	29	30
12 POINT	4	7	11	14	18	20	21	22	25	26	28	30	32	33	35	37	39	41	42	44	46	48	49	51	53
10 POINT	13	15	17	19	21	23	25	27	29	31	33	35	37	39	41	43	45	47	49	51	53	55	57	60	62

8/8

Besides the three principal properties which we have mentioned, the following (like Satellites to good letter) are not undeserving the purchaser's examination, who ought to take notice, 1. Whether the letter stands even, and in line; which is the chief good quality in letter, and makes the face thereof sometimes to pass, though otherwise ill-shaped. 2. Whether it stands parallel; and whether it drives out or gets in, either at the head, or the foot, and is, as Printers call it, bottle-arsed; which is a fault that cannot be mended but by rubbing the whole fount over again. 3. Whether the thin lower-case letters, especially the dots over the i and j, are come in casting. 4. Whether the break is ploughed away and smoothened. 5. Whether it be well scraped, so as not to want rubbing down by the compositor. 6. Whether each letter has a due proportion, as to thick**ness; and whether they are not so thin as to hinder each other from appearing with a full**

6/6

Besides the three principal properties which we have mentioned, the following (like Satellites to good letter) are not undeserving the purchaser's examination, who ought to take notice, 1. Whether the letter stands even, and in line; which is the chief good quality in letter, and makes the face thereof sometimes to pass, though otherwise ill-shaped. 2. Whether it stands parallel; and whether it drives out or gets in, either at the head, or the foot, and is, as Printers call it, bottle-arsed; which is a fault that cannot be mended but by rubbing the whole fount over again. 3. Whether the thin lower-case letters, especially the dots over the i and j, are come in casting. 4. Whether the break is ploughed away and smoothened. 5. Whether it be well scraped, so as not to want rubbing down by the compositor. 6. Whether each letter has a due proportion, as to thickness; and whether they are not so thin as to hinder each other from appearing with a full face; or so thick as to occasion a gap between letter and letter. 7. Whether it be well bearded: which founders in France are obliged to do, to their own disadvantage, on account of their shallow letter. 8. Whetner it have a deep and open, single or double nick, different from other founts of the same body, and in tne same printing-house.
We cannot too strongly urge the advantage to be derived from letter having a deep nick, and also that the **nick should differ from other founts of that body in the same house. This may appear a trifling consideration;**

8/10

Besides the three principal properties which we have mentioned, the following (like Satellites to good letter) are not undeserving the purchaser's examination, who ought to take notice, 1. Whether the letter stands even, and in line; which is the chief good quality in letter, and makes the face thereof sometimes to pass, though otherwise ill-shaped. 2. Whether it stands parallel; and whether it drives out or gets in, either at the head, or the foot, and is, as Printers call it, bottle-arsed; which is a fault that cannot be mended but by rubbing the whole fount over again. 3. Whether the thin lower-case letters, especially the dots over the i and j, are come in casting. 4. Whether the **ness; and whether they are not so thin as to hinder each other from appearing with a full**

6/8

Besides the three principal properties which we have mentioned, the following (like Satellites to good letter) are not undeserving the purchaser's examination, who ought to take notice, 1. Whether the letter stands even, and in line; which is the chief good quality in letter, and makes the face thereof sometimes to pass, though otherwise ill-shaped. 2. Whether it stands parallel; and whether it drives out or gets in, either at the head, or the foot, and is, as Printers call it, bottle-arsed; which is a fault that cannot be mended but by rubbing the whole fount over again. 3. Whether the thin lower-case letters, especially the dots over the i and j, are come in casting. 4. Whether the break is ploughed away and smoothened. 5. Whether it be well scraped, so as not to want rubbing down by the compositor. 6. Whether each letter has a due proportion, as to thickness; and whether they are not so thin as to hinder each other from appearing with a full face; or so thick as to occasion a gap between letter and letter. 7. Whether it be **nick should differ from other founts of that body in the same house. This may appear a trifling consideration;**

8/12

Besides the three principal properties which we have mentioned, the following (like Satellites to good letter) are not undeserving the purchaser's examination, who ought to take notice, 1. Whether the letter stands even, and in line; which is the chief good quality in letter, and makes the face thereof sometimes to pass, though otherwise ill-shaped. 2. Whether it stands parallel; and whether it drives out or gets in, either at the head, or the foot, and is, as Printers call it, bottle-arsed; which is a fault that cannot be mended but by rubbing the **ness; and whether they are not so thin as to hinder each other from appearing with a full**

6/10

Besides the three principal properties which we have mentioned, the following (like Satellites to good letter) are not undeserving the purchaser's examination, who ought to take notice, 1. Whether the letter stands even, and in line; which is the chief good quality in letter, and makes the face thereof sometimes to pass, though otherwise ill-shaped. 2. Whether it stands parallel; and whether it drives out or gets in, either at the head, or the foot, and is, as Printers call it, bottle-arsed; which is a fault that cannot be mended but by rubbing the whole fount over again. 3. Whether the thin lower-case letters, especially the dots over the i and j, are come in casting. 4. Whether the break is ploughed away and smoothened. 5. Whether it be well scraped, so as not to want rubbing down by the compositor. 6. Whether **nick should differ from other founts of that body in the same house. This may appear a trifling consideration;**

ABCDEFGHIJKLMNOPQRSTUVWXYZ
ABCDEFGHIJKLMNOPQRSTUVWXYZ
&.,"-:;!?1234567890$
&.,"-:;!?1234567890$
abcdefghijklmnopqrstuvwxyz
abcdefghijklmnopqrstuvwxyz

ABCDEFGHIJKLMNOPQRSTUVWXYZ
ABCDEFGHIJKLMNOPQRSTUVWXYZ
&.,"-:;!?""1234567890$
&.,"-:;!?""1234567890$
abcdefghijklmnopqrstuvwxyz
abcdefghijklmnopqrstuvwxyz

TRADE GOTHIC EXTENDED: LINOTYPE

PICAS	6	7	8	9	10	11	12	13	14	15	16	17	18	19	20	21	22	23	24	25	26	27	28	29	30
8 POINT	15	18	20	22	24	26	28	31	33	35	38	40	42	45	47	49	52	55	57	59	61	64	66	69	71
6 POINT	19	21	23	26	28	31	33	36	39	42	44	47	50	53	55	58	61	64	66	69	72	75	77	80	83

ABCDEFGHIJKLMNOPQ
RSTUVWXYZ&abcdefg
hijklmnopqrstuvwxyz
1234567890$.,'-:;!?

48 POINT AURORA BOLD CONDENSED, AMSTERDAM CONTINENTAL

ABCDEFGHIJKLMNOPQRSTUV
WXYZ&abcdefghijklmnopqrst
uvwxyz1234567890$.,'-:;!?

36 POINT AURORA BOLD CONDENSED, AMSTERDAM CONTINENTAL

ABCDEFGHIJKLMNOPQRSTUVWXYZ&ab
cdefghijklmnopqrstuvwxyz12345678
90$.,'-:;!?

28 POINT AURORA BOLD CONDENSED, AMSTERDAM CONTINENTAL

ABCDEFGHIJKLMNOPQRSTUVWXYZ&abcdef
ghijklmnopqrstuvwxyz1234567890$.,'-:;!?

24 POINT AURORA BOLD CONDENSED, AMSTERDAM CONTINENTAL

ABCDEFGHIJKLMNOPQRSTUVWXYZ&abcdefghijklmnopqrstuvw
xyz1234567890$.,'-:;!?

16 POINT AURORA BOLD CONDENSED, AMSTERDAM CONTINENTAL

*Aurora Bold Condensed is a re-cut of Anzeigen-Grotesk in sizes from 60 point down to 14 point. Sizes above or below these are called Anzeigen-Grotesk.

ABCDEFGHIJKLMNOPQRSTUVWXYZ&abcdefghijklmnopqrstuvwxyz12345
67890$.,'-:;!?

14 POINT AURORA BOLD CONDENSED, AMSTERDAM CONTINENTAL

ABCDEFGHIJKLMNOPQRSTUV
WXYZ&abcdefghijklmnopqrst
uvwxyz1234567890$.,'-:;!?

60 POINT AURORA CONDENSED, AMSTERDAM CONTINENTAL

ABCDEFGHIJKLMNOPQRSTUVWXYZ&a
bcdefghijklmnopqrstuvwxyz1234567
890$.,'-:;!?

48 POINT AURORA CONDENSED, AMSTERDAM CONTINENTAL

ABCDEFGHIJKLMNOPQRSTUVWXYZ&abcdefghijkl
mnopqrstuvwxyz1234567890$.,'-:;!?

36 POINT AURORA CONDENSED, AMSTERDAM CONTINENTAL

ABCDEFGHIJKLMNOPQRSTUVWXYZ&abcdefghijklmnopqrstu
vwxyz1234567890$.,'-:;!?

28 POINT AURORA CONDENSED, AMSTERDAM CONTINENTAL

*Aurora Condensed is a re-cut of Inserat Grotesk in sizes from 60 point down to 14 point. Sizes above or below these are called Inserat Grotesk.

ABCDEFGHIJKLMN OPQRSTUVWXYZ &abcdefghijklmnopqrstuv wxyz1234567890$.,-':;!?

48 POINT CHELTENHAM OLDSTYLE, LUDLOW

ABCDEFGHIJKLMN OPQRSTUVWXYZ &abcdefghijklmnopqrstu vwzyz1234567890$.,-':;!?

48 POINT CHELTENHAM OLDSTYLE ITALIC, LUDLOW

ABCDEFGHIJKLMNOPQRS TUVWXYZ&abcdefghijklmnopqrs tuvwxyz1234567890$.,-':;!?

36 POINT CHELTENHAM OLDSTYLE, LUDLOW

ABCDEFGHIJKLMNOPQRS
TUVWXYZ&abcdefghijklmnop
qrstuvwxyz1234567890$.,-';:!?

36 POINT CHELTENHAM OLDSTYLE ITALIC, LUDLOW

ABCDEFGHIJKLMNOPQRSTUVWXYZ&ab
cdefghijklmnopqrstuvwxyz1234567890$.,-';,!?

24 POINT CHELTENHAM OLDSTYLE, LUDLOW

ABCDEFGHIJKLMNOPQRSTUVWXYZ&
abcdefghijklmnopqrstuvwxyz1234567890$.,-';:!?

24 POINT CHELTENHAM OLDSTYLE ITALIC, LUDLOW

ABCDEFGHIJKLMNOPQRSTUVWX
YZ&abcdefghijklmnopqrstuvwxyz1234
567890$.,-';:!?

36 POINT CHELTENHAM OLDSTYLE CONDENSED, LUDLOW

ABCDEFGHIJKLMNOPQRSTUVWXYZ&abcdefghijklm
nopqrstuvwxyz1234567890$.,-';:!?

24 POINT CHELTENHAM OLDSTYLE CONDENSED, LUDLOW

ABCDEFGHIJKLMNOPQRSTUVWX
YZ&abcdefghijklmnopqrstuvwxyz123
4567890$.,-';:;!?

36 POINT CHELTENHAM BOLD CONDENSED, LUDLOW

*ABCDEFGHIJKLMNOPQRSTUV
WXYZ&abcdefghijklmnopqrstuvw
xyz1234567890$.,-';:;!?*

36 POINT CHELTENHAM BOLD CONDENSED ITALIC, LUDLOW

ABCDEFGHIJKLMNOPQRSTUVWXYZ&abcdefghijkl
mnopqrstuvwxyz1234567890$.,-';:;!?

24 POINT CHELTENHAM BOLD CONDENSED, LUDLOW

*ABCDEFGHIJKLMNOPQRSTUVWXYZ&abcdefghi
jklmnopqrstuvwxyz1234567890$.,-';:;!?*

24 POINT CHELTENHAM BOLD CONDENSED ITALIC, LUDLOW

ABCDEFGHIJKLMNOPQRSTUVWXYZ&abc
defghijklmnopqrstuvwxyz1234567890$
.,-';:;!?

36 POINT CHELTENHAM BOLD EXTRA CONDENSED, LUDLOW

ABCDEFGHIJKLMNOPQRSTUVWXYZ&abcdefghijklmnopqrstuv
wxyz1234567890$.,-';:;!?

24 POINT CHELTENHAM BOLD EXTRA CONDENSED, LUDLOW

258

ABCDEFGHIJKLMN OPQRSTUVWXYZ&a bcdefghijklmnopqrst uvwxyz1234567890 $.,-';:,!?

36 POINT CHELTENHAM BOLD EXTENDED, LUDLOW

ABCDEFGHIJKLMNOPQRSTUV WXYZ&abcdefghijklmnopqrstu vwxyz1234567890$.,-';:,!?

24 POINT CHELTENHAM BOLD EXTENDED, LUDLOW

ABCDEFGHIJKLMNOPQRS TUVWXYZ&abcdefghijklmn opqrstuvwxyz1234567890$.,-':;!?

36 POINT CHELTENHAM WIDE, LUDLOW

ABCDEFGHIJKLMNOPQRSTUVWXYZ&a bcdefghijklmnopqrstuvwxyz1234567890$.,-':;!?

24 POINT CHELTENHAM WIDE, LUDLOW

ABCDEFGHIJKLMNOPQR
STUVWXYZ&abcdefghijkl
mnopqrstuvwxyz123456789
0$.,-'::!?

36 POINT CHELTENHAM BOLD OUTLINE, LUDLOW

ABCDEFGHIJKLMNOPQRSTUVWXYZ&
abcdefghijklmnopqrstuvwxyz1234567890$
.,-'::!?

24 POINT CHELTENHAM BOLD OUTLINE, LUDLOW

ABCDEFGHIJKL
MNOPQRSTU
VWXYZ

48 POINT CHELTENHAM CURSIVE, LUDLOW

ABCDEFGHIJKLMNO
PQRSTUVWXYZ

36 POINT CHELTENHAM CURSIVE, LUDLOW

ABCDEFGHIJKLMNOPQRSTU
VWXYZ

24 POINT CHELTENHAM CURSIVE, LUDLOW

ABCDEFGHIJK
LMNOPQRSTUV
WXYZ&abcdefgh
ijklmnopqrstuv
wxyzfl123456789
0$.,"'-.:;!?"''

60 POINT CHISEL, STEPHENSON BLAKE

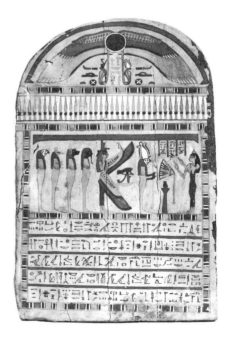

Stela of the lady Ta-Byet-Mut.
Egyptian twenty-second dynasty.

ABCDEFGHIJKLMNO PQRSTUVWXYZ&abc defghijklmnopqrstuvw xyzfl1234567890$.,'"-:; !?""''

48 POINT CHISEL, STEPHENSON BLAKE

ABCDEFGHIJKLMNOPQRSTUVWXYZ &abcdefghijklmnopqrstuvwxyz12345 67890$.,'"-:;!?""''

30 POINT CHISEL, STEPHENSON BLAKE

ABCDEF
GHIJKL
MNOPQR
STUVWX
YZ&abcde
fghijklmn
opqrstuv
wxyz123
4567890
$.,' " '' - ;;!?'' '' ''

48 POINT CHISEL EXPANDED, STEPHENSON BLAKE

ABCDEFGHIJ
KLMNOPQRS
TUVWXYZ&a
bcdefghijklm
nopqrstuvwx
yz1234567890
$.,'%-:;!?''''

36 POINT CHISEL EXPANDED, STEPHENSON BLAKE

ABCDEFGHIJKLM
NOPQRSTUVWXYZ
&abcdefghijklmnopq
rstuvwxyz123456789
O$.,'%-:;!?''''

18 POINT CHISEL EXPANDED, STEPHENSON BLAKE

CITY

ABCDEFGHIJKLMNOPQRSTUVWXYZ&
abcdefghijklmnopqrstuvwxyz1234567
890$.,'-:;!?"

30 POINT CITY LIGHT, AMSTERDAM CONTINENTAL

ABCDEFGHIJKLMNOPQRSTUVWXYZ&abcdefghijklmn
opqrstuvwxyz1234567890$.,'-:;!?"

24 POINT CITY LIGHT, AMSTERDAM CONTINENTAL

ABCDEFGHIJKLMNOPQRSTUVWXYZ&abcdefghijklmnopqrstuvwxyz1234567890$
.,'-:;!?"
12 POINT CITY LIGHT, AMSTERDAM CONTINENTAL

ABCDEFGHIJKLMNOP
QRSTUVWXYZ&abcde
fghijklmnopqrstuvwxy
z1234567890$.,'-:;!?"

48 POINT CITY MEDIUM, AMSTERDAM CONTINENTAL

ABCDEFGHIJKLMNOPQRSTUVWXYZ&abcdefghijk
lmnopqrstuvwxyz1234567890$.,'-:;!?"

24 POINT CITY MEDIUM, AMSTERDAM CONTINENTAL

ABCDEFGHIJKLMNOPQRSTUVWXYZ&abcdefghijklmnopqrstuvwxyz12345678
90$.,'-:;!?"
12 POINT CITY MEDIUM, AMSTERDAM CONTINENTAL

ABCDEFGHIJKLMN
OPQRSTUVWXYZ&a
bcdefghijklmnopqrst
uvwxyz1234567890
$.,'-:,!?"

48 POINT CITY BOLD, AMSTERDAM CONTINENTAL

ABCDEFGHIJKLMNOPQRSTUVWXYZ&abcdefg
hijklmnopqrstuvwxyz1234567890$.,'-:,!?"

24 POINT CITY BOLD, AMSTERDAM CONTINENTAL

ABCDEFGHIJKLMNOPQRSTUVWXYZ&abcdefghijklmnopqrstuvwxyz1234
567890$.,'-:,!?"

12 POINT CITY BOLD, AMSTERDAM CONTINENTAL

ABCDEFGHIJKL
MNOPQRSTUV
WXYZ&abcdefgh
ijklmnopqrstuvw
xyzfifffl12345678
90$.,'"-:;!?""

48 POINT CLARENDON (HAAS), AMSTERDAM CONTINENTAL

ABCDEFGHIJKLMN
OPQRSTUVWXYZ&a
bcdefghijklmnopqrstu
vwxyzfifl1234567890
$.,'"-:;!?""

36 POINT CLARENDON (HAAS), AMSTERDAM CONTINENTAL

ABCDEFGHIJKLMNOPQRS
TUVWXYZ&abcdefghijklm
nopqrstuvwxyzfifl12345678
90$.,'"-:;!?""

28 POINT CLARENDON (HAAS), AMSTERDAM CONTINENTAL

ABCDEFGHIJKLMNOPQRSTUV WXYZ&abcdefghijklmnopqrstuv wxyzfifl1234567890$.,'‘-:;!?"“

24 POINT CLARENDON (HAAS), AMSTERDAM CONTINENTAL

ABCDEFGHIJKLMNOPQRSTUVWXYZ&abcdefghijklm
nopqrstuvwxyzfifl1234567890$.,'‘-:;!?"“

16 POINT CLARENDON (HAAS), AMSTERDAM CONTINENTAL

ABCDEFGHIJKLMNOPQRSTUVWXYZ&abcdefghijklmnopqrstuvwxyzfifl
1234567890$.,'‘-:;!?"“

12 POINT CLARENDON (HAAS), AMSTERDAM CONTINENTAL

ABCDEFGHIJK LMNOPQRSTU VWXYZ&abcdef ghijklmnopqrst uvwxyzfifl12345 67890$.,'‘-:;!?"“

48 POINT CLARENDON BOLD (HAAS), AMSTERDAM CONTINENTAL

ABCDEFGHIJKLMN
OPQRSTUVWXYZ&a
bcdefghijklmnopqrst
uvwxyzfifl123456789
0$.,"-:;!?""

36 POINT CLARENDON BOLD (HAAS), AMSTERDAM CONTINENTAL

ABCDEFGHIJKLMNOPQ
RSTUVWXYZ&abcdefghijk
lmnopqrstuvwxyzfifl12345
67890$.,"-:;!?""

28 POINT CLARENDON BOLD (HAAS), AMSTERDAM CONTINENTAL

ABCDEFGHIJKLMNOPQRSTU
VWXYZ&abcdefghijklmnopqrst
uvwxyzfifl1234567890$.,"-:;!?""

24 POINT CLARENDON BOLD (HAAS), AMSTERDAM CONTINENTAL

ABCDEFGHIJKLMNOPQRSTUVWXYZ&abcdefghijkl
mnopqrstuvwxyzfifl1234567890$.,"-:;!?""

16 POINT CLARENDON BOLD (HAAS), AMSTERDAM CONTINENTAL

ABCDEFGHIJKLMNOPQRSTUVWXYZ&abcdefghijklmnopqrstuvwxyzfifl
1234567890$.,"-:;!?""

12 POINT CLARENDON BOLD (HAAS), AMSTERDAM CONTINENTAL

ABCDEFGHIJKLMNO
PQRSTUVWXYZ&abc
defghijklmnopqrstuvwxy
zfifffllffiffl1234567890$
.,"‘-:;!?"“

48 COLUMBIA, AMSTERDAM CONTINENTAL

ABCDEFGHIJKLMNOPQRS
TUVWXYZ&abcdefghijklmnop
qrstuvwxyzfifffllffiffl1234567890$
.,"‘-:;!?"“

36 COLUMBIA, AMSTERDAM CONTINENTAL

ABCDEFGHIJKLMNOPQRSTUVWXYZ&ab
cdefghijklmnopqrstuvwxyzfifffllffiffl1234567890$
.,"‘-:;!?"“

24 COLUMBIA, AMSTERDAM CONTINENTAL

ABCDEFGHIJKLMNO PQRSTUVWXYZ&ab cdefghijklmnopqrstuvw xyzfiflfffffiffl1234567890 $.,"'-.:;!?"''

48 POINT COLUMBIA BOLD, AMSTERDAM CONTINENTAL

ABCDEFGHIJKLMNOPQRS TUVWXYZ&abcdefghijklmno pqrstuvwxyzfifffflffiffl12345678 90$.,"'-.:;!?"''

36 POINT COLUMBIA BOLD, AMSTERDAM CONTINENTAL

ABCDEFGHIJKLMNOPQRSTUVWXYZ& abcdefghijklmnopqrstuvwxyzfifffflffiffl1234567 890$.,"'-.:;!?"''

24 POINT (large) COLUMBIA BOLD, AMSTERDAM CONTINENTAL

ABCDEFGHIJKLMNOPQRSTUV
WXYZ&abcdefghijklmnopqrstu
vwxyz1234567890$.,-'··!?

48 POINT CONDENSED GOTHIC OUTLINE 6-CO-LUDLOW

ABCDEFGHIJKLMNOPQRSTUVWXYZ&abcd
efghijklmnopqrstuvwxyz1234567890$
.,'··!?

36 POINT CONDENSED GOTHIC OUTLINE 6-CO-LUDLOW

ABCDEFGHIJKLMNOPQRSTUVWXYZ&abcdefghijklmnopqrs
tuvwxyz1234567890$.,-'··!?

24 POINT CONDENSED GOTHIC OUTLINE 6-CO-LUDLOW

CONSORT

ABCDEFGHIJKLMNOP
QRSTUVWXYZ&abcdefg
hijklmnopqrstuvwxyzfiffl
ffiffl1234567890$.,"-:;!?""''

36 POINT CONSORT, STEPHENSON BLAKE

ABCDEFGHIJKLMNOPQRSTUVWX
YZ&abcdefghijklmnopqrstuvwxyzfiffl
ffiffl1234567890$.,"-:;!?""''

24 POINT CONSORT, STEPHENSON BLAKE

ABCDEFGHIJKLMNOPQRSTUVWXYZ&abcdefghijklmnopqrstuv
wxyzfifffffiffiffl1234567890$.,'-:;!?''"'
12 POINT CONSORT, STEPHENSON BLAKE

ABCDEFGHIJKLMNOPQRS
TUVWXYZ&abcdefghijklmn
opqrstuvwxyzfifffflffiffl12345
67890$.,''-:;!?''"'
30 POINT CONSORT LIGHT, STEPHENSON BLAKE

ABCDEFGHIJKLMNOPQRSTUVWX
YZ&abcdefghijklmnopqrstuvwxyzfiff
flffiffi1234567890$.,''-:;!?''"'
24 POINT CONSORT LIGHT, STEPHENSON BLAKE

ABCDEFGHIJKLMNOPQRSTUVWXYZ&abcdefghijklmnopqrst
uvwxyzfifffflffiffi1234567890$.,'-:;!?''"'
12 POINT CONSORT LIGHT, STEPHENSON BLAKE

ABCDEFGHIJKLMNOPQRSTUVW
XYZ&abcdefghijklmnopqrstuvwxy
zfifffflffiffl1234567890$.,''-:;!?''"'
36 POINT CONSORT CONDENSED, STEPHENSON BLAKE

ABCDEFGHIJKLMNOPQRSTUVWXYZ&abcdefghijk
lmnopqrstuvwxyzfifffflffiffl1234567890$.,''-:;!?''"'
24 POINT CONSORT CONDENSED, STEPHENSON BLAKE

ABCDEFGHIJKLMNOPQRSTUVWXYZ&abcdefghijklmnopqrstuvwxyzfifffflffiffl1234567
890$.,'-:;!?''"'
12 POINT CONSORT CONDENSED, STEPHENSON BLAKE

ABCDEFGHIJKLMN
OPQRSTUVWXYZ&
abcdefghijklmnopqrstu
vwxyzfifffflft1234567890
$.,''-:;!?''''

54 POINT DIDOT, AMSTERDAM CONTINENTAL

ABCDEFGHIJKLMNOPQRST
UVWXYZ&abcdefghijklmnop
qrstuvwxyzfifffflft1234567890$
.,''-:;!?''''

42 POINT DIDOT, AMSTERDAM CONTINENTAL

ABCDEFGHIJKLMNOPQRSTUVW
XYZ&abcdefghijklmnopqrstuvwxyzfiff
flft1234567890$.,''-:;!?''''

30 POINT (large) DIDOT, AMSTERDAM CONTINENTAL

ABCDEFGHIJKLMNOPQRSTUV WXYZ&abcdefghijklmnopqrstuvwxyz 1234567890$.,'-:;!?''''

30 POINT (large) DIDOT ITALIC, AMSTERDAM CONTINENTAL

ABCDEFGHIJKLMNOPQRSTUVWXYZ&abcdefghi jklmnopqrstuvwxyzfifffflft1234567890$.,'-:;!?''''

24 POINT DIDOT, AMSTERDAM CONTINENTAL

ABCDEFGHIJKLMNOPQRSTUVWXYZ&abcd efghijklmnopqrstuvwxyz1234567890$.,'-:;!?''''

24 POINT DIDOT ITALIC, AMSTERDAM CONTINENTAL

ABCDEFGHIJKLMNOPQRSTUVWXYZ&abcdefghijklmnopqrstuv wxyzfifffflft1234567890$.,'-:;!?''''

18 POINT (large) DIDOT, AMSTERDAM CONTINENTAL

ABCDEFGHIJKLMNGPQRSTUVWXYZ&abcdefghijklmnopq rstuvwxyz1234567890$.,'-:;!?''''

18 POINT (large) DIDOT ITALIC, AMSTERDAM CONTINENTAL

ABCDEF
GHIJKL
MNOPQR
STUVWX
YZ&abcde
fghijklmn
opqrstuvw
xyzzfifffflffi
ffl1234 56
7890$.,"-:;
!?""''

36 POINT EGYPTIAN EXPANDED, STEPHENSON BLAKE

ABCDEFGHIJ
KLMNOPQRS
TUVWXYZ&a
bcdefghijklmno
pqrstuvwxyzfiff
flffiffl12345678
90$.,"-:;!?""''

24 POINT EGYPTIAN EXPANDED, STEPHENSON BLAKE

ABCDEFGHIJKLMNOPQ
RSTUVWXYZ&abcdefgh
ijklmnopqrstuvwxyzfifffl
ffiffl1234567890$.,"-:;!?""''

18 POINT EGYPTIAN EXPANDED, STEPHENSON BLAKE

ABCDEFGHIJKLMNOPQRSTUVW
XYZ&abcdefghijklmnopqrstuvwx
yzfiflfffffffl1234567890$.,'-:;!?

18 POINT EGYPTIAN EXPANDED, STEPHENSON BLAKE

ABCDEFGHIJKLMNOPQRSTUVWXYZ&ab
cdefghijklmnopqrstuvwxyzfiflfffffffl123
4567890$.,'-:;!?

12 POINT EGYPTIAN EXPANDED, STEPHENSON BLAKE

36 POINT EGYPTIAN EXPANDED OPEN, STEPHENSON BLAKE

ABCDEFGH
IJKLMNOP
QRSTUVW
XYZ&abcde
fghijklmnop
qrstuvwxyz
fiffflffifflffl1234
567890$.,'-:;!?

30 POINT EGYPTIAN EXPANDED OPEN, STEPHENSON BLAKE

ABCDEFGHIJ
KLMNOPQRST
UVWXYZ&abc
defghijklmnopq
rstuvwxyzfiffflffifli
ffl1234567890$.
,'-:;!?

24 POINT EGYPTIAN EXPANDED OPEN, STEPHENSON BLAKE

ABCDEFGHIJ KLMNOPQRS TUVWXYZ&12 34567890$.,"- .;!?""``

36 POINT ENGRAVERS BOLD, ATF

ABCDEFGHIJKLMNO PQRSTUVWXYZ&123 4567890$.,"-:;!?""``

24 POINT ENGRAVERS BOLD, ATF

ABCDEFGHIJKLMNOPQRSTUVWXYZ&123456789 0$.,'-:;!?""``

12 POINT NO. 2 ENGRAVERS BOLD, ATF

EUROSTILE

ABCDEF GHIJKL

72 POINT EUROSTILE BOLD EXTENDED 415-22, AMSTERDAM CONTINENTAL

MNOPQ
RSTUV
WXYZ&
abcdefg
hijklmno
pqrstuv
wxyz123
456789
0$.,'"–-;,!?"

72 POINT EUROSTILE BOLD EXTENDED 415-22, AMSTERDAM CONTINENTAL

ABCDEFGHI
JKLMNOPQ
RSTUVWXY
Z&abcdefghij
klmnopqrstu
vwxyz12345
67890$.,'"-;;
!?"''''

48 POINT EUROSTILE BOLD EXTENDED 415-22, AMSTERDAM CONTINENTAL

ABCDEFGHIJKLMNOP
QRSTUVWXYZ&abcd
efghijklmnopqrstuvwxy
z1234567890$.,'"-;;!?"''''

30 POINT EUROSTILE BOLD EXTENDED 415-22, AMSTERDAM CONTINENTAL

ABCDEFGHIJKLMNOPQRSTUVWXYZ
&abcdefghijklmnopqrstuvwxyz123456
7890$.,'"-;;!?"''''

18 POINT EUROSTILE BOLD EXTENDED 415-22, AMSTERDAM CONTINENTAL

ABCDEFGHIJKLMNOPQRSTUVWXYZ&abcdefghij
klmnopqrstuvwxyz1234567890$.,'"-;;!?"''''

12 POINT EUROSTILE BOLD EXTENDED 415-22, AMSTERDAM CONTINENTAL

281

ABCDEFGHIJ
KLMNOPQRS
TUVWXYZ&
abcdefghijklmn
opqrstuvwxyz
1234567890
$.,"-:;!?"""

48 POINT EUROSTILE EXTENDED 415-12, AMSTERDAM CONTINENTAL

ABCDEFGHIJKLMNOP
QRSTUVWXYZ&abcdef
ghijklmnopqrstuvwxyz12
34567890$.,'-:;!?"""

30 POINT EUROSTILE EXTENDED 415-12, AMSTERDAM CONTINENTAL

ABCDEFGHIJKLMNOPQRSTUVWXYZ&
abcdefghijklmnopqrstuvwxyz12345678
90$.,'-:;!?"""

18 POINT EUROSTILE EXTENDED 415-12, AMSTERDAM CONTINENTAL

ABCDEFGHIJKLMNOPQRSTUVWXYZ&abcdefghijklmno
pqrstuvwxyz1234567890$.,'-:;!?"""

12 POINT EUROSTILE EXTENDED 415-12, AMSTERDAM CONTINENTAL

"Dioscorides De Materia Medica"
and other texts, in Greek,
early tenth century.

ABCDEFGHIJK LMNOPQRRST UVWXYZ&abc defghijklmnopqr stuvwxyz12345 67890$.,'-:;!?""''

66 POINT FOLIO MEDIUM, BAUER

ABCDEFGHIJKLM NOPQRRSTUVWX YZ&abcdefghijklmn opqrstuvwxyz12345 67890$.,'-:;!?""''

54 POINT FOLIO MEDIUM, BAUER

ABCDEFGHIJKLMNOPQRRSTU
VWXYZ&abcdefghijklmnopqrstu
vwxyz1234567890$.,'-:;!?""

36 POINT FOLIO MEDIUM, BAUER

ABCDEFGHIJKLMNOPQRRSTUVWXYZ&abc
defghijklmnopqrstuvwxyz1234567890$.,'-:;!?""

24 POINT FOLIO MEDIUM, BAUER

ABCDEFGHIJKLM
NOPQRRSTUVWX
YZ&abcdefghijklmno
pqrstuvwxyz1234567
890$.,'-:;!?

54 POINT FOLIO LIGHT, BAUER

ABCDEFGHIJKLMN OPQRSTUVWXYZ &abcdefghijklmnopq rstuvwxyz12345678 90$.,'-:!?

54 POINT FOLIO LIGHT ITALIC, BAUER

ABCDEFGHIJKLMNOPQRRSTU VWXYZ&abcdefghijklmnopqrstuv wxyz1234567890$.,'-:;!?

36 POINT FOLIO LIGHT, BAUER

ABCDEFGHIJKLMNOPQRSTUV WXYZ&abcdefghijklmnopqrstuv wxyz1234567890$.,'-:;!?

36 POINT FOLIO LIGHT ITALIC, BAUER

ABCDEFGHIJKLMNOPQRRSTUVWXYZ&abc
defghijklmnopqrstuvwxyz1234567890$.,'-:;!?

24 POINT FOLIO LIGHT, BAUER

*ABCDEFGHIJKLMNOPQRSTUVWXYZ&abcd
efghijklmnopqrstuvwxyz1234567890$.,'-:;!?*

24 POINT FOLIO LIGHT ITALIC, BAUER

ABCDEFGHIJ
KLMNOPQR
RSTUVWXYZ
&abcdefghijkl
mnopqrstuvw
xyz1234567
890$.,'-:;!?""''

66 POINT FOLIO BOLD, BAUER

ABCDEFGHIJKL MNOPQRRSTUV WXYZ&abcdefgh ijklmnopqrstuvw xyz1234567890 $.,'-:;!?""

54 POINT FOLIO BOLD, BAUER

ABCDEFGHIJKLMNOPQRR STUVWXYZ&abcdefghijklm nopqrstuvwxyz1234567890 $.,'-:;!?""

36 POINT FOLIO BOLD, BAUER

ABCDEFGHIJKLMNOPQRRSTUVWXYZ &abcdefghijklmnopqrstuvwxyz12345678 90$.,'-:;!?""

24 POINT FOLIO BOLD, BAUER

ABCDEFGHIJKLMNOPQRST UVWXYZ&abcdefghijklmn opqrstuvwxyz1234567890 $.,'-:;!?""''

36 POINT FOLIO EXTRABOLD, BAUER

ABCDEFGHIJKLMNOP QRSTUVWXYZ&abcd efghijklmnopqrstuv wxyz1234567890 $.,'-:;!?

66 POINT FOLIO BOLD CONDENSED, BAUER

ABCDEFGHIJKLMNOPQRST UVWXYZ&abcdefghijklm nopqrstuvwxyz12345678 90$.,'-:;!?

54 POINT FOLIO BOLD CONDENSED, BAUER

ABCDEFGHIJKLMNOPQRSTUVWXYZ&abcdef ghijklmnopqrstuvwxyz1234567890 $.,'-:;!?

36 POINT FOLIO BOLD CONDENSED, BAUER

ABCDEFGHIJKLMNOPQRSTUVWXYZ&abcdefghijklmnopqrstu vwxyz1234567890$.,'-:;!?

24 POINT FOLIO BOLD CONDENSED, BAUER

AaBCDEEFG
HIJKLMMmNn
OPQRrSTUV
WXYZ&abcd
efghijklmnop
qrstuvwxyz
1234567890
$.,'-:;!?""''

66 POINT FOLIO MEDIUM EXTENDED (& alternate characters), BAUER

ABCDEFGHI
JKLMNOPQ
RSTUVWXY
Z&abcdefgh
ijklmnopqrs
tuvwxyz
1234567890
$.,'-:;!?""

66 POINT FOLIO MEDIUM EXTENDED ITALIC, BAUER

AaBCDEeFGHIJ KLMMNNOPQ RrSTUVWXYZ& abcdefghijklmn opqrstuvwxyz $.,'-:;!?""''

54 POINT FOLIO MEDIUM EXTENDED (& alternate characters), BAUER

ABCDEFGHIJKL MNOPQRSTUV WXYZ&abcdef ghijklmnopqrst uvwxyz1234567 890$.,'-:;!?""''

54 POINT FOLIO MEDIUM EXTENDED ITALIC, BAUER

AaBCDEEFGHIJKLMMnn OPQRrSTUVWXYZ&abcdef ghijklmnopqrstuvwxyz1234 567890$.,'-:;!?""

36 POINT FOLIO MEDIUM EXTENDED (& alternate characters), BAUER

ABCDEFGHIJKLMNOPQRS TUVWXYZ&abcdefghijklm nopqrstuvwxyz1234567890 $.,'-:;!?""

36 POINT FOLIO MEDIUM EXTENDED ITALIC, BAUER

AaBCDEEFGHIJKLMMnnOPQRrSTU VWXYZ&abcdefghijklmnopqrstuvwx yz1234567890$.,'-:;!?""

24 POINT FOLIO MEDIUM EXTENDED (& alternate characters), BAUER

ABCDEFGHIJKLMNOPQRSTUVWXYZ &abcdefghijklmnopqrstuvwxyz12345 67890$.,'-:;!?""

24 POINT FOLIO MEDIUM EXTENDED ITALIC, BAUER

ABCDEFGHIJ
KLMNOPQRS
TUVWXYZ&abc
defghijklmnopqrst
uvwxyz1234567890
.,='·:,!?

48 POINT FRAKTUR 16-2, LUDLOW

ABCDEFGHIJKLMNOPQRST
UVWXYZ&abcdefghijklmnopqrstuvw
xyz1234567890.,='·:,!?

24 POINT FRAKTUR 16-2, LUDLOW

ABCDEFGHIJKLMNOPQ
RSTUVWXYZ&abcdefghijklm
nopqrstuvwxyz1234567890
.,='·:,!?

48 POINT FRAKTUR 16-1, LUDLOW

ABCDEFGHIJKLMNOPQRSTUVWXYZ&abcdefghijflmno
pqrstuvwxyz1234567890.,=':;!?

24 POINT FRAKTUR 16-1, LUDLOW

ABCDEFGHIJK
LMNOPQRSTU
VWXYZ&abcdefgh
ijflmnopqrstuvwxyz1
234567890.;-':;!?

48 POINT FRAKTUR 16-3, LUDLOW

ABCDEFGHIJKLMNOPQRSTU
VWXYZ&abcdefghijflmnopqrstuvwxyz
1234567890.,-':;!?

24 POINT FRAKTUR 16-3, LUDLOW

ABCDEFGHIJK LMNOPQRSTU VWXYZ&abcd efghijklmnopqr stuvwxyz1234 567890$.,-';:,!?

60 POINT FRANKLIN GOTHIC, LUDLOW

ABCDEFGHIJKLMNOPQR STUVWXYZ&abcdefghijkl mnopqrstuvwxyz123456 7890$.,-';:,!?

36 POINT FRANKLIN GOTHIC, LUDLOW

ABCDEFGHIJKLMNOPQRSTUVWXYZ &abcdefghijklmnopqrstuvwxyz12345 67890$.,-,:;!?

24 POINT FRANKLIN GOTHIC, LUDLOW

ABCDEFGHIJKLMNOPQ RSTUVWXYZ&abcdefg hijklmnopqrstuvwxyz 1234567890$.,-':;!?

60 POINT FRANKLIN GOTHIC EXTRA CONDENSED, LUDLOW

ABCDEFGHIJKLMNOPQRSTUVWXYZ& abcdefghijklmnopqrstuvwxyz 1234567890$.,-':;!?

36 POINT FRANKLIN GOTHIC EXTRA CONDENSED, LUDLOW

ABCDEFGHIJKLMNOPQRSTUVWXYZ&abcdefghijklmnopqrst uvwxyz1234567890$.,-,:;!?

24 POINT FRANKLIN GOTHIC EXTRA CONDENSED, LUDLOW

ABCDEFG
HIJKLMNO
PQRSTUV
WXYZ&ab
cdefghijklm
nopqrstuvw
xyzfifffffl123
4567890$
.,"'-:;!?"'"
·,

42 POINT HELLENIC WIDE, BAUER

ABCDEFGHIJK
LMNOPQRSTU
VWXYZ&abcde
fghijklmnopqrstu
vwxyzfifffll12345
67890$.,"'-:;!?"'"

30 POINT HELLENIC WIDE, BAUER

ABCDEFGHIJKLMNOP
QRSTUVWXYZ&abcde
fghijklmnopqrstuvwxyzfi
fffl1234567890$.,"-:;!?""

24 POINT HELLENIC WIDE, BAUER

ABCDEFGHIJKLMNOPQRSTUVW
XYZ&abcdefghijklmnopqrstuvwxy
zfiffffl1234567890$.,"-:;!?""

18 POINT HELLENIC WIDE, BAUER

ABCDEFGHIJKLMNOPQRSTUVWXYZ&abc
defghijklmnopqrstuvwxyzfiffffl1234567890
$.,"-:;!?""

14 POINT HELLENIC WIDE, BAUER

ABCDEFGHIJKLMNOPQRSTUVWXYZ&abcdefghijklmnopqrstuvwxyz
fiffffl1234567890$.,"-:;!?""

10 POINT HELLENIC WIDE, BAUER

ABCDEFGHIJKLM
NOPQRSTUVWX
YZ&abcdefghijklm
nopqrstuvwxyzfffifl
ft1234567890
$.,´-:;!?

60 POINT HORIZON LIGHT, BAUER

ABCDEFGHIJKLMNO
PQRSTUVWXYZ&abc
defghijklmnopqrstuvwx
yzfffiflft1234567890
$.,´-:;!?

48 POINT HORIZON LIGHT, BAUER

ABCDEFGHIJKLMN
OPQRSTUVWXYZ&
abcdefghijklmnopqrstuv
wxyzfffiflft1234567890
$.,´-:;!?

48 POINT HORIZON LIGHT ITALIC, BAUER

ABCDEFGHIJKLMNOPQRS
TUVWXYZ&abcdefghijklmn
opqrstuvwxyzfffiflft12345678
90$.,´-:;!?

36 POINT HORIZON LIGHT, BAUER

ABCDEFGHIJKLMNOPQR
STUVWXYZ&abcdefghijklm
nopqrstuvwxyzfffiflft12345678
90$.,´-:;!?

36 POINT HORIZON LIGHT ITALIC, BAUER

ABCDEFGHIJKLMNOPQRSTUVWX
YZ&abcdefghijklmnopqrstuvwxyz
fffiflflft1234567890$.,´-:;!?

30 POINT HORIZON LIGHT, BAUER

*ABCDEFGHIJKLMNOPQRSTUVW
XYZ&abcdefghijklmnopqrstuvwxyz
fffiflft1234567890$.,´-:;!?*

30 POINT HORIZON LIGHT ITALIC, BAUER

ABCDEFGHIJKLMNOPQRSTUVWXYZ&abcdefgh
ijklmnopqrstuvwxyzfffiflflft1234567890$.,´-:;!?

24 POINT HORIZON LIGHT, BAUER

*ABCDEFGHIJKLMNOPQRSTUVWXYZ&abcdefg
hijklmnopqrstuvwxyz fffiflft1234567890$.,´-:;!?*

24 POINT HORIZON LIGHT ITALIC, BAUER

ABCDEFGHIJKLMNOPQRSTUVWXYZ&abcdefghijklmnopqrst
uvwxyzfffiflflft1234567890$.,´-:;!?

18 POINT HORIZON LIGHT, BAUER

*ABCDEFGHIJKLMNOPQRSTUVWXYZ&abcdefghijklmnopqrs
tuvwxyz fffiflft1234567890$.,´-:;!?*

18 POINT HORIZON LIGHT ITALIC, BAUER

ABCDEFGHIJKLMNOPQRSTUVWXYZ&abcdefghijklmnopqrstuvwx
yzfffiflflft1234567890$.,´-:;!?

16 POINT HORIZON LIGHT, BAUER

*ABCDEFGHIJKLMNOPQRSTUVWXYZ&abcdefghijklmnopqrstuvw
xyzfffiflft1234567890$.,´-:;!?*

16 POINT HORIZON LIGHT ITALIC, BAUER

ABCDEFGHIJKL MNOPQRSTUV WXYZ&abcdefghi jklmnopqrstuvwxy zfffiflft1234567890 $.,´-:;!?

60 POINT HORIZON MEDIUM, BAUER

ABCDEFGHIJKLMNOPQRSTUVW
XYZ&abcdefghijklmnopqrstuvwxyz
fffiflft1234567890$.,´-:;!?

30 POINT HORIZON MEDIUM, BAUER

ABCDEFGHIJKLMNOPQRSTUVWXYZ&abcdefghijklmnopqrs
tuvwxyzfffiflft1234567890$.,´-:;!?

18 POINT HORIZON MEDIUM, BAUER

ABCDEFGHIJK
LMNOPQRSTU
VWXYZ&abcde
fghijklmnopqrst
uvwxyzfffifflft123
4567890$.,´-:;!?

60 POINT HORIZON BOLD, BAUER

ABCDEFGHIJKLMNOPQRSTU
VWXYZ&abcdefghijklmnopqrst
uvwxyzfffifflft1234567890$.,´-:;!?

30 POINT HORIZON BOLD, BAUER

ABCDEFGHIJKLMNOPQRSTUVWXYZ&abcdefghijkl
mnopqrstuvwxyzfffifflft1234567890$.,´-:;!?

18 POINT HORIZON BOLD, BAUER

305

ABCDEF
GHIJKL
MNOPQR
STUVWX
YZ&abcde
fghijklmn
opqrstuv
wxyzfiffffl
ffiffl12345
67890$.,"
-:;!?""""

48 POINT LATIN WIDE, STEPHENSON BLAKE

ABCDEFGHIJ KLMNOPQRS TUVWXYZ&a bcdefghijklm nopqrstuvwx yzfifffffiffiffl123 4567890$.,"-:; !?""

36 POINT LATIN WIDE, STEPHENSON BLAKE

ABCDEFGHIJKLM NOPQRSTUVWXYZ &abcdefghijklmnopq rstuvwxyzfiffffiffiffl12 34567890$.,"-:;!?""

18 POINT LATIN WIDE, STEPHENSON BLAKE

ABCDEFGHIJKLMNOPQRSTUVWXYZ&abcd
efghijklmnopqrstuvwxyzfiffffiffiffl123456789
0$.,"-:;!?""

12 POINT LATIN WIDE, STEPHENSON BLAKE

ABCDEFGHIJKLMNOPQRSTUVWXYZ&abcdefghijklmnopqrstuvwxyzfiffffl
ffiffl1234567890$.,"-:;!?""

6 POINT LATIN WIDE, STEPHENSON BLAKE

ABCDEFGHIJKLMNOPQR
STUVWXYZ&abcdefghijkl
mnopqrstuvwxyzfifffflffffiffl12
34567890$.,"-:;!?""

36 POINT LATIN BOLD CONDENSED, STEPHENSON BLAKE

ABCDEFGHIJKLMNOPQRSTUVWXYZ&abcdefgh
ijklmnopqrstuvwxyzfifffflffffiffl1234567890$.,"-:;!?""

24 POINT LATIN BOLD CONDENSED, STEPHENSON BLAKE

ABCDEFGHIJKLMNOPQRSTUVWXYZ&abcdefghijklmnopqrstuvwxyzfifffflffffiffl123456
7890$.,"-:;!?""

12 POINT LATIN BOLD CONDENSED, STEPHENSON BLAKE

ABCDEFGHIJKLMNOPQRSTUVWXYZ
&abcdefghijklmnopqrstuvwxyzfifffflffi
ffl1234567890$.,'"-:;!?""

48 POINT LATIN ELONGATED, STEPHENSON BLAKE

ABCDEFGHIJKLMNOPQRSTUVWXYZ&abcdef
ghijklmnopqrstuvwxyzfifffflffiffl1234567890$
.,'"-:;!?""

36 POINT LATIN ELONGATED, STEPHENSON BLAKE

ABCDEFGHIJKLMNOPORSTUVWXYZ&abcdefghijklmnopqrstuvwxyz
fiﬀﬂﬃﬄﬀﬂ1234567890$.,''-:;!?''''
24 POINT LATIN ELONGATED, STEPHENSON BLAKE

ABCDEFGHIJKLMNOPQRSTUVWXYZ&abcdefghijklmnopqrstuvwxyzfiﬀﬂﬃﬄ1234567890$
.,''-:;!?''''
18 POINT LATIN ELONGATED, STEPHENSON, BLAKE

ABCDEFGHIJKLMNOPQRSTUVWXYZ&abcdefghijklmnopqrstuvwxyzfiﬀﬂﬃﬄ1234567890$.,''-:;!?''''
12 POINT LATIN ELONGATED, STEPHENSON BLAKE

LIGHTLINE GOTHIC

ABCDEFGHIJKLMNOPQRSTUV
WXYZ&abcdefghijklmnopqrstuvw
xyz1234567890$.,''-:;!?''''
36 POINT LIGHTLINE GOTHIC, ATF

ABCDEFGHIJKLMNOPQRSTUVWXYZ
&abcdefghijklmnopqrstuvwxyz1234567
890$.,''-:;!?''''
30 POINT LIGHTLINE GOTHIC, ATF

ABCDEFGHIJKLMNOPQRSTUVWXYZ&abcdefg
hijklmnopqrstuvwxyz1234567890$.,''-:;!?''''
24 POINT LIGHTLINE GOTHIC, ATF

ABCDEFGHIJKLMNOPQRSTUVWXYZ&abcdefghijklmnopqr
stuvwxyz1234567890$.,''-:;!?''''
18 POINT LIGHTLINE GOTHIC, ATF

ABCDEFGHIJKLMNOPQRSTUVWXY
Z&1234567890$.,-';:!?

18 POINT #2 LINING LITHO LIGHT 45-L, LUDLOW

ABCDEFGHIJKLMNOPQRSTUVWX
YZ&1234567890$.,-';:!?

18 POINT #2 LINING LITHO BOLD 45-B, LUDLOW

LINING PLATE GOTHIC

ABCDEFGHIJKLMNOPQRSTUV
WXYZ&1234567890$.-,';:!?

24 POINT #1 LINING PLATE GOTHIC BOLD, LUDLOW

ABCDEFGHIJKLMNOPQRSTUVWXYZ&
1234567890$.,-';:!?

12 POINT #4 LINING PLATE GOTHIC BOLD, LUDLOW

ABCDEFGHIJKLMNOPQRS
TUVWXYZ&1234567890$
.,-';:!?

24 POINT #2 LINING PLATE GOTHIC HEAVY, LUDLOW

ABCDEFGHIJKLMNOPQRSTUVWXYZ&1234
567890$.,-';:!?

18 POINT #1 LINING PLATE GOTHIC HEAVY, LUDLOW

ABCDEFGHIJKLMNOPQRSTUVWXYZ&
1234567890$.,-';:!?

18 POINT #2 LINING PLATE GOTHIC HEAVY CONDENSED, LUDLOW

ABCDEFGHIJKLMNOPQRSTUVWXYZ&1234567890$.,-';:!?

12 POINT #4 LINING PLATE GOTHIC HEAVY CONDENSED, LUDLOW

ABCDEFGHIJKLMNOPQRSTUVWXYZ&
1234567890$.,-’:;!?
12 POINT #4 LINING PLATE GOTHIC HEAVY EXTENDED, LUDLOW

ABCDEFGHIJKLMNOPQRSTUVWXYZ&
1234567890$.,-’:;!?
12 POINT #2 LINING PLATE GOTHIC HEAVY EXTENDED, LUDLOW

ABCDEFGHIJKLMNOPQRS
TUVWXYZ&1234567890$
.,-’:;!?
24 POINT #2 LINING PLATE GOTHIC LIGHT, LUDLOW

ABCDEFGHIJKLMNOPQRSTUVWXYZ&1234
567890$.,-’:;!?
18 POINT #1 LINING PLATE GOTHIC LIGHT, LUDLOW

ABCDEFGHIJKLMNOPQRSTUVWXYZ&
1234567890$.,-’:;!?
18 POINT #2 LINING PLATE GOTHIC LIGHT CONDENSED, LUDLOW

ABCDEFGHIJKLMNOPQRSTUVWXYZ&
1234567890$.,-’:;!?
12 POINT #4 LINING PLATE GOTHIC LIGHT EXTENDED, LUDLOW

ABCDEFGHIJKLMNOPQRSTUVWXYZ&1234567890$.,-’:;!?
12 POINT #2 LINING PLATE GOTHIC LIGHT EXTENDED, LUDLOW

MICROGRAMMA

ABCDEFGHIJKLMNO
PQRSTUVWXYZ&12
34567890$.,”-:;!?”“
36 POINT MICROGRAMMA NORMAL, AMSTERDAM CONTINENTAL

311

ABCDEFGHIJKLMNOPQRSTU
VWXYZ&1234567890$.,"-:;!?""''

30 POINT (small) MICROGRAMMA NORMAL, AMSTERDAM CONTINENTAL

ABCDEFGHIJKLMNOPQRSTUVWXYZ&1234
567890$.,'-:;!?""''

18 POINT MICROGRAMMA NORMAL, AMSTERDAM CONTINENTAL

ABCDEFGHIJKLMNOPQRSTU
VWXYZ&1234567890$.,"-:;!?""''

36 POINT MICROGRAMMA CONDENSED, AMSTERDAM CONTINENTAL

ABCDEFGHIJKLMNOPQRSTUVWXYZ&
1234567890$.,"-:;!?""''

30 POINT (small) MICROGRAMMA CONDENSED, AMSTERDAM CONTINENTAL

ABCDEFGHIJKLMNOPQRSTUVWXYZ&1234567890$.,'-:;!?""''

18 POINT MICROGRAMMA CONDENSED, AMSTERDAM CONTINENTAL

ABCDEFGHIJK
LMNOPQRSTU
VWXYZ&1234
567890$.,"-:;!?""''

36 POINT MICROGRAMMA EXTENDED, AMSTERDAM CONTINENTAL

ABCDEFGHIJKLMNO
PQRSTUVWXYZ&12
34567890$.,''-:;!?''''

30 POINT (small) MICROGRAMMA EXTENDED, AMSTERDAM CONTINENTAL

ABCDEFGHIJKLMNOPQRSTUV
WXYZ&1234567890$.,''-:;!?''''

18 POINT MICROGRAMMA EXTENDED, AMSTERDAM CONTINENTAL

ABCDEFGHIJKLM
NOPQRSTUVWXY
Z&1234567890$
.,''-:;!?''''

36 POINT MICROGRAMMA BOLD, AMSTERDAM CONTINENTAL

ABCDEFGHIJKLMNOPQR
STUVWXYZ&123456789
0$.,''-:;!?''''

30 POINT (small) MICROGRAMMA BOLD, AMSTERDAM CONTINENTAL

ABCDEFGHIJKLMNOPQRSTUVWXYZ&
1234567890$.,''-:;!?''''

18 POINT MICROGRAMMA BOLD, AMSTERDAM CONTINENTAL

ABCDEFGHIJ KLMNOPQRS TUVWXYZ&1 234567890$.,''-;;!?,,''

36 POINT MICROGRAMMA BOLD EXTENDED, AMSTERDAM CONTINENTAL

ABCDEFGHIJKLM NOPQRSTUVWXY Z&1234567890$.,''-;;!?,,''

30 POINT (small) MICROGRAMMA BOLD EXTENDED, AMSTERDAM CONTINENTAL

ABCDEFGHIJKLMNOPQRSTU VWXYZ&1234567890$.,''-;;!?,,''

18 POINT MICROGRAMMA BOLD EXTENDED, AMSTERDAM CONTINENTAL

ABCDEFGHIJKL
MNOPQRSTUVW
XYZ&abcdefghijkl
mnopqrstuvwxyzfffi
flffiffl1234567890$.,"-
:;!?""

48 POINT MODERN 20, STEPHENSON BLAKE

ABCDEFGHIJKLMNOPQRSTU
VWXYZ&abcdefghijklmnopqrstuv
wxyzfffiflffiffl1234567890$.,"-:;!?""

30 POINT MODERN 20, STEPHENSON BLAKE

ABCDEFGHIJKLMNOPQRST
UVWXYZ&abcdefghijklmnopqrstu
vwxyzfffiflffiffl1234567890$.,"-:;!?""

30 POINT MODERN 20 ITALIC, STEPHENSON BLAKE

ABCDEFGHIJKLMNOPQRSTUVWXYZ&abcdefghij
klmnopqrstuvwxyzfffiflffiffl1234567890$.,"-:;!?""

18 POINT MODERN 20, STEPHENSON BLAKE

ABCDEFGHIJKLMNOPQRSTUVWXYZ&abcdefgh
ijklmnopqrstuvwxyzfffiflffiffl1234567890$.,"-:;!?""

18 POINT MODERN 20 ITALIC, STEPHENSON BLAKE

ABCDEFGHIJKLMNOP QRSTUVWXYZ&abcdef ghijklmnopqrstuvwxyz 1234567890$.,-':;!?

48 POINT RECORD GOTHIC, LUDLOW

ABCDEFGHIJKLMNOPQRSTU VWXYZ&abcdefghijklmnopqrst uvwxyz1234567890$.,-':;!?

36 POINT RECORD GOTHIC, LUDLOW

ABCDEFGHIJKLMNOPQRSTUVWXYZ&abcdef
ghijklmnopqrstuvwxyz1234567890$.,-':;!?

24 POINT RECORD GOTHIC, LUDLOW

ABCDEFGHIJKLM
NOPQRSTUVWXY
Z&abcdefghijklmn
opqrstuvwxyz123
4567890$.,-';;.!?

60 POINT RECORD GOTHIC BOLD, LUDLOW

ABCDEFGHIJKLM
NOPQRSTUVWXY
Z&abcdefghijklmn
opqrstuvwxyz123
4567890$.,-';;.!?

60 POINT RECORD GOTHIC BOLD ITALIC, LUDLOW

ABCDEFGHIJKLMNOPQRSTU
VWXYZ&abcdefghijklmnopqrs
tuvwxyz1234567890$.,-':;!?

36 POINT RECORD GOTHIC BOLD, LUDLOW

ABCDEFGHIJKLMNOPQRSTU
VWXYZ&abcdefghijklmnopqrst
uvwxyz1234567890$.,-':;!?

36 POINT RECORD GOTHIC BOLD ITALIC, LUDLOW

ABCDEFGHIJKLMNOPQRSTUVWXYZ&abcde
fghijklmnopqrstuvwxyz1234567890$.,-':;!?

24 POINT RECORD GOTHIC BOLD, LUDLOW

ABCDEFGHIJKLMNOPQRSTUVWXYZ&abcde
fghijklmnopqrstuvwxyz1234567890.,-':;!?

24 POINT RECORD GOTHIC BOLD ITALIC, LUDLOW

ABCDEFGHIJKLMNOPQ
RSTUVWXYZ&abcdefgh
ijklmnopqrstuvwxyz123
4567890$.,-':;!?

60 POINT RECORD GOTHIC THINLINE CONDENSED, LUDLOW

ABCDEFGHIJKLMNOPQRSTUVWXYZ&
abcdefghijklmnopqrstuvwxyz12345678
90$.,-':;!?

36 POINT RECORD GOTHIC THINLINE CONDENSED, LUDLOW

ABCDEFGHIJKLMNOPQRSTUVWXYZ&abcdefghijklmnopqrst
uvwxyz1234567890$.,-':;!?

24 POINT RECORD GOTHIC THINLINE CONDENSED, LUDLOW

ABCDEFGHIJKLMNOPQRSTUVWXYZ&abcdefgh
ijklmnopqrstuvwxyz1234567890$.,-':;!?

48 POINT RECORD GOTHIC EXTRA CONDENSED, LUDLOW

ABCDEFGHIJKLMNOPQRSTUVWXYZ&abcdefghijklmnopqrstuv
wxyz1234567890$.,-':;!?

36 POINT RECORD GOTHIC EXTRA CONDENSED, LUDLOW

ABCDEFGHIJKLMNOPQRSTUVWXYZ&abcdefghijklmnopqrstuvwxyz1234567890$.,-':;!?

24 POINT RECORD GOTHIC EXTRA CONDENSED, LUDLOW

ABCDEFGHIJKLMNOPQ
RSTUVWXYZ&abcdefghi
jklmnopqrstuvwxyz1234
567890$.,-':;!?

60 POINT RECORD GOTHIC CONDENSED, LUDLOW

ABCDEFGHIJKLMNOPQRSTU
VWXYZ&abcdefghijklmnopqr
stuvwxyz1234567890$.,-':;!?

60 POINT RECORD GOTHIC CONDENSED ITALIC, LUDLOW

ABCDEFGHIJKLMNOPQRSTUVWXYZ&ab
cdefghijklmnopqrstuvwxyz1234567890
$.,-':;!?

36 POINT RECORD GOTHIC CONDENSED, LUDLOW

*ABCDEFGHIJKLMNOPQRSTUVWXYZ&ab
cdefghijklmnopqrstuvwxyz1234567890
$.,-':;!?*

36 POINT RECORD GOTHIC CONDENSED ITALIC, LUDLOW

ABCDEFGHIJKLMNOPQRSTUVWXYZ&abcdefghijklmnopqrs
tuvwxyz1234567890$.,-':;!?

24 POINT RECORD GOTHIC CONDENSED, LUDLOW

*ABCDEFGHIJKLMNOPQRSTUVWXYZ&abcdefghijklmnopqrst
uvwxyz1234567890$.,-':;!?*

24 POINT RECORD GOTHIC CONDENSED ITALIC, LUDLOW

ABCDEFGHIJKL
MNOPQRSTUVW
XYZ&abcdefghijkl
mnopqrstuvwxyz
1234567890$.,-':;!?

48 POINT RECORD GOTHIC EXTENDED, LUDLOW

321

ABCDEFGHIJKLM
NOPQRSTUVWXY
Z&abcdefghijklm
nopqrstuvwxyz12
34567890$.,-';:!?

48 POINT RECORD GOTHIC EXTENDED ITALIC, LUDLOW

ABCDEFGHIJKLMNOPQ
RSTUVWXYZ&abcdefghi
jklmnopqrstuvwxyz123
4567890$.,-';:!?

36 POINT RECORD GOTHIC EXTENDED, LUDLOW

ABCDEFGHIJKLMNOPQ
RSTUVWXYZ&abcdefghi
jklmnopqrstuvwxyz123
4567890$.,-';:!?

36 POINT RECORD GOTHIC EXTENDED ITALIC, LUDLOW

ABCDEFGHIJKLMNOPQRSTUVWXY
Z&abcdefghijklmnopqrstuvwxyz123
4567890$.,-';:!?

24 POINT RECORD GOTHIC EXTENDED, LUDLOW

ABCDEFGHIJKLMNOPQRSTUVWXY
Z&abcdefghijklmnopqrstuvwxyz
1234567890$.,-';:!?

24 POINT RECORD GOTHIC EXTENDED ITALIC, LUDLOW

ABCDEFGHIJKL
MNOPQRSTUV
WXYZ&abcdefg
hijklmnopqrstuvw
xyz1234567890
$.,-':,!?

60 POINT RECORD GOTHIC MEDIUM EXTENDED, LUDLOW

ABCDEFGHIJKLMNOPQRS
TUVWXYZ&abcdefghijklmn
opqrstuvwxyz1234567890$
.,-’:;!?

36 POINT RECORD GOTHIC MEDIUM EXTENDED, LUDLOW

ABCDEFGHIJKLMNOPQRSTUVWXYZ&
abcdefghijklmnopqrstuvwxyz123456789
0$.,-’:;!?

24 POINT RECORD GOTHIC MEDIUM EXTENDED, LUDLOW

ABCDEFGHIJKL
MNOPQRSTUV
WXYZ&abcdefg
hijklmnopqrstuv
wxyz12345678
90$.,-’:;!?

60 POINT RECORD GOTHIC BOLD MEDIUM EXTENDED, LUDLOW

ABCDEFGHIJKLMNOPQRS
TUVWXYZ&abcdefghijklm
nopqrstuvwxyz12345678
90$.,-';:,!?

36 POINT RECORD GOTHIC BOLD MEDIUM EXTENDED, LUDLOW

ABCDEFGHIJKLMNOPQRSTUVWXYZ&a
bcdefghijklmnopqrstuvwxyz12345678
0$.,-';:,!?

24 POINT RECORD GOTHIC BOLD MEDIUM EXTENDED, LUDLOW

ABCDEFGHIJ
KLMNOPQR
STUVWXYZ&
abcdefghijkl
mnopqrstuv
wxyz123456
7890$.,-';:,!?

60 POINT RECORD GOTHIC BOLD EXTENDED, LUDLOW

ABCDEFGHIJ
KLMNOPQR
STUVWXYZ&
abcdefghijkl
mnopqrstuv
wxyz123456
7890$.,-';:!?

60 POINT RECORD GOTHIC BOLD EXTENDED ITALIC, LUDLOW

ABCDEFGHIJKLMNOP
QRSTUVWXYZ&abcde
fghijklmnopqrstuvwxy
z1234567890$.,-';:!?

36 POINT RECORD GOTHIC BOLD EXTENDED, LUDLOW

ABCDEFGHIJKLMNOP
QRSTUVWXYZ&abcde
fghijklmnopqrstuvwx
yz1234567890$.,-';;!?

36 POINT RECORD GOTHIC BOLD EXTENDED ITALIC, LUDLOW

ABCDEFGHIJKLMNOPQRSTUVWX
YZ&abcdefghijklmnopqrstuvwxyz
1234567890$.,-';;!?

24 POINT RECORD GOTHIC BOLD EXTENDED, LUDLOW

ABCDEFGHIJKLMNOPQRSTUVW
XYZ&abcdefghijklmnopqrstuvw
xyz1234567890$.,-';;!?

24 POINT RECORD GOTHIC BOLD EXTENDED ITALIC, LUDLOW

ROMAN COMPRESSED 3

ABCDEFGHIJKLMNOPQRST
UVWXYZ&abcdefghijklmno
pqrstuvwxyzffffifflffflffi123456
7890$.,"-:;!?""''

48 POINT ROMAN COMPRESSED 3, STEPHENSON BLAKE

327

ABCDEFGHIJKLMNOPQRSTUVWXYZ&
abcdefghijklmnopqrstuvwxyzfiflffffiffl1234567
890$.,"-:;!?""

30 POINT ROMAN COMPRESSED 3, STEPHENSON BLAKE

ABCDEFGHIJKLMNOPQRSTUVWXYZ&abcdefghijklmnopqrstuvw
xyzfiflffffiffl1234567890$.,"-:;!?""

18 POINT ROMAN COMPRESSED 3, STEPHENSON BLAKE

STENCIL

ABCDEFGHIJKL
MNOPQRSTUVWX
YZ&1234567890$
.,-';:;!?

36 POINT STENCIL, LUDLOW

TORINO

ABCDEFGHIJKLMNO
PQRSTUVWXYZ&abc
defghijklmnopqrstuvw
xyzfiflffffiflffifffi1234567890
$.,"-:;!?""

48 POINT TORINO, AMSTERDAM CONTINENTAL

328

ABCDEFGHIJKLMN
OPQRSTUVWXYZ&
abcdefghijklmnopqrst
uvwxyzfiffflffiffl12345
67890$.,"-:;!?""

48 POINT TORINO ITALIC, AMSTERDAM CONTINENTAL

ABCDEFGHIJKLMNOPQRSTUVWXYZ&ab
cdefghijklmnopqrstuvwxyzfiffflffifffl1234567
890$.,"-:;!?""

24 POINT (large) TORINO, AMSTERDAM CONTINENTAL

ABCDEFGHIJKLMNOPQRSTUVWXYZ
&abcdefghijklmnopqrstuvwxyzfiffflffiffl12
34567890$.,"-:;!?""

24 POINT (large) TORINO ITALIC, AMSTERDAM CONTINENTAL

ABCDEFGHIJKLMNOPQRSTUVWXYZ&abcdefghijklmnopqrstuvwxyzfiffflffifffl
1234567890$.,"-:;!?""

14 POINT TORINO, AMSTERDAM CONTINENTAL

ABCDEFGHIJKLMNOPQRSTUVWXYZ&abcdefghijklmnopqrstuvwxyz
fiffflffiffl1234567890$.,"-:;!?""

14 POINT TORINO ITALIC, AMSTERDAM CONTINENTAL

ABCDEFGHIJKLMN
OPQRSTUVWXYZ&
abcdefghijklmnopqr
stuvwxyz12345678
90!?$.,:;)''

48 POINT UNIVERS 55, ATF

ABCDEFGHIJKLM
NOPQRSTUVWXY
Z&abcdefghijklmno
pqrstuvwxyz12345
67890!?$.,:;(''

48 POINT UNIVERS 56, ATF

ABCDEFGHIJKLMNOPQR
STUVWXYZ&abcdefghijkl
mnopqrstuvwxyz1234567
890!?$.,:;()''

36 POINT UNIVERS 55, ATF

ABCDEFGHIJKLMNOPQR
STUVWXYZ&abcdefghijkl
mnopqrstuvwxyz1234567
890!?$.,:;(''

36 POINT UNIVERS 56, ATF

ABCDEFGHIJKLMNOPQRSTUV
WXYZ&abcdefghijklmnopqrstuv
wxyz1234567890!?$.,:;)''

30 POINT UNIVERS 55, ATF

ABCDEFGHIJKLMNOPQRSTU
VWXYZ&abcdefghijklmnopqrst
uvwxyz1234567890!?$.,:;(''

30 POINT UNIVERS 56, ATF

Created by Deberny et Peignot, Paris, for ATF.

ABCDEFGHIJKLMNOPQRSTUVWXYZ&
abcdefghijklmnopqrstuvwxyz12345678
90!?$.,:;)''

24 POINT (large) UNIVERS 55, ATF

*ABCDEFGHIJKLMNOPQRSTUVWXYZ
&abcdefghijklmnopqrstuvwxyz1234567
890!?$.,:;('' *

24 POINT (large) UNIVERS 56, ATF

ABCDEFGHIJKLMNOPQRSTUVWXYZ&abcdefghijk
lmnopqrstuvwxyz1234567890!?$.,:;)''

24 POINT (small) UNIVERS 55, ATF

*ABCDEFGHIJKLMNOPQRSTUVWXYZ&abcdefghi
jklmnopqrstuvwxyz1234567890!?$.,:;()'' *

24 POINT (small) UNIVERS 56, ATF

ABCDEFGHIJKLMNOPQRSTUVWXYZ&abcdefghijklmnopqrstuv
wxyz1234567890!?$.,:;()''

18 POINT UNIVERS 55, ATF

*ABCDEFGHIJKLMNOPQRSTUVWXYZ&abcdefghijklmnopqrstuv
wxyz1234567890!?$.,:;()'' *

18 POINT UNIVERS 56, ATF

ABCDEFGHIJKLMNOPQRSTUVWXYZ&abcdefghijklmnopqrstuvwxyz12345
67890!?$.,:;()''

14 POINT UNIVERS 55, ATF

*ABCDEFGHIJKLMNOPQRSTUVWXYZ&abcdefghijklmnopqrstuvwxyz12345
67890!?$.,:;()'' *

14 POINT UNIVERS 56, ATF

ABCDEFGHIJKLMNOPQRSTUVWXYZ&abcdefghijklmnopqrstuvwxyz1234567890!?$.,.:;()''

12 POINT UNIVERS 55, ATF

ABCDEFGHIJKLMNOPQRSTUVWXYZ&abcdefghijklmnopqrstuvwxyz1234567890!?$.,.:;()''

12 POINT UNIVERS 56, ATF

ABCDEFGHIJKLMN OPQRSTUVWXYZ& abcdefghijklmnopqrs tuvwxyz123456789 0!?$.,.:;)''

48 POINT UNIVERS 45, ATF

ABCDEFGHIJKLMN OPQRSTUVWXYZ& abcdefghijklmnopqr stuvwxyz12345678 90!?$.,.:;(''

48 POINT UNIVERS 46, ATF

Created by Deberny et Peignot, Paris, for ATF.

ABCDEFGHIJKLMNOPQRS
TUVWXYZ&abcdefghijklmn
opqrstuvwxyz1234567890
!?$.,:;)''

36 POINT UNIVERS 45, ATF

ABCDEFGHIJKLMNOPQR
STUVWXYZ&abcdefghijkl
mnopqrstuvwxyz1234567
890!?$.,:;(''

36 POINT UNIVERS 46, ATF

ABCDEFGHIJKLMNOPQRSTUVWXYZ&a
bcdefghijklmnopqrstuvwxyz1234567890
!?$.,:;)''

24 POINT (large) UNIVERS 45, ATF

ABCDEFGHIJKLMNOPQRSTUVWXYZ&
abcdefghijklmnopqrstuvwxyz12345678
90!?$.,:;(''

24 POINT (large) UNIVERS 46, ATF

ABCDEFGHIJKL MNOPQRSTUVW XYZ&abcdefghijkl mnopqrstuvwxyz1 234567890!?$.,.:;)"

48 POINT UNIVERS 65, ATF

ABCDEFGHIJKL MNOPQRSTUVW XYZ&abcdefghijk lmnopqrstuvwxyz 1234567890!?$.,.:;("

48 POINT UNIVERS 66, ATF

Created by Deberny et Peignot, Paris, for ATF.

ABCDEFGHIJKLMNOP QRSTUVWXYZ&abcdefg hijklmnopqrstuvwxyz123 4567890!?$.,:;()''

36 POINT UNIVERS 65, ATF

ABCDEFGHIJKLMNOP QRSTUVWXYZ&abcdef ghijklmnopqrstuvwxyz1 234567890!?$.,:;(''

36 POINT UNIVERS 66, ATF

ABCDEFGHIJKLMNOPQRSTUVWXY Z&abcdefghijklmnopqrstuvwxyz1234 567890!?$.,:;)''

24 POINT (large) UNIVERS 65, ATF

ABCDEFGHIJKLMNOPQRSTUVWX YZ&abcdefghijklmnopqrstuvwxyz123 4567890!?$.,:;(''

24 POINT (large) UNIVERS 66, ATF

ABCDEFGHIJKL MNOPQRSTUV WXYZ&abcdefgh ijklmnopqrstuvwx yz1234567890!?$.,.:;)"

48 POINT UNIVERS 75, ATF

ABCDEFGHIJKL MNOPQRSTUV WXYZ&abcdefg hijklmnopqrstuv wxyz123456789 0!?$.,.:;(''

48 POINT UNIVERS 76, ATF

Created by Deberny et Peignot, Paris, for ATF.

ABCDEFGHIJKLMNOP
QRSTUVWXYZ&abcde
fghijklmnopqrstuvwxyz
1234567890!?$.,:;)''

36 POINT UNIVERS 75, ATF

ABCDEFGHIJKLMNOP
QRSTUVWXYZ&abcde
fghijklmnopqrstuvwxy
z1234567890!?$.,:;(''

36 POINT UNIVERS 76, ATF

ABCDEFGHIJKLMNOPQRSTUVW
XYZ&abcdefghijklmnopqrstuvwxyz
1234567890!?$.,:;)''

24 POINT (large) UNIVERS 75, ATF

ABCDEFGHIJKLMNOPQRSTUVW
XYZ&abcdefghijklmnopqrstuvwxy
z1234567890!?$.,:;(''

24 POINT (large) UNIVERS 76, ATF

ABCDEFGHIJKLMNOPQRS TUVWXYZ&abcdefghijklmnop qrstuvwxyz1234567890!?$.,: ;("

48 POINT UNIVERS 47, ATF

ABCDEFGHIJKLMNOPQRS TUVWXYZ&abcdefghijklmn opqrstuvwxyz1234567890 !?$.,:;("

48 POINT UNIVERS 48, ATF

ABCDEFGHIJKLMNOPQRSTUVWXYZ &abcdefghijklmnopqrstuvwxyz1234567 890!?$.,:;("

36 POINT UNIVERS 47, ATF

Created by Deberny et Peignot, Paris, for ATF.

ABCDEFGHIJKLMNOPQRSTUVWXY Z&abcdefghijklmnopqrstuvwxyz1234 567890!?$.,:;("

36 POINT UNIVERS 48, ATF

ABCDEFGHIJKLMNOPQRSTUVWXYZ&abcdefghijklmnopqr stuvwxyz1234567890!?$.,:;("

24 POINT (large) UNIVERS 47, ATF

ABCDEFGHIJKLMNOPQRSTUVWXYZ&abcdefghijklmno pqrstuvwxyz1234567890!?$.,:;("

24 POINT (large) UNIVERS 48, ATF

ABCDEFGHIJKLMNOPQR STUVWXYZ&abcdefghijkl mnopqrstuvwxyz1234567 890!?$.,:;)"

48 POINT UNIVERS 57, ATF

ABCDEFGHIJKLMNOP
QRSTUVWXYZ&abcdefg
hijklmnopqrstuvwxyz12
34567890!?$.,:;("

48 POINT UNIVERS 58, ATF

ABCDEFGHIJKLMNOPQRSTUVW
XYZ&abcdefghijklmnopqrstuvwxyz
1234567890!?$.,:;)"

36 POINT UNIVERS 57, ATF

ABCDEFGHIJKLMNOPQRSTUV
WXYZ&abcdefghijklmnopqrstuv
wxyz1234567890!?$.,:;("

36 POINT UNIVERS 58, ATF

ABCDEFGHIJKLMNOPQRSTUVWXYZ&abcdefghijkl
mnopqrstuvwxyz1234567890!?$.,:;)"

24 POINT (large) UNIVERS 57, ATF

ABCDEFGHIJKLMNOPQRSTUVWXYZ&abcdefghi
jklmnopqrstuvwxyz1234567890!?$.,:;("

24 POINT (large) UNIVERS 58, ATF

Created by Deberny et Peignot, Paris, for ATF.

ABCDEFGHIJKLMNOP
QRSTUVWXYZ&abcdef
ghijklmnopqrstuvwxyz12
34567890!?$.,:;(''

48 POINT UNIVERS 67, ATF

ABCDEFGHIJKLMNO
PQRSTUVWXYZ&abc
defghijklmnopqrstuv
wxyz1234567890!?$.,
:;)''

48 POINT UNIVERS 68, ATF

ABCDEFGHIJKLMNOPQRSTU
VWXYZ&abcdefghijklmnopqrstu
vwxyz1234567890!?$.,:;(''

36 POINT UNIVERS 67, ATF

ABCDEFGHIJKLMNOPQRSTU
VWXYZ&abcdefghijklmnopqrs
tuvwxyz1234567890!?$.,:;)''

36 POINT UNIVERS 68, ATF

ABCDEFGHIJKLMNOPQRSTUVWXYZ
&abcdefghijklmnopqrstuvwxyz1234567
890!?$.,:;(''

30 POINT UNIVERS 67, ATF

ABCDEFGHIJKLMNOPQRSTUVWX
YZ&abcdefghijklmnopqrstuvwxyz12
34567890!?$.,:;)''

30 POINT UNIVERS 68, ATF

Created by Deberny et Peignot, Paris, for ATF.

ABCDEFGHIJKLMNOPQR
STUVWXYZ&abcdefghijklm
nopqrstuvwxyz1234567890$
.,:;-'!?

42 POINT VENUS MEDIUM, BAUER

ABCDEFGHIJKLMNOPQRSTUVW
XYZ&abcdefghijklmnopqrstuvwxyz12
34567890$.,:;-'!?

36 POINT VENUS MEDIUM, BAUER

ABCDEFGHIJKLMNOPQRSTUVWXYZ&
abcdefghijklmnopqrstuvwxyz1234567890
$.,:;-'!?

30 POINT VENUS MEDIUM, BAUER

ABCDEFGHIJKLMNOPQRSTUVWXYZ&abcdefg
hijklmnopqrstuvwxyz1234567890$.,:;-'!?

24 POINT VENUS MEDIUM, BAUER

*ABCDEFGHIJKLMNOPQRSTUVWXYZ&abcdefgh
ijklmnopqrstuvwxyz1234567890$.,:;-'!?*

24 POINT VENUS MEDIUM ITALIC, BAUER

ABCDEFGHIJKLMNOPQRSTUVWXYZ&abcdefghijklmnop
qrstuvwxyz1234567890$.,:;-'!?

18 POINT VENUS MEDIUM, BAUER

*ABCDEFGHIJKLMNOPQRSTUVWXYZ& abcdefghijklmnop
qrstuvwxyz1234567890$.,:;-'!?*

18 POINT VENUS MEDIUM ITALIC, BAUER

ABCDEFGHIJKLMNOPQRSTUVWXYZ&abcdefghijklmnopqrstuvw
xyz1234567890$.,:;-'!?

16 POINT VENUS MEDIUM, BAUER

*ABCDEFGHIJKLMNOPQRSTUVWXYZ& abcdefghijklmnopqrstuvw
xyz1234567890$.,:;-'!?*

16 POINT VENUS MEDIUM ITALIC, BAUER

ABCDEFGHIJKLMNOPQRSTUVWXYZ&abcdefghijklmnopqrstuvwxyz123456
7890$.,:;-'!?

14 POINT VENUS MEDIUM, BAUER

*ABCDEFGHIJKLMNOPQRSTUVWXYZ& abcdefghijklmnopqrstuvwxyz123456
7890$.,:;-'!?*

14 POINT VENUS MEDIUM ITALIC, BAUER

ABCDEFGHIJKLMNOPQRSTUVWXYZ& abcdefghijklmnopqrstuvwxyz1234567890$.,:;-'!?

12 POINT VENUS MEDIUM, BAUER

ABCDEFGHIJKLMNOPQRSTUVWXYZ& abcdefghijklmnopqrstuvwxyz1234567890$.,:;-'!?

12 POINT VENUS MEDIUM ITALIC, BAUER

ABCDEFGHIJKLMNOPQRSTUVWXYZ& abcdefghijklmnopqrstuvwxyz1234567890$.,:;-'!?

10 POINT VENUS MEDIUM, BAUER

ABCDEFGHIJKLMNOPQRSTUVWXYZ& abcdefghijklmnopqrstuvwxyz 1234567890$.,:;-'!?

10 POINT VENUS MEDIUM ITALIC, BAUER

ABCDEFGHIJKLMNOPQRSTUVWXYZ&abcdefghijklmnopq
rstuvwxyz1234567890$.,'-:;!?)

18 POINT VENUS LIGHT, BAUER

*ABCDEFGHIJKLMNOPQRSTUVWXYZ&abcdefghijklmnopqrs
tuvwxyz1234567890$.,:;-'!?*

18 POINT VENUS LIGHT ITALIC, BAUER

ABCDEFGHIJKLMNOPQRSTUVWXYZ&abcdefghijklmnopqrstuvwxyz1234567890$.,'-:;!?)

12 POINT VENUS LIGHT, BAUER

ABCDEFGHIJKLMNOPQRSTUVWXYZ&abcdefghijklmnopqrstuvwxyz1234567890$.,:;-'!?

12 POINT VENUS LIGHT ITALIC, BAUER

ABCDEFGHIJKLMNOPQ RSTUVWXYZ&abcdefghi jklmnopqrstuvwxyz12345 67890$.,:;-'!?

42 POINT VENUS BOLD, BAUER

ABCDEFGHIJKLMNOPQRSTU VWXYZ&abcdefghijklmnopqrstu vwxyz1234567890$.,:;-'!?

36 POINT VENUS BOLD, BAUER

ABCDEFGHIJKLMNOPQR STUVWXYZ&abcdefghijklm nopqrstuvwxyz1234567890$.,:;-'!?

36 POINT VENUS BOLD ITALIC, BAUER

ABCDEFGHIJKLMNOPQRSTUVWXYZ &abcdefghijklmnopqrstuvwxyz1234567 890$.,:;-'!?

30 POINT VENUS BOLD, BAUER

ABCDEFGHIJKLMNOPQRSTUV WXYZ&abcdefghijklmnopqrstuvw xyz1234567890$.,:;-'!?

30 POINT VENUS BOLD ITALIC, BAUER

ABCDEFGHIJKLMNOPQRSTUVWXYZ&abc
defghijklmnopqrstuvwxyz1234567890$.,:;-'!?

24 POINT VENUS BOLD, BAUER

*ABCDEFGHIJKLMNOPQRSTUVWXYZ&
abcdefghijklmnopqrstuvwxyz123456789
0$.,:;-'!?*

24 POINT VENUS BOLD ITALIC, BAUER

ABCDEFGHIJKLMNOPQRSTUVWXYZ&abcdefghijklmn
opqrstuvwxyz1234567890$.,:;-'!?

18 POINT VENUS BOLD, BAUER

347

ABCDEFGHIJKLMNOPQRSTUVWXYZ&abcdefghij klmnopqrstuvwxyz1234567890$.,:;-'!?

18 POINT VENUS BOLD ITALIC, BAUER

ABCDEFGHIJKLMNOPQRSTUVWXYZ& abcdefghijklmnopqrs tuvwxyz1234567890$.,:;-'!?

16 POINT VENUS BOLD, BAUER

ABCDEFGHIJKLMNOPQRSTUVWXYZ& abcdefghijklmn opqrstuvwxyz1234567890$.,:;-'!?

16 POINT VENUS BOLD ITALIC, BAUER

ABCDEFGHIJKLMNOPQRSTUVWXYZ&abcdefghijklmnopqrstuvwxyz1234 567890$.,:;-'!?

14 POINT VENUS BOLD, BAUER

ABCDEFGHIJKLMNOPQRSTUVWXYZ&abcdefghijklmnopqrst uvwxyz1234567890$.,:;-'!?

14 POINT VENUS BOLD ITALIC, BAUER

ABCDEFGHIJKLMNOPQRSTUVWXYZ&abcdefghijklmnopqrstuvwxyz1234567890 $.,:;-'!?

12 POINT VENUS BOLD, BAUER

ABCDEFGHIJKLMNOPQRSTUVWXYZ&abcdefghijklmnopqrstuvwxyz123 4567890$.,:;-'!?

12 POINT VENUS BOLD ITALIC, BAUER

ABCDEFGHIJKLMNOPQRSTUVWXYZ&abcdefghijklmnopqrstuvwxyz1234567890$.,:;-'!?

10 POINT VENUS BOLD, BAUER

ABCDEFGHIJKLMNOPQRSTUVWXYZ&abcdefghijklmnopqrstuvwxyz1234567890$.,:;-'!?

10 POINT VENUS BOLD ITALIC, BAUER

Note: Venus Bold Italic matches the weight of Venus Extra Bold in the Roman.

ABCDEFGHIJKLMNOPQRSTUVWXYZ&abcdefghijk
lmnopqrstuvwxyz1234567890$.,'-:;!?

18 POINT VENUS EXTRA BOLD, BAUER

ABCDEFGHIJKLMNOPQRSTUVWXYZ&abcdefghijklmnopqrstuvwxyz12345
67890$.,'-:;!?

12 POINT VENUS EXTRA BOLD, BAUER

ABCDEFGHIJKLMNOPQRSTU
VWXYZ&abcdefghijklmnopqr
stuvwxyz1234567890$.,.;-'!?

66 POINT VENUS LIGHT CONDENSED, BAUER

ABCDEFGHIJKLMNOPQRSTUVWX
YZ&abcdefghijklmnopqrstuvwxyz
1234567890$.,.;-'!?

54 POINT VENUS LIGHT CONDENSED, BAUER

ABCDEFGHIJKLMNOPQRSTUVWXYZ&abc
defghijklmnopqrstuvwxyz1234567890$.,:
;-'!?

42 POINT VENUS LIGHT CONDENSED, BAUER

ABCDEFGHIJKLMNOPQRSTUVWXYZ&abcdefghijklmno
pqrstuvwxyz1234567890$.,:;-'!?

36 POINT VENUS LIGHT CONDENSED, BAUER

ABCDEFGHIJKLMNOPQRSTUVWXYZ&abcdefghijklmnopqrstuv
wxyz1234567890$.,:;-'!?

30 POINT VENUS LIGHT CONDENSED, BAUER

ABCDEFGHIJKLMNOPQRSTUVWXYZ&abcdefghijklmnopqrstuvwxyz123
4567890$.,:;-'!?

24 POINT VENUS LIGHT CONDENSED, BAUER

ABCDEFGHIJKLMNOPQRSTUVWXYZ&abcdefghijklmnopqrstuvwxyz1234567890$.,:;-'!?

18 POINT VENUS LIGHT CONDENSED, BAUER

ABCDEFGHIJKLMNOPQRSTUVWXYZ&abcdefghijklmnopqrstuvwxyz1234567890$.,:;-'!?

16 POINT VENUS LIGHT CONDENSED, BAUER

ABCDEFGHIJKLMNOPQRSTUVWXYZ&abcdefghijklmnopqrstuvwxyz1234567890 $.,:;-'!?

14 POINT VENUS LIGHT CONDENSED, BAUER

ABCDEFGHIJKLMNOPQRSTUVWXYZ&abcdefghijklmnopqrstuvwxyz 1234567890 $.,:;-'!?

12 POINT VENUS LIGHT CONDENSED, BAUER

ABCDEFGHIJKLMNOPQRSTUVWXYZ& abcdefghijklmnopqrstuvwxyz1234567890 $.,:;-'!?

10 POINT VENUS LIGHT CONDENSED, BAUER

ABCDEFGHIJKLMNOPQ
RSTUVWXYZ&abcdefg
hijklmnopqrstuvwxyz
1234567890$.,:;-'!?

84 POINT VENUS BOLD CONDENSED, BAUER

ABCDEFGHIJKLMNOPQRST
UVWXYZ&abcdefghijklmno
pqrstuvwxyz1234567890
$.,:;-'!?

66 POINT VENUS BOLD CONDENSED, BAUER

ABCDEFGHIJKLMNOPQRSTUVWX YZ&abcdefghijklmnopqrstuvwx yz1234567890$.,:;-'!?

54 POINT VENUS BOLD CONDENSED, BAUER

ABCDEFGHIJKLMNOPQRSTUVWXYZ&abc defghijklmnopqrstuvwxyz1234567890$.,:;-'!?

42 POINT VENUS BOLD CONDENSED, BAUER

ABCDEFGHIJKLMNOPQRSTUVWXYZ&abcdefghijkl mnopqrstuvwxyz1234567890$.,:;-'!?

36 POINT VENUS BOLD CONDENSED, BAUER

ABCDEFGHIJKLMNOPQRSTUVWXYZ&abcdefghijklmnopqrs tuvwxyz1234567890$.,:;-'!?

30 POINT VENUS BOLD CONDENSED, BAUER

ABCDEFGHIJKLMNOPQRSTUVWXYZ&abcdefghijklmnopqrstuvwxyz 1234567890$.,:;-'!?

24 POINT VENUS BOLD CONDENSED, BAUER

ABCDEFGHIJKLMNOPQRSTUVWXYZ&abcdefghijklmnopqrstuvwxyz1234567890$.,:;
-'!?

18 POINT VENUS BOLD CONDENSED, BAUER

ABCDEFGHIJKLMNOPQRSTUVWXYZ&abcdefghijklmnopqrstuvwxyz1234567890$.,:;-'!?

16 POINT VENUS BOLD CONDENSED, BAUER

ABCDEFGHIJKLMNOPQRSTUVWXYZ&abcdefghijklmnopqrstuvwxyz1234567890$.,:;-'!?

14 POINT VENUS BOLD CONDENSED, BAUER

ABCDEFGHIJKLMNOPQRSTUVWXYZ&abcdefghijklmnopqrstuvwxyz1234567890$.,:;-'!?

12 POINT VENUS BOLD CONDENSED, BAUER

ABCDEFGHIJKLMNOPQRSTUVWXYZ& abcdefghijklmnopqrstuvwxyz1234567890$.,:;-'!?

10 POINT VENUS BOLD CONDENSED, BAUER

ABCDEFGHIJKLMNO
PQRSTUVWXYZ&ab
cdefghijklmnopqrst
uvwxyz1234567890
$.,:;-'!?

84 POINT VENUS EXTRA BOLD CONDENSED, BAUER

ABCDEFGHIJKLMNOPQR STUVWXYZ&abcdefghij klmnopqrstuvwxyz123 4567890$.,:;-'!?

66 POINT VENUS EXTRA BOLD CONDENSED, BAUER

ABCDEFGHIJKLMNOPQRSTU VWXYZ&abcdefghijklmnopq rstuvwxyz1234567890$.,:;-' !?

54 POINT VENUS EXTRA BOLD CONDENSED, BAUER

ABCDEFGHIJKLMNOPQRSTUVWXYZ&
abcdefghijklmnopqrstuvwxyz123456
7890$.,:;-'!?

42 POINT VENUS EXTRA BOLD CONDENSED, BAUER

ABCDEFGHIJKLMNOPQRSTUVWXYZ&abcdefgh
ijklmnopqrstuvwxyz1234567890$.,:;-'!?

36 POINT VENUS EXTRA BOLD CONDENSED, BAUER

ABCDEFGHIJKLMNOPQRSTUVWXYZ&abcdefghijklmnop
qrstuvwxyz1234567890$.,:;-'!?

30 POINT VENUS EXTRA BOLD CONDENSED, BAUER

ABCDEFGHIJKLMNOPQRSTUVWXYZ&abcdefghijklmnopqrstuvwx
yz1234567890$.,:;-'!?

24 POINT VENUS EXTRA BOLD CONDENSED, BAUER

ABCDEFGHIJKLMNOPQRSTUVWXYZ& abcdefghijklmnopqrstuvwxyz1234567890
$.,:;-'!?

18 POINT VENUS EXTRA BOLD CONDENSED, BAUER

ABCDEFGHIJKLMNOPQRSTUVWXYZ&abcdefghijklmnopqrstuvwxyz1234567890$.,:;-'!?

16 POINT VENUS EXTRA BOLD CONDENSED, BAUER

ABCDEFGHIJKLMNOPQRSTUVWXYZ& abcdefghijklmnopqrstuvwxyz1234567890$.,:;-'!?

14 POINT VENUS EXTRA BOLD CONDENSED, BAUER

ABCDEFGHIJKLMNOPQRSTUVWXYZ& abcdefghijklmnopqrstuvwxyz1234567890$.,:;-'!?

12 POINT VENUS EXTRA BOLD CONDENSED, BAUER

355

ABCDEFGHIJKLMNOPQRSTUVWXYZ& abcdefghijklmnopqrstuvwxyz1234567890$.,:;-'!?

10 POINT VENUS EXTRA BOLD CONDENSED, BAUER

ABCDEFGHIJKLMNOPQRS
TUVWXYZ&abcdefghijklmno
pqrstuvwxyz1234567890$.,:;-'
!?

36 POINT VENUS LIGHT EXTENDED, BAUER

ABCDEFGHIJKLMNOPQRSTUV
WXYZ&abcdefghijklmnopqrstuvwx
yz1234567890$.,:;-'!?

30 POINT VENUS LIGHT EXTENDED, BAUER

ABCDEFGHIJKLMNOPQRSTUVWXYZ
&abcdefghijklmnopqrstuvwxyz123456789
0$.,:;-'!?

24 POINT VENUS LIGHT EXTENDED, BAUER

ABCDEFGHIJKLMNOPQRSTUVWXYZ&abcdef
ghijklmnopqrstuvwxyz1234567890$.,:;-'!?

18 POINT VENUS LIGHT EXTENDED, BAUER

ABCDEFGHIJKLMNOPQRSTUVWXYZ&abcdefghijk
lmnopqrstuvwxyz1234567890$.,:;-'!?

16 POINT VENUS LIGHT EXTENDED, BAUER

ABCDEFGHIJKLMNOPQRSTUVWXYZ&abcdefghijklmnopqrstu
vwxyz1234567890$.,:;-'!?

14 POINT VENUS LIGHT EXTENDED, BAUER

ABCDEFGHIJKLMNOPQRSTUVWXYZ&abcdefghijklmnopqrstuvwxyz12
34567890$.,:;-'?!

12 POINT VENUS LIGHT EXTENDED, BAUER

ABCDEFGHIJKLMNOPQRSTUVWXYZ&abcdefghijklmnopqrstuvwxyz1234567890$
.,:;-'!?

10 POINT VENUS LIGHT EXTENDED, BAUER

ABCDEFGHIJKLMN
OPQRSTUVWXYZ&
abcdefghijklmnopqrstu
vwxyz1234567890$.,:
;-'!?

42 POINT VENUS MEDIUM EXTENDED, BAUER

ABCDEFGHIJKLMNOPQR
STUVWXYZ&abcdefghijklm
nopqrstuvwxyz1234567890
$.,:;-'!?

36 POINT VENUS MEDIUM EXTENDED, BAUER

ABCDEFGHIJKLMNOPQRSTU
VWXYZ&abcdefghijklmnopqrstu
vwxyz1234567890$.,:;-'!?

30 POINT VENUS MEDIUM EXTENDED, BAUER

ABCDEFGHIJKLMNOPQRSTUVWXYZ&abcdefghijklmnopqrstuvwxyz1234567890$.,:;-'!?

24 POINT VENUS MEDIUM EXTENDED, BAUER

ABCDEFGHIJKLMNOPQRSTUVWXYZ&abcdefghijklmnopqrstuvwxyz1234567890$.,:;-'!?

18 POINT VENUS MEDIUM EXTENDED, BAUER

ABCDEFGHIJKLMNOPQRSTUVWXYZ&abcdefghijklmnopqrstuvwxyz1234567890$.,:;-'!?

16 POINT VENUS MEDIUM EXTENDED, BAUER

ABCDEFGHIJKLMNOPQRSTUVWXYZ&abcdefghijklmnopqrstuvwxyz1234567890$.,:;-'!?

14 POINT VENUS MEDIUM EXTENDED, BAUER

ABCDEFGHIJKLMNOPQRSTUVWXYZ&abcdefghijklmnopqrstuvwxyz1234567890$.,:;-'!?

12 POINT VENUS MEDIUM EXTENDED, BAUER

ABCDEFGHIJKLMNOPQRSTUVWXYZ&abcdefghijklmnopqrstuvwxyz1234567890$.,:;-'!?

10 POINT VENUS MEDIUM EXTENDED, BAUER

ABCDEFGHIJKL MNOPQRSTUVW XYZ&abcdefghijk lmnopqrstuvwxyz 1234567890$.,:; -'!?

42 POINT VENUS BOLD EXTENDED, BAUER

ABCDEFGHIJKLMNO PQRSTUVWXYZ&abc defghijklmnopqrstuvw xyz1234567890$.,:;-' !?

36 POINT VENUS BOLD EXTENDED, BAUER

ABCDEFGHIJKLMNOPQRS TUVWXYZ&abcdefghijklm nopqrstuvwxyz123456789 0$.,:;-'!?

30 POINT VENUS BOLD EXTENDED, BAUER

ABCDEFGHIJKLMNOPQRSTUV WXYZ&abcdefghijklmnopqrstu vwxyz1234567890$.,:;-'!?

24 POINT VENUS BOLD EXTENDED, BAUER

ABCDEFGHIJKLMNOPQRSTUVWXYZ&a bcdefghijklmnopqrstuvwxyz123456789 0$.,:;-'!?

18 POINT VENUS BOLD EXTENDED, BAUER

ABCDEFGHIJKLMNOPQRSTUVWXYZ&abcde fghijklmnopqrstuvwxyz1234567890$.,:;-'!?

16 POINT VENUS BOLD EXTENDED, BAUER

ABCDEFGHIJKLMNOPQRSTUVWXYZ&abcdefghijkl mnopqrstuvwxyz1234567890$.,:;-'!?

14 POINT VENUS BOLD EXTENDED, BAUER

ABCDEFGHIJKLMNOPQRSTUVWXYZ&abcdefghijklmnopqrstuv wxyz1234567890$.,:;-'!?

12 POINT VENUS BOLD EXTENDED, BAUER

ABCDEFGHIJKLMNOPQRSTUVWXYZ&abcdefghijklmnopqrstuvwxyz1234567 890 $.,:;-'!?

10 POINT VENUS BOLD EXTENDED, BAUER

ABCDEFGHIJK LMNOPQRSTU VWXYZ&abcde fghijklmnopqrs tuvwxyz12345 67890$.,:;-'!?

42 POINT VENUS EXTRA BOLD EXTENDED, BAUER

ABCDEFGHIJKLMN OPQRSTUVWXYZ& abcdefghijklmnopq rstuvwxyz1234567 890$.,:;-'!?

36 POINT VENUS EXTRA BOLD EXTENDED, BAUER

ABCDEFGHIJKLMNOPQ RSTUVWXYZ&abcdefg hijklmnopqrstuvwxyz12 34567890$.,:;-'!?

30 POINT VENUS EXTRA BOLD EXTENDED, BAUER

ABCDEFGHIJKLMNOPQRST UVWXYZ&abcdefghijklmno pqrstuvwxyz1234567890$.,:;-'!?

24 POINT VENUS EXTRA BOLD EXTENDED, BAUER

ABCDEFGHIJKLMNOPQRSTUVWXYZ &abcdefghijklmnopqrstuvwxyz1234 567890$.,:;-'!?

18 POINT VENUS EXTRA BOLD EXTENDED, BAUER

ABCDEFGHIJKLMNOPQRSTUVWXYZ&ab cdefghijklmnopqrstuvwxyz1234567890 $.,:;-'!?

16 POINT VENUS EXTRA BOLD EXTENDED, BAUER

ABCDEFGHIJKLMNOPQRSTUVWXYZ&abcdefghij klmnopqrstuvwxyz1234567890$.,:;-'!?

14 POINT VENUS EXTRA BOLD EXTENDED, BAUER

ABCDEFGHIJKLMNOPQRSTUVWXYZ&abcdefghijklmnopqrs tuvwxyz1234567890$.,:;-'!?

12 POINT VENUS EXTRA BOLD EXTENDED, BAUER

ABCDEFGHIJKLMNOPQRSTUVWXYZ&abcdefghijklmnopqrstuvwxyz123 4567890$.,:;-'!?

10 POINT VENUS EXTRA BOLD EXTENDED, BAUER

BANK SCRIPT

A B C D E F G H I J K L M N O P Q R S T U V W X Y Z & abcdefghijklmnopq rstuvwxyz1234567890$.,'=.;.!?"''

48 POINT BANK SCRIPT, ATF

A B C D E F G H I J K L M N O P Q R S T U V W X Y Z & abcdefghijklmnopqrstuvwxyz12345 67890$.,'=.;.!?"''

24 POINT BANK SCRIPT, ATF

A B C D E F G H I J K L M N O P Q R S T U V W X Y Z & abcdefghijklmnopqrstuvwx yz1234567890$.,'=.;.!?"''

14 POINT BANK SCRIPT, ATF

ABCDEF GHIJKLM NOPQRSTUVWXYZ Vabcdefghijklmnopqrstuvw xyz1234567890$.,'‹=:;!?''"

48 POINT COMMERCIAL SCRIPT, ATF

ABCDEFGHIJKLMNOPQRSTUVWX YZVabcdefghijklmnopqrstuvwxyz1234567890$.,'‹=:;!?''"

24 POINT COMMERCIAL SCRIPT, ATF

ABCDEFGHIJKLMNOPQRSTUVWXYZVabcdefghijklmnopqrstuvwxyz 1234567890$.,'‹=:;!?''"

14 POINT COMMERCIAL SCRIPT, ATF

DUTCH INITIALS

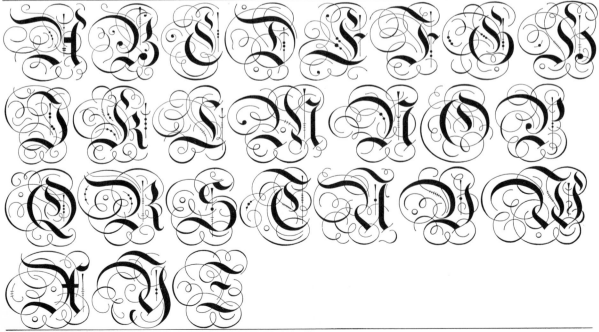

60 POINT DUTCH INITIALS, ATF

364

AABCDDEE
FFGHHIJKLLM
NOPQRKSSTT
UVWXYZThErabcdefgh
ijkl mnopqrstuvwxyz th 1234
567890$.,'-:;!?

60 POINT LEGEND, BAUER

AABCCDDEFFG
HHIJKLLMNOPQR
RSSTTUVWXYZThEr
abcdefghijklmnopqrstuvwxyzth123
4567890$.,'-:;!?

48 POINT LEGEND, BAUER

AABBCDDEEFfGHAIJKLLMNOPQRRRSSTTUVWXYZTh
Et abcdefghijklmnopqrstuvwxyzth1234567890$.,'-:;!?

18 POINT LEGEND, BAUER

LIBRA

abcdefghijklmnopqrstu
vwxyz&1234567890$.,"-:;!?""

36 POINT LIBRA, AMSTERDAM CONTINENTAL

abcdefghijklmnopqrstuvwxyz&1234567890$
.,"-:;!?""

24 POINT LIBRA, AMSTERDAM CONTINENTAL

abcdefghijklmnopqrstuvwxyz&1234567890$.,"-:;!?""

12 POINT LIBRA, AMSTERDAM CONTINENTAL

MISTRAL

ABCDEFGHIJKLMNOPQRSTUVWXY
Z&abcdefghijklmnopqrstuvwxyz123
4567890$.,''-:;!?"''

36 POINT MISTRAL, AMSTERDAM CONTINENTAL

ABCDEFGHIJKLMNOPQRSTUVWXYZ&abcdefghijklm
nopqrstuvwxyz1234567890$.,''-:;!?"''

24 POINT MISTRAL, AMSTERDAM CONTINENTAL

ABCDEFGHIJKLMNOPQRSTUVWXYZ&abcdefghijklmnopqrstuvwxyz123456789
0$.,''-:;!?"''

18 POINT MISTRAL, AMSTERDAM CONTINENTAL

366

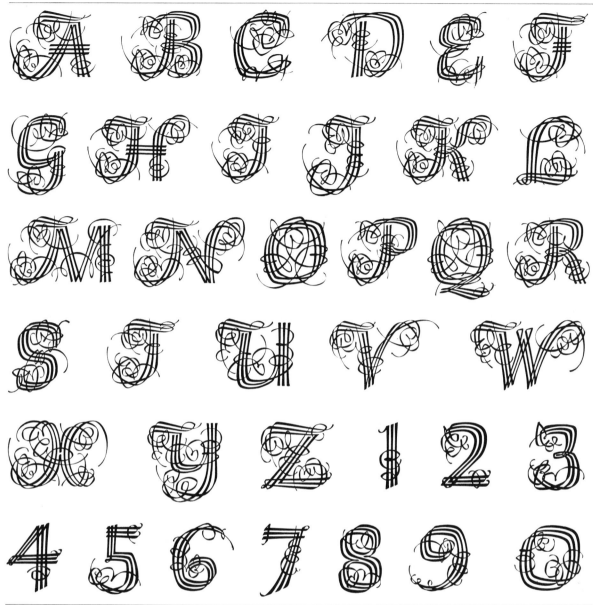

60/66 POINT RAFFIA INITIALS, AMSTERDAM CONTINENTAL

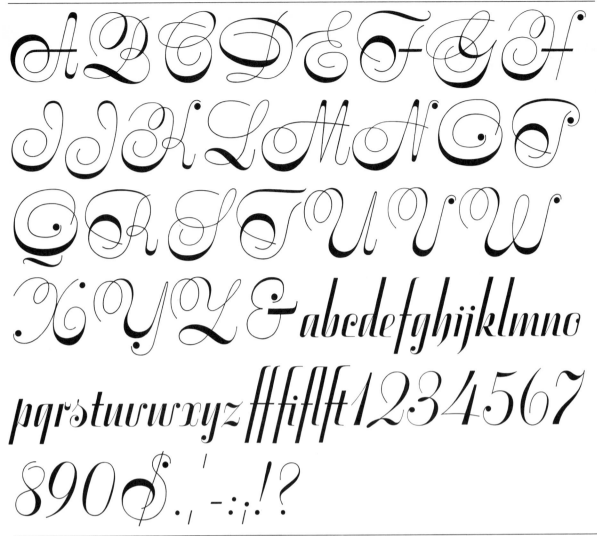

60 POINT STRADIVARIUS, BAUER

36 POINT STRADIVARIUS, BAUER

18 POINT STRADIVARIUS, BAUER

ABCDEFGHIJKLMNOPQRSTUVWX
YZ&abcdefghijklmnopqrstuvwxyz1234567890$
.,"-:;!?"""

30 POINT THOMPSON QUILLSCRIPT, ATF

ABCDEFGHIJKLMNOPQRSTUVWXYZ&abcdefgh
ijklmnopqrstuvwxyz1234567890$.,"-:;!?"""

24 POINT THOMPSON QUILLSCRIPT, ATF

ABCDEFGHIJKLMNOPQRSTUVWXYZ&abcdefghijklmnopqrstuvwxyz
1234567890$.,"-:;!?"""

18 POINT THOMPSON QUILLSCRIPT, ATF

TYPO SCRIPT

ABCDEFGHIJKLM
NOPQRSTUVWXYZ
& abcdefghijklmnopqrstuvwxyz1234
567890$.,"-:;!?"""

60 POINT TYPO SCRIPT, ATF

ABCDEFGHI JKLMNOP

QRSTUVWXYZ& abcdefghijklm

nopqrstuvwxyz1234567890$., "=:;!? ""''

48 POINT TYPO SCRIPT, ATF

ABCDEFGHI JKLMNOPQRSTUVWXYZ& abcdefghijklmnopqrstuvwxyz

fiffffffiffl1234567890$., "=:;!? ""''

18 POINT TYPO SCRIPT, ATF

ALBERTUS

ABCDEFGHIJKLMN
OPQRSTUVWXYZ&
abcdefghijklmnopqrst
uvwxyzfiffffflffififfl12345
67890$.,"-:;!?""''

48 POINT ALBERTUS, MOULDTYPE FOUNDRY LTD

ABCDEFGHIJKLMNOPQRST
UVWXYZ&abcdefghijklmno
pqrstuvwxyzfiffffflffififfl1234567
890$.,"-:;!?""''

36 POINT ALBERTUS, MOULDTYPE FOUNDRY LTD.

ABCDEFGHIJKLMNOPQRSTUVWXYZ&ab
cdefghijklmnopqrstuvwxyzfiffffflffififfl12345678
90$.,"-:;!?""''

24 POINT ALBERTUS, MOULDTYPE FOUNDRY LTD.

ABCDEFGHIJKL
MNOPQRSTUV
WXYZ&123456
7890$.,'-:;!9""`

48 POINT AUGUSTEA, AMSTERDAM CONTINENTAL

ABCDEFGHIJKLMNOPQRSTUVWXY
Z&1234567890$.,'-:;!9""`

24 POINT AUGUSTEA, AMSTERDAM CONTINENTAL

ABCDEFGHIJKLMNOPQRSTUVWXYZ&123456
7890$.,'-:;!9""`

18 POINT AUGUSTEA, AMSTERDAM CONTINENTAL

ABCDEFGHIJK
LMNOPQRST
UVWXYZ&123
4567890$.,'-:;!9

48 POINT AUGUSTEA SHADED, AMSTERDAM CONTINENTAL

ABCDEFGHIJKLMNOPQRSTUVWXY
Z&1234567890$.,'-:;!9""`

24 POINT AUGUSTEA SHADED, AMSTERDAM CONTINENTAL

ABCDEFGHIJKLMNOPQRSTUVWXYZ&123
4567890$.,'₌₌;!9""«

18 POINT AUGUSTEA SHADED, AMSTERDAM CONTINENTAL

EGIZIO

ABCDEFGHIJ
KLMNOPQRS
TUVWXYZ&a
bcdefghijklmno
pqrstuvwxyzfiff
flffifffl1234567890
$.," -:;!?""«

60 POINT EGIZIO MEDIUM, AMSTERDAM CONTINENTAL

ABCDEFGHIJKL
MNOPQRSTUVW
XYZ&abcdefghijkl
mnopqrstuvwxyzfi
ffflffifffl1234567890$
.," "-..!?""“
•, -•;••

48 POINT EGIZIO MEDIUM, AMSTERDAM CONTINENTAL

ABCDEFGHIJKL
MNOPQRSTUVW
XYZ&abcdefghijkl
mnopqrstuvwxyzfiff
flffifffl1234567890$
.," "-.;!?"”“
•, -•;••

48 POINT EGIZIO MEDIUM ITALIC, AMSTERDAM CONTINENTAL

ABCDEFGHIJKLMNOPQRSTUVW
XYZ&abcdefghijklmnopqrstuvwxyz
fifflffiffl1234567890$.,'-:;!?""''

24 POINT (large) EGIZIO MEDIUM, AMSTERDAM CONTINENTAL

ABCDEFGHIJKLMNOPQRSTUVWX
YZ&abcdefghijklmnopqrstuvwxyzfifffl
ffiffl1234567890$.,''-:;!?""''

24 POINT (large) EGIZIO MEDIUM ITALIC, AMSTERDAM CONTINENTAL

ABCDEFGHIJKLMNOPQRSTUVWXYZ&abcdefghijklm
nopqrstuvwxyzfifflffiffl1234567890$.,'-:;!?""''

18 POINT EGIZIO MEDIUM ITALIC, AMSTERDAM CONTINENTAL

ABCDEFGHIJKLMNOPQRSTUVWXYZ&abcdefghijk
lmnopqrstuvwxyzfifflffiffl1234567890$.,'-:;!?""''

18 POINT EGIZIO MEDIUM, AMSTERDAM CONTINENTAL

ABCDEFGHIJKLMNO
PQRSTUVWXYZ&abc
defghijklmnopqrstuvwxy
zfifffflffiffl1234567890$.,"-:
.!?""
,''

60 POINT EGIZIO MEDIUM CONDENSED, AMSTERDAM CONTNENTAL

ABCDEFGHIJKLMNOPQRS
TUVWXYZ&abcdefghijklmno
pqrstuvwxyzfifffflffifffl12345678
90$.,"-:;!?""

48 POINT EGIZIO MEDIUM CONDENSED, AMSTERDAM CONTNENTAL

ABCDEFGHIJKLMNOPQRSTUVWXYZ&abcdefghijklmn
opqrstuvwxyzfifffflffiffl1234567890$.,"-:;!?""

24 POINT (large) EGIZIO MEDIUM CONDENSED, AMSTERDAM CONTINENTAL

ELIZABETH

ABCDEFGHIJKLMNOP
QRSTUVWXYZ&abcdef
ghijklmnopqrstuvwxyzfffi
flft1234567890$.,'-:;!?

48 POINT ELIZABETH, BAUER

ABCDEFGHIJKLMNOP
QRSTUVWXYZ&abcdefgh
ijklmnopqrstuvwxyz fffifl ft 123
4567890$.,'-:;!?

48 POINT ELIZABETH ITALIC, BAUER

ABCDEFGHIJKLMNOPQRSTUVWXY
Z&abcdefghijklmnopqrstuvwxyzfffifl ft 12345
67890$.,'-:;!?

30 POINT ELIZABETH, BAUER

ABCDEFGHIJKLMNOPQRSTUVWXYZ
&abcdefghijklmnopqrstuvwxyz fffifl ft 12345678
90$.,'-:;!?

30 POINT ELIZABETH ITALIC, BAUER

ABCDEFGHIJKLMNOPQRSTUVWXYZ&abcdefghijklmnopqrstuvwx
yzfffifl ft 1234567890$.,'-:;!?

18 POINT ELIZABETH, BAUER

ABCDEFGHIJKLMNOPQRSTUVWXYZ&abcdefghijklmnopqrstuvwxyz fffifl ft
1234567890$.,'-:;!?

18 POINT ELIZABETH ITALIC, BAUER

377

ABCDEFGH IJKLMNOP QRSTUVW XYZ&abcdef ghijklmnopq rstuvwxyz12 34567890.,'-:;!?

60 POINT FORTUNE LIGHT, BAUER

ABCDEFGHIJKLM NOPQRSTUVWXY Z&abcdefghijklmnop qrstuvwxyz12345678 90$.,"-:;!?""

42 POINT FORTUNE LIGHT, BAUER

ABCDEFGHIJKLMNOPQRSTUVW
XYZ&abcdefghijklmnopqrstuvwxyz
1234567890$.,"-:;!?""

24 POINT FORTUNE LIGHT, BAUER

ABCDEFG
HIJKLMNO
PQRSTUV
WXYZ&abc
defghijklmn
opqrstuvwx
yz123456789
0$.,"-:;!?""

60 POINT FORTUNE BOLD, BAUER

ABCDEFGH
IJKLMNOP
QRSTUVWX
YZ&abcdefg
hijklmnopqr
stuvwxyzfifi
fl1234567890
$.,"-:;!?"''"

60 POINT FORTUNE BOLD ITALIC, BAUER

ABCDEFGHIJKL MNOPQRSTUVW XYZ&abcdefghijkl mnopqrstuvwxyz 1234567890$.,"-:;!?""

42 POINT FORTUNE BOLD, BAUER

ABCDEFGHIJKLM NOPQRSTUVWXYZ &abcdefghijklmnopq rstuvwxyzfifffl12345 67890$.,"-:;!?""

42 POINT FORTUNE BOLD ITALIC, BAUER

ABCDEFGHIJKLMNOPQRSTU
VWXYZ&abcdefghijklmnopqrstu
vwxyz1234567890$.,"-:;!?""

24 POINT FORTUNE BOLD, BAUER

ABCDEFGHIJKLMNOPQRSTUVWX
YZ&abcdefghijklmnopqrstuvwxyz
fifffl1234567890$.,"-:;!?""

24 POINT FORTUNE BOLD ITALIC, BAUER

ABCDEF
GHIJKLM
NOPQRS
TUVWXY
Z&abcdef
ghijklmn
opqrstuv
wxyz1234
567890$.,"-
.;!?""""

60 POINT FORTUNE EXTRA BOLD, BAUER

ABCDEFGHIJK LMNOPQRSTU VWXYZ&abcdef ghijklmnopqrst uvwxyz1234567 890$.,"-:;!?""

42 POINT FORTUNE EXTRA BOLD, BAUER

ABCDEFGHIJKLMNOPQR STUVWXYZ&abcdefghijklm nopqrstuvwxyz1234567890$.,"-:;!?""

24 POINT FORTUNE EXTRA BOLD, BAUER

ABCDEFGHIJKLMNO
PQRSTUVWXYZ&ab
cdefghijklmnopqrstuv
wxyzfifffl1234567890$
.,"-:;!?""

54 POINT PALATINO, AMSTERDAM CONTINENTAL

ABCDEFGHIJKLMNO
PQRSTUVWXYZ&ab
cdefghijklmnopqrstuvwxyz
fifffl1234567890$.,"-:;!?""

54 POINT PALATINO ITALIC, AMSTERDAM CONTINENTAL

ABCDEFGHIJKLMNOPQRSTUVW
XYZ&abcdefghijklmnopqrstuvwxyz
fifffl1234567890$.,"-:;!?""

30 POINT PALATINO, AMSTERDAM CONTINENTAL

ABCDEFGHIJKLMNOPQRSTUVW
XYZ&abcdefghijklmnopqrstuvwxyzfifffl
1234567890$.,"-:;!?""

30 POINT PALATINO ITALIC, AMSTERDAM CONTINENTAL

ABCDEFGHIJKLMNOPQRSTUVWXYZ&abcdefghijklmnopqrstuvwxyzfifffl
1234567890$.,"-:;!?""

14 POINT PALATINO, AMSTERDAM CONTINENTAL

ABCDEFGHIJKLMNOPQRSTUVWXYZ&abcdefghijklmnopqrstuvwxyzfifffl123456
7890$.,"-:;!?""

14 POINT PALATINO ITALIC, AMSTERDAM CONTINENTAL

ABCDEFGHIJKLMN
OPQRSTUVWXYZ&
abcdefghijklmnopqrst
uvwxyzfifffl12345678
90$.,"-:;!?""

54 POINT PALATINO SEMI BOLD, AMSTERDAM CONTINENTAL

ABCDEFGHIJKLMNOPQRSTUV
WXYZ&abcdefghijklmnopqrstuvw
xyzfifffl1234567890$.,"-:;!?""

30 POINT PALATINO SEMI BOLD, AMSTERDAM CONTINENTAL

ABCDEFGHIJKLMNOPQRSTUVWXYZ&abcdefghijklmnopqrstuvwxyz fifffl1234567890$.,"-:;!?""

14 POINT PALATINO SEMI BOLD, AMSTERDAM CONTINENTAL

PERPETUA

ABCDEFGHIJKLM NOPQRSTUVWX YZ&abcdefghijklmn opqrstuvwxyzfifffflffi ffl1234567890$.,"-:;!?""

60 POINT PERPETUA, MONOTYPE

ABCDEFGHIJKLMN
OPQRSTUVWXYZ
& abcdefghijklmnopqr
stuvwxyzfiffffflffiffl123
4567890$.,'"-:;!?""''

60 POINT PERPETUA ITALIC, MONOTYPE

ABCDEFGHIJKLMNOPQR
STUVWXYZ&abcdefghijklm
nopqrstuvwxyzfiffflffiffl1234
567890$.,'"-:;!?""''

42 POINT PERPETUA, MONOTYPE

ABCDEFGHIJKLMNOPQRST
UVWXYZ& abcdefghijklmnop
qrstuvwxyzfiffffflffiffl12345678
90$.,'"-:;!?""''

42 POINT PERPETUA ITALIC, MONOTYPE

ABCDEFGHIJKLMNOPQRSTUVWXYZ&abcdefg
hijklmnopqrstuvwxyzfiffflffiffl1234567890$.,"-:;!?""''

24 POINT PERPETUA, MONOTYPE

*ABCDEFGHIJKLMNOPQRSTUVWXYZ& abcdefghijklmn
opqrstuvwxyzfiffflffiffl1234567890$.,"-:;!?""''*

24 POINT PERPETUA ITALIC, MONOTYPE

ABCDEFGHIJKL MNOPQRSTUV WXYZ&abcdefg hijklmnopqrstuv wxyzfiffffl1234567 890$.,"-:;!?""''

60 POINT PERPETUA BOLD, MONOTYPE

**ABCDEFGHIJKLMNOPQRSTUVWXYZ&abc
defghijklmnopqrstuvwxyzfiffflffiffl12345678
90$.,"-:;!?""''**

24 POINT PERPETUA BOLD, MONOTYPE

Helvetica Light Roman
Helvetica Light Italic
Helvetica Roman
Helvetica Italic
Helvetica Bold Roman
Helvetica Bold Italic
Helvetica Bold Roman No. 2
Helvetica Black Roman
Helvetica Black Italic
Helvetica Light Condensed Roman
Helvetica Light Condensed Italic
Helvetica Condensed Roman
Helvetica Condensed Italic
Helvetica Bold Condensed Roman
Helvetica Bold Condensed Italic
Helvetica Black Condensed Roman
Helvetica Black Condensed Italic
Helvetica Bold Outline
Helvetica Inserat Roman
Helvetica Inserat Italic
Helvetica Compressed
Helvetica Extra Compressed
Helvetica Ultra Compressed

A virtual signature of many outstanding designers, Helvetica has had universal acceptance in the past decade. Used in many variations, and as display copy or as text in combination with other display faces, this beautiful and versatile type demands room in this book.

An historical factor, with subtle, far reaching implications, occurred during the 1960's. Phototype and the earnest onset of automated computerized typesetting gathered the momentum that has, after 500 years, changed the typesetter's art forever. By the end of this decade, hot metal and foundry type may be on its way to becoming a kind of folk art.

Computerized, automated typesetting became possible because the electronic technology for it was at hand. That same technology also paved the way for information gathering in a new sense. Those characteristics that make high speed, quality typesetting possible, also opened the door on a range of potential for communication as yet only partially explored.

Remote input stations, international information banks accumulating data from routine typesetting chores, more efficient storage and recall of political, scientific, military, and financial information, and world wide instant dissemination of trends, experience and creative effort have suddenly burst on the scene. Formerly thought of as futuristic technology, these techniques are now well beyond the theoretic stage.

But the route to understanding type will probably always include a preliminary study of traditional wood and metal types, their origins and development for centuries.

Phototype, being unrestricted by the conditions governing the production and use of metal type will, in time, alter its design characteristics. But for the present, phototypesetting, like any evolving technology, carries over most of the characteristics of the faces from which it derives. In many cases the original drawings for alphabets were simply rephotographed and put on film.

Yet slight differences in visual character developed, especially in the spacing of individual characters of text settings. The use of light sensitive surfaces to pick up the specific weight and character of each face gave a more precise rendition of alphabets that previously had to go through the typographer's repro-proving process. The question of aesthetic superiority may be argued for years to come.

To the left, is an abbreviated one line series of currently available variations on Helvetica, set on Mergenthaler V.I.P. (Variable Input Phototypesetter) for both display and text settings. And on the following pages, a relatively full showing of four basic weights of Helvetica, set on the V.I.P., a piece of equipment that responds to a computer, or may be directly activated by punched tapes representing original copy. The V.I.P. in turn produces the printouts you see reproduced on the following pages.

ABCDEFGHIJKLM NOPQRSTUVWXY Z&abcdefghijklmno pqrstuvwxyz12345 67890$.,"-:;!?""

60 POINT HELVETICA LIGHT, MERGENTHALER V.I.P.

ABCDEFGHIJKLMNOP QRSTUVWXYZ&abcdef ghijklmnopqrstuvwxyz1 234567890$.,"-:;!?""

48 POINT HELVETICA LIGHT, MERGENTHALER V.I.P.

ABCDEFGHIJKLMNOPQRSTUVWXY Z&abcdefghijklmnopqrstuvwxyz1234 567890$.,"-:;!?""

30 POINT HELVETICA LIGHT, MERGENTHALER V.I.P.

ABCDEFGHIJKLMNOPQRSTUVWXYZ&abc
defghijklmnopqrstuvwxyz1234567890$.,"-:;!?
24 POINT HELVETICA LIGHT, MERGENTHALER V.I.P.

ABCDEFGHIJKLMNOPQRSTUVWXYZ&abcdefghijkl
mnopqrstuvwxyz1234567890$.,"-:;!?""
20 POINT HELVETICA LIGHT, MERGENTHALER V.I.P.

ABCDEFGHIJKLMNOPQRSTUVWXYZ&abcdefghijklmnopq
rstuvwxyz1234567890$.,"-:;!?""
18 POINT HELVETICA LIGHT, MERGENTHALER V.I.P.

ABCDEFGHIJKLMNOPQRSTUVWXYZ&abcdefghijklmnopqrstuvwxyz123
4567890$.,"-:;!?""
14 POINT HELVETICA LIGHT, MERGENTHALER V.I.P.

*ABCDEFGHIJKLMNOPQR
STUVWXYZ&abcdefghijklm
nopqrstuvwxyz1234567890
$.,"-:;!?""*
42 POINT HELVETICA LIGHT, MERGENTHALER V.I.P.

*ABCDEFGHIJKLMNOPQRSTUVWXYZ&abcdefg
hijklmnopqrstuvwxyz1234567890$.,"-:;!?""*
22 POINT HELVETICA LIGHT, MERGENTHALER V.I.P.

*ABCDEFGHIJKLMNOPQRSTUVWXYZ&abcdefghijklmnopqrstuvwxyz123
4567890$.,"-:;!?""*
14 POINT HELVETICA LIGHT, MERGENTHALER V.I.P.

ABCDEFGHIJKLM NOPQRSTUVWX YZ&abcdefghijklmn opqrstuvwxyz1234 567890$.,"-:;!?""

60 POINT HELVETICA REGULAR, MERGENTHALER V.I.P.

ABCDEFGHIJKLMNOP QRSTUVWXYZ&abcd efghijklmnopqrstuvwxyz 1234567890$.,"-:;!?""

48 POINT HELVETICA REGULAR, MERGENTHALER V.I.P.

ABCDEFGHIJKLMNOPQRSTUVWX
YZ&abcdefghijklmnopqrstuvwxyz123
4567890$.,"-:;!?""

30 POINT HELVETICA REGULAR, MERGENTHALER V.I.P.

ABCDEFGHIJKLMNOPQRSTUVWXYZ&abc
defghijklmnopqrstuvwxyz1234567890$.,"-:;!?

24 POINT HELVETICA REGULAR, MERGENTHALER V.I.P.

ABCDEFGHIJKLMNOPQRSTUVWXYZ&abcdefghijkl
mnopqrstuvwxyz1234567890$.,"-:;!?"""

20 POINT HELVETICA REGULAR, MERGENTHALER V.I.P.

ABCDEFGHIJKLMNOPQRSTUVWXYZ&abcdefghijklmnop
qrstuvwxyz1234567890$.,"-:;!?"""

18 POINT HELVETICA REGULAR, MERGENTHALER V.I.P.

ABCDEFGHIJKLMNOPQRSTUVWXYZ&abcdefghijklmnopqrstuvwxyz123
4567890$.,"-:;!?"""

14 POINT HELVETICA REGULAR, MERGENTHALER V.I.P.

ABCDEFGHIJKLMNOPQR
STUVWXYZ&abcdefghijklm
nopqrstuvwxyz1234567890
$.,"-:;!?"""

42 POINT HELVETICA REGULAR, MERGENTHALER V.I.P.

ABCDEFGHIJKLMNOPQRSTUVWXYZ&abcdef
ghijklmnopqrstuvwxyz1234567890$.,"-:;!?"""

22 POINT HELVETICA REGULAR, MERGENTHALER V.I.P.

ABCDEFGHIJKLMNOPQRSTUVWXYZ&abcdefghijklmnopqrstuvwxyz12
34567890$.,"-:;!?"""

14 POINT HELVETICA REGULAR, MERGENTHALER V.I.P.

ABCDEFGHIJKL MNOPQRSTUVW XYZ&abcdefghijkl mnopqrstuvwxyz 1234567890$.,"-:;!

60 POINT HEGVETICA BOLD, MERGENTHALER V.I.P.

ABCDEFGHIJKLMNO PQRSTUVWXYZ&abc defghijklmnopqrstuvw xyz1234567890$.,"-:;! ?""

48 POINT HELVETICA BOLD, MERGENTHALER V.I.P.

ABCDEFGHIJKLMNOPQRSTUVW XYZ&abcdefghijklmnopqrstuvwxy z1234567890$.,"-:;!?""

30 POINT HELVETICA BOLD, MERGENTHALER V.I.P.

394

ABCDEFGHIJKLMNOPQRSTUVWXYZ&ab
cdefghijklmnopqrstuvwxyz1234567890$.,"
-:;!?""

24 POINT HELVETICA BOLD, MERGENTHALER V.I.P.

ABCDEFGHIJKLMNOPQRSTUVWXYZ&abcdefghij
klmnopqrstuvwxyz1234567890$.,"-:;!?""

20 POINT HELVETICA BOLD, MERGENTHALER V.I.P.

ABCDEFGHIJKLMNOPQRSTUVWXYZ&abcdefghijklmn
opqrstuvwxyz1234567890$.,"-:;!?""

18 POINT HELVETICA BOLD, MERGENTHALER V.I.P.

ABCDEFGHIJKLMNOPQRSTUVWXYZ&abcdefghijklmnopqrstuvwxyz
1234567890$.,"-:;!?""

14 POINT HELVETICA BOLD, MERGENTHALER V.I.P.

*ABCDEFGHIJKLMNOPQR
STUVWXYZ&abcdefghijkl
mnopqrstuvwxyz1234567
890$.,"-:;!?""*

42 POINT HELVETICA BOLD, MERGENTHALER V.I.P.

*ABCDEFGHIJKLMNOPQRSTUVWXYZ&abcdef
ghijklmnopqrstuvwxyz1234567890$.,"-:;!?""*

22 POINT HELVETICA BOLD, MERGENTHALER V.I.P.

*ABCDEFGHIJKLMNOPQRSTUVWXYZ&abcdefghijklmnopqrstuvwxyz
1234567890$.,"-:;!?""*

14 POINT HELVETICA BOLD, MERGENTHALER V.I.P.

ABCDEFGHIJK LMNOPQRSTU VWXYZ&abcde fghijklmnopqrst uvwxyz123456

60 POINT HELVETICA BLACK, MERGENTHALER V.I.P.

ABCDEFGHIJKLMN OPQRSTUVWXYZ &abcdefghijklmnop qrstuvwxyz123456 7890$.,"-.;;!?"''

48 POINT HELVETICA BLACK, MERGENTHALER V.I.P.

ABCDEFGHIJKLMNOPQRSTU VWXYZ&abcdefghijklmnopqrs tuvwxyz1234567890$.,"-.;;!?"''

30 POINT HELVETICA BLACK, MERGENTHALER V.I.P.

ABCDEFGHIJKLMNOPQRSTUVWXY Z&abcdefghijklmnopqrstuvwxyz123 4567890$.,"-:;!?""''

24 POINT HELVETICA BLACK, MERGENTHALER V.I.P.

ABCDEFGHIJKLMNOPQRSTUVWXYZ&abc defghijklmnopqrstuvwxyz1234567890$.,"-:; !?""''

20 POINT HELVETICA BLACK, MERGENTHALER V.I.P.

ABCDEFGHIJKLMNOPQRSTUVWXYZ&abcdefghi jklmnopqrstuvwxyz1234567890$.,"-:;!?""''

18 POINT HELVETICA BLACK, MERGENTHALER V.I.P.

ABCDEFGHIJKLMNOPQRSTUVWXYZ&abcdefghijklmnopqrst uvwxyz1234567890$.,"-:;!?""''

14 POINT HELVETICA BLACK, MERGENTHALER V.I.P.

ABCDEFGHIJKLMNOP QRSTUVWXYZ&abcdef ghijklmnopqrstuvwxyz1 234567890$.,"-:;!?""''

42 POINT HELVETICA BLACK, MERGENTHALER V.I.P.

ABCDEFGHIJKLMNOPQRSTUVWXYZ&a bcdefghijklmnopqrstuvwxyz1234567890 $.,"-:;!?""''

22 POINT HELVETICA BLACK, MERGENTHALER V.I.P.

ABCDEFGHIJKLMNOPQRSTUVWXYZ&abcdefghijklmnopqrs tuvwxyz1234567890$.,"-:;!?""''

14 POINT HELVETICA BLACK, MERGENTHALER V.I.P.

14/15 Typography is closely allied to the fine arts, and types have always reflected the taste or feeling of their time. The charm of the early Italian types has perhaps never been equalled; and the like is true of the Renaissance manuscripts on which they were based — and of many other departments of art in that same wonderful time. Note, too,
Typography is closely allied to the fine arts, and types have always re-

14/18 Typography is closely allied to the fine arts, and types have always reflected the taste or feeling of their time. The charm of the early Italian types has perhaps never been equalled; and the like is true of the Renaissance manuscripts on which they were based —
Typography is closely allied to the fine arts, and types have always re-

11/12 Typography is closely allied to the fine arts, and types have always reflected the taste or feeling of their time. The charm of the early Italian types has perhaps never been equalled; and the like is true of the Renaissance manuscripts on which they were based — and of many other departments of art in that same wonderful time. Note, too, the relation of the French manuscripts and types of a slightly later date to the manuscripts
Typography is closely allied to the fine arts, and types have always reflected the taste or

11/15 Typography is closely allied to the fine arts, and types have always reflected the taste or feeling of their time. The charm of the early Italian types has perhaps never been equalled; and the like is true of the Renaissance manuscripts on which they were based — and of many other departments of art in that same wonderful time. Note,
Typography is closely allied to the fine arts, and types have always reflected the taste or

12/13 Typography is closely allied to the fine arts, and types have always reflected the taste or feeling of their time. The charm of the early Italian types has perhaps never been equalled; and the like is true of the Renaissance manuscripts on which they were based — and of many other departments of art in that same wonderful time. Note, too, the relation of the French manuscripts and types of a slightly later date to the manuscripts and
Typography is closely allied to the fine arts, and types have always reflected the

12/16 Typography is closely allied to the fine arts, and types have always reflected the taste or feeling of their time. The charm of the early Italian types has perhaps never been equalled; and the like is true of the Renaissance manuscripts on which they were based — and of many other departments of art in that same wonderful time. Note, too, the
Typography is closely allied to the fine arts, and types have always reflected the

10/11 Typography is closely allied to the fine arts, and types have always reflected the taste or feeling of their time. The charm of the early Italian types has perhaps never been equalled; and the like is true of the Renaissance manuscripts on which they were based — and of many other departments of art in that same wonderful time. Note, too, the relation of the French manuscripts and types of a slightly later date to the manuscripts and the types of the Italian Renaissance.
Typography is closely allied to the fine arts, and types have always reflected the taste or feeling of

10/14 Typography is closely allied to the fine arts, and types have always reflected the taste or feeling of their time. The charm of the early Italian types has perhaps never been equalled; and the like is true of the Renaissance manuscripts on which they were based — and of many other departments of art in that same wonderful time. Note, too, the relation of the French manuscripts and types of a slightly later
Typography is closely allied to the fine arts, and types have always reflected the taste or feeling of

HELVETICA: PHOTOTYPE, V.I.P.

14 Abcdefghijklmnopqrstu
12 Abcdefghijklmnopqrstuvwx
11 Abcdefghijklmnopqrstuvwxyz
10 Abcdefghijklmnopqrstuvwxyz12

14 Abcdefghijklmnopqrstuvw
12 Abcdefghijklmnopqrstuvwxyz
11 Abcdefghijklmnopqrstuvwxyz1
10 Abcdefghijklmnopqrstuvwxyz12

14 Abcdefghijklmnopqrstuv
12 Abcdefghijklmnopqrstuvwx
11 Abcdefghijklmnopqrstuvwxyz
10 Abcdefghijklmnopqrstuvwxyz1

NORMAL METAL SPACING

NORMAL PHOTOTYPE SPACING

TIGHT PHOTOTYPE SPACING

9/10 Typography is closely allied to the fine arts, and types have always reflected the taste or feeling of their time. The charm of the early Italian types has perhaps never been equalled; and the like is true of the Renaissance manuscripts on which they were based — and of many other departments of art in that same wonderful time. Note, too, the relation of the French manuscripts and types of a slightly later date to the manuscripts and the types of the Italian Renaissance.

In spite of the increasing interest in the history of printing, and the attention paid in many quarters to the work of famous typographers, a knowledge of standards among the rank and file of printers is still greatly lacking. To the average printer of to-day, type is type, printing is *Typography is closely allied to the fine arts, and types have always reflected the taste or feeling of their time. The*

8/9 Typography is closely allied to the fine arts, and types have always reflected the taste or feeling of their time. The charm of the early Italian types has perhaps never been equalled; and the like is true of the Renaissance manuscripts on which they were based — and of many other departments of art in that same wonderful time. Note, too, the relation of the French manuscripts and types of a slightly later date to the manuscripts and the types of the Italian Renaissance.

In spite of the increasing interest in the history of printing, and the attention paid in many quarters to the work of famous typographers, a knowledge of standards among the rank and file of printers is still greatly lacking. To the average printer of to-day, type is type, printing is printing — it is all about alike; and he concerns himself only with alleged labour-saving contrivances, or new type-faces that ensure convenience at the expense of proper design. In a more advanced class is to be found the printer who, *Typography is closely allied to the fine arts, and types have always reflected the taste or feeling of their time. The charm of the*

9/13 Typography is closely allied to the fine arts, and types have always reflected the taste or feeling of their time. The charm of the early Italian types has perhaps never been equalled; and the like is true of the Renaissance manuscripts on which they were based — and of many other departments of art in that same wonderful time. Note, too, the relation of the French manuscripts and types of a slightly later date to the manuscripts and the types of the Italian Renaissance.

In spite of the increasing interest in the history of *Typography is closely allied to the fine arts, and types have always reflected the taste or feeling of their time. The*

8/12 Typography is closely allied to the fine arts, and types have always reflected the taste or feeling of their time. The charm of the early Italian types has perhaps never been equalled; and the like is true of the Renaissance manuscripts on which they were based — and of many other departments of art in that same wonderful time. Note, too, the relation of the French manuscripts and types of a slightly later date to the manuscripts and the types of the Italian Renaissance.

In spite of the increasing interest in the history of printing, and the attention paid in many quarters to the work of famous typographers, a knowledge of standards among the rank and file *Typography is closely allied to the fine arts, and types have always reflected the taste or feeling of their time. The charm of the*

7/8 Typography is closely allied to the fine arts, and types have always reflected the taste or feeling of their time. The charm of the early Italian types has perhaps never been equalled; and the like is true of the Renaissance manuscripts on which they were based — and of many other departments of art in that same wonderful time. Note, too, the relation of the French manuscripts and types of a slightly later date to the manuscripts and the types of the Italian Renaissance.

In spite of the increasing interest in the history of printing, and the attention paid in many quarters to the work of famous typographers, a knowledge of standards among the rank and file of printers is still greatly lacking. To the average printer of to-day, type is type, printing is printing — it is all about alike; and he concerns himself only with alleged labour-saving contrivances, or new type-faces that ensure convenience at the expense of proper design. In a more advanced class is to be found the printer who, knowing something of the historical side of printing and *Typography is closely allied to the fine arts, and types have always reflected the taste or feeling of their time. The charm of the early Italian*

6/7 Typography is closely allied to the fine arts, and types have always reflected the taste or feeling of their time. The charm of the early Italian types has perhaps never been equalled; and the like is true of the Renaissance manuscripts on which they were based — and of many other departments of art in that same wonderful time. Note, too, the relation of the French manuscripts and types of a slightly later date to the manuscripts and the types of the Italian Renaissance.

In spite of the increasing interest in the history of printing, and the attention paid in many quarters to the work of famous typographers, a knowledge of standards among the rank and file of printers is still greatly lacking. To the average printer of to-day, type is type, printing is printing — it is all about alike; and he concerns himself only with alleged labour-saving contrivances, or new type-faces that ensure convenience at the expense of proper design. In a more advanced class is to be found the printer who, knowing something of the historical side of printing and realizing intellectually that there is a standard of excellence, yet has never considered the question as applying in any practical way to himself or his work.

Typography is closely allied to the fine arts, and types have always reflected the taste or feeling of their time. The charm of the early Italian types has perhaps never *Typography is closely allied to the fine arts, and types have always reflected the taste or feeling of their time. The charm of the early Italian types has perhaps never*

7/11 Typography is closely allied to the fine arts, and types have always reflected the taste or feeling of their time. The charm of the early Italian types has perhaps never been equalled; and the like is true of the Renaissance manuscripts on which they were based — and of many other departments of art in that same wonderful time. Note, too, the relation of the French manuscripts and types of a slightly later date to the manuscripts and the types of the Italian Renaissance.

In spite of the increasing interest in the history of printing, and the attention paid in many quarters to the work of famous typographers, a knowledge of standards among the rank and file of printers is still greatly lacking. To the average printer of to-day, type is type, printing is printing *Typography is closely allied to the fine arts, and types have always reflected the taste or feeling of their time. The charm of the early Italian*

6/10 Typography is closely allied to the fine arts, and types have always reflected the taste or feeling of their time. The charm of the early Italian types has perhaps never been equalled; and the like is true of the Renaissance manuscripts on which they were based — and of many other departments of art in that same wonderful time. Note, too, the relation of the French manuscripts and types of a slightly later date to the manuscripts and the types of the Italian Renaissance.

In spite of the increasing interest in the history of printing, and the attention paid in many quarters to the work of famous typographers, a knowledge of standards among the rank and file of printers is still greatly lacking. To the average printer of to-day, type is type, printing is printing — it is all about alike; and he concerns himself only with alleged labour-saving contrivances, or new type-faces that ensure convenience at the expense of proper design. In a more advanced class is *Typography is closely allied to the fine arts, and types have always reflected the taste or feeling of their time. The charm of the early Italian types has perhaps never*

HELVETICA: PHOTOTYPE, V.I.P.

9 Abcdefghijklmnopqrstuvwxyz1234
8 Abcdefghijklmnopqrstuvwxyz12345678
7 Abcdefghijklmnopqrstuvwxyz1234567890
6 Abcdefghijklmnopqrstuvwxyz1234567890

NORMAL METAL SPACING

9 Abcdefghijklmnopqrstuvwxyz12345
8 Abcdefghijklmnopqrstuvwxyz123456789
7 Abcdefghijklmnopqrstuvwxyz1234567890
6 Abcdefghijklmnopqrstuvwxyz1234567890

NORMAL PHOTOTYPE SPACING

9 Abcdefghijklmnopqrstuvwxyz12345
8 Abcdefghijklmnopqrstuvwxyz123456789
7 Abcdefghijklmnopqrstuvwxyz1234567890
6 Abcdefghijklmnopqrstuvwxyz1234567890

TIGHT PHOTOTYPE SPACING

14/15 Typography is closely allied to the fine arts, and types have always reflected the taste or feeling of their time. The charm of the early Italian types has perhaps never been equalled; and the like is true of the Renaissance manuscripts on which they were based — and of many other departments of art in that same wonderful time. Note, too,

Typography is closely allied to the fine arts, and types have always re-

14/18 Typography is closely allied to the fine arts, and types have always reflected the taste or feeling of their time. The charm of the early Italian types has perhaps never been equalled; and the like is true of the Renaissance manuscripts on which they were based —

Typography is closely allied to the fine arts, and types have always re-

12/13 Typography is closely allied to the fine arts, and types have always reflected the taste or feeling of their time. The charm of the early Italian types has perhaps never been equalled; and the like is true of the Renaissance manuscripts on which they were based — and of many other departments of art in that same wonderful time. Note, too, the relation of the French manuscripts and types of a slightly later date to the manuscripts and

Typography is closely allied to the fine arts, and types have always reflected the

12/16 Typography is closely allied to the fine arts, and types have always reflected the taste or feeling of their time. The charm of the early Italian types has perhaps never been equalled; and the like is true of the Renaissance manuscripts on which they were based — and of many other departments of art in that same wonderful time. Note, too, the

Typography is closely allied to the fine arts, and types have always reflected the

11/12 Typography is closely allied to the fine arts, and types have always reflected the taste or feeling of their time. The charm of the early Italian types has perhaps never been equalled; and the like is true of the Renaissance manuscripts on which they were based — and of many other departments of art in that same wonderful time. Note, too, the relation of the French manuscripts and types of a slightly later date to the manuscripts and the

Typography is closely allied to the fine arts, and types have always reflected the taste or

11/15 Typography is closely allied to the fine arts, and types have always reflected the taste or feeling of their time. The charm of the early Italian types has perhaps never been equalled; and the like is true of the Renaissance manuscripts on which they were based — and of many other departments of art in that same wonderful time. Note, too, the

Typography is closely allied to the fine arts, and types have always reflected the taste or

10/11 Typography is closely allied to the fine arts, and types have always reflected the taste or feeling of their time. The charm of the early Italian types has perhaps never been equalled; and the like is true of the Renaissance manuscripts on which they were based — and of many other departments of art in that same wonderful time. Note, too, the relation of the French manuscripts and types of a slightly later date to the manuscripts and the types of the Italian Renaissance.

Typography is closely allied to the fine arts, and types have always reflected the taste or feeling of

10/14 Typography is closely allied to the fine arts, and types have always reflected the taste or feeling of their time. The charm of the early Italian types has perhaps never been equalled; and the like is true of the Renaissance manuscripts on which they were based — and of many other departments of art in that same wonderful time. Note, too, the relation of the French manuscripts and types of a slightly later date to the

Typography is closely allied to the fine arts, and types have always reflected the taste or feeling of

HELVETICA: PHOTOTYPE, V.I.P.

14 Abcdefghijklmnopqrstuv
12 Abcdefghijklmnopqrstuvwxy
11 Abcdefghijklmnopqrstuvwxyz1
10 Abcdefghijklmnopqrstuvwxyz123

NORMAL METAL SPACING

14 Abcdefghijklmnopqrstuvw
12 Abcdefghijklmnopqrstuvwxyz
11 Abcdefghijklmnopqrstuvwxyz12
10 Abcdefghijklmnopqrstuvwxyz123

NORMAL PHOTOTYPE SPACING

14 Abcdefghijklmnopqrstuvwx
12 Abcdefghijklmnopqrstuvwxyz1
11 Abcdefghijklmnopqrstuvwxyz12
10 Abcdefghijklmnopqrstuvwxyz1234

TIGHT PHOTOTYPE SPACING

9/10 Typography is closely allied to the fine arts, and types have always reflected the taste or feeling of their time. The charm of the early Italian types has perhaps never been equalled; and the like is true of the Renaissance manuscripts on which they were based — and of many other departments of art in that same wonderful time. Note, too, the relation of the French manuscripts and types of a slightly later date to the manuscripts and the types of the Italian Renaissance.

In spite of the increasing interest in the history of printing, and the attention paid in many quarters to the work of famous typographers, a knowledge of standards among the rank and file of printers is still greatly lacking. To the average printer of to-day, type is type, printing is printing — it is all about alike; and he concerns himself only with *Typography is closely allied to the fine arts, and types have always reflected the taste or feeling of their time. The*

8/9 Typography is closely allied to the fine arts, and types have always reflected the taste or feeling of their time. The charm of the early Italian types has perhaps never been equalled; and the like is true of the Renaissance manuscripts on which they were based — and of many other departments of art in that same wonderful time. Note, too, the relation of the French manuscripts and types of a slightly later date to the manuscripts and the types of the Italian Renaissance.

In spite of the increasing interest in the history of printing, and the attention paid in many quarters to the work of famous typographers, a knowledge of standards among the rank and file of printers is still greatly lacking. To the average printer of to-day, type is type, printing is printing — it is all about alike; and he concerns himself only with alleged labour-saving contrivances, or new type-faces that ensure convenience at the expense of proper design. In a more advanced class is to be found the printer who, *Typography is closely allied to the fine arts, and types have always reflected the taste or feeling of their time. The charm of the*

9/13 Typography is closely allied to the fine arts, and types have always reflected the taste or feeling of their time. The charm of the early Italian types has perhaps never been equalled; and the like is true of the Renaissance manuscripts on which they were based — and of many other departments of art in that same wonderful time. Note, too, the relation of the French manuscripts and types of a slightly later date to the manuscripts and the types of the Italian Renaissance.

In spite of the increasing interest in the history of printing, and the attention paid in many quarters to the work of *Typography is closely allied to the fine arts, and types have always reflected the taste or feeling of their time. The*

8/12 Typography is closely allied to the fine arts, and types have always reflected the taste or feeling of their time. The charm of the early Italian types has perhaps never been equalled; and the like is true of the Renaissance manuscripts on which they were based — and of many other departments of art in that same wonderful time. Note, too, the relation of the French manuscripts and types of a slightly later date to the manuscripts and the types of the Italian Renaissance.

In spite of the increasing interest in the history of printing, and the attention paid in many quarters to the work of famous typographers, a knowledge of standards among the rank and file of *Typography is closely allied to the fine arts, and types have always reflected the taste or feeling of their time. The charm of the*

7/8 Typography is closely allied to the fine arts, and types have always reflected the taste or feeling of their time. The charm of the early Italian types has perhaps never been equalled; and the like is true of the Renaissance manuscripts on which they were based — and of many other departments of art in that same wonderful time. Note, too, the relation of the French manuscripts and types of a slightly later date to the manuscripts and the types of the Italian Renaissance.

In spite of the increasing interest in the history of printing, and the attention paid in many quarters to the work of famous typographers, a knowledge of standards among the rank and file of printers is still greatly lacking. To the average printer of to-day, type is type, printing is printing — it is all about alike; and he concerns himself only with alleged labour-saving contrivances, or new type-faces that ensure convenience at the expense of proper design. In a more advanced class is to be found the printer who, knowing something of the historical side of printing and *Typography is closely allied to the fine arts, and types have always reflected the taste or feeling of their time. The charm of the early Italian*

6/7 Typography is closely allied to the fine arts, and types have always reflected the taste or feeling of their time. The charm of the early Italian types has perhaps never been equalled; and the like is true of the Renaissance manuscripts on which they were based — and of many other departments of art in that same wonderful time. Note, too, the relation of the French manuscripts and types of a slightly later date to the manuscripts and the types of the Italian Renaissance.

In spite of the increasing interest in the history of printing, and the attention paid in many quarters to the work of famous typographers, a knowledge of standards among the rank and file of printers is still greatly lacking. To the average printer of to-day, type is type, printing is printing — it is all about alike; and he concerns himself only with alleged labour-saving contrivances, or new type-faces that ensure convenience at the expense of proper design. In a more advanced class is to be found the printer who, knowing something of the historical side of printing and realizing intellectually that there is a standard of excellence, yet has never considered the question as applying in any practical way to himself or his work.

Typography is closely allied to the fine arts, and types have always reflected the taste or feeling of their time. The charm of the early Italian types has perhaps never been *Typography is closely allied to the fine arts, and types have always reflected the taste or feeling of their time. The charm of the early Italian types has perhaps never*

7/11 Typography is closely allied to the fine arts, and types have always reflected the taste or feeling of their time. The charm of the early Italian types has perhaps never been equalled; and the like is true of the Renaissance manuscripts on which they were based — and of many other departments of art in that same wonderful time. Note, too, the relation of the French manuscripts and types of a slightly later date to the manuscripts and the types of the Italian Renaissance.

In spite of the increasing interest in the history of printing, and the attention paid in many quarters to the work of famous typographers, a knowledge of standards among the rank and file of printers is still greatly lacking. To the average printer of to-day, type is type, printing is printing — *Typography is closely allied to the fine arts, and types have always reflected the taste or feeling of their time. The charm of the early Italian*

6/10 Typography is closely allied to the fine arts, and types have always reflected the taste or feeling of their time. The charm of the early Italian types has perhaps never been equalled; and the like is true of the Renaissance manuscripts on which they were based — and of many other departments of art in that same wonderful time. Note, too, the relation of the French manuscripts and types of a slightly later date to the manuscripts and the types of the Italian Renaissance.

In spite of the increasing interest in the history of printing, and the attention paid in many quarters to the work of famous typographers, a knowledge of standards among the rank and file of printers is still greatly lacking. To the average printer of to-day, type is type, printing is printing — it is all about alike; and he concerns himself only with alleged labour-saving contrivances, or new type-faces that ensure convenience at the expense of proper design. In a more advanced class is *Typography is closely allied to the fine arts, and types have always reflected the taste or feeling of their time. The charm of the early Italian types has perhaps never*

HELVETICA: PHOTOTYPE, V.I.P.

9 Abcdefghijklmnopqrstuvwxyz12345
8 Abcdefghijklmnopqrstuvwxyz123456789
7 Abcdefghijklmnopqrstuvwxyz1234567890
6 Abcdefghijklmnopqrstuvwxyz1234567890

9 Abcdefghijklmnopqrstuvwxyz123456
8 Abcdefghijklmnopqrstuvwxyz123456789
7 Abcdefghijklmnopqrstuvwxyz1234567890
6 Abcdefghijklmnopqrstuvwxyz1234567890

9 Abcdefghijklmnopqrstuvwxyz123456
8 Abcdefghijklmnopqrstuvwxyz1234567890
7 Abcdefghijklmnopqrstuvwxyz1234567890
6 Abcdefghijklmnopqrstuvwxyz1234567890

NORMAL METAL SPACING

NORMAL PHOTOTYPE SPACING

TIGHT PHOTOTYPE SPACING

14/15 Typography is closely allied to the fine arts, and types have always reflected the taste or feeling of their time. The charm of the early Italian types has perhaps never been equalled; and the like is true of the Renaissance manuscripts on which they were based — and of many other departments of art in that
Typography is closely allied to the fine arts, and types have always re-

12/13 Typography is closely allied to the fine arts, and types have always reflected the taste or feeling of their time. The charm of the early Italian types has perhaps never been equalled; and the like is true of the Renaissance manuscripts on which they were based — and of many other departments of art in that same wonderful time. Note, too, the relation of the French manuscripts and types of a slightly later
Typography is closely allied to the fine arts, and types have always reflected the

14/18 Typography is closely allied to the fine arts, and types have always reflected the taste or feeling of their time. The charm of the early Italian types has perhaps never been equalled; and the like is true of the Renaissance manuscripts on which
Typography is closely allied to the fine arts, and types have always re-

12/16 Typography is closely allied to the fine arts, and types have always reflected the taste or feeling of their time. The charm of the early Italian types has perhaps never been equalled; and the like is true of the Renaissance manuscripts on which they were based — and of many other depart-ments of art in that same wonderful time.
Typography is closely allied to the fine arts, and types have always reflected the

11/12 Typography is closely allied to the fine arts, and types have always reflected the taste or feeling of their time. The charm of the early Italian types has perhaps never been equalled; and the like is true of the Renais-sance manuscripts on which they were based — and of many other departments of art in that same wonderful time. Note, too, the rela-tion of the French manuscripts and types of a
Typography is closely allied to the fine arts, and types have always reflected the taste or

10/11 Typography is closely allied to the fine arts, and types have always reflected the taste or feeling of their time. The charm of the early Italian types has perhaps never been equalled; and the like is true of the Renaissance manuscripts on which they were based — and of many other departments of art in that same wonderful time. Note, too, the relation of the French manuscripts and types of a slightly later date to the manuscripts and the types of the Italian Renaissance.
Typography is closely allied to the fine arts, and types have always reflected the taste or feeling of

11/15 Typography is closely allied to the fine arts, and types have always reflected the taste or feeling of their time. The charm of the early Italian types has perhaps never been equalled; and the like is true of the Renais-sance manuscripts on which they were based — and of many other departments of art in
Typography is closely allied to the fine arts, and types have always reflected the taste or

10/14 Typography is closely allied to the fine arts, and types have always reflected the taste or feeling of their time. The charm of the early Italian types has perhaps never been equalled; and the like is true of the Renaissance manuscripts on which they were based — and of many other departments of art in that same wonderful time. Note, too, the relation of the French manuscripts and types of a
Typography is closely allied to the fine arts, and types have always reflected the taste or feeling of

HELVETICA: PHOTOTYPE, V.I.P.

14 **Abcdefghijklmnopqrs**
12 **Abcdefghijklmnopqrstuv**
11 **Abcdefghijklmnopqrstuvwx**
10 **Abcdefghijklmnopqrstuvwxyz**
NORMAL METAL SPACING

14 **Abcdefghijklmnopqrstu**
12 **Abcdefghijklmnopqrstuvw**
11 **Abcdefghijklmnopqrstuvwxy**
10 **Abcdefghijklmnopqrstuvwxyz**
NORMAL PHOTOTYPE SPACING

14 **Abcdefghijklmnopqrstuv**
12 **Abcdefghijklmnopqrstuvwx**
11 **Abcdefghijklmnopqrstuvwxyz**
10 **Abcdefghijklmnopqrstuvwxyz1**
TIGHT PHOTOTYPE SPACING

9/10 Typography is closely allied to the fine arts, and types have always reflected the taste or feeling of their time. The charm of the early Italian types has perhaps never been equalled; and the like is true of the Renaissance manuscripts on which they were based — and of many other departments of art in that same wonderful time. Note, too, the relation of the French manuscripts and types of a slightly later date to the manuscripts and the types of the Italian Renaissance.

In spite of the increasing interest in the history of printing, and the attention paid in many quarters to the work of famous typographers, a knowledge of standards among the rank and file of printers is still greatly lacking. To the average printer of to-day, type is type,
Typography is closely allied to the fine arts, and types have always reflected the taste or feeling of their time.

8/9 Typography is closely allied to the fine arts, and types have always reflected the taste or feeling of their time. The charm of the early Italian types has perhaps never been equalled; and the like is true of the Renaissance manuscripts on which they were based — and of many other departments of art in that same wonderful time. Note, too, the relation of the French manuscripts and types of a slightly later date to the manuscripts and the types of the Italian Renaissance.

In spite of the increasing interest in the history of printing, and the attention paid in many quarters to the work of famous typographers, a knowledge of standards among the rank and file of printers is still greatly lacking. To the average printer of to-day, type is type, printing is printing — it is all about alike; and he concerns himself only with alleged labour-saving contrivances, or new type-faces that ensure convenience at the expense of proper design. In a more advanced class is to
Typography is closely allied to the fine arts, and types have always reflected the taste or feeling of their time. The charm of

9/13 Typography is closely allied to the fine arts, and types have always reflected the taste or feeling of their time. The charm of the early Italian types has perhaps never been equalled; and the like is true of the Renaissance manuscripts on which they were based — and of many other departments of art in that same wonderful time. Note, too, the relation of the French manuscripts and types of a slightly later date to the manuscripts and the types of the Italian Renaissance.

In spite of the increasing interest in the history of
Typography is closely allied to the fine arts, and types have always reflected the taste or feeling of their time.

8/12 Typography is closely allied to the fine arts, and types have always reflected the taste or feeling of their time. The charm of the early Italian types has perhaps never been equalled; and the like is true of the Renaissance manuscripts on which they were based — and of many other departments of art in that same wonderful time. Note, too, the relation of the French manuscripts and types of a slightly later date to the manuscripts and the types of the Italian Renaissance.

In spite of the increasing interest in the history of printing, and the attention paid in many quarters to the work of famous typographers, a knowledge of standards among the rank and
Typography is closely allied to the fine arts, and types have always reflected the taste or feeling of their time. The charm of

7/8 Typography is closely allied to the fine arts, and types have always reflected the taste or feeling of their time. The charm of the early Italian types has perhaps never been equalled; and the like is true of the Renaissance manuscripts on which they were based — and of many other departments of art in that same wonderful time. Note, too, the relation of the French manuscripts and types of a slightly later date to the manuscripts and the types of the Italian Renaissance.

In spite of the increasing interest in the history of printing, and the attention paid in many quarters to the work of famous typographers, a knowledge of standards among the rank and file of printers is still greatly lacking. To the average printer of to-day, type is type, printing is printing — it is all about alike; and he concerns himself only with alleged labour-saving contrivances, or new type-faces that ensure convenience at the expense of proper design. In a more advanced
Typography is closely allied to the fine arts, and types have always reflected the taste or feeling of their time. The charm of the early

6/7 Typography is closely allied to the fine arts, and types have always reflected the taste or feeling of their time. The charm of the early Italian types has perhaps never been equalled; and the like is true of the Renaissance manuscripts on which they were based — and of many other departments of art in that same wonderful time. Note, too, the relation of the French manuscripts and types of a slightly later date to the manuscripts and the types of the Italian Renaissance.

In spite of the increasing interest in the history of printing, and the attention paid in many quarters to the work of famous typographers, a knowledge of standards among the rank and file of printers is still greatly lacking. To the average printer of to-day, type is type, printing is printing — it is all about alike; and he concerns himself only with alleged labour-saving contrivances, or new type-faces that ensure convenience at the expense of proper design. In a more advanced class is to be found the printer who, knowing something of the historical side of printing and realizing intellectually that there is a standard of excellence, yet has never considered the question as applying in any practical way to himself or his work.
Typography is closely allied to the fine arts, and types have always reflected the taste or feeling of their time. The charm of the early Italian types has

7/11 Typography is closely allied to the fine arts, and types have always reflected the taste or feeling of their time. The charm of the early Italian types has perhaps never been equalled; and the like is true of the Renaissance manuscripts on which they were based — and of many other departments of art in that same wonderful time. Note, too, the relation of the French manuscripts and types of a slightly later date to the manuscripts and the types of the Italian Renaissance.

In spite of the increasing interest in the history of printing, and the attention paid in many quarters to the work of famous typographers, a knowledge of standards among the rank and file of printers is still
Typography is closely allied to the fine arts, and types have always reflected the taste or feeling of their time. The charm of the early

6/10 Typography is closely allied to the fine arts, and types have always reflected the taste or feeling of their time. The charm of the early Italian types has perhaps never been equalled; and the like is true of the Renaissance manuscripts on which they were based — and of many other departments of art in that same wonderful time. Note, too, the relation of the French manuscripts and types of a slightly later date to the manuscripts and the types of the Italian Renaissance.

In spite of the increasing interest in the history of printing, and the attention paid in many quarters to the work of famous typographers, a knowledge of standards among the rank and file of printers is still greatly lacking. To the average printer of to-day, type is type, printing is printing — it is all about alike; and he concerns himself only with alleged labour-saving
Typography is closely allied to the fine arts, and types have always reflected the taste or feeling of their time. The charm of the early Italian types has

HELVETICA: PHOTOTYPE, V.I.P.

9 **Abcdefghijklmnopqrstuvwxyz12**
8 **Abcdefghijklmnopqrstuvwxyz12345**
7 **Abcdefghijklmnopqrstuvwxyz123456789**
6 **Abcdefghijklmnopqrstuvwxyz1234567890**

NORMAL METAL SPACING

9 **Abcdefghijklmnopqrstuvwxyz123**
8 **Abcdefghijklmnopqrstuvwxyz123456**
7 **Abcdefghijklmnopqrstuvwxyz1234567890**
6 **Abcdefghijklmnopqrstuvwxyz1234567890**

NORMAL PHOTOTYPE SPACING

9 **Abcdefghijklmnopqrstuvwxyz123**
8 **Abcdefghijklmnopqrstuvwxyz1234567**
7 **Abcdefghijklmnopqrstuvwxyz1234567890**
6 **Abcdefghijklmnopqrstuvwxyz1234567890**

TIGHT PHOTOTYPE SPACING

14/15 **Typography is closely allied to the fine arts, and types have always reflected the taste or feeling of their time. The charm of the early Italian types has perhaps never been equalled; and the like is true of the Renaissance manuscripts on which they were based — and** *Typography is closely allied to the fine arts, and types have*

14/18 **Typography is closely allied to the fine arts, and types have always reflected the taste or feeling of their time. The charm of the early Italian types has perhaps never been equalled; and the like is true of the Ren-** *Typography is closely allied to the fine arts, and types have*

12/13 **Typography is closely allied to the fine arts, and types have always reflected the taste or feeling of their time. The charm of the early Italian types has perhaps never been equalled; and the like is true of the Renaissance manuscripts on which they were based — and of many other departments of art in that same wonderful time. Note, too, the** *Typography is closely allied to the fine arts, and types have always re-*

12/16 **Typography is closely allied to the fine arts, and types have always reflected the taste or feeling of their time. The charm of the early Italian types has perhaps never been equalled; and the like is true of the Renaissance manuscripts on which they were based — and of many** *Typography is closely allied to the fine arts, and types have always re-*

11/12 **Typography is closely allied to the fine arts, and types have always reflected the taste or feeling of their time. The charm of the early Italian types has perhaps never been equalled; and the like is true of the Renaissance manuscripts on which they were based — and of many other departments of art in that same wonderful time. Note, too, the** *Typography is closely allied to the fine arts, and types have always reflected*

10/11 **Typography is closely allied to the fine arts, and types have always reflected the taste or feeling of their time. The charm of the early Italian types has perhaps never been equalled; and the like is true of the Renaissance manuscripts on which they were based — and of many other departments of art in that same wonderful time. Note, too, the relation of the French manuscripts and types of a slightly later date to the manu-** *Typography is closely allied to the fine arts, and types have always reflected the*

11/15 **Typography is closely allied to the fine arts, and types have always reflected the taste or feeling of their time. The charm of the early Italian types has perhaps never been equalled; and the like is true of the Renaissance manu-scripts on which they were based — and** *Typography is closely allied to the fine arts, and types have always reflected*

10/14 **Typography is closely allied to the fine arts, and types have always reflected the taste or feeling of their time. The charm of the early italian types has perhaps never been equalled; and the like is true of the Renais-sance manuscripts on which they were based — and of many other departments of art in that same wonderful time. Note, too,** *Typography is closely allied to the fine arts, and types have always reflected the*

HELVETICA: PHOTOTYPE, V.I.P.

14	**Abcdefghijklmnopq**	14	**Abcdefghijklmnopqr**	14	**Abcdefghijklmnopqrs**
12	**Abcdefghijklmnopqrst**	12	**Abcdefghijklmnopqrstu**	12	**Abcdefghijklmnopqrstuv**
11	**Abcdefghijklmnopqrstuv**	11	**Abcdefghijklmnopqrstuv**	11	**Abcdefghijklmnopqrstuvw**
10	**Abcdefghijklmnopqrstuvw**	10	**Abcdefghijklmnopqrstuvw**	10	**Abcdefghijklmnopqrstuvwx**

NORMAL METAL SPACING

NORMAL PHOTOTYPE SPACING

TIGHT PHOTOTYPE SPACING

9/10
Typography is closely allied to the fine arts, and types have always reflected the taste or feeling of their time. The charm of the early Italian types has perhaps never been equalled; and the like is true of the Renaissance manuscripts on which they were based — and of many other departments of art in that same wonderful time. Note, too, the relation of the French manuscripts and types of a slightly later date to the manuscripts and the types of the Italian Renaissance.

In spite of the increasing interest in the history of printing, and the attention paid in many quarters to the work of famous typographers, a
Typography is closely allied to the fine arts, and types have always reflected the taste or

8/9
Typography is closely allied to the fine arts, and types have always reflected the taste or feeling of their time. The charm of the early Italian types has perhaps never been equalled; and the like is true of the Renaissance manuscripts on which they were based — and of many other departments of art in that same wonderful time. Note, too, the relation of the French manuscripts and types of a slightly later date to the manuscripts and the types of the Italian Renaissance.

In spite of the increasing interest in the history of printing, and the attention paid in many quarters to the work of famous typographers, a knowledge of standards among the rank and file of printers is still greatly lacking. To the average printer of to-day, type is type, printing is printing — it is all about alike; and he concerns himself only with alleged labour-saving con-
Typography is closely allied to the fine arts, and types have always reflected the taste or feeling of their

9/13
Typography is closely allied to the fine arts, and types have always reflected the taste or feeling of their time. The charm of the early Italian types has perhaps never been equalled; and the like is true of the Renaissance manuscripts on which they were based — and of many other departments of art in that same wonderful time. Note, too, the relation of the French manuscripts and types of a slightly later date to the manuscripts and the types of the Italian Renaissance.

Typography is closely allied to the fine arts, and types have always reflected the taste or

8/12
Typography is closely allied to the fine arts, and types have always reflected the taste or feeling of their time. The charm of the early Italian types has perhaps never been equalled; and the like is true of the Renaissance manuscripts on which they were based — and of many other departments of art in that same wonderful time. Note, too, the relation of the French manuscripts and types of a slightly later date to the manuscripts and the types of the Italian Renaissance.

In spite of the increasing interest in the history of printing, and the attention paid in many quarters to
Typography is closely allied to the fine arts, and types have always reflected the taste or feeling of their

7/8
Typography is closely allied to the fine arts, and types have always reflected the taste or feeling of their time. The charm of the early Italian types has perhaps never been equalled; and the like is true of the Renaissance manuscripts on which they were based — and of many other departments of art in that same wonderful time. Note, too, the relation of the French manuscripts and types of a slightly later date to the manuscripts and the types of the Italian Renaissance.

In spite of the increasing interest in the history of printing, and the attention paid in many quarters to the work of famous typographers, a knowledge of standards among the rank and file of printers is still greatly lacking. To the average printer of to-day, type is type, printing is printing — it is all about alike; and he concerns himself only with
Typography is closely allied to the fine arts, and types have always reflected the taste or feeling of their time. The charm

6/7
Typography is closely allied to the fine arts, and types have always reflected the taste or feeling of their time. The charm of the early Italian types has perhaps never been equalled; and the like is true of the Renaissance manuscripts on which they were based — and of many other departments of art in that same wonderful time. Note, too, the relation of the French manuscripts and types of a slightly later date to the manuscripts and the types of the Italian Renaissance.

In spite of the increasing interest in the history of printing, and the attention paid in many quarters to the work of famous typographers, a knowledge of standards among the rank and file of printers is still greatly lacking. To the average printer of to-day, type is type, printing is printing — it is all about alike; and he concerns himself only with alleged labour-saving contrivances, or new type-faces that ensure convenience at the expense of proper design. In a more advanced class is to be found the printer who, knowing something of the historical side of printing and realizing intellectually that there
Typography is closely allied to the fine arts, and types have always reflected the taste or feeling of their time. The charm of the early

7/11
Typography is closely allied to the fine arts, and types have always reflected the taste or feeling of their time. The charm of the early Italian types has perhaps never been equalled; and the like is true of the Renaissance manuscripts on which they were based — and of many other departments of art in that same wonderful time. Note, too, the relation of the French manuscripts and types of a slightly later date to the manuscripts and the types of the Italian Renaissance.

In spite of the increasing interest in the history of printing, and the attention paid in many quarters to the work of
Typography is closely allied to the fine arts, and types have always reflected the taste or feeling of their time. The charm

6/10
Typography is closely allied to the fine arts, and types have always reflected the taste or feeling of their time. The charm of the early Italian types has perhaps never been equalled; and the like is true of the Renaissance manuscripts on which they were based — and of many other departments of art in that same wonderful time. Note, too, the relation of the French manuscripts and types of a slightly later date to the manuscripts and the types of the Italian Renaissance.

In spite of the increasing interest in the history of printing, and the attention paid in many quarters to the work of famous typographers, a knowledge of standards among the rank and file of printers is still greatly lacking. To the average printer of to-day, type is type,
Typography is closely allied to the fine arts, and types have always reflected the taste or feeling of their time. The charm of the early

HELVETICA: PHOTOTYPE, V.I.P.

9 **Abcdefghijklmnopqrstuvwxy**
8 **Abcdefghijklmnopqrstuvwxyz12**
7 **Abcdefghijklmnopqrstuvwxyz12345**
6 **Abcdefghijklmnopqrstuvwxyz123456789**

NORMAL METAL SPACING

9 **Abcdefghijklmnopqrstuvwxyz**
8 **Abcdefghijklmnopqrstuvwxyz123**
7 **Abcdefghijklmnopqrstuvwxyz123456**
6 **Abcdefghijklmnopqrstuvwxyz1234567890**

NORMAL PHOTOTYPE SPACING

9 **Abcdefghijklmnopqrstuvwxyz**
8 **Abcdefghijklmnopqrstuvwxyz123**
7 **Abcdefghijklmnopqrstuvwxyz123456**
6 **Abcdefghijklmnopqrstuvwxyz1234567890**

TIGHT PHOTOTYPE SPACING

SOURCES OF ILLUSTRATIONS

Pages 2 (left & below), 161.
Courtesy of the American Museum
of Natural History.

Pages 14, 15, 16.
Courtesy of American Type Founders Co., Inc.

Page 83.
Courtesy of Columbia University,
Special Collections Library.

Page 13.
Courtesy of Cooper Union Art Library.

Pages 2 (Above), 5, 136, 191, 261.
Courtesy of The Metropolitan Museum of Art.

Pages 7, 9, 10, 11, 108, 185, 283.
Courtesy of The Pierpont Morgan Library.

Pages 48, 57.
Courtesy of The New York Public Library.

SOURCES OF TEXT QUOTATIONS

A CONCISE HISTORY OF THE ORIGIN AND
PROGRESS OF PRINTING, Philip Luckombe, London,
1770. Courtesy of The New York Public Library.
From page 228 **Caledonia** (p. 41)

A DISSERTATION UPON ENGLISH TYPOGRAPHICAL
FOUNDERS AND FOUNDRIES, Edward Rowe Mores,
1778. Courtesy of The New York Public Library.
From page 65 **Bookman** (pp. 63-5)

Baskerville's preface to PARADISE LOST, John Milton,
Burmingham, England, 1758. Courtesy of Columbia
University, Special Collections Library.
From page 25 **Baskerville**

FOURNIER ON TYPEFOUNDING; THE TEXT OF THE
MANUALE TYPOGRAPHIQUE (1764-1766), Harry Carter,
London, 1930. Courtesy of The New York Public Library.
From page 103 **Century Schoolbook** (pp. 289-91)

Giambattista Bodoni — To the Reader. G. B. BODONI'S
PREFACE TO THE MANUALE TIPOGRAFICO OF 1818,
H. V. Marrot, London, 1925. Courtesy of
The New York Public Library.
From page 252 **Trade Gothic**

HISTORIC PRINTING TYPES, Theodore L. DeVinne,
1886. Courtesy of Cooper Union Art Library.
From page 115 **Futura** (pp. 106-7)
From page 202 **Weiss** (pp. 108-9)

Reprinted by permission of the publishers from
PRINTING TYPES, Daniel Berkeley Updike; Cambridge,
Mass.: The Belknap Press of Harvard University Press,
Copyright, 1922, 1937, 1962, by The President and
Fellows of Harvard College.
From page 231 **Cheltenham** (p. 15)
From page 235 **DeVinne** (p. 7)
From page 238 **Electra** (p. 11)
From page 241 **Fairfield** (p. 13)
From page 244 **Helvetica** (Introduction)
From page 247 **Janson** (p. 38)
From page 250 **Scotch 2** (p. 41)

TYPOGRAPHIA, J. Johnson, Vol. 2; England, 1824.
Courtesy of Cooper Union Museum Library.
From page 170 **Akzidenz Grotesk** (pp. 96-7)
From page 152 **News Gothic** (p. 6)
From page 192 **Times Roman** (pp. 89-91)
From page 18 **Proofreader's marks** (Frontispiece)

Translation of a letter to Mr. Francis Rosaspina
in Bologna by Bodoni, 1813. Courtesy of Columbia
University, Special Collections Library.
From page 36 **Bodoni**

From a letter to John Baskerville by Benjamin Franklin,
1760. THE WRITINGS OF BENJAMIN FRANKLIN,
A. H. Smyth, MacMillan Co., 1905. Courtesy of
The New York Public Library.
From page 76 **Caslon**

From a letter to B. Vaughan Esq. by Benjamin Franklin,
1785. Courtesy of the Library of Congress.
From page 96 **Century Expanded**

From a letter to Noah Webster by Benjamin Franklin,
1789. THE WRITINGS OF BENJAMIN FRANKLIN,
A. H. Smyth, MacMillan Co., 1905. Courtesy of
The New York Public Library.
From page 137 **Garamond**

Designed by Ben Rosen
Original typographers: the Composing Room, Inc.,
York Typesetting Company and Kenro, Inc.
Phototypesetting by Words, Inc.
Text set in 9 point Akzidenz-Grotesk
Phototype is 9 point Helvetica light (V.I.P.)
Other credits listed below showings.